REGIONALIZATION OF WATER MANAGEMENT

A Revolution in England and Wales

WATER AUTHORITY BOUNDARIES

Areas in England within
Welsh National Water
Development Authority

Areas in Wales within
Severn Trent Water Authority

NORTHUMBRIAN

NORTH
WEST

YORKSHIRE

WELSH
NATIONAL
WATER
DEVELOPMENT
AUTHORITY

SEVERN TRENT

ANGLIAN

THAMES

WESSEX

SOUTHERN

SOUTH WEST

Miles
0 10 20 30 40 50

0   20   40   60   80
Kilometres

The ten Water Authorities in England and Wales
(reproduced by permission of the Controller of Her Majesty's Stationery Office)

REGIONALIZATION OF WATER MANAGEMENT

A Revolution in England and Wales

DANIEL A. OKUN

Kenan Professor of Environmental Engineering,
University of North Carolina at Chapel Hill, USA

APPLIED SCIENCE PUBLISHERS LTD
LONDON

APPLIED SCIENCE PUBLISHERS LTD
RIPPLE ROAD, BARKING, ESSEX, ENGLAND

ISBN: 0 85334 738 7

WITH 32 TABLES AND 20 ILLUSTRATIONS
© APPLIED SCIENCE PUBLISHERS LTD 1977

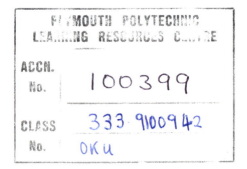
Printed in Great Britain by Galliard (Printers) Ltd, Great Yarmouth

Preface

While on sabbatical leave at University College London during the 1966–67 academic year, I became aware of a significant but unheralded evolutionary change in water supply management that had taken place in England and Wales following World War II. In a span of less than 20 years, the number of separate water supply undertakings had been reduced from more than 1200 to fewer than 200 while at the same time public water supply service was extended to more than 99 percent of the total population in England and Wales. (Meanwhile, in the United States, small water supply systems had proliferated, almost doubling in number, with little increase in the 75 percent of the total population served by public water supply systems.) By 1966 this reorganization of water supply services had been accepted and lauded by all involved, although it had been initially beset with difficulties because of the understandable reluctance of local authority members and water supply officials to yield their sovereignty over the only realm of local government that pays its own way, or may even yield profits. An American observer could not help but wonder how such institutional changes, which would be most difficult to initiate in the United States, could have been undertaken so successfully in Britain.

When further, far more comprehensive, regionalization was contemplated, building on the regrouping of water supplies, but extending to water resources, sewerage, water pollution control and the recreational and other uses of water, I became interested in studying this reorganization. Assessment of its success would necessarily need to wait for many years; but as interesting, it seemed to me, was the process by which this revolution in water management, encompassed in the Water Act 1973, was to be effected. Ten water authorities in England and Wales were to take over, on 1 April 1974, the complete ownership of all dams and reservoirs, water supply transmission mains, water treatment plants, water distribution systems, sewerage systems, wastewater treatment facilities, river works and the management of the rivers themselves, all of which had been invested in some 1600 separate local authorities, water supply undertakings and river authorities. In 1973, I had just relinquished administrative responsibilities at the University of North Carolina after 18 years, and the time appeared to be propitious to take leave to observe the events accompanying this reorganization.

The stimulus for this interest in regional water management came, as did so much other stimulation in my professional life, from the late Professor Gordon Maskew Fair of Harvard University who, in 1966, inaugurated a study of regional water supply in Western Europe resulting in a document *Piped Water for All—A Study of Regional Water Supply in Western Europe*. Because he wrote of the necessity for the functional and administrative integration of regionalization of water supply and wastewater disposal, the sound financing of water services and the water quality goals that need to be attained, Professor Fair would have applauded the ambition of this reorganization of water management in England and Wales and would have been pleased to have its story told, if not by himself, by his student. Those principles here espoused are those that were learned from my quarter-century of association with Professor Fair, master teacher, historian and philosopher, whose life was devoted to educating engineers to the goal of managing water in the service of people.

Unless attributed to another, the views expressed in this volume are my own, distilled from interviews, meetings, official, commercial and professional publications, publications of the National Water Council and the water authorities, the minutes of meetings of the Severn Trent, Southern and Thames Water Authorities, and a melange of biases brought with me to this study.

With Britain well along and the United States just embarking on the road toward metrication, both the Imperial system, with Imperial gallons (which are 20 percent larger than US gallons) and SI (Système International) units are used, with the former given precedence because of its still easier understanding by both professional and lay people in Britain and the United States.

American spelling is used throughout, even when quoting British sources, except that British spelling is used for British proper names and titles. British and Americans often use different words to express the same meaning and give different meanings to the same words. Accordingly, a glossary of technical terms is appended.

A word of advice to the reader. Inasmuch as this volume is organized both chronologically and topically, some repetition is inevitable if excessive and tedious cross-referencing is to be avoided. Readers are advised to use the index freely so as to be able to turn readily to those sections of the volume that are of particular interest. For example, the debates on metering that arose from the consultation papers and in parliament are discussed in Chapters 3 and 4, while the substantive discussion of the metering issue is in Chapter 9 on Finance.

Opportunities for the preparation of this book were made possible through the generous support of many individuals and their agencies: Professor Kenneth J. Ives of University College London, where I was extended a visiting professorship from 1973 to 1975; Dr Ralph W. Richardson, Jr of the Rockefeller Foundation and Dr Edward H. Bryan of the RANN (Research Applied to National Needs) program of the National Science Foundation, whose organizations provided research grants for the study; John Herrington of the United States–United Kingdom Educational Commission which granted me a Fulbright–Hays lectureship at University College; and Dr Russell F. Christman, chairman of the Department of Environmental Sciences and Engineering at the University of North Carolina who made it possible for me to give time to the writing upon my return to Chapel Hill. A fine setting to inaugurate the writing was provided by the Rockefeller Foundation Study Center in Bellagio, Italy, where the helpful ministrations of its director, Dr William Olson, made embarking upon this effort considerably more pleasant than it would otherwise have been, particularly as this book represents my first substantial writing in a subject area not primarily technical.

This study would have been impossible without the gracious hospitality and cooperation of a host of professional colleagues in the United Kingdom: F. Needham Green, general manager of the North Surrey Water Company, advised me of the impending reorganization and kept me informed by sending me the consultation papers from the Department of the Environment as they appeared, so providing the basis for making application for the several grants that supported the study; David J. Kinnersley, then executive secretary of the Association of River Authorities, upon my arrival in London in August 1973, less than two weeks after passage of the Act, helped me to understand what transpired during the legislative process and what was transpiring during the creation of the 'shadow' National Water Council and water authorities, and in addition, made an office available to me at ARA headquarters where I could peruse the documentation leading to the Water Act 1973 at my leisure; J. E. Beddoe, then Under Secretary, and J. R. Niven, of the Department of the Environment gave freely of their time in advising me on the reorganization; A. H. M. Smyth, chairman, and Brian Thorpe, chief executive, of the Southern Water Authority made me welcome at all the meetings of the authority, to the extent of including me among their number at a meeting held with representatives of the local authorities and the press where their first confrontation with the public took place; Peter Black, chairman, Alex Morrison, chief executive, Eric Gilliland, director of finance, and Hugh Fish, director of scientific services of the Thames Water Authority, in addition to inviting me to meetings of the authority and its committees, entered into extended discussion and debate with me on issues involved in the reorganization; Peter F. Stott, director general of the National Water

Council invited me to participate in the first National Water Conference in Bournemouth in March 1975 after one year's experience with the reorganization; J. R. Buckenham, former director of the British Waterworks Association and now secretary of the National Water Council, with Elizabeth Brazendale, made the voluminous publications of the BWA and NWC readily available to me; H. W. Barker and H. G. Giles, then of the Water Supply Industry Training Board, invited me to participate in many of the sessions conducted for officers of the water industry from throughout the country at Tadley Court, which gave me an opportunity to learn their feelings about the reorganization; and the members of an *ad hoc* advisory committee, who graciously agreed to meet with me to discuss the issues of the reorganization and to review this document in draft form, including Messrs Black, Fish, Ives, Niven, Thorpe, and in addition: Peter Banks, of John Taylor and Sons, who made available to me the file of columns that he had prepared for *Municipal Engineering* on all aspects of the reorganization; Douglas H. Banks and L. R. Gray, who let me see something of their divisional organizations and facilities in the field; R. le G. Hetherington of Binnie and Partners, who made his firm's library available; Trevor P. Hughes, the director general, water engineering, of the Department of the Environment; R. C. Jenking, director of finance of the North West Water Authority; Barry Rydz, then director of resource planning of the Severn Trent Water Authority; D. H. Sharp, secretary of the Institution of Chemical Engineers; H. S. Tricker, senior technical adviser of the National Water Council; and David H. A. Price, of the Department of the Environment, long a personal friend and professional colleague, who throughout my stay in Britain offered significant personal insights into the reorganization. Many others gave of their time in extended interviews including: Lord Ashby, first chairman of the Royal Commission on Environmental Pollution; Sir Leonard Millis, the doyen of the British water industry and a member of the National Water Council; Charles Simeons, then a Member of Parliament from Luton who had been a member of Standing Committee D that studied the Water Bill; Dr Ron Allen, director of the Water Research Centre; H. C. Butcher of the Confederation of British Industry; and Sir Norman Rowntree, director of the Water Resources Board throughout its existence. Particular thanks go to David L. Walker, assistant director general of the National Water Council who provided opportunities for stimulating discussions of the new organization and its problems and who made a painstaking review of the draft of this document.

Appreciation is extended to my colleagues on the faculty who examined portions of the draft and were free with their critical comments; to Peter J. Kolsky, a British graduate student who brought a perceptive mind to a detailed examination of the entire manuscript; and especially to Phyllis E. Carlton who typed and retyped the manuscript, seemingly without end, with patience and good humor.

Lastly, to all of my colleagues and students at the University who were so understanding when I was closeted in my study and not available, I offer apologies, thanks and this volume in partial compensation.

It is with great pleasure that I dedicate this book to the late Professor Gordon Maskew Fair.

DANIEL A. OKUN
Chapel Hill, North Carolina

Contents

xi

CHAPTER 1

Introduction

The first issue of *Time* for 1971 featured the 'Issue of the Year: the Environment'.[1] *Time's* essay congratulated Suffolk County, a New York City suburb on Long Island, for spotting '... a way to combat both the money shortage and water pollution. Instead of building costly new sewerage and treatment plants, they banned the sale of detergents containing phosphates, prime source of water contamination.' The residents of Suffolk County, living cheek by jowl, depend upon individual household wells for their water supply and for septic tanks or cesspools on their properties for disposal of their household wastewaters. The contamination of the wells by the wastewaters containing detergents caused foaming at the water tap, evidence of the connection between the septic tank and the well. Thus the detergents constituted a useful 'marker' of contamination, while phosphates create no problem whatsoever when discharged into the ground. A ban on detergents only assured that the tap would be free of foam, but not free of sewage. Little enthusiasm was expressed for the only rational approach to the problem, the provision of public water supply and sewerage systems.

On 18 January 1972 the *New York Times* carried a photograph showing a conservation officer in campaign hat, pistol at his hip, in the company of the Commissioner of the New York State Department of Environmental Conservation, searching the shelves of a New York City supermarket for household detergents containing more than 8·7 percent phosphorus.[2] In all, some 100 agents were assigned to this 'round-up'. With all New York City's difficulties, the militant action against phosphorus in detergents represented absurdity of a high order.

A concern for the environment became a national issue in the United States. The promise of political capital to be made from legislating against pollution resulted in the overwhelming passage of Public Law 92–500 in October 1972, just before the national elections, with the avowed goal of eliminating the discharge of pollutants into the nation's waters by 1985. To implement this legislation, $18 000 million was authorized in federal construction grant funds for treatment facilities to be spent over a period of three years.

While concern for water pollution in the United States, at least as expressed through the torrent of laws and regulations and commitments of funds, was in the ascendancy in the early 1970s, concern for water supply had virtually disappeared. Except for water used on interstate carriers, the federal government had had no responsibility for the quality of water supply, this responsibility resting with the states. The state regulatory agencies, overwhelmed by requirements to match the federal financial commitment in water pollution control, found their capacity to provide surveillance over public water seriously abridged. In 1963 some 20 000 separate public community water supply systems had served 150 million people, with about half of these systems serving populations under 1000. By 1975, the number of systems and the number serving fewer than 1000 people doubled, while the total population served increased only 6 percent.[3] The quality of water service in these small communities, to say nothing of the quality of water service to the 50 million people not served from public systems at all, received little attention from government or from public health authorities generally until passage of the Safe Drinking Water Act in December 1974.

In the United Kingdom, public water supply has received high priority since World War II. By 1973, as a result of an active program of regrouping water supply undertakings, only 177 public water supply systems served almost 50 million people in England and Wales, more than 99 percent of the total population. By almost any measure, the quality of water supply service available generally over England and Wales can be said to be superior to the quality of water service afforded to people in the United States.

In the preservation of the quality and appearance of their surface waters for fishing and as amenities, the British have no equals. A visitor cannot help being impressed with the tidiness and attractiveness of the landscape and its streams and the very heavy use that is made of these waters by sailors, rowers, paddlers, anglers and picnickers. The growing concern for the quality of the environment resulted in the creation of the Royal Commission on Environmental Pollution in 1970, but no flood of ill-considered, costly legislation ensued. Lord Ashby, first chairman of the Royal Commission, illustrated the difference in approach between Britain and the United States by focusing on the detergent problem.[4] A dramatic development in his lifetime had been the replacement of soap by synthetic detergents. No attention was paid to the second-order effects of detergents, one of which was that their surface-active materials did not degrade as readily as soap. The detergent foam, while impressive to the housewife, carried into streams, rendering them unfit for recreation. In 1957 the government set up a committee that pressed manufacturers to find a biodegradable surface-active material. By 1959 they had replaced the 'hard' branched-chain alkyl benzene sulfonates (ABS) with the 'soft' straight-chain linear alkyl sulfonates (LAS) which are degradable at about the same rate as organic matter in domestic wastewaters. The new material would cost more, so after proceeding with successful trials in two communities to ascertain that the new formulation would have the beneficial effects anticipated and that it would be acceptable to housewives, the manufacturers agreed to replace the hard detergents with soft detergents for domestic use.

'In contrast to this story of unostentatious success', Lord Ashby went on, 'the story of political reaction to the second-order effects of phosphates in detergents on the other side of the Atlantic is a cautionary tale.' The dangers of phosphate pollution were sensationally described in popular accounts of lakes dying from eutrophication. Housewives were urged not to buy detergents containing phosphates. The industry took fright and hastily sought and found a substitute, nitrilo-tri-acetate (NTA), and a crash program for its manufacture was undertaken. Some state and city legislators, anxious to win public approbation at little cost to the public treasury, enacted 'panic legislation', even where eutrophication could not occur. Federal legislation to ban phosphate detergents was barely averted.

Meanwhile, it was learned that NTA could react in man with nitrates to produce nitrosamines, some of which are known to be carcinogenic. Furthermore, NTA is a chelating agent that can take toxic heavy metals into solution, thereby endangering drinking water supplies. Overnight the capital investment in manufacturing facilities for NTA was abandoned. In time, it was appreciated that phosphorus in detergents is of only local significance and can be removed more effectively in wastewater treatment.[5]

Lord Ashby asserted that while the costs of pollution abatement fall on the public in taxes or higher prices for goods and services, 'the people of Britain willingly allowed their elected rulers to pass laws to abate pollution, in the knowledge that these laws will put up the cost of heat and light, cars, beer, paper and the rates'. The public allows this for one of three reasons: fear, rising aesthetic values, and altruism for the sake of future generations, and the governments of industrialized countries have been in the mood to respond to public pressure to improve and conserve the environment as, in a period of affluence, the costs appeared to be of little consequence. However, when economic constraints hit the United States, the high goals of environmental quality were quietly lowered and timetables quietly extended. In the United Kingdom, the responsible leadership has been considerably more prudent in committing massive funds to reaping doubtful benefits in the first place, and in promising unachievable goals in the second place.

Differences in approach between the United States and the United Kingdom are illuminated in their policies on water management. This volume traces the development of the regional approach to water management taken in England and Wales, culminating in a veritable revolution in water management. K. F. Roberts, chief executive of the Wessex Water Authority, expressed a widely held feeling that '... the changes now made in England and Wales are likely to be viewed with great interest by, and have repercussions on, many friends and colleagues away from these shores. Ours is a truly pioneering exercise and I venture to predict that others may follow in our tracks'.[6]

PRINCIPLES OF SOUND WATER MANAGEMENT

The reader will find that the author is not a dispassionate observer of the water reorganization, but a believer in the promise of regionalization.†

Five general principles for water quality management run through this document, principles embodied in the new organization and which most professionals in the water field would endorse, at least in part:

1. The uniqueness of water projects

The optimum solution to any specific water problem, whether a water supply for a city or region, or effluent treatment and disposal for an industry, is unique. Requirements for a uniform approach nationwide, whether for water or effluent treatment, or in applying standards, are not likely to be most efficient for all projects, nor are they likely to use resources of water, materials, men, or money most economically. Uniformity under the guise of equity may appear to provide easier regulation and administration, but they are obtained at high social cost. Climate, precipitation, topography, density and distribution of population, industrial development, land use, recreational interests, and cultural pursuits vary from place to place throughout England and Wales, and certainly throughout the United States, so that a standard that may be entirely appropriate in one place is not likely to be appropriate in another. Institutional, regulatory and financial arrangements that permit variations across a country are to be preferred over regulatory patterns that prescribe a uniform approach nationwide.

2. Efficiencies and economies of scale

The technological problems associated with providing a water supply or with disposing of municipal and industrial wastewaters are as complex for

† The author was a minor participant on the scene with articles in British journals immediately before and after reorganization day (Daniel A. Okun, 'Reorganization: Water—Formidable Problems Lie Ahead', *New Civil Engineer* (Britain), pp. 21–4, 28 March 1974), (Daniel A. Okun, 'The Promise of Water Reorganization', *Water*, The National Water Council, No. 1, pp. 3–7, October 1974) and with presentation of a paper at the first National Water Conference in Bournemouth, sponsored by the National Water Council (D. A. Okun, 'Management in the Water Industry', National Water Conference, Bournemouth, *Proceedings Report*, pp. 24–7, 1975).

small systems as for large, but are often more intractable for small systems. Water operations exhibit significant economies and efficiencies of scale such that the incorporation of larger populations or industries into a project, up to an optimum size, are likely to reduce unit costs and to enlarge opportunities for achieving an optimal use of resources. A number of communities acting together can more easily afford to go a longer distance to develop a high quality water resource than individual communities acting alone. The efficacy of this approach has already been well demonstrated by the success of water supply regrouping effected by the Water Act 1945 in England and Wales. The loss of local sovereignty over water supply or sewage disposal with the concomitant loss of accountability will generally be unimportant to a consumer if the quality of his service is high and the cost low. In the United States, consolidations of rural school districts, a most emotional and highly charged arena of public service, have been accepted in the face of a loss of local accountability because of the promise of superior educational opportunities. School consolidations were responsible for busing long before busing was introduced for racial integration.

3. Integration of water supply, sewerage and pollution control services

As wastewaters are treated to higher and higher degrees, the effluent products become important water resources for non-potable purposes, particularly where natural water resources are fully exploited. If water resources are to be managed efficiently, all elements of the hydrological cycle should fall within the purview of a single agency so that the wastewater of one community on a river may be an asset rather than a problem to its downstream neighbor.

4. Sound financial policies

Water services in an industrial society have changed from being primarily a public health responsibility to being a public utility. Accordingly, the philosophy for financing the service has shifted from governmental subsidies on behalf of public health to a system that reflects the cost of providing the service. If the quality of water service is to be maintained, it must be adequately financed. Any sound financing program should generate sufficient funds to cover the costs of the services, should promote the efficient utilization and allocation of the available resources, and should not discriminate among classes of consumers. Furthermore, the charges imposed should reflect the true costs incurred, and water services should not be the vehicle for the amelioration of social ills. If subsidies for some are desired, these should be identified and not hidden in the charges for water services. In other words, subsidies from central government or cross-subsidies among classes of consumers are not believed to be appropriate in a sound charging scheme.

5. A preference for pure rather than polluted sources for potable water

Since the mid-19th century, when Dr John Snow demonstrated the relationship between contaminated water supplies and cholera, and since the turn of the century when Sir Alexander Houston demonstrated the effectiveness of water treatment for the removal of bacterial pathogens, the industrialized countries of the world have become sanguine about their ability to render even highly polluted sources of water free of any threat of water-borne infectious disease. Water treatment processes, capped by disinfection with chlorine or ozone, if properly applied, assures water free from infectious micro-organisms. While most water engineers have opted for protected sources when selecting amongst alternatives, in some instances polluted sources were developed by engineers confident that the savings in cost and the expediency of this option were fully justified because the polluted waters would be rendered potable. However, in the post-World War II period, the explosion of the synthetic chemical industry, with some 500 new synthetic organic chemicals being introduced into commerce annually, a new threat to drinking water quality has appeared. Neither sewage and industrial effluent treatment, nor water supply treatment, have been designed to remove these chemicals, nor are they removed in transport down a water course or in storage in a reservoir, processes which in the past have been depended upon for improving water quality for potable purposes. Many of the chemicals now found in rivers used for sources of potable water have been identified as being mutagenic, carcinogenic, or teratogenic, although the concentrations that place a population at risk have not been established. The significance of the life-long ingestion of low levels of these chemicals will probably not be revealed for many years. In the absence of technology for effectively monitoring or removing these chemicals, and with uncertainty as to health risks, prudence would require that the highest quality of protected sources, such as upland impounded reservoirs or groundwaters, be used for potable purposes. Where such supplies are not sufficient for all purposes, polluted sources or reclaimed wastewaters might well be used for industrial water supplies or other purposes not requiring water of potable quality. The choice, as put by the late Professor Gordon M. Fair of Harvard University, between the 'virginal' and 'repentent' would still seem to call for a preference for the virginal, at least in drinking water supplies.

In the United States, none of the five principles is now widely observed and, in fact, the trend is to ignore the issues they raise. Neither were these principles being followed in England and Wales prior to the reorganization, although some small moves towards satisfying some of them were being made. There was still some nationwide standardization, with the Royal Commission standards for sewage disposal; still some fragmentation of services as in the local authority responsibility for sewerage and sewage disposal; water service charging schemes incorporated hidden subsidies from the exchequer with no incentives for reductions in water use or effluent discharges for optimal resource use; and the expedient course for enlarging abstractions for water supply from the polluted downstream reaches of rivers was being promoted.

The promise of the Water Act 1973 is that it provides a framework for implementation of these principles. While critical of some elements of the Act the author cannot help being an advocate for the revolution in water management here described.[7]

WATER IN ENGLAND AND WALES

The water situation in England and Wales is not substantially different from that in the United States. England and Wales, with an area of 58 350 square miles (151 000 square km), has a population of about 50 million, some 850 per square mile. Comparable to this is the northeast area of the United States, extending from the northern boundary of Massachusetts, including Rhode Island, Connecticut, New Jersey, and Delaware, and the southern portion of New York and the eastern sections of Pennsylvania and Maryland, with a 1970 population of 42 400 000 living on 55 850 square miles (144 600 square km) for a density of 760 per square mile. In the United States, excluding Alaska and Hawaii, the 1970 population was 202 100 000 on 3 022 000 square miles (7 824 000 square km).

The average annual rainfall in the United States varies from below 10 inches (25 mm) in some states to above 60 inches (1520 mm) in others although the range is more limited in the northeast, about 40 to 45 inches (1040 to 1140 mm) per year (Fig. 1.1). Rainfall in England and Wales also varies considerably, with the lowest precipitation in the populous eastern areas of the country, from 23 inches (580 mm) per year in London to over 100 inches (2500 mm) in Wales and the Lake District of the northwest (Fig. 1.2). The average annual rainfall in England and Wales is about 35·5 inches (900 mm) as compared with 29·5 inches (750 mm) over the United States. Despite the high precipitation in England and Wales, problems result from its uneven distribution over the country, with the density of population precisely inverse to the precipitation.

Accordingly, transfers of water from the water-rich areas to the centers of population began in the 19th century, with Birmingham and Liverpool developing resources in Wales, and Manchester in the Lake District.

The technology of water supply is much the same in the United States as in Britain. However, a much larger proportion of the population in England and Wales, more than 99 percent, receives supplies from public systems, as compared to only 75 percent served from public systems in the United

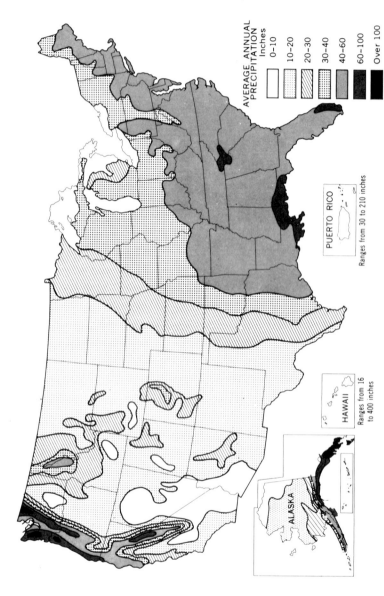

FIG. 1.1 Average annual precipitation in the United States.

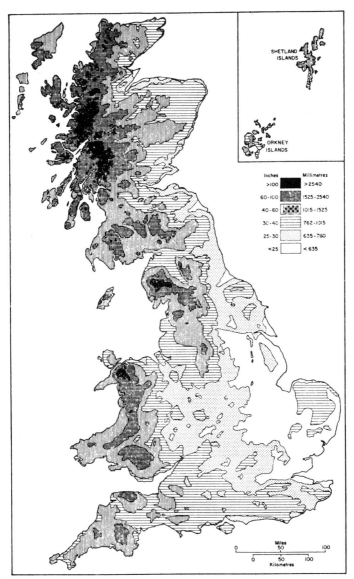

FIG. 1.2   Average annual precipitation in Britain. Reproduced by permission of
the Controller of Her Majesty's Stationery Office.

States. In the comparable densely populated region of the United States, the northeast, only 85 percent of the population is served from public systems.

Also, the administration of the water supply service tends to be substantially different in the two countries. For example, by the time of reorganization on 1 April 1974, only 177 water supply undertakings served almost 50 million people in England and Wales, with very few undertakings serving fewer than 100 000 people. By contrast, in the United States in 1975 some 40 000 systems served 159 million people, with 99 percent of these systems serving fewer than 50 000 persons each.

In Britain, each local authority continued, until the 1974 reorganization, to be responsible for its own sewerage and sewage disposal with only a few joint boards serving larger metropolitan areas. In the United States, the situation is the same. On the other hand, the proportion of the population in Britain being served by sewers, about 94 percent, is almost double that in the United States.

With the rivers being generally small, and dilution limited, most municipalities that discharge to inland waters in England and Wales provide a higher degree of biological treatment, with nitrification, than is customary in the United States. Because of the more extensive use of beaches and estuaries for recreational purposes in the United States, where water and air temperatures are higher than in England and Wales, these waters have tended to be better protected. Except for the southern coast, coastal waters of England are not used extensively for bathing, whereas bathing is enjoyed along almost the entire coastline of the United States.

On the other hand, the British have attempted to protect the amenity quality of their inland waters far more extensively than in the United States, because they are used intensively for water-based recreation. When more than conventional biological treatment is required to protect these waters, the British use a tertiary stage of 'polishing', often by filtration, which clarifies the effluents discharged and so protects the aesthetic quality of the receiving streams. In the United States, with approximately one-third of the total population drawing from rivers and lakes that receive effluents, more attention is given to chlorination of wastewaters and to a tertiary phase, not yet introduced widely, that would remove nutrients and/or dissolved organic compounds.

In Britain, even effluents discharged into a body of water that is the source of public potable water supply are not chlorinated. The British hold that chlorination of effluents destroys the beneficial oragnisms along with the pathogens, and slows stabilization in the river. The chlorination of effluents is now being examined in the United States, as chlorine has been found to react with organics to create chlorinated hydrocarbons that are difficult to remove and that may be carcinogenic.

THE BRITISH AND AMERICAN GOVERNMENTAL SETTINGS

Volumes have been written about the British and American governmental systems and their differences. Of particular concern in the development of water services are the federal–state relations in the United States and the problems of nationalism and devolution in the United Kingdom.

Federal–state relations in the United States

Under the United States Constitution and federal system of government, the protection of the health and welfare is the responsibility of the states with the federal government to intercede only when interstate issues arise. For example, water law in the United States originally had been exclusively state law except for navigation on interstate waterways. However, the power of the federal government had grown substantially in the last half century, concomitant with the massive growth of federal financial resources. The uncertainties of householders, local authorities, and industries faced with laws and regulations emanating from the state and federal governments are now being exacerbated by the growing power of the latter. The National Water Commission, in its evaluation of federal–state jurisdictions, quotes an expert in water law:[8]

'If [federal law] fits with the state law into a single pattern it creates no problems. When it and state law clash, when gaps appear, when federal law upsets that which state law has set up, when federal law undoes the tenure security that states give to property rights, when federal rights override instead of meshing with private rights, then there is a federal–state conflict in the field of water rights, there is confusion, uncertainty, bad feeling, jealousy and bitterness. To a substantial degree, this is what exists today.'[9]

Aside from the confusion created by the duality of state and federal laws and regulations, the growing dependence upon federal subsidy and the control that such subsidy gives to the federal government has shifted the balance of power to the federal government. Two aspects of this shift are particularly troublesome:

1. Federal laws and regulations tend to require uniform standards of performance throughout the country. In a nation as diverse as the United States, with 10-fold differences in precipitation between one state and another, with 1000-fold differences in density of population, with almost 100 percent differences in *per capita* income and with vast differences in size, to say nothing of historic and cultural differences, laws calling for uniform standards of treatment make any attempt at optimizing the use of resources or minimizing costs virtually impossible. For example, Public Law 92–500, the Federal Water Pollution Control Act Amendments of 1972, requires

that all municipalities provide a minimum of secondary treatment, which poses no burden in densely populated land-bound states where such treatment was already required by the state, but is quite unreasonable for sparsely populated coastal states or states on large rivers such as the Mississippi where secondary treatment can provide no perceptible benefit.

2. The federal government has assumed the burden for many water projects through subsidy, thereby concealing the true costs from the beneficiaries. For example, reservoirs built throughout the United States by the Corps of Engineers, which are intended primarily for flood control, but which also provide for water-based recreation and water supply, are constructed and operated with almost 100 percent federal funds. In the case of municipal sewerage interceptors and sewage treatment plants, federal funds provide 75 percent of the construction costs. When faced with the opportunity of receiving such beneficences, states and local authorities are hesitant to 'look a gift horse in the mouth'. If that state or local government does not accept the gratuity, another will. When the benefits are local and costs federal, states and local authorities are in no position to forego projects or reduce their size based upon optimal use of resources or highest benefit–cost ratios. In an attempt, largely unsuccessful, to assure some degree of optimization and cost effectiveness, and to ensure responsible use of the grant funds, the federal government has established a huge bureaucracy with voluminous regulations which the grateful recipient must observe if these funds are to be won.

The nationalism issue in the United Kingdom

The issue of devolution, or decentralization of government amongst the constituent countries of the United Kingdom, will inevitably have an impact on the water reorganization. The United Kingdom of Great Britain and Northern Ireland, as it is properly identified, comprises the countries of England and Wales, Scotland and Northern Ireland (Table 1.1).

The parliament, in London, is the legislative governing body for the United Kingdom although some delegation of authority is already evident. For example, except for foreign relations and defense, which are the responsibility of the United Kingdom Parliament, Northern Ireland with its own parliament controlled its own affairs until these powers were suspended during the current Irish troubles.

Scotland, although it does not have its own parliament, has its own legal system and is not included with England and Wales in any common approach to water management or local government. The Water Act 1945, the Water Resources Act 1963, the Water Act 1973, and the Local Government Act 1972 apply only to England and Wales. Regrouping of water supplies in Scotland was initiated more than 20 years after it had been initiated in England and Wales. The Control of Pollution Act 1974 does apply to Scotland with modifications to recognize the different institutional

TABLE 1.1
Population of the United Kingdom

	Estimated population 1970	%	Area	
			sq. miles	sq. km
England	46 254 000	83	19 441	50 333
Wales	2 734 000	5	3 096	8 017
Scotland	5 199 000	9	11 747	30 414
Northern Ireland	1 524 000	3	2 106	5 452
TOTALS	55 711 000	100	36 390	94 216
Total England and Wales	48 988 000	88	22 538	58 350

arrangements in Scotland, but it does not apply to Northern Ireland with respect to water.

Wales is administered with England as a unit and does not have a separate Local Government Act as does Scotland. Cymru, Welsh for Wales, is the only one of the four countries of the United Kingdom that has its own language, spoken by about one-fourth of the population along with English. With a distinctive cultural, social, and economic history, Wales exhibits many of the problems encountered by the underdeveloped nations of the world while not enjoying the political independence that would permit dealing with their problems locally. Understandably, the lack of independence has become a political issue for the Plaid Cymru, the Welsh Nationalist Party, which is committed to achieving a measure of political independence that envisages Wales with its own parliament as part of a federal United Kingdom. Devolution of administration has become an accepted policy of the major British political parties. The post of Secretary of State for Wales was created in 1964 with an administrative unit in Cardiff as well as London. Devolution would see the creation of separate assemblies in Wales and Scotland to provide greater local autonomy.

Dependent upon small farming and heavy industry related to mining, Wales is an economic problem area. Nationalists bridle at the dependency of Wales upon central government and its regulatory posture. The government is committed to extending greater independence to Wales.[10] That decisions will need to be made by government is clear from the position taken by some Welsh and Scots with regard to their resources of water and North Sea oil respectively. Are these to be national resources to be developed by and for all the people of the United Kingdom, or are they to be resources of the Welsh and Scots to exploit at the expense of the English?

The British and American Civil Services

The changing of the guard with new administrations, when these new administrations involve a change in political party, are much the same in the two countries. Members of the President's cabinet, who are secretaries of the executive departments, and the under secretaries and the assistant secretaries are appointed by the President with the approval of the Senate. The British secretaries of state and ministers, who also head departments, are appointed by the Prime Minister, but they are selected from amongst members of parliament. The impact of changes of government in Britain tend to be less severe on the Civil Service than in the United States, as the opposition party maintains a shadow cabinet often made up of those who served in the cabinet under that party's administration or those who would serve in a new cabinet if the opposition were to win power. Thus the new secretaries of state and ministers are generally familiar with their departments.

From initial conception through its passage and implementation, many different groups were vociferous in their denunciation of all or parts of the Water Act and those responsible for it. These critical comments resulted from true differences of professional opinion and not from any disrespect for the Civil Service officers responsible for preparing the Bill. Most British professionals hold their Civil Service colleagues in high regard, regardless of the party in power. The British Civil Service, in contrast with its American counterpart, is largely free of political infiltration and serves to provide continuity in effecting legislative change, although some may charge elements of the Civil Service with becoming 'fossilized'.

The high esteem in which the British Civil Service is held, may be gleaned from a bit of dialogue from a popular mystery novel.[11] The protagonist is a young Welshman reared on a farm who escaped to pursue higher education, including the reading of politics, philosophy, and economics at the London School of Economics, a prestigious institution of higher learning. He had hoped to join the Civil Service, but enjoyed summer work riding and became a jockey. His probity on the track is challenged and he organizes his own investigation in a way that stirs the admiration of a 'Lord Ferth' who concludes '. . . it's a pity you didn't join the Civil Service. You'd have gone all the way.'

It is difficult to imagine that an American novelist would choose to characterize his hero's high qualities by asserting that he would have been a good civil servant.

The American columnist, Jack Anderson, asserted that 36 senators and 32 congressmen pushed a single federal agency to find civil service jobs for their friends. While federal law prohibits preferential treatment in civil service hiring in the United States, flexibility in the law permits all types of violations. Anderson asserted that the General Services Administration's files showed that more than 300 people got their jobs in that one agency through political favoritism and that a special unit was created within the agency to handle the illegal patronage referrals. The Civil Service Commission itself reported that political interests influence appointments 'in a style that approximates a patronage system' concluding that many officials of one agency were hired illegally during the Nixon years because of their political contacts.[12]

The problems of the Civil Service are magnified when a new agency is created and many new positions become available to be filled. A case in point is the Environmental Protection Agency which was created in 1970 from several existing agencies, including the Federal Water Pollution Control Administration, during the Nixon Republican Party administration. Established at a time when many Republican candidates for Congress were defeated, and with a new and enlarged mandate requiring huge increases in personnel, the EPA became a haven for defeated politicians and their aides. For many, these positions were merely way-stations pending more successful campaigns for other political posts. Not only was the efficiency of EPA seriously reduced by having key positions filled by inexperienced appointees with no career aspirations in the agency, but highly qualified professional civil servants who had transferred to the EPA felt obliged to resign from the Civil Service or to take early retirement.

New regulatory agencies in the United States often build up staff from among those to be regulated. The EPA, one of nine regulatory agencies that responded to a questionnaire from the investigations subcommittee of the House of Representatives commerce committee, indicated that 51 employees of its staff had been previously employed by industries regulated by EPA.[13] While such individuals can bring important qualifications to regulatory agencies, they may bring an industry bias as well. The differences between the two civil services are more a reflection of the times than of inherent dissimilarities. A revitalization of the US Civil Service, along with the development of greater trust between the federal government and the states leading to a return of powers to the states, may improve the respect in which government is held by those governed, an essential ingredient to rational legislation and enforcement.

CHRONOLOGY AND BACKGROUND FOR THE WATER REORGANIZATION IN ENGLAND AND WALES

Proposals for regional water management in England and Wales were initiated a century ago. A series of essays was published in the *Journal of the Society of Arts* in 1879 on the subject 'Suggestions for dividing England and Wales into watershed districts', apparently as a competition. One proposal, the winner of a silver medal, called for 12 watershed districts with boundaries not much different from those now adopted, each containing one or more complete river basins, managed by commissioners who would have charge of all the rivers and water works in their district so 'that every drop of water falling in their district should be more or less under their control, from the time it falls on the land until it reaches the sea'.[14] This proposal recommended conterminous districts, with separate commissioners, for sewerage and sewage treatment because '. . . the Commisioners of Water Supply will be much more likely to guard the rivers jealously from pollution if they have not themselves the task of purifying the polluted waters of the sewers'. Thus, the 'poacher–gamekeeper' conflict, which we discuss in Chapter 8, was seen to be an issue from the start.

The story of the modern revolution in water management begins with the successful regrouping of water supplies under the Water Act 1945 and follows with the Water Resources Act 1963 which created the now defunct Water Resources Board and river authorities (Chapter 2). (A chronology of the precursors to the reorganization is in Appendix 1.) The prompt action on the reorganization can be attributed to the reorganization of local government, itself a most revolutionary step, under the Local Government Act 1972, which called for two-tier government, with many fewer local authorities, as of 1 April 1974. Because many local authorities that were being reorganized were responsible for water services, the water reorganization was timed to take place on the same date.

The government's move towards regionalization began with a series of consultation papers which were widely distributed amongst individuals and organizations that were to be affected either directly or indirectly, with their responses having a significant impact on the final form of the Water Bill (Chapter 3). The debates on the Water Bill in parliament illuminated the issues although few changes were made (Chapter 4). With Royal Assent on 18 July 1973, only nine months were available for preparing for implementation of the Act, during which shadow water authorities were created, staffs were assembled, organizational structures were developed, and budgets were prepared (Chapter 5). Changes that would ordinarily take place over decades were compressed into a few months. Thus the first half of this volume examines the process of reorganization. (A timetable of the reorganization is in Appendix 2.)

A description of each of the ten water authorities (WAs) and how they organized themselves follows (Chapter 6) along with the agencies at the national level, such as the National Water Council and the Water Research Centre (Chapter 7).

A major issue addressed by the water reorganization is improved water quality management and the control of water pollution (Chapter 8). The true costs of water service, and particularly water pollution control, have always been masked by central government subsidies. The reorganization eliminated such subsidies and placed upon consumers the burden of meeting the true costs of the service. Methods for meeting the revenue requirements while maintaining equity among consumers became the key issue upon which the success of the reorganization will inevitably rest (Chapter 9).

The significance of the reorganization for the water industry in the United States is discussed, in part on the basis of the five principles enunciated in the introduction (Chapter 10). Finally, the problems of the reorganization, including the government's review of the reorganization and the prospects for the future, are reviewed (Chapter 11).[15]

CHAPTER 2

Prelude to Regionalization

Unheralded at the time, both in the United Kingdom and abroad, the Water Act 1945 was the essential first step leading to the regionalization of all water management in England and Wales, with the Rivers Board Act 1948 being the second. Preparatory studies leading to these Acts were initiated and conducted during the height of the military engagements of World War II. The Central Advisory Water Committee, the Milne Committee, in 1943 recommended the establishment of river authorities to integrate water pollution control, water conservation, and rivers control.[1] A government White Paper, A National Water Policy (1944), accepted the essence of the Milne Committee report, while recommending that the Minister of Health be given responsibility for central planning and water conservation.[2]

These studies revealed several major concerns:

1. Adequacy of water supply, particularly in industrialized urban areas, was being threatened.
2. The large number of local authorities, each responsible for providing its own water supply and wastewater collection, were not generally up to addressing the problems that often required joint action.
3. Government exerted little influence on the passage or implementation of local acts for water management.
4. A confusion of authorities, responsibilities and controls over the water in the river and the river itself prevailed.
5. No national strategy for water management existed and the necessary data upon which such a strategy might be based were not available.

In terms of the national consciousness, attention to water supply at that time may not be as strange to an Englishman as to an American. (Groundwork had been laid during the war for the new National Health Service.) The war, and particularly the bombings, may have accentuated the need for more adequate water supplies for fire-fighting.

THE WATER ACT 1945

These elements of the Water Act 1945 were most significant:

1. A single Minister, the Minister of Health, was charged with the responsibility 'to promote the conservation and proper use of water resources and the provision of water supplies in England and Wales and to secure the effective execution by water undertakers, under his control and direction' of a national policy relating to water.

2. The Central Advisory Water Committee was created to advise the Government in matters related to water. (CAWC was eventually to prepare the way for the Water Resources Act 1963 and the Water Act 1973, the latter calling for the demise of the Water Resources Board created by the former and the demise of CAWC itself.)

3. The Minister was authorized to order, without an application of any of the local authorities concerned, the constitution of a united district of all or parts of local authorities or joint water boards for the purpose of providing water supply for areas larger than that of any single local authority. The Act empowered the Minister 'where it appears . . . expedient for the purpose of securing a more efficient supply of water to . . . by order provide compulsorily for any of these matters'.

The last authorization led to the extensive regrouping or regionalization of water supply undertakings.[3] Originally, the water undertakings were expected to initiate the regrouping but, in 1956, because of resistance and its slow pace, the Ministry of Housing and Local Government, which had taken over water responsibilities from the Ministry of Health, embarked upon an aggressive program to accelerate the process. From an original 1186 water undertakings in 1945 and 1030 in 1956, the number dropped precipitously to 260 in 1968. By the time of the reorganization of 1 April 1974, the number of water supply undertakings had been reduced to only 187 separate agencies serving almost 50 000 000 people. This regrouping was to provide a foundation without which reorganization on the scale proposed in the Water Act 1973 might not have been attempted.

Initially, this regrouping had been bitterly fought throughout the water supply industry. Organizations with long histories of service, and positions of authority within these organizations, were to disappear. Local identification with local water supply undertakings and the people operating them were to be replaced by the anonymity of larger and presumably less responsive agencies. However, the fact that about 20 percent of public water supply in England and Wales had been provided by private statutory water companies suggested that a managerial form of organization is as suitable as a so-called democratic local authority organization for providing water service.

Regrouping was implemented very gradually by persuasion rather than fiat. Following the 1950 election, the Labour government did not enact legislation compelling regrouping and, even when government policy was to push regrouping, only about ten percent of the regrouping orders were made compulsorily. By contrast, in Scotland in 1968, regrouping was effected by Act of Parliament, reducing the number of undertakings from 199 to 14 almost overnight. Had there been more pressure for regrouping, the number of water supply undertakings at the time of reorganization might have been halved.

Nevertheless, even the most prejudiced observer would agree that regrouping was a great success, creating strong water supply undertakings and excellent service to the public. Because of their large size, and with financial assistance under the Rural Water Supplies and Sewerage Acts 1944 and 1955, water supply undertakings were able to reach out into rural communities to the extent that more than 99 percent of the total population of England and Wales are served with piped water from well-operated public systems, a statistic that is matched by only one or two other countries in the world. Difficulties with water supply undertakings were not responsible for the initiatives leading to further regionalization. Rather, their success accounted in large measure for an appreciation of what might be accomplished by further consolidation. The process produced a body of professionals familiar with the trauma associated with massive restructuring who were prepared to give leadership in what, inevitably, was bound to be a most trying period.

Opposition to the 1974 reorganization emanated principally from those who had not been regrouped, principally in the wastewater collection and disposal fields, represented by officers of the Institute of Water Pollution Control who were still decrying the Water Act 1973 long after it had been passed.

Had a formal study and report of the process and significance of the regrouping of water supply been made, with both qualitative and quantitative assessments of the changes between 1945 and 1973, much of the ammunition would have been removed from the opponents of the 1974 reorganization. Hopefully, studies of regionalization of water management under the Water Act 1973 will be mounted, not only for the benefit of the government and water industry officials in England and Wales, but also for the benefit of their colleagues elsewhere in the world.

THE RIVER BOARDS ACT 1948

While the Water Act 1945 addressed the recommendations of the 1944 White Paper as related to water supply, the River Boards Act 1948 gave legislative attention to the recommendations concerning the establishment of river boards. Functions previously undertaken by local authorities, catchment boards, and fisheries boards relating to land drainage and flood control, navigation, fisheries and pollution control were consolidated into 32 river boards in England and Wales. The river boards were also to initiate programs of data collection on river abstractions and discharges.

Until passage of the Rivers (Prevention of Pollution) Acts 1951 and 1961, the river boards' powers embraced only the limited scope of the Rivers (Prevention of Pollution) Act 1876. These new Acts, '... to make new provision for maintaining or restoring the wholesomeness of the rivers and other inland or coastal waters of England and Wales ...' put restrictions upon the discharges of pollutants to rivers and established a system of consent by river boards for discharges to rivers. Essentially, these Acts applied to discharges to non-tidal rivers. Control over tidal rivers and estuaries under the Clean Rivers (Estuaries and Tidal Waters) Act 1960 was restricted to new or substantially altered discharges. All discharges could, in theory, be controlled with a Tidal Waters Order but, up to 1970, only 14 such orders had been made and none on any of the major polluted estuaries.[4] Discharges to the tidal Thames have been controlled since 1968 by local legislation.

The 1951 Act, in Section 9, authorized the regrouping of sewerage functions. However, except for a total of only 27 joint boards, sewerage and sewage disposal remained a local authority function, with almost 1400 separate undertakings providing service until the 1974 reorganization.

THE WATER RESOURCES ACT 1963

Prodded by a most serious drought in the summer of 1959 that caused severe restrictions on the use of water and threatened many industrial operations, the Central Advisory Water Committee authorized by the Water Act 1945 and established in 1955 came out with its Proudman Committee Report in 1962 that drew attention to the need for national policy planning for water.[5] The existence of a large number of authorities, each acting in an isolated fashion without regard to the situation nearby or nationally, was deplored.

CAWC saw the need for new administrative devices that would permit and encourage comprehensive water planning and recommended the creation of river authorities that would replace the river boards with additional responsibility for water conservation (water resources development). The river authorities were to be authorized to assess resources, to execute water development works, to license river abstractions and to introduce a system of charges to finance their operations. CAWC also recommended the creation of a central executive body to promote an active policy for water, to coordinate the activities of the river authorities, and to construct works for water conservation.

A government White Paper that same year (1962) accepted most of these recommendations, excepting only the proposal for a central executive body, substituting an advisory body with a mandate only for water conservation planning but without power to execute projects.[6]

The Proudman Committee had recommended compact river authorities with only 10 to 15 members: 'We attach less importance to representation as such than to the efficient and expeditious discharge of the wide range of functions involved'. The Government recommended instead, using an argument that was to become familiar in connection with the constitution of the new water authorities in 1973, river authorities with 21 to 31 members to be appointed by both local authorities and the Minister of Housing and Local Government and the Minister of Agriculture, Fisheries and Food.

In a review of the history of the Water Resources Act 1963 by Barr,[7] Lord Hastings, then Joint Parliamentary Secretary of the Ministry of Housing and Local Government, is quoted as identifying its purpose as securing '. . . that sufficient water is made available for any reasonable use in any part of the country. It does this by providing for a national plan for the development of water resources, and national supervision over its execution.' In the debate, proposals for maintaining minimum flows in the rivers and for charging for abstractions from the rivers were affirmed.

Regrets were widely expressed that the government did not propose to centralize power, recast the water undertakings, or combine water conservation and supply and distribution. Denis Howell (to become Minister of State for the Environment in a Labour government) pointed out that it is administratively wasteful to have separate water supply and wastewater disposal organizations, an idea that was somewhat ahead of its time.

The Government claimed that the central advisory body it projected, the Water Resources Board, was to be given sufficient powers to undertake its duties with respect to the collection of information, the coordination of the activities of the river authorities, and national planning for water resources development. In the words of Lord Hastings, introducing the bill in the House of Lords, '. . . surely this is a Board of real strength, and one with the duty of taking the initiative'.[8]

Opposition to proposals for the WRB was vehement, with claims that it would lack punch and drive; and that, as conceived, it would certainly not be as important a body as a central water authority for the nation should be. The government claimed that a strong central authority could not avoid cutting across Ministerial accountability, and therefore should not be created. The WRB's limited functional scope also came under attack with the assertion that it could not approach its mandate properly without also being responsible for control of pollution.

Despite the heavy criticism of the WRB, the Water Resources Act of 1963, when made law, received a wide range of encomiums: 'An important milestone in our history', 'A great step forward in our water legislation', and 'an immensely important and imaginative measure'.

The landmark nature of the Water Resources Act of 1963 lay in the conception of the 29 river authorities and their functions. Despite some strong pressures for consolidation into larger areal entities, they were little different in area from the existing river boards, generally having the same boundaries, based on watershed areas, with some consolidation (Fig. 2.1).

The river authorities would have responsibility in their areas for land drainage (including flood control), fisheries and prevention of pollution, as performed by the river boards and would add responsibilities for the development of water resources. They also were to initiate hydrologic data collection programs, and surveys of current resources and anticipated requirements preparatory to initiating programs of development.

Most important, while continuing to have power to grant consents for discharges into their rivers, the new river authorities were to have, through licensing, and charges for licenses and abstraction, complete control over the abstraction and impounding of waters in their domains. They were also to have the power to acquire land and control new discharges into underground strata.

The river authorities were to derive their income from several sources: precepts upon the general rates collected by local authorities; precepts upon rates levied by drainage boards; license fees and charges for water abstraction; land drainage charges; and fees for fishing licenses. It was the charging for water abstractions that was the novel concept and these charges were intended to meet the costs of water resources development.

The Water Resources Act 1963 consolidated executive power and responsibility, limited though these might have been, in the river authorities with their consent control of pollution and their power to charge for abstractions and use these financial resources for water resource development. The Water Resources Board was to achieve considerably more renown but its mandate and its powers were sharply restricted.

The Water Resources Board

The first tasks of the Water Resources Board were associated with the inauguration of 'intelligence' gathering. Beginning with their *Second Annual Report*, in 1965 (the *pro forma First Annual Report* being submitted only a few months after its formation) to the *Tenth Annual Report* (the last) for the year ending 30 September 1973,[9] major attention was given to a continuing assessment of the water resources of England and Wales. Without question, an important legacy of the Water Resources Act 1963 and the WRB will have been the institutionalizing of the data gathering so essential to rational water planning.

Fig. 2.1   River authorities in England and Wales.

Over the years of its existence, the attention of the WRB focused increasingly on water resource planning. Their first study, *Water Supplies in Southeast England*, was published in 1966.[10] This was followed over its lifetime by reports extending the studies to all areas of England and Wales culminating in its comprehensive study, *Water Resources in England and Wales*.[11] In addition, a wide variety of special reports was prepared, including wash and estuarial storage schemes, desalination, underground recharge, and the wide-ranging Trent Research Programme. The substantive recommendations of the WRB are discussed in Chapter 8.

The WRB research program was directed toward providing the basis for its reports, with some 80 to 90 percent of its funds being devoted to an assessment of new water sources and their development, data acquisition and operational research. The ecological effect of water resources projects and water demand and engineering studies accounted for the remainder. No investment was made in water quality or water pollution studies, as these were not within the purview of WRB.

The neglect of water quality and water pollution by WRB can be attributed to its limited mandate in the Act, and its frustration was articulated in its *Seventh Annual Report* in 1970:[12] 'We cannot deal competently with problems of managing water resources without going beyond our strict terms of reference. ... The Board's terms of reference do not include ... prevention of pollution, but water quality is a crucial factor in nearly all our work. The two operations of providing water for use and disposing of it after use are clearly interrelated and inseparable. The importance of this will grow in the future as reuse of water in rivers plays an increasing part in meeting needs, i.e. as effluent contributes increasingly to the supply of water ... the most serious defect in the present system is the lack of any national authority charged with planning and coordinating the work of the 1400 sewage treatment authorities...'.†

One measure of the interest of WRB in water quality considerations was the qualifications and/or interests of its technical staff. Of a total of 151 published professional and scientific papers prepared by staff members during the life of the WRB, only nine can be said to have any relationship to water quality, and most of these were authored or co-authored by the same individual. Publications of the WRB itself, extensive as they were, included no reports with any emphasis on water quality other than several volumes of the twelve-volume report of the Trent Research Programme and one of 12 Technical Notes. In the *Ninth Annual Report*, a summary of the register of

† However, in Section 12 of the Act, the WRB was charged 'to bring to the notice of the river authority concerned any case where it appeared to the Board that, for the purpose of securing the proper use of water resources in a river authority area, the quality of the water contained in inland water in that area needs to be improved, and that the requisite improvement could be obtained through the exercise of powers conferred by the Rivers (Prevention of Pollution) Acts 1951 to 1961.

research projects listed only 11 of 128 research projects with any concern for water quality, and half of these were part of the Trent Research Programme.[13]

In its final report, the WRB summarized it accomplishments, some of which are paraphrased below, with parenthetical comments by the author.[14]

Retrospect

The WRB was concerned from the start to get to know the people with whom it was to deal. Cordial relations were established with the river authorities and the statutory water supply undertakers. (No mention was made of relations with the local authorities responsible for wastewater disposal.)

The primary task laid on the WRB by the Water Resources Act of 1963 was to provide advice as to the development and use of water resources in England and Wales. This required a broader outlook than merely the cheapest way of meeting water demand; the Act required a concern for amenity. (No reference here made to water quality, other than to preserve amenity. Quality for protection of sources of water used for drinking was not mentioned.)

The use of rivers as aqueducts, the use of reservoirs to regulate river flows, and the successive uses of water by a sequence of abstractions and discharges made the problems of water quality and wastewater disposal inseparable from the problems of providing clean water for abstraction. (A recognition, in words, of the quality issue.)

Last thoughts

'Our concern under the Water Resources Act has been to secure the proper use in the widest sense of water resources in England and Wales. This has necessarily involved us in such fundamental issues as the interrelation of *water quality* and water quantity and the needs of amenity and recreation, especially fisheries.' (Italics mine.)

While it was hoped that the WRB's work would lead to the right choices for water development in the future, many problems remain for the new authorities, '. . . none more urgent or of greater importance for the future than water quality'.

In its brief nine-year history, the WRB may well have been frustrated by a limited mandate flowing from the 1963 Act. Also, it suffered from changes in Ministries to which it had been responsible: initially, the Ministry of Housing and Local Government; in 1965, the Ministry of Land and Natural Resources and the Secretary of State for Wales; in 1967, the Ministry of Land and Natural Resources was dissolved, and responsibility reverted to the Ministry of Housing and Local Government and the

Secretary of State for Wales; and in 1970, Secretaries of State for the Environment and for Wales.

However, there can be no gainsaying that the WRB ventured the first comprehensive examination of water resources needs and prospects for meeting these needs in England and Wales. In institutionalizing data collection, and in examining a wide range of options, WRB did much to facilitate the next phase of water resources development. Exclusion of water quality from its consideration, as mandated in the 1963 Act, does open its specific national strategy to question.

The river authorities

The river authorities were a logical extension toward multipurpose agencies; beginning with the original single-purpose catchment boards, followed by a broadening function in their immediate predecessors, the river boards. In addition to the functions usually exercised by the river boards for land drainage, fisheries, river pollution, and navigation, the river authorities were to act '. . . for the purpose of conserving, redistributing or otherwise augmenting water resources in their area, of securing the proper use of water resources in their area, or of transferring any such resources to the area of another river authority'.

The river authorities' land drainage responsibilities included flood control in both urban and rural areas. They executed the maintenance of river banks, the clearing of river obstructions, reshaping river beds and construction of new channels, including flood relief channels and sluices, and in some instances sea defense (coastal protection) works. In discharging their pollution prevention responsibilities, the river authorities performed detailed analyses of samples of river water. Where pollution was a major problem, river authority inspectors made periodic visits to wastewater treatment works and factories to ensure that operations were satisfactory. They would advise on the capacity of a treatment works to handle projected additional housing, or whether a trade waste was acceptable even after treatment. The river authority might request that county planning authorities put a 'standing-still order' on an area until facilities were acceptable, but this approach was abandoned as a misuse of the planning power relegated to the local authorities.

Under the Water Resources Act 1963, the river authorities became responsible for developing water resources for water supply undertakings that formerly were themselves responsible for finding and developing their own sources and that were resentful at having lost this responsibility.

From 1 July 1965, the abstraction of water from a surface or underground source was not permitted without a license. Licenses of right were issued to those who were already abstracting. In general, the larger abstractors were required to meter their abstractions. Except for cooling waters, water supply undertakings represented the major abstractors.

TABLE 2.1
Number of Licenses for Water Abstractions as of 31 December 1972

	Surface water	*Ground water*	*Total*
Water supply			
Statutory Water			
Undertakings	1 263	1 624	2 887
Other	1 633	926	2 559
Agriculture	7 927	23 867	31 794
Irrigation, other than			
agriculture	200	150	350
Industry	3 680	3 945	7 625
TOTAL	14 703	30 512	45 215

Agricultural users had extensive numbers of licenses, but the amounts that they were permitted to abstract, and the amounts that in fact they did abstract, were quite small. Data on licensing and abstractions are shown in Tables 2.1, 2.2, and 2.3.

The river authority licensing procedures served to pinpoint, for purposes of national planning, where the demands were. The river authorities with the greater water demands in England and Wales were the Trent River Authority, Mersey and Weaver River Authority, Thames Conservancy and Severn River Authority.

TABLE 2.2
Total Quantity of Water Authorized for Abstraction as of 31 December 1972
(In 1000 million cubic meters per year)

	Surface water	*Ground water*	*Total*	%
Water supply				
Statutory Water				
Undertakings	5·4	2·7	8·1	31
Other	0·2	—	0·2	1
Agriculture	0·2	0·1	0·3	1
Industry				
Central Electricity				
Generating Board	11·4	—	11·4	44
Other	5·0	1·1	6·1	23
TOTAL	22·2	3·9	26·1	100

TABLE 2.3
Actual Quantity of Water Abstracted in 1972
(in 1000 million cubic meters)

	Surface water	*Ground water*	*Total*	*%*
Water supply	3·6	1·8	5·4	36
Agriculture	<0·1	—	<0·1	1
Industry				
Central Electricity				
Generating Board				
Cooling	5·9	—	5·9	39
Other	0·2	—	0·2	2
Evaporation	0·2	—	0·2	2
Other				
Cooling	2·3	0·2	2·5	16
Other	0·2	0·1	0·3	2
Evaporation	0·2	0·1	0·3	2
TOTAL	12·7	2·2	14·9	100

Control of discharges

The river authorities inherited the responsibility for issuing consents (permits) for wastewater discharges authorized by the Rivers (Prevention of Pollution) Acts of 1951 and 1961 and the Clean Rivers (Estuaries and Tidal Waters) Act of 1960. Each consent contained conditions based upon the particular circumstances, including volumes to be discharged and limits of toxic substances. The Royal Commission (1915) 30/20 Standard, which requires that the effluent not exceed 30 milligrams per liter of suspended solids (SS) or 20 milligrams per liter of biochemical oxygen demand (BOD) was widely adopted for municipal effluents. With trade effluents or where dilution was limited, as in the rivers Thames and Lee which are used as sources of water supply for London, special conditions could be established.

Although violators could be fined, the general practice had been to pursuade polluters, and to adjust conditions to a compromise comfortable to all. Only a strong public outcry was likely to induce the river authorities to precipitate action, and even then the fines were trivial, and far less than damages won by the Anglers' Co-operative Association on behalf of their members' riparian angling interests. Despite this, a gradual but well-defined rate of improvement was observed in the rivers of England and Wales.

Greater attention was traditionally given to rivers that serve as sources of potable water supply. The institutional agreements, with river authority regulators maintaining surveillance, seemed to assure that more rapid progress would have been made had there been more public pressure.

Charging for abstractions

The most innovative aspect of the Water Resources Act 1963 was the authority for the river authorities to initiate charges for abstractions: 'The charges ... shall be levied at such rates ... as appear to the River Authority to be requisite for balancing their water resources account'. Charges would be levied on all persons at the same rate with respect to the same quantity of water authorized to be abstracted in the same relevant circumstances. Among the 'relevant circumstances' were the following:

1. the characteristics of the source of supply,
2. the season of the year in which the water was to be abstracted,
3. the purposes for which the water was authorized to be used, and
4. the way in which the water was to be disposed of after use.

Under the implied mandate of the Act, the charges were intended only to meet the expenses of the river authorities on their water resources accounts. With the minimal charges initiated, they were not intended to exert influence upon water use. According to Rees, two river authorities had in fact stated that it would be unethical to think of water charges as a rationing device.[15]

Some license holders, with no real need, were encouraged to give up their licenses and some abstractors were encouraged to reduce the level of their

TABLE 2.4
River Authority Charges for Abstractions in Pence Per 1000 Gallons (4·55 cubic meters)

River authority	Number of categories of charges[a]	1970–71 Industry and public water supply			
		Surface water		Ground water	
		Winter	Summer	Winter	Summer
Avon & Dorset	4	0·12	0·36	0·12	0·22
Essex	6	0·43	2·16	1·73	1·73
Great Ouse	3	0·31	1·25	0·62	0·62
Hampshire	3	0·14	0·14	—	—
Lea	3	0·14	0·42	0·14	0·42
Kent	2	0·20	0·60	—	—
East Suffolk & Norfolk	3	0·15	1·01	0·46	0·46
Sussex	1	0·14	1·74	—	—
Thames	2	0·28	1·12	—	—
Welland & Nene	3	0·17	1·7	0·04	0·4

[a] includes various surface and ground waters, classified by quality, reach, tidal or non-tidal, storage facilities, point of return, etc.

authorization rather than the level of use. The quantity licensed for abstraction was not guaranteed to be available, but the license holder was assured that no other license, prejudicing his right, would be issued by the river authority. Table 2.4 is illustrative of charges of some of the river authorities.†

A thorough assessment of the Water Resources Act 1963 is beyond the scope of this volume, but can be found in a study by Craine.[16]

Perhaps the most significant contribution of the short-lived river authorities was their operating experience as true multifunctional agencies, the only such in the water field in the United Kingdom. One not unimportant benefit was the large number of professionals, relative to their total number in the water industry, that the river authorities contributed to the higher echelons of the new water authorities. In a country where sharp distinctions had always been made between the 'clean' and 'dirty' water fields, the river authorities developed leadership with an understanding of both, a resource sorely needed in the reorganized water industry.

THE LOCAL GOVERNMENT ACT 1972

The Local Government Act, 1972, calling for the reorganization of local authorities on 1 April 1974, with health services reorganization taking place on the same date, gave urgency to consideration of water reorganization. Many local authorities were responsible for water supply and almost all were responsible for sewerage and sewage disposal. The alleged poor performance of local authorities in discharging their sewerage and sewage disposal functions was given as one of the major reasons for water reorganization. If water reorganization were to follow long after 1 April 1974, then local government would have to suffer two successive and equally traumatic reorganizations over a very short period.

History of local government in England

'At the opening of the 19th century certain towns had municipal corporations with a variety of powers, and appointed or elected in a variety of ways. Elsewhere ... functions were exercised by unpaid justices of the peace, ... by a weak parish organization, and by a mass of separate authorities—such as turnpike trusts, improvement commissioners and local boards—with powers over a limited area to deal with each problem as and when it arose. The result has been described as "a chaos of areas, a chaos of franchises, a chaos of authorities, and a chaos of rates". In certain districts there were no authorities of any kind to run the necessary services. In others the newly created and old established authorities often found

---

† The gallons used in the text are Imperial gallons, equal to 1·2 US gallons, or 4·55 liters.

themselves with similar or overlapping functions. Usually, each separate authority had power to levy a rate to pay for its special purposes; the rate-payer, however, had no way of exercising supervison or control.'[17]

Reforms during the 19th century culminated in the creation of the county councils in 1888 and in the Local Government Act 1894, establishing urban and rural district councils. Not until the conclusion of World War II were changes in local government structure seen to be necessary. The first effort, a Local Boundary Commission in 1945, was unsuccessful. The Local Government Act 1958 created local government commissions for England and Wales, but recommendations were only partially implemented. A Royal Commission on Local Government in 1969 finally provided an acceptable basis for local government reorganization. The Labour government that had been responsible for earlier proposals for reform was replaced in 1970 by a Conservative government. Revised proposals announced in 1971 were incorporated in the Local Government Act 1972, which established new systems of local government for England and Wales, excepting London which had been reorganized in 1965 with the creation of the Greater London Council.

Prior to 1 April 1974, local government in England and Wales comprised a total of 1424 local authorities, comprising single-tier and two-tier local governments, including 83 county boroughs whose councils were responsible for major services with other services being delegated to 259 borough councils, 522 urban district councils, and 469 rural district councils.

In addition to these authorities, some 10 000 parishes, primarily in the rural areas, exercise limited responsibilities such as for community halls, recreational facilities, footway lighting, tourism, cemeteries, and crema-toria often by agreement with the district and/or county councils. Parish councils are generally given an opportunity to comment on planning applications and may spend up to two pence in the pound for the general benefit of their areas, obtaining these funds through 'precepts' on the district councils. The role of parishes was not substantially changed by local government reorganization and presumably continues much as before.

The new organization of local government

All local government in England and Wales now operates under a two-tier system of local authorities, into which the existing London government fits quite well. The top tier of local government is made up of 47 county councils plus the Greater London Council and 6 Metropolitan County Councils.

The second tier for London constitutes 32 London Boroughs plus the City of London (in which the financial district is located). The metropolitan counties, with 36 district councils, include six conurbations shown in Fig. 2.2 centered on Newcastle, Liverpool, Manchester, Leeds, Sheffield, and

County boundary
Metropolitan county
National boundary

Northumberland
Tyne and Wear
Cleveland
Cumbria
Durham
North Yorkshire
Lancashire
West Yorkshire
Humberside
Greater Manchester
Merseyside
South Yorkshire
Cheshire
Derbyshire
Nottinghamshire
Lincolnshire
Clwyd
Gwynedd
Staffordshire
Leicestershire
Norfolk
Salop
West Midlands
Warwickshire
Northamptonshire
Cambridgeshire
Suffolk
Powys
Hereford and Worcester
Bedfordshire
Dyfed
Gloucestershire
Oxfordshire
Buckinghamshire
Hertfordshire
Essex
Gwent
GREATER LONDON
West Glamorgan
Mid Glamorgan
South Glamorgan
Avon
Berkshire
Surrey
Kent
Wiltshire
Somerset
Hampshire
West Sussex
East Sussex
Dorset
Devon
Isle of Wight
Cornwall

0   20   40   60   80   100 MILES
0   20   40   60   80   100 120 KILOMETRES

FIG. 2.2   Counties in England and Wales as of 1 April 1974. Greater London has its own local government structure, different from that in the rest of England and Wales. Reproduced by permission of the Controller of Her Majesty's Stationery Office.

Birmingham. The metropolitan county areas were established with each metropolitan county extended for most part to the edge of the continuously built-up area of the conurbation enclosed by the county. Thus, for the first time, each of the conurbations outside London has one local authority to administer strategic functions over the entire metropolitan area.

The 47 counties governed by county councils include 333 district councils at the second tier. The total of 456 local authorities ranges in size from the Greater London Council with a resident population of 7·3 million to non-metropolitan counties of as few as 283 000 (Northumberland). In Wales, the counties range in population from 99 000 to 536 000.

The second-tier metropolitan district councils serve populations ranging from an average size of 227 000 for a London borough to 1·1 million in the Birmingham metropolitan district. The non-metropolitan district councils cover areas with populations ranging in general between 60 000 and 100 000. Twelve of the new districts have populations below 40 000 as compared with 75 percent of the former local authorites having populations below this figure.

Classification of functions

The broad divisions of functions between the two tiers for each of the three general area classifications, the metropolitan areas, non-metropolitan areas and Greater London, are shown in Fig. 2.3. In general, the larger strategic and planning functions are assigned to the county councils, while the direct services are assigned to the district councils. The amenities such as museums, recreational facilities, tourism and the like are authorized functions for all levels of government, including the parishes.

The functions related to water, such as development and housing, are responsibilities of the second-tier district councils, which deal with local plans and deal with most applications for planning permission and other matters concerned with local development.

With the water reorganization, the water, sewerage and sewage disposal functions of the local authorities were transferred to the water authorities as of 1 April 1974. The one continuing local authority water responsibility is their service as agents for the WAs in the discharge of the sewerage functions. For the first two or three years after reorganization, these councils were also to collect charges on behalf of the WAs.

Water authorities and local authorities

The Royal Commission on Local Government was shocked to learn, at quite a late stage in its deliberations, that the section of the Ministry of Housing and Local Government (the predecessor to the Department of the Environment) responsible for sewerage and water supply was urging that these functions should be taken out of local government no matter what changes in local government structure the Commission might propose and

FUNCTION	METROPOLITAN AREAS		NON-METROPOLITAN AREAS		GREATER LONDON	
	County Council	District Council	County Council	District Council	Greater London Council	London Borough Council
Planning						
structure plans	●		●		●	
local plans		●		●		●
development control		●		●		●
country parks	●	●	●	●		
national parks	●		●			
derelict land	●	●	●	●	●	●
Transport						
transport planning	●		●		●	
highways	●		●		●	●
traffic regulation	●		●		●	
road safety	●		●		●	
parking	●		●		●	●
public transport	●		●		●	
Education		●	●		● inner London	● outer London
Social Services		●	●			●
Housing		●		●	●	●
Fire Service	●		●		●	
Police Service	●		●			
Consumer Protection	●		●			●
Environmental Health						
building regulations		●		●	● inner London	● outer London
clean air		●		●		●
control of disease		●		●		●
food hygiene		●		●		●
refuse collection		●		●		●
refuse disposal	●		●		●	
street cleansing		●		●		●
Libraries		●	●			●
Museums and the Arts	●	●	●	●	●	●
Recreational Facilities	●	●	●	●	●	●
Encouragement of Tourism	●	●	●	●	●	●
Cemeteries and Crematoria		●		●		●
Footpaths	●	●	●	●		●
Smallholdings	●		●		●	
Allotments		●		●		●

FIG. 2.3 Allocation of the main local government functions in England. Reproduced by permission of the Controller of Her Majesty's Stationery Office.

the government adopt.[18] The Ministry of Housing and Local Government had initially testified to the advantages of entrusting water distribution to the local authorities who were responsible for planning the location of new houses and factories. The design and timing of major new schemes for water supply and sewerage should develop from the best possible estimates of future needs, and the choice amongst various options should take account of all relevant considerations and not solely those of the water and sewerage undertakings. Local opinion and democratic control should weigh heavily in the balance in such decisions as:

The extent to which expenditures should be made in bringing piped water to remote rural properties.

The selection between two reservoir schemes, with the less expensive scheme perhaps doing more damage to the landscape or interfering more with the agricultural potential for land use.

The disposal of wastewaters from a coastal town as between discharge to the sea with limited treatment or discharge to inland waters with complete treatment.

The Ministry had claimed that the only way in which all relevant factors could be considered would be to have the water and sewerage programs administered by directly-elected multipurpose authorities, preferably regional authorities of adequate size.

In yielding this approach to one that would sever all water responsibilities from local government, Senior pointed out 'it was evidently characteristic of the department in charge of housing and planning . . . that what its left hand was up to remained unknown to its right hand, or even to its erstwhile head'.

That the Government in the end shifted all water functions into the new WAs outside local government is not hard to understand: local government had demonstrated a poor record of perfomance in the sewerage field, as it had not taken advantage of opportunities for regrouping of sewerage and sewage disposal facilities that had been generated by the Rivers (Prevention of Pollution) Act 1951. Under the press of requirements for local authority expenditure, sewage treatment enjoyed a low priority, as the benefits to be derived accrued generally to the ratepayers of another authority downstream. Even protecting local coastal waters stirred no great enthusiasm: '. . . the richest and most civilized of our cities are not ashamed to be among the worst offenders in what can only be described as a stinking morass of municipal delinquency, relieved only here and there by an island of altruism'.[18] In the light of the institutional arrangements in existence, local government officials were undoubtedly exerting perceived priorities in promoting the interests of their own communities and not subordinating them to those of their neighbors.

Shortly after the Water Act 1973 was passed, the Department of the Environment delineated the relationships between the local authorities and the new WAs.[19] As part of their responsibility for environmental health and consumer protection, the district councils and the London borough councils retain the functions that the local authorities have had under the Public Health Act 1936 for taking such steps as may be necessary for ascertaining the sufficiency and wholesomeness of water supplies within their areas. Where a local authority wishes to secure a supply of piped water or sewerage for part of its area, WAs are required to construct the facilities with an agreement that the local authority would reimburse the WA over a period of 12 years for any deficits that the WA incurs in providing the services.

Close cooperation between the WAs and local authorities at all levels would be necessary if the reorganizations of local government and water management were to succeed. Five factors were to contribute to this close cooperation:

1. the appointment of a majority of members on each WA from local authorities,
2. the local authorities' service as agents of the WAs for discharging the sewerage function,
3. the relationship of planning in the WAs to the system of land use planning,
4. cooperation in the provision of goods and services by one authority to another, and
5. arrangements for emergencies and disasters.

The role of local government in the future

On 1 April 1974 the local government correspondent for *The Times* stated: 'If local government, reorganized, is to be a force in the future, it must keep its functions and its independence. In both cases, the evidence weighs against local government.'[20] The Governments had always declared in favor of greater independence for local authorities but in fact had continuously eroded that independence by increasing both centralization of functions and financial dependence of local government on central government. The latter is effected by rejection of alternative sources of finance for local government. One forecast predicted that there would be no local government in England in 30 years time.

Local government reorganization had been supported by local authorities because they believed that increasing size and responsibility would renew their strength and would prevent further erosion of their functions. The local authorities rejected the idea that their larger size would make them more remote, claiming that their councillors would have more time for their constituents. However, with simultaneous deletion of local authorities' responsibilities for both water and public health, whether sufficient services remain to permit the new local authorities to continue viable poses a serious question.

Conflicts over functions between the two tiers, the district councils and the county councils, created additional difficulties. Further, uncertainty as to the future financial arrangements for local government resulted in a Government study of local government finance.

Government was charged with grossly ignoring its responsibilities to local government in preparing guidelines for their relations with the WAs, with grave problems arising from delays in project development and with machinery clogged by standards and regulations rigidly applied. The conflicts between the two tiers of local government '. . . will be as nothing compared with the conflicts being soaked up by the *ad hoc* water authorities.'[21]

Interviews with officials of local government illuminated other problems:[22]

1. many small authorities with poor records and personnel were not easily incorporated into larger structures;
2. agency agreements with the WAs for sewerage were giving difficulty;
3. staffing and policy guidelines for long-term programs needed to be initiated;
4. modern equipment, requisite for modern organizations, is not available in the office or in the field;
5. district and county councils are often incompatible, particularly as regards district council schemes that require county council approval; and
6. the larger units have difficulty in the recruitment of qualified staff not formerly used by the small local authorities, particularly in planning. Many of the more qualified personnel in local authorities were recruited to other positions because of uncertainties of the future.

Despite these difficulties, most articulate local authority personnel agreed that the reorganization was a move in the right direction and would, in time, serve the public better than the smaller local authorities had in the past.

HEALTH SERVICE REORGANIZATION

The National Health Service, created under the leadership of Aneurin Bevan in 1948, is one of the hallmarks of modern Britain. Visitors may be unaware of the local government serving them or of the water industry supplying them with water, but they almost always become aware of the health services available to the people of Britain and to the visitors themselves. Despite vociferous critics and detractors, the NHS unquestionably had become a model which to lesser or greater degree has been emulated elsewhere in the world. That it served so long without major reorganization may well be testimony to the quality of service it rendered.

The launching of a new and innovative health services program required that the initial NHS be a compromise. Local authorities at that time were so upset at losing control over their hospitals that it was essential to leave them the community health services. The newly created regional hospital boards and hospital management committees were responsible for voluntary and local authority hospitals but not for teaching hospitals. General practitioners were so fearful of losing their independence that they would not serve the National Health Service directly but would become independent under executive councils made up of medical professionals and laymen.

Thus, three branches of the NHS came under separate administrations. Not only was this inefficient from a management standpoint, but the patients were not served as well as would be expected from a unified health industry. For the bulk of his lifetime a patient would be under the care of his general practitioner, but when he went to hospital for treatment or

The Bevan NHS

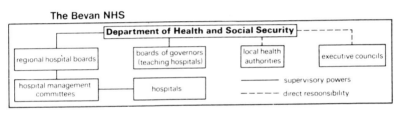

The NHS from 1 April 1974 —England only

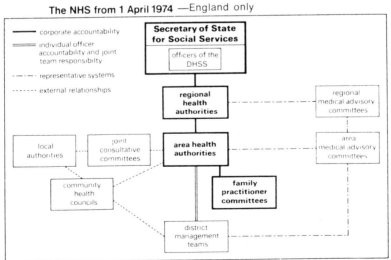

FIG. 2.4 Reorganization of the National Health Service.

diagnosis he would move under other auspices, which often were not in close contact with his GP. Unrelated to both of these were the community health services and the welfare services being managed by the local authorities. Often the needs of individuals would be lost betweeen these separate bureaucracies.

Those who initiated the major health reform had intended that the NHS would transform the health of the nation within a generation, while the cost of the service would decline in time because, as the population became more healthy, national expenditures on medical care would fall. This expectation has not been entirely fulfilled, but many improvements in health have been accomplished as a result of improved technology and the virtual elimination of malnutrition in children. The most impressive achievement claimed for the National Health Service is the steady decline in maternal and infant mortality.[23]

Despite the significant quality of improvement in health care for the mass of the population in Britain, the problems bespoke the need for a reorganization leading to a unification of health care so that patients would not suffer from the failures of competing bureaucracies. Reorganization studies were initiated by the Labour government in 1968, with subsequent parliamentary debate leading to a new NHS, with the aim of creating a management system that would utilize efficiently the 800 000 employees of the service and the £3000 million annual budget. Three major objectives of the reorganization were: unification of the various forms of health services available to patients, coordination between the NHS and local authorities, and improvement in management.[24]

The unification accomplished by the reorganization is seen in Fig. 2.4. Under the new organization, the services are brought together into a three-tier organization under the Secretary of State for Social Services. The local authorities lose control of personal health services, which are now a direct responsibility of area health authorities which are responsible to regional health authorities. Fourteen regional authorities in England are responsible for all the health services carried out by a total of 90 area health authorities, with 205 district management teams. The district management team is the basic operational unit, serving populations ranging from 80 000 to 410 000 people. This represents a consolidation of 15 regional hospital boards, 36 boards of governors of teaching hospitals, 330 hospital management committees and 175 local health authorities, all of which disappear.

The traditional responsibility of the local medical officer of health for the wholesomeness of drinking water, which continues under the water reorganization, comes under the jurisdiction of the new area health authorities, along with decisions in the highly charged matter of fluoridation.

CHAPTER 3

Creation of the Water Bill

In 1973, Britain was suffering the throes of crises that would have brought down many governments, and in fact did bring down the Conservative government early in 1974: an oil crisis brought on by the Middle East war of October, a coal crisis brought on by the National Miners' Union's refusal to work overtime, a rail crisis brought on by adherence of motormen to 'work to rule', IRA bombs everywhere, and runaway inflation. Why should the government have taken on the headache of reorganization of the water industry when, so far as could be observed, the general public had perceived no crisis that demanded precipitate action?

J. E. Beddoe, then Under Secretary in the Department of the Environment (DoE), and generally acclaimed (or damned) as 'chief architect' of the water reorganization, responded that Water Resources Board studies had indicated that, unless additional water resources were developed, there might well be serious water problems in the mid-1980s. Any major reorganization is bound to be accompanied by initial disorganization, and the government believed it better to reorganize well before the crisis was at hand.[1]

The need for new organizational arrangements had been made clear by the WRB in 1970. Not only was the range of its mandate limited but it had no power other than to publish. Its reports had little force, other than their own arguments, and the WRB had no constituency or machinery to force consideration of their recommendations, let alone to push for their implementation. In fact, this lack of executive power and concomitant executive responsibility led to inevitable conflicts between the WRB and those with the powers and responsibilities for implementation of water resources schemes, namely the DoE, the water supply undertakings, and the river authorities.

Even parliament did not appear to be too anxious to move the WRB's recommendations, largely because the WRB, being entirely technical in character, did not always assess political realities adequately, and parliament is primarily a political body.

The other major factor urging consideration of water reorganization was that the government had already committed itself to local government and health services reorganization. If anything was to be done about reorganizing the sewage disposal functions, it had best be done simultaneously with local government reorganization.

In appreciation of the need for study of the existing situation in the water industry, the government established the Working Party on Sewage Disposal in February 1969, chaired by Lena M. Jeger, MP, and in September 1969 reactivated the Central Advisory Water Committee (CAWC), authorized by the Water Act 1945. Meanwhile, in March 1969, a joint symposium was held in London on 'Future Organization of River, Sewage, and Water Authorities' under sponsorship of the Institution of Water Engineers, the Institution of Public Health Engineers, and the Institute of Water Pollution Control.

The proceedings of the Symposium, published in 1969,[2] the report of the Jeger Committee, published in 1970,[3] and especially the report of the CAWC, issued in April 1971,[4] all contributed significantly to the government's decision to move ahead. These documents helped shape the government's proposals for reorganization which were published before the end of 1971.[5]

The presence of the then sitting Royal Commission on Local Government in England, if not its recommendations which were not yet available, hung heavy over discussions of water reorganization. Fear was expressed that water reorganization might need to be adapted to decisions made for local government rather than for local government to be molded to permit sound reorganization of the water services.

C. H. Spens, chairman of the symposium and for almost ten years previously chief engineer of the Ministry of Housing and Local Government, concluded that '... change was necessary and change was bound to come'. The consensus was that despite its many positive features, in failing to define clearly the river authorities' responsibilities for developing water sources, the Water Resources Act 1963 undermined clearly designated responsibilities of the water undertakers as spelled out in the 1945 Act.

Wide differences of opinion were expressed at the symposium, in part because the water engineers participated almost exclusively in the first day's sessions, the sewerage and sewage disposal people in the second, and the river people in the third, with little interaction.

Most significantly, a changing concept was that the water industry no longer served solely a public health function; water was a commodity to be sold for public use. Therefore, water management on a regional basis might well be in the hands of small and efficient boards of directors with highly competent technical staffs rather than under the control of elected local authority representatives.

There was less general agreement on how wastewater collection and disposal functions might be managed. Some favored including these functions in those of the water authority responsible for rivers and water supply. Most seemed to favor joint sewerage boards formed by regrouping existing facilities under the general direction of elected local authority representatives. With 1400 separate authorities this would be cumbersome; if local government reorganization resulted in 60 or 70 local authorities, this might be feasible.

In general, the river and water supply professionals at the symposium were prepared for quite substantial reorganization with large multipurpose authorities and complete abandonment of local authority management of any phase of the water industry. On the other hand, many of the wastewater professionals appeared reluctant to abandon the local authority management responsibility and preferred single-purpose operations.

Spens concluded that only drastic reorganization would suffice, with a small number of autonomous regional water authorities which would:

control the whole of the hydrological cycle,
be based on river catchments or groups of catchments,
control river flows, both in quantity and quality,
be responsible for conservation and development of resources,
abstract water for public supply, and treat and distribute it to consumers,
collect wastewaters and conduct them to treatment works, and
construct and manage treatment works and accept the effluents back into
    the rivers.

That the reorganization was ultimately to adopt this framework reflects well upon the participants of the symposium and particularly upon Mr Spens' percipience.

Not all observers on the scene were without reservations concerning the prospect of large and all-embracing authorities. A paper, emanating from Resources for the Future,[6] that presented the proposition that single all-purpose regional authorities were the most efficient and economic means of managing water resources was criticised by Peter Banks, a consulting engineer who wrote: 'As with so many superficially attractive economic arguments in support of large and all embracing bodies the neatness of the solution blinds its advocates to the fact that the fundamental principles of our society are being abandoned. The checks and balances ... are swept away all too easily in pursuit of the best economic and administrative solutions'.[7]

Banks was to continue to be an articulate critic of the reorganization. He defended the small rural district councils which were often accused of ineffectiveness in discharging their wastewater disposal functions:[8] 'In a multipurpose authority (such as a rural district council) the members ensure how the priorities are decided ... they can opt for a swimming pool before a new sewage works. A single-purpose authority might well see to it that they had the sewage works anyway, and its precept would enforce economies elsewhere.

'Rightly or wrongly many authorities spend very little on sewage disposal. Who can doubt that spending would increase if a specialist authority took over the function?'

Perhaps it is the changing expectations of people for water quality that has determined that water pollution control, particularly if the investment is to benefit only another community downstream, no longer should compete helplessly with investments such as swimming pools that benefit the rate-payer in the community creating the wastes.

The Jeger Committee, led largely by professionals, addressed itself less to schemes for organization and administration and more to the need to achieve a higher quality of water in rivers, estuaries and along the coast.

The more significant of the Jeger Committee recommendations, as they affected reorganization, were:

> while larger sewerage authorities were needed, wastewater disposal must be considered a part of the whole water cycle, together with water conservation and the control of quality and quantity of flow in waterways,
>
> powers for pollution control should be extended to include tidal rivers, estuaries and the sea,
>
> planning authorities must consult with authorities responsible for wastewater collection, treatment and disposal before planning new construction, and
>
> trade effluent discharges into public sewers should be subject to control and liability for charges, which should be applicable throughout the country.

In general, the Jeger Committee endorsed the idea that reorganization, as well as specific additional regulatory legislation, was necessary to help address the pollution problems of the country.

THE CENTRAL ADVISORY WATER COMMITTEE (CAWC) REPORT

The terms of reference for the committee were:

'To consider in the light of the report of the Royal Commission on Local Government in England and of technological and other developments, how the functions related to water conservation, management of water resources, water supply, sewerage, sewage disposal, and the prevention of pollution now exercised by water authorities, public water supply undertakings, and sewage disposal authorities can best be organized, and to make recommendations.'

By the time of their deliberations, the report of the Royal Commission on Local Government in England (1969) had appeared and it recommended that water supply and wastewater collection and disposal be local authority responsibilities.[9]

CAWC's report, *The Future Management of Water in England and Wales*,[4] confirmed the view that the responsibility for water was fragmented among many separate bodies, with conflicts between them and inadequate machinery for resolving these conflicts. The main problems were:

inflexibility in the use of resources,
division of responsibility between river authorities and water supply undertakings for development of new sources,
promotion of large schemes, and
inadequate levels of wastewater treatment.

They concluded that reduction in the number of operating units and changing relationships amongst authorities were necessary to permit the formation and implementation of comprehensive water management plans.

A wide range of options for reorganization was considered but, perhaps gun-shy from the implication that their earlier recommendations leading to the Water Resources Act 1963 were so soon to be discarded, they could not agree upon a preferred option. Some favored single-purpose authorities, essentially the *status quo*, as they decried the loss of intimate contact between the public and local authorities that would be inevitable with the creation of large multipurpose authorities. Others favored multipurpose authorities that would take over the work of the river authorities, the water supply undertakings, the local authority responsibilities for sewerage and wastewater treatment and disposal, the British Waterways Board responsibility for canals, and land drainage and fisheries.

CAWC recognized the value of a central national water authority to replace the WRB with enlarged responsibilities, particularly to include water quality, and in certain instances to execute water conservation works.

The one area of general agreement within CAWC was that there should be a sharp reduction in the number of operating entities. If regional water authorities were to be established, the right number would be about ten. They would be small, with a 10 to 15 member, managerial-type board appointed by the Ministers, although the idea was entertained that some could be appointed by local authorities. Chairmen would be appointed on the basis of demonstrated administrative competence, a departure from the election of chairmen for the river authorities from among authority members.

The most significant recommendation of CAWC was with regard to financing. Charges reflecting actual costs were to be levied for all the services provided and a single bill might be rendered that would combine the cost of providing water to the premises and the cost of removing and treating it prior to disposal.

CAWC was not of one mind with regard to the implementation of reorganization, with some favoring step-by-step change and others urging a more radical, one-time surgical operation.

In reviewing the CAWC report, Banks identified a central issue:[10] 'Essentially, the question is how much say our future local authorities should have in the control of water resources.' Many may argue that water should be regarded just like gas and electricity. However water does have amenity value in its natural state and tapping it as a utility may interfere with this value. (Another important difference is the public health significance of wholesome water which depends to a considerable extent on its source.)

Lord Nugent of Guildford, a member of CAWC, Chairman of the Thames Conservancy, and to become the chairman of the to-be-created National Water Council, also indicated a preference for 'an accelerated evolution of the present structure with its roots firmly grounded in local government.'[11]

The greatest criticism of the CAWC report was that it did not come to any hard decision as between single-purpose and multipurpose authorities. It set out the advantages of each and left the government to choose.

GOVERNMENT PROPOSALS FOR REORGANIZATION OF WATER AND SEWAGE SERVICES

The Secretary of State for the Environment, on 2 December 1971, announced to the House of Commons the government's intention of reorganizing the water services on the basis of ten all-purpose regional water authorities (WAs), and subject to approval by parliament, this would take effect on 1 April 1974, the date of local government reorganization.[5] The frontispiece shows the boundaries and Table 3.1 a statistical analysis of the proposed WAs.

The DoE advised that they intended to circulate a series of consultation papers to associations and organizations concerned, inviting comments on all aspects of the reorganization.

The water services to be included in the reorganization were water resources development, water supply, collection, treatment and disposal of sewage, pollution control, inland navigation, and provision of facilities for water-based recreation. Land drainage (flood control) and fisheries were excluded.

The government believed the time had come to bring together all aspects of the hydrological cycle under all-purpose management structures. While, in the six years of their existence, the river authorities had made a useful

TABLE 3.1
Water Authority Statistics (after Ogden)

		North West	Northumbrian	Severn Trent	Yorkshire	Anglian	Thames	Southern	Wessex	South West	WNWDA	Total
Estimated population	(millions)	7·0	2·7	8·5	4·5	4·1	12·1	3·7	2·0	1·3	2·9	48·8
	(%)	14·3	5·5	17·4	9·2	8·4	24·8	7·6	4·1	2·7	6·0	100
Rateable value	(£ million)	290	110	350	170	190	950	200	110	50	120	2540
	(%)	11·4	4·3	13·8	6·7	7·5	37·4	7·9	4·3	2·0	4·7	100
Water supplies per day	(million gal)	520	210	450	250	310	700	220	150	80	240	3130
	(million m³)	2·4	0·9	2·0	1·2	1·4	3·2	1·0	0·7	0·3	1·1	14·2
	(%)	16·7	6·6	14·4	8·1	10·0	22·3	7·1	4·7	2·4	7·7	100
Number or river authorities		3	1	2	1	5	2	4	3	2	6	29
Number of water undertakers		24	8	26	22	25	18	16	11	8	29	187
Water boards		18	2	14	11	17	6	3	6	7	16	100
Local authorities		6	2	7	10	3	4	6	1	1	10	50
Water companies		0	3	2	1	4	8	6	4	0	2	30
Bulk suppliers		0	1	3	0	1	0	1	0	0	1	7
Number of sewerage and sewage disposal authorities		204	75	173	144	196	163	106	86	72	174	1393
Local authorities		197	73	171	141	196	160	102	86	72	168	1366
Joint borads		7	2	2	3	0	3	4	0	0	6	27

start, problems had arisen from the separate responsibility for water supply, river management, water conservation, pollution control, sewerage and wastewater disposal. The government concluded, and the Royal Commission on Environmental Pollution concurred, that WAs concerned with all relevant aspects of water management should replace the many and diverse public authorities in the field. One option, single-purpose authorities, would be more cumbersome and less economical in their use of resources and, because conflicts would continue to arise, would require constant intervention by central government. Regional coordinating bodies, the other option, if given real power, would deprive the operating bodies of autonomy. These options would presage further reorganization in the near future, an unconscionable idea. The government believed that the proposed reorganization should move to establish the institutions that are necessary as best they could be foreseen at this time.

The water authorities

Regional WAs would take over the water conservation, water quality control, navigation and recreation functions of the river authorities as well as those of the British Waterways Board for canals and navigation. They would replace the existing joint water boards and joint sewerage boards but the statutory (privately owned) water companies would continue, provided a satisfactory arrangement could be made for them to serve as agents of the WAs.

Local authorities would continue to be responsible for local sewerage, although the WAs would control the discharge of industrial effluents to these sewers. Local authorities would also retain the responsibility for independent testing of public water supplies to assure that water delivered by the WAs would be wholesome.

The main activities of the WAs would be the provision of water supply and the reclamation or disposal of used water. In their planning and operations, the WAs would take account of needs for navigation, recreation, land drainage, sea defenses, fisheries and conservation of amenities and wildlife. They would be under specific statutory obligation to maintain and, where possible, improve the quality of rivers and canals in their areas.

Inland navigation and recreation

In general, the network of canals administered by the British Waterways Board were said to no longer fulfil major transport functions, but the canals do serve as aqueducts for water supply undertakings and for recreation. Because they are of local and regional value, they should no longer be administered as a national enterprise. Hence, the government proposed that the British Waterways Board functions be shifted to the WAs.

Financing

The revenues for the new WAs would come from charges for the services they would provide, except for exchequer grants for very specific purposes. The idea of a single combined charge for all water services to a consumer warranted further study. The administrative cost of pollution control, collected for the river authorities by precepts levied on local authorities, would be incorporated into the overall costs of providing clean water and disposing of used water. Charges for abstractions of water from surface and underground sources would be continued.

To meet the additional costs of recreation and navigation, the WAs would look to tolls and contributions from local authorities, national park authorities, the Sports Council, and other using bodies.

While it was intended that statutory safeguards assure the equitable distribution of costs of various water services, the WAs would be responsible for their detailed schedules of charges. No longer would there be a necessity for acquiring loan sanctions from government for individual projects. The WAs would be able to raise money from government sources to meet their needs for outside capital, but the minister would retain control on matters of major financial policy. Control of investment programs for the purpose of national economic policy direction would be exercised through approval of seven-year rolling programs by the government. The WAs would assume the obligations of servicing the debts of the bodies they replace.

Constitution of the WAs

The government agreed with the CAWC that WA areas should be hydrological and that their boundaries would therefore not coincide with those of local government. The WAs should comprise a limited number of members appointed by both local authorities and by the Ministers. The government proposed that WA chairmen be appointed by the Ministers.

Within the area of each WA, one or more consumer councils would reflect the various interests involved in the WAs, such as local authorities, industry, farming, amenities and recreation. The Was would report to these councils and the councils, if dissatisfied, would have direct access to the Ministers.

The Secretary of State for Wales announced his intention of establishing a Welsh National Water Development Authority that would serve as the WA for the exclusively Welsh river basins and for areas of Welsh rivers that lie partly in England. In the remainder of Wales, the Severn Trent Water Authority was to have responsibility, in consultation with the WNWDA.

Organization at national level

The government, while agreeing that there should be a national strategy for water development, did not believe that a strong national body needed to be interposed between the Ministers and the small number of WAs projected. The WRB had done indispensable work, necessary when 29 river authorities existed, but the new WAs would be largely self-sufficient. Where inter-regional arrangements needed to be made the WAs should be able to make them.

The government, recognizing the need for a body to speak for the water industry and to provide essential services for the WAs, proposed a water council consisting of a chairman appointed by the Ministers, the chairmen of the WAs, and appointed members having specialized knowledge of industry, agriculture, amenity, recreation, and other matters of concern to the WAs. This national body would promote efficiency in the industry by comparing practices and performance of the WAs and help the WAs to profit from one another's experiences.

Timetable

The government's aim was to conduct extensive consultations in 1972, so as to have adequate time for drafting legislation that would permit the organization to take effect with local government reorganization on 1 April 1974. The Bill because of its complexity and the limited time available to meet the deadline, would be confined to reorganization. Other aspects of needed legislation, particularly that for pollution control, would be handled subsequently.

Banks, representing the views of many professional engineers who had favored the adoption of single-purpose authorities, was far more accepting of the projected reorganization following the Government's proposals than might have been anticipated:[12] 'As a long term solution to the water problem, the proposals have much to commend them. Sewage treatment and pollution control are closely related to water supply, and all three can affect the provision of recreational facilities and amenities, the importance of which is emphasized again and again in the memorandum'. While many within the water industry would be disappointed at the selection of multipurpose instead of single-purpose authorities, Banks pointed out, again running against the grain of most observers, that the new legislation should be brought into operation as rapidly as possible. He then reflected the spirit of many of those involved: 'It now remains for all workers in the industry whether they agree with the decision or not to make every effort to make the scheme effective and to ensure that we have adequate water, clean rivers and pleasant recreational amentities'.

CONSULTATION PAPERS AND RESPONSES

In early 1972, the DoE began to distribute a series of consultation papers, 17 in all, to some 180 organizations and associations, in a total of about

3000 copies each, to assure adequate dissemination and discussion of each issue. About two months were allowed for the submission of written responses. The titles of the consultation papers are listed in Table 3.2.

Views on their responses to the consultation papers were solicited from 31 major organizations and answers were received from 25. The six that did not respond were organizations with only a peripheral interest in the reorganization or with no permanent secretariat. The consultation papers are discussed in turn, in each instance followed by the more typical comments of respondents. Where many organizations expressed a particular viewpoint, representative comments are cited.

TABLE 3.2
Consultation Papers and Dates of Publication in 1972

1. The place of water companies in the new system	January 6
2. Safeguards for staff	January 20
3. The Welsh National Water Development Authority	January 20
4. Practical arrangements for implementation	February 7
5. Operational areas: Fringe problems	March 6
6. Local law and related matters	March 6
7. Public Health functions relating to local authorities	March 27
8. Constitution of regional water authorities	March 29
9. Public participation in water management	April 18
10. Economics and finance	April 18
11. The National Water Council	August 10
12. The amenity use of water space and the reorganization of the British Waterways Board	August 9
13. Staff commission for England and Wales	August 22
14. Grant	September 25
15. Future organization of land drainage	September 18
16. Fisheries	September 18
17. Pollution Control	June–July

1. The place of water companies in the new system

The Government proposed to retain the statutory (privately owned) water companies as these companies could continue to play a valuable role as agents of the WAs. The WAs would be obliged to make sufficient water available to these companies (either in bulk supply or by authorizing direct abstractions) to enable the companies to meet their obligations to their customers.

A capital investment program for the companies would be agreed upon between the companies and the WAs and included in the capital investment program submitted by the WAs to the Secretary of State.

Response

Retaining these islands of private enterprise in a sea of nationalized functions was anomalous. The staff of the DoE might well have preferred that WAs take over the functions and assets of the companies to make the control of the hydrological cycle complete. However, the Conservative government responsible for the legislation was dedicated to authorizing no further nationalization of private enterprise in the United Kingdom. Although the magnitude of the companies in private hands is small by contrast with industries already nationalized, the philosophy of nationalization is anathema to the Conservative party. Departure from what was claimed to be a rational proposal for bringing together all water-related enterprises into single authorities prompted a strong outcry in opposition.

The Association of Municipal Corporations, the Rural District Councils Association and the Urban Distric Councils Association expressed firm opposition to only the statutory water companies being kept outside the WAs. Once having breached the basic principle, the government's proposal provides ample justification for the retention of local authority water supply undertakings. They recommended establishing the WAs as regional bodies with a limited range of executive functions but with a strong coordinating supervisory role over local authorities. The statutory water companies would then have a place. Otherwise, they would not.

The British Waterworks Association pointed out that, while it was accepted that water companies are generally reliable and efficient, equally sound performance has been obtained from a good many local government authorities engaged in water supply. They too might serve as agents for WAs without actually being taken over.

While almost all the organizations that responded to this consultation paper were in strong opposition to the continuation of the statutory water companies, the Institute of Public Health Engineers and the Confederation of British Industry approved the proposal. IPHE, wishfully, saw this arrangement as being extended to sewerage, wastewater treatment and other services.

It seemed quite clear that were the Labour Party to have a firm hold on government for an extended period, this anomaly of water companies outside the WAs would not long continue.

2. Safeguards for staff

In presenting the reorganization to the House of Commons, the Secretary of State for the Environment said that 'staff interest will be safeguarded . . .'. The staff would be guaranteed terms and conditions of employment by the WAs to which they were to be transferred no less favorable than those they had enjoyed. Where an individual might suffer loss of employment or a decrease in emoluments because of reorganization, he would be entitled to compensation.

The DoE proposed a special measure, applicable also to the other major reorganizations, that senior officers would have the option of retirement with full benefits if they had reached age 50 (rather than 65) by 1 April 1974 if they were otherwise eligible for retirement by virtue of length of service. This 'golden handshake' was intended to reduce the number of officers in the higher echelons who would have had to have been accommodated in the new organizations. It was, in fact, instrumental in encouraging many senior officials to take early retirement, some to emigrate and others to take private employment, resulting in a loss of experienced professionals to the new authorities.

Response

The National Association of Local Government Officers (NALGO) was not happy with the Government proposals, and wanted guarantees on pay and conditions of service being maintained. No one should be made to accept redundancy (dismissal), but conditions should be such as to encourage voluntary redundancy. NALGO emphasized the anxiety of staff so that early assurances for staff were important to maintain morale. Further, NALGO believed that a single negotiating body for the industry would be important.

The Institution of Municipal Engineers pointed out that only in the larger local authorities would it likely be practicable to identify professional staff wholly connected with sewerage. In the smaller local authorities, the senior professional staff carry responsibilities for a wide range of technical functions, of which sewerage is only one.

The Institution of Water Engineers recognized that the reorganization would present many staff with new opportunities. Some, for one reason or another, will feel aggrieved because of the loss of status or the need to move their domiciles and it is better that staff should feel free to leave with adequate compensation if they prefer to do so. The risk that many may wish to leave would not materialize provided that the opportunities offered by the WAs at least met those available elsewhere.

3. The Welsh National Water Development Authority

The Government proposed to set up the Welsh National Water Development Authority to serve as the WA for the Welsh rivers which would include some areas in England while the Severn Trent Water Authority would be responsible for the upper Severn River basin in Wales. In addition to its WA functions, the WNWDA was to exercise other functions throughout Wales, including the upper Severn, such as promotion of recreation and tourism related to reservoirs, rivers, and canals.

The Severn Trent Water Authority would have a statutory obligation to consult with WNWDA on matters of substance related to its obligations in

Wales, particularly in the upper Severn. Final decisions would be subject to joint ratification by the Secretary of State for Wales and the Secretary of State for the Environment.

Response

The Institution of Water Engineers was not happy with the arrangement whereby the assets of the water supply undertakings that draw water from Wales would be transferred to the WNWDA, which would furnish bulk supplies to the other WAs. Such bulk transfer arrangements were considered to be unsatisfactory because the day-to-day management of the system would present great difficulty if the sources were under the control of one WA and the treatment under another. These difficulties would be overcome if WNWDA could lease their reservoirs to the appropriate WAs.

4. Practical arrangements for implementation

It was proposed that the WAs be brought into shadow existence well before the anicipated date of transfer of functions on 1 April 1974, as soon as possible after the Water Bill received Royal Assent. During this period the WAs were to make preparations for transfer of assets and functions, approve budgets, fix charges for 1974–75, and make long-term policy and management decisions, particularly with regard to the organization of the WAs and appointment of chief officers.

Although the government would provide guidelines, each WA was to determine its own structure and internal organization.

Personnel

The government proposed that each WA have a single chief executive, who would be the first appointed and who would then be responsible for putting proposals for internal organization before his WA. The government further proposed that the finance officer be the only other officer appointed during this 'shadow' period.

Because the chosen chief executives were to be overridingly important to the operation of the WAs, it was proposed that candidates be sought from far and wide, including private industry, government, and nationalized industry outside the 'ring fence' as well as from the water industry. Also, as matters of budgets and charges would have to be settled early on, arrangements for appointments of the finance officers were to be similar to those for the chief executives.

Provisional organization

To minimize transitional problems, existing organizations such as river authorities and joint water boards would transfer intact as 'provisional management units' (PMUs).

With regard to wastewater collection and disposal, only a few joint boards were of sufficient size to become provisional management units. Each WA was expected to inherit, on the average, about 130 portions of local authority departments responsible for sewerage and sewage treatment, plus some related administrative personnel. Most would not be large enough to form PMUs but in combination they would be and when agreements were reached for groupings, working parties would be established for each group which would draw up detailed written reports covering assets and staff requirements. After the initial consultation paper was issued, another consultation paper outlining procedures was issued in May 1972, with reports to be available early in 1973, even before the Water Bill was passed. The role of the working parties can be gathered from the suggested section headings in the reports they were to render, as shown in Table 3.3. The government suggested that, in addition to the 15 or so working parties per WA area, a steering committee be established together with one multi-functional working party for each WA.

TABLE 3.3
Report of Working Parties to Chief Executive

Section headings

Constitution
Boundaries
Existing organization modules
Future organization modules
Present staff
Existing accommodation
Provisional organization, staff and accommodation requirements
Plant and equipment
Maintenance of stores organizations
Work under construction and in course of design
Land
Miscellaneous
Recommendations

Response

The major objections related to the timetable. The Institute of Municipal Treasurers and Accountants (IMTA) stated that it was impossible and inadvisable for the WAs to make long-term policy and management decisions before 1 April 1974, in advance of the appointment of all the chief officers. IMTA believed that local authorities should be under statutory obligations to act as agents for the WAs in the provision of financial and administrative services for three years unless a WA agreed otherwise.

The local authority associations expressed concern with the precipitate haste to implement proposals which disregarded the human side of the reorganization. The time available for reorganization of the government of Greater London in 1966 had been insufficient and, in consequence, well nigh intolerable strains were imposed on members and on senior officers to the extent that, in some cases, health was seriously impaired. The time available for the local government reorganization did not materially differ from that available to the reorganization of London, and the imposition of water reorganization in addition was something that did not need to be contended with in London. Also, continuing reorganization in the water industry in regrouping had led to more continued unsettling of personnel. The timing, they concluded, 'appears to carry optimism to a point beyond the exercise of reasonable judgement'.

All the respondents objected strenuously to the provision to go outside the 'ring fence' for the chief executives as a slur on the current staff. They believed that the chief executives and the finance officers could be found within the industry.

All the technical organizations such as the Institution of Water Engineers and the Institute of Water Pollution Control, as well as the associations representing the local authorities, decried the initial appointment of only two chief officers. They emphasized the need for technical advice before long-term decisions were made and indicated that the appointment of the chief engineer should accompany the appointment of the finance officer and chief executive. Budget preparation should not be the prerogative solely of the finance officer.

5. Operational areas—fringe problems

The boundaries of the WAs, based upon natural watersheds, would in many instances not be identical with the boundaries of water service areas or sewerage areas of local authorities. The government suggested that any two or more WAs have the power to do jointly anything that a single WA would have the power to do, or that one might act as an agent for another.

Where a source of water supply is in one WA and the area served in another, the former would be under an obligation to provide a bulk supply to the latter, for the time being at least. Where a distribution system straddles boundary lines between WAs, the WA enclosing the larger area might well take over the whole. In the case of sewers crossing WA boundaries, the location of the treatment plant or outfall might determine the WA to which the system would be assigned.

6. Local law and related matters

This consultation paper was not expected to be at all controversial, as river authorities had been operating to a significant extent under local enactments, which powers would continue to be exercised under the appropriate WAs.

7. Public health functions remaining with local authorities

In the context of British practice, 'public health functions' are essentially sewerage functions. The government's initial proposal had been that local authorities continue to provide local sewerage functions.[5]

The WAs are to finance their sewerage and wastewater disposal activities through an extension of the existing system of water charges, as contrasted with the system of rates or taxes previously used. Home owners and developers could requisition sewerage from the WAs if the annual revenue from the charges is no less than one-eighth the cost of the necessary sewers. Where the charge would be insufficient, district councils would be authorized to requisition the sewers by making up the difference over a period of twelve years.

Each WA would have overall responsibility for sewerage within its area, implying that it should have powers to coordinate design of new systems provided by others. It would further be necessary for the WA to own certain trunk-sewers as well as to own and operate treatment works and to control admission of trade wastes to sewers, even if the latter are owned by others, in order to protect treatment facilities and to ensure the quality of effluent. The difficult question was how the local authority responsibility for local sewerage should be distinguished from WA responsibility for the remainder of the system for the purposes of planning, design, construction, operation, and charging. Three options were presented without recommendation:

1. Division in terms of function: an obvious type of arrangement, but difficult to implement. Where this split now exists, as for the Greater London Council or a joint sewerage board, the authority responsible for treatment and disposal owns trunk or principal sewers. Problems are involved in defining trunk or principal sewers, in controlling discharges from industry which would go into sewers generally owned by the local authority, in controlling discharges from overflows from combined systems, and in finance, because charges from industry would have to be proportioned between the local authorities and WAs.

2. Division in terms of size: this might give responsibilities to WAs for domestic sewers nine inches or larger, pumping stations and force mains, stormwater overflows from combined storm sewers and possibly any sewer to which a trade waste is discharged. Such a definition would be simple and straightforward to apply. However, most local authorities would then be left with little to manage and might have difficulty in establishing a suitable organization.

3. Agency arrangements: all statutory responsibilities under an agency arrangement would rest with the WAs, but local sewerage functions would be delegated to the local authorities, the new district councils. Agency arrangements would not appear to be efficient, as the agent, spending WA funds, would not have any incentive to be economical. The WAs would have

to involve themselves in most of the decision-making and there might be problems of staff duplication or the local authorities would be merely contractors providing plant and labor.

Local authorities would continue to be responsible for ascertaining sufficiency and wholesomeness of water supplies. Under the Public Health Act 1936, the district councils would retain the powers to require water supply to be provided to housing, and to close or restrict the use of polluted water sources.

Response

Some members of the Institute of Water Pollution Control favored the WAs taking over the complete control of all sewerage, but the consensus was for a division of responsibility between local authorities and WAs with separation by function. Whilst trade effluent control would be a function of the WAs, they need not own the sewers. Charges for trade wastes discharges to sewers can be collected by the local authorities on behalf of the WAs.

The Greater London Council which, with other large main drainage authorities, had operated in much the same way that was being proposed for the WAs, stated that their experiences should not be disregarded. The WAs should take over all sewage treatment plants of meaningful size, take over contributing sewers to assure monitoring of discharges from local authorities, and set and enforce standards for discharges from local authorities.

The associations representing the local authorities claimed that this consultation paper revealed more clearly than any other the failure of government to realize the full implications of its reorganization proposals. Water supply has tended to dominate the government's thinking, with sewerage relegated to a secondary position. For example, the initial DoE circular 92/71, referring to '... all aspects of the hydrological cycle, literally from the source to the tap' obviously omits that portion of the cycle from the tap back to the source.[5]

The associations objected to the idea that the WAs should be responsible for trunk sewers while local authorities were responsible for other sewers, as this would require two maintenance organizations in the same area. They agreed that the WAs have a large range of responsibilities, but the government, by its insistence on the WAs owning and operating the services, was confusing the controls needed for planning, coordination, and the prevention of pollution with operational management. By placing so much emphasis on pollution, the government failed to take sufficient account of the interaction of sewerage and other local services such as public health and development and the need to have an effective local body to receive and remedy complaints. Inefficiency is not only likely to affect individual customers (as it may, for example, in gas and electricity undertakings); inefficiency could rapidly become a major public health problem. The government did not appreciate the volume of work that the WAs would be required to accomplish in providing sewerage for new construction. The need to have control of sewerage in connection with local development suggests that the dividing line in responsibility be between sewerage, which should be with local authorities, and wastewater treatment and the main outfall sewers, which might be in the hands of the WAs.

The Institution of Municipal Engineers expressed grave concern that removal of the responsibilities for sewerage from local authorities would tend to decrease local authority responsibility in the public works area to the extent that they would not be able to attract professional staff and maintain efficient organizations. Therefore, proposals for local government should be integrated with proposals for reorganization of water and sewerage services. Only if the district councils have significant functions would they be capable of undertaking local sewerage functions. Such councils would then also be well equipped to retain the operation of wastewater disposal works acting on behalf of the WAs, thus avoiding the artificial division between sewerage and sewage disposal and ensuring continued economic use of manpower and resources.

NALGO disagreed with all proposals in the consultation paper and preferred that the WAs take over all the sewerage beyond the property line. Functions to be assigned to local governments for sewerage are not enough to provide worthwhile careers in local authorities in this field. All rational consideration justifies complete take over: trade waste control, conflicts that would be created by division of responsibility and by duplication, single maintenance responsibility, and control of infiltration.

The British Waterworks Association was in full support of the proposal that local authorities continue their responsibilities under the Public Health Acts relating to water supply. In particular, the district councils would retain the power to require provision of adequate quantity of wholesome water to new houses. The responsibility for initiating fluoridation would continue to rest with the local authorities as at present.

8. Constitution of the Water Authorities

The new tasks of the WAs—broader than the sum of their predecessor agencies—their new relationships, and their new managerial responsibilities, demanded a fresh approach to the task of determining their composition and structure. The WAs were anticipated to have annual budgets on the order of £250 million in capital and £350 million in operations and a total of about 65 000 employees. To secure effective management of these comprehensive and large bodies, the members of the WAs should be chosen for their demonstrated competence and their number should be small. The chairmen should be appointed by the Ministers for five years.

Although the total WA membership should be small, local government members should be represented in substantial numbers, considering the area of the WA and the number of local authorities within each WA. Members could not feasibly be drawn from the new second-tier district councils, but county councils would be expected to nominate members from among their number, although not every county council could be represented in the larger WAs. Representation might be by rotation, election, or appointment by the Ministers from among those nominated by county councils.

The appointed members should represent other than local interests: industry, agriculture, sports, recreation, amenities, navigation, and if included in the purview of the WAs, land drainage and fisheries, but not on a narrow basis, as the intent is to keep the membership small.

It was proposed that chief executives be appointed by the WAs and be *ex officio* members of the WAs. The chairmen and appointed members should be remunerated, but the Government was uncertain as to whether local authority members should be remunerated or receive the allowances for councillors as proposed in the local government bill.

Because the WAs would be different from the agencies whose functions and assets they inherit, and not like any other agencies in Britain, the government proposed to establish a management structure committee to provide advice to the WAs.

Response

The associations representing the local authorities believed that the authority membership should not be so small that the WAs would be remote and inaccessible. They believed that the local authority representation on the WAs should be a majority and preferably at least two-thirds to insure local democratic control and local participation. The strong predilection for a small membership should not be allowed to have precedence over the needs for adequate representation. The associations believed that the size should depend on the particular authority, but in any event should not be fewer than 30. The chief executives appointed by the WAs ought not be *ex officio* members of the WAs. Local government organizations have always drawn a clear line between members and officers and experience has shown that this arrangement has many practical advantages.

NALGO believed that consumers would best be served by having 75 to 80 percent of the WA membership appointed from among elected local government representatives. Others might represent special interests including at least two representing trade unions. If this arrangement were to be accepted, there would be no need for the proposed regional consumer councils.

The British Waterworks Association expressed very strongly the vital need to preserve local democratic control in the water industry. The interests of the consumers would not be served by the government proposals. BWA would prefer the WAs to be wholly elected and that the basis for membership should be experience and knowledge, rather than their capacity for management, as the latter would be the function of a strong team of officers.

The Metropolitan Water Board (London) asserted that the WAs should be large enough to be representative, and local authority members should be a majority. Every WA should have at least one representative from each county within its area. MWB considered the proposed WA a hybrid, in that members are neither wholly elected for their value as representatives of the population served nor wholly nominated for their management capabilities. These two types of management organizations could not be mixed.

The Institution of Water Engineers asserted that management should be the responsibility of the full-time staff and WA members should confine themselves to policy. The maximum number of members in each authority should be 15, which would be small enough to be an effective decision-making group and would not need to be divided into a number of single-interest committees to conduct their business. The Confederation of British Industries agreed that, to secure effective management, the membership of each WA should be not more than 10 to 12.

All of the organizations responding were in agreement that the chairmen of the WAs should be elected from among WA members.

9. Public participation in water management

The activities of the WAs will relate to the public in many ways, and although each WA will include a substantial portion of members drawn from local government, the numbers will be small to keep the WA small and some form of organized public participation may be advisable.

The government proposed regional consultative councils, independent of the WAs, with their status defined in legislation. The WAs would be required to report annually to their RCCs on plans and arrangements for exercising their functions. The councils would respond to the WAs and if dissatisfied they might take the matter up with the appropriate Minister.

Response

The associations representing local authorities, the Metropolitan Water Board, and others, decried the need for the RCCs, as it demonstrated the basic unsoundness of the policy of creating large regional authorities having functions at local level. Local democratic involvement and accountability should be a central factor in the organization of the WAs. Strong local government representation would require less special consultative arrangements, which at best are likely to be ineffective and unresponsive to public opinion. The consumer councils for the nationalized industries have proven to be of little value.

The Institute of Water Pollution Control did agree that strong consultative councils would be helpful, particularly if they comprised substantial membership from local government. IPHE also supported this approach but was concerned that adequate servicing of the consultative council did not appear to be provided.

The Confederation of British Industries endorsed RCCs. They should be large, drawn from a wide range of interested bodies and they should not have a majority of local government members.

The Institute of Municipal Treasurers and Accountants accepted the government's proposal but recommended that the expenses of the RCCs be met by the National Water Council or the DoE and not by the WAs, in order that they might be completely independent.

10. Economics and finance

The consultation paper states immediately: 'The main economic objective of the WAs will be to get the appropriate economy in the use of resources . . . This will entail assessing the future demand for water, and for increased capacity for the disposal of dirty water, on the basis of charges likely to be made: and comparing the cost of alternative methods of providing the services required . . . Methods of quantifying the social and amenity benefits . . . will need to be further developed so that these too can be included in the comparison as far as possible on a par with financial outgoings and income.'

The financial objectives for water supply and water abstraction in the past had been that revenue should balance recurrent expenditure and that there should be a uniform tariff throughout a service area. Charges have been based on historic costs, without a return on fixed assets, or provision for replacement.

The DoE proposed a study of financial objectives and the relationship of charges to costs. It was not intended that the WAs make any substantial changes in the pattern of charges for the first year or two, although it would be necessary for them to develop sufficient income to match their expenditures.

The government proposed that WAs should plan to eliminate variations in charges that derive simply from variations in historic costs over a period of seven years and, at least early on, attempt to moderate the extreme charges (either high or low).

After pointing out that charging for water by flat rate is inequitable and provides no incentive for economy in its use, the government proposed that the WAs charging powers be wide enough to enable them to initiate metering. Installing residential meters in England and Wales was estimated to cost £500 million, with annual costs of £15 million per year for repairs and replacements, exclusive of meter reading and billing, so that universal metering is unlikely to be achieved for a considerable number of years.

The government proposed that river abstractions, wastewater disposal and the other water services also be charged for on the basis of volumes established by metering. Although charges will likely be different in different parts of the country, the principles upon which they are based should be similar. In any case, customers are to receive an inclusive unit charge for all water services. The basis for charging would, of course, be different for those who do not receive all the services. Responding to the Jeger Committee report,[3] the DoE indicated that industry should bear the full cost of collection and treatment of its wastewaters.

Response

The Institute of Municipal Treasurers and Accountants recognized the implied change from 'taxation' to a 'market' approach. They concluded that demands should then be significantly influenced by pricing policies. This impact has not yet been quantified and more background data are needed. Studies were proposed to support the idea of metering, although authority for metering should not be withheld. Would funds be better invested in new sources than in meters? Would there be adverse health repercussions from resident metering? Would metering reduce inequities?

IMTA, joined by the British Waterworks Association, believed that the WAs, to be really free to manage their own affairs and to fix their own charges, should be given power to borrow money from anywhere, rather than being limited to borrowing from government loan funds as proposed.

The associations representing the local government authorities believed that economic objectives should not be regarded as the overwhelming guideline for services such as water, which have developed within a public health framework and now are intended to provide amenity. The implied criticism of existing financial policies was unwarranted, because these policies had resulted in the average household receiving unlimited supplies of wholesome water for less than £10 per year.

The establishment of revenue targets based upon invested capital similar to what has been done in the nationalized industries should not apply to water services as there are no alternative ways of providing water services and the return must be expressed in terms of social benefits. However, they did concur with a program of phased equalization of charges over WA areas for each type of service provided.

Metering of household water is anathema to any public health approach. Those most likely to use less water would be those who should use more as the charges would fall most heavily on the elderly and those with small incomes.

The Institution of Water Engineers urged caution in the determination of investment policies indicating that they could not be compared with the other single-purpose nationalized industries inasmuch as, irrespective of cost, a minimum amount of service must be afforded all households for public health reasons. They supported the need for metering and the establishment of comprehensive charges for all water services. However, they were concerned about the method of arriving at charges for amenity and recreational services.

The British Waterworks Association was in general agreement with the economic objectives outlined by the government. They too were concerned that the government intended to use the price mechanism as a means of influencing water demand, a practice which contrasts with general policy throughout the industry of providing resources to meet all domestic demands. The BWA member undertakings were almost all opposed to universal metering of water at residential premises. Despite the apparent fairness of this approach, its implementation would be quite impracticable and would entail greater charges to consumers without any related benefits. The money would be better used in extending development and distributing of water.

11. The National Water Council and other central units

The government 'attach considerable importance to the role of the National Water Council'. It is to be the main source of advice to the government on national water policy and is to provide the WAs with a forum for discussion of common problems. NWC is to provide certain common services: statistical data, training, negotiating machinery for pay and conditions of service, liaison between the WAs and other national bodies, and standardizing and testing of fittings.

The government would appoint the chairman of the NWC, and the membership would consist of the ten WA chairmen with additional members appointed by the Ministers for their expertise in various aspects of the water industry.

Research was to be integrated into a new organization, the Water Research Centre, which would comprise the Water Research Association, the Technology Division of the Water Resources Board, the Development Division of the Directorate General–Water Engineering of the DoE, and the Water Pollution Research Laboratory. The form would be similar to that of the Water Research Association, a membership organization. It would be governed by a council including representatives of the WAs, the NWC, the government, Scotland, Northern Ireland, industry, etc., and would be financed primarily by the WAs with contributions from the other members. The WAs would conduct their own research, but WRC, with a budget of some £4 million per year, would be responsible for tackling the common problems of the industry.

The strategic planning role of the WRB needed to be retained but modified, with regional planning being the responsibility of the WAs. For national planning, a new Central Water Planning Unit reporting to the DoE would take over the planning division of the WRB and be concerned with the quality as well as the quantity. The CWPU would be steered by a committee on which the NWC, the WRC and government departments are represented. The chairman, to be appointed by the Secretary of State in consultation with the chairman of NWC would be multidisciplinary and capable of relating technical, scientific and economic aspects of water resource planning and operation. An initial staff of 35 to 40 at Reading, the site of the expiring WRB, was contemplated.

A new Data Collection Unit would take over the quantitative data collection responsibilities of the WRB and the quality data collection responsibilities of the Director General–Water Engineering of the DoE. While data from within the regions would be collected by the WAs, the accumulation and analysis of data on a national basis would be the responsibility of the DCU. It would advise concerning data to be collected and assure common standards of analytical methods and data collection. It would be sited also at Reading with an initial staff of 30 to 35 professionals.

Response

The British Waterworks Association considered that the proposals on the role of the NWC were unsatisfactory. NWC should be stronger, with planning, advisory and coordinating functions, and a greater degree of independence from Government than proposed. The BWA was particularly disappointed that its recommendations that the NWC be given powers to carry out executive functions, particularly in inter-regional projects, was rejected. The strategic planning capacity developed by the WRB should be retained and broadened to include water quality but within the NWC, with the regional planning carried out by the WAs. Having central planning under the DoE would militate against the provision of an independent service.

Lastly, the BWA expressed concern over the lack of adequate local authority representation on the NWC, inasmuch as all of its members would be appointed by government. The BWA did agree that its own executive staff should be transferred to the NWC, as its reason for being would terminate on 1 April 1974.

In expressing similar concerns, the Institution of Water Engineers stated that the NWC would be hampered by its personnel being without technical competence. For example, with planning in the DoE and within the WAs, the NWC would be in the middle without resources to address either regional or national planning problems.

The associations representing the local authorities decried the organizational structure, with policy-making dominated by civil servants operating under the cloak of the Secretary of State for the Environment. Planning in the Central Water Planning Unit in the government would detract from the responsibilities of the NWC, leaving it in the situation of an observer. The associations supported the CAWC in its proposal for a strong central body which would be more than just a façade to conceal the reality of control by the Secretary of State and his department. The associations were also concerned with what appeared to be a proliferation of new bodies at the national level. As NWC would seem to have a strong government bias, financing its functions from central government rather than the WAs would have appeared more seemly. With transfer of the BWA and the Association of River Authorities to the NWC, the WAs would be deprived of any independent forum in which to discuss their problems and through which to make representations to government.

The Greater London Council feared that the government intended to exercise complete control of the water industry, with the NWC being allowed no real power over policy. This consultation paper reinforced the GLC's fears that local government will have a negligible voice in policy matters. The NWC should be made up of elected WA chairmen and it then could accept responsibility for policy, resources development, etc.

Many organizations joined in asserting that national activities of planning and research should be within the NWC. The thrust of all the comments was that the NWC as proposed would not be sufficiently strong or independent to be effective.

12. Amenity use of water space and the British Waterways Board

In this consultation paper, the government for the first time committed itself to using water resources, such as rivers, lakes, canals, reservoirs, and other man-made waters, as environmental amenities and recreational assets for the use of the public.

The WAs were to have the new statutory duty to make the best possible use of all waters under their control for recreation and amenity in its widest sense. They were to provide facilities, make regulations, and create a system of charges for the facilities. Close liaison would be maintained with local authorities in these efforts.

The government proposed to establish, under the aegis of the NWC, a Water Space Amenity Commission. The amenity member of the NWC would be *ex officio* chairman of WSAC. Members are to be WA representatives and persons appointed by the Secretary of State for their specialized competence. While the WAs are expected to finance their operations from revenues, outside support may be justified for particular activities, such as establishing and preserving amenities. For example, local authority contributions to the amenity use of water in their areas may warrant exchequer grants. Also, the Sports Council might make grants for activities within their purview.

The British Waterways Board has required subsidies, despite the lessening use of waterways for navigation, to keep the canals from becoming nuisances or hazards. The government proposed that the waterways under the British Waterways Boards be integrated into the WAs.

Response

The Countryside Commission and the Sports Council urged that legislation provide for close liaison between the WAs and the regional sports councils, the latter having been set up over the years to work closely with local authorities, other public bodies and commercial undertakings. One of the major difficulties hindering the development of water-based recreation is the financing of land-based facilities. Up to now, the river authorities and water undertakings have been unable to assist, and local authorities have been reluctant to contribute capital for the provision of facilities outside their boundaries. Therefore, it would seem essential that the WAs have power to acquire land adjacent to water areas and should possess adequate financial resources to promote land-based facilities for water recreation. Furthermore, fees for licenses should not have to cover all the costs of management and development of facilities for waterway amenities.

Existing administrative organizations, including the Countryside Commission and Sports Council were adequate to promote recreation including the use of water resources, and the WSAC would only create problems. They were reluctant to see the disappearance of the British Waterways Board. If it were to be retained, there would be no need for the WSAC, as the BWB together with the existing organizations would be adequate.

The Greater London Council feared that amenity and recreation might be given a low priority, for amenities would be regarded as an extra to be paid for through charges, by grants from local authorities and by exchequer grants. They strongly urged that recreation be treated equally with the other functions of the WAs. The GLC proposed that the legislation make it clear that the primary responsibility for the amenity and recreational use of the Thames, the largest open space in London, rest with existing planning authorities. All activities of the Thames Water Authority and the WSAC should be directed to assisting these authorities in their duties, both financially and otherwise.

The British Waterworks Association accepted the idea of the addition of amenity and recreational objectives for the WAs but objected strenuously to the creation of another body at the national level in the form of the WSAC. This task should be allocated to the NWC. Safeguards should be included in legislation to make sure that interest in recreation will not prevent the WAs from fulfilling their first and foremost duty to maintain a wholesome public water supply. If the WSAC is created, it should not have powers that would threaten the responsibilities of the WAs.

13. Staff Commission for England and Wales

The government proposed a staff commission to promote arrangements for transfer of staff to the WAs, to encourage recruitment, to safeguard staff and to keep them informed. This was to be modeled on the Staff Commission for Local Government, which was involved in similar activities for the local government reorganization.

14. Grant

Exchequer grants had been available to local authorities for the first-time provision of piped water and sewerage in rural localities, with the obligation of the local authorities to make a contribution. Such grants were henceforth to be made to the WAs for the same purpose.

Response

The Institute of Municipal Treasurers and Accountants and most of the other respondents were concerned that no mention was made of a continuation of rate support grants. These grants provide funds for local authorities for sewerage and sewage disposal services, precepted expenditures of river authorities on pollution prevention, fisheries, and navigation, and precepted deficits of many water boards. In south Wales and southwest England, a number of water boards receive a large part of their income from rate support grants in addition to levying the maximum permitted charges. This grant has been in excess of £100 million annually, including 57 percent of the costs of sewerage and sewage disposal across England and Wales. The ending of rate support grants for water-related services could double or even treble the charges to WA customers in some areas. It would leave the WAs in a most invidious position at the very outset. The DoE should consider continuing rate support grants in some form for at least a few years.

The British Waterworks Association spoke for many in its concern that there would be an increase in water charges without a corresponding reduction in general rate demands. BWA considered it essential that the system of grants for rural water supplies and sewerage be maintained at existing levels after the reorganization, with continuation of county council contributions to the cost of the rural schemes. If the county councils do not continue such payments, the cost to the WAs and their consumers would increase substantially.

15. Land drainage

The Ministry of Agriculture, Fisheries and Food, in setting out the government's position on land drainage, including flood control, asserted that, because of the important involvement of local authorities in land drainage, with a tradition of local participation, and because of the relations with other services, all land drainage should continue to be its responsibility. To coordinate with water management, the MAFF would appoint to each WA two members who would be qualified in agriculture, land drainage, or fisheries.

Land drainage would become a WA responsibility, with the MAFF having power to give direction on land drainage matters. The functions of the WAs would be:

1. control over main rivers, including drainage and flood protection,
2. improvement of sea defenses,
3. control of structures in water courses, and
4. provision of flood warning systems.

The regional land drainage committees would consist of 15 members, with a chairman to be one of the MAFF-appointed members of the WA. The WA would appoint two from its own number, with local authorities appointing the others who would be a majority. In addition, an area land drainage committee would be established for each of the river authority areas.

Land drainage activities have been financed by precepts on local authorities and drainage boards, by drainage charges on owners of land, and by grants where needed. The government was not certain how this should be handled in the future.

Response

Charging for land drainage should be separate from water services, according to the associations representing the local authorities. The WAs should have a common financial policy, continuing existing arrangements for paying for land drainage, avoiding changing the system on a piecemeal basis.

The Greater London Council felt it should be the authority responsible for land drainage in London, as London's problems are those involved with the Thames estuary.

While most organizations agreed that the WAs should incorporate responsibilities for land drainage, the British Waterworks Association opposed the proposal that land drainage be run by statutory committees virtually separate from the WAs. The proposal stemmed from a desire to keep the tradition of successful local participation alive, although the government had rejected this argument when it was applied to water supply undertakings. This separateness of land drainage committees also threatened the original concept of the WAs as all-purpose management bodies.

The Institution of Water Engineers found the proposals for land drainage to be complex and would prefer that all land drainage within the river basins be the sole responsibility of the WAs and that ultimate responsibility for WA operations in this area as well as in others be borne by the same Ministers.

16. Fisheries

Because of the close relationship between fisheries and the other WA functions, the government proposed that the WAs take over the river authority responsibilities in this field. Each WA would be expected to establish a small fisheries committee, normally under the chairmanship of a WA member appointed by the MAFF. Fisheries would continue to be financed in the main from licenses, but deficiencies would be made good from charges for water services.

Response

The Association of Municipal Corporations urged a substantial representation of local authorities on regional and local advisory fisheries committees, with the MAFF continuing to be responsible for the fisheries functions of the WAs.

17. Water pollution control

As the last of the consultation papers, the government issued a series of six papers on pollution control. In general, these were addressed to matters that were not to be included in the Water Bill, because of the press of time, but would appear in subsequent legislation and would inevitably become responsibilities of the WAs.

1. *Existing control of discharges and deposits*

At the time, there was no general prohibition against pollution of tidal rivers and estuaries, as there was against pollution of non-tidal rivers. Under the Clean Rivers (Estuaries and Tidal Waters) Act 1960, the consent of the river authorities had to be obtained for new or altered discharges, and they could attach conditions to these discharges. On application by a river authority, full pollution prevention powers could have been obtained for these waters by means of Tidal Waters Orders, but this power had not been much used.

Within the 3-mile limit, 12 sea fisheries committees exercised some control of pollution. The Secretary of State for the Environment examined new outfall schemes when large loan sanctions were involved. A sanction was not given unless the scheme avoids risk to public health or amenity.

The government indicated that it shared in the Jeger Committee recommendation that routine pollution control be extended to tidal rivers, estuaries and the sea. In assigning responsibility for controlling these new discharges, the government felt that the WAs would be most appropriate, although the government (the Secretary of State and the MAFF) would have the ultimate decision in instances that drew their attention. In all respects, the same rules, regulations, and procedures would apply to tidal rivers, estuaries, and the sea as had applied to non-tidal rivers, with the additional participation of the MAFF and the sea fisheries committees.

2. *Pollution from boats*

The River (Prevention of Pollution) Act 1951 authorized river authorities to control the discharges from boats on non-tidal rivers. The British

Waterways Board had power to register boats for fees and to provide on-shore sanitary facilities. These divided responsibilities have not been adequate.

The Jeger Committee had recommended that discharges from boats into fresh waters used for recreation be prohibited and such discharges into estuaries and tidal rivers be controlled.[3] The government agreed with the recommendations for fresh waters but thought that control of discharges to tidal rivers and the sea should be left to local initiative. Accordingly, legislation was proposed that would prohibit vessels on fresh waters to have appliances that would permit discharges, and to enable the WAs to provide necessary shore-based facilities for boat registration. Also, the WAs were to be given the power to regulate discharges from boats into tidal waters and the sea.

3. *Full control of all trade effluent discharges to public sewers*

The consultation paper on economics and finance dealt with charges, while this consultation paper dealt with the power to charge. Trade effluents had fallen into three categories: those started, or substantially altered, after 3 March 1937 which are fully controlled; those existing at the time, which could be charged for and controlled as to temperature and acidity and alkalinity, but could not otherwise be controlled as to volume or composition; and those governed by agreement between industry and local authorities, which were exempt from control.

The Jeger Committee recommended,[3] and the government fully supported, that all discharges of trade effluents be subject to control and liability for charges and that the WAs should be given the appropriate powers.

4. *Risk from accidents*

A wide range of laws and regulations apply to those who accidentally pollute surface waters, but underground waters, which are often used without treatment, were not so protected. The Jeger Committee recommended better safety precautions against accidental pollution and provisions for prosecution of those permitting pollution.[3]

The WAs are to be given strong powers for control of accidents. They are to be permitted to designate an area in which, for the purposes of protecting water resources against accidental damage, certain activities are to be prohibited, such as oil refining or storage, deposits of refuse or sludge, wastewater treatment, burial of human or animal remains, manufacture of poisons, etc.

5. *Publication of information about discharges to inland water courses*

The Rivers (Prevention of Pollution) Act 1961 makes it a criminal offense to disclose any information obtained in connection with an application for consent to discharge or the imposition of conditions on a polluter, or information concerning a sample of effluent. The earlier Act (1951) requires each river authority to maintain a register of conditions attached to consents, but restricts persons from inspection of premises. The Acts, however, preserved the common law right of a riparian owner to obtain an injunction against an upstream polluter without having to prove actual damage.

The Royal Commission on Environmental Pollution urged publication of information about discharges because the waters into which the discharges are made are public property.[13] The only value of confidentiality to industry is to protect themselves against action if they had been given a consent by a regulatory authority.

The Secretary of State accepted the view of the Royal Commission. The use of rivers as receiving waters is unavoidable. The cost of removing *all* impurities from wastewaters so as to retain clean water in streams would be too high to accept. Even only meeting current standards, which are far short of clean water, would cost in the order of £500 million. The government did not believe, therefore, that riparian owners should continue to be able, under common law, to obtain injunctions to stop a discharge which conformed to conditions imposed by a WA.

The government proposed that applications for consents for discharges be made public and that the WAs consider any representation before granting consent. A riparian owner downstream of a discharge would have the right to apply to the WA to revoke or vary the consent if he considered it to be damaging and he could go to the Secretary of State for redress. Included would be public access to analyses of effluents, consents and the like. Where sought by an industry, the Secretary of State can in rare cases grant confidentiality.

A polluter would be held free of responsibility to a riparian owner if he operated within a consent condition.

6. *Control of discharges of mine waters*

Mine waters had in general been exempt from pollution laws. The Government proposed that exemptions be repealed so as to bring mine waters into the same class as other pollutants.

Response

The Confederation of British Industry made a comprehensive analysis of these consultation papers, concluding that:

1. Full allowance should be made for the dilution and dispersion available in the sea and for the little utility of sea water in setting conditions.

2. A five-year consent is preferred to a two-year consent for forward planning, with provision for appeal to the Secretary of State.

3. Exemption of certain existing trade wastes from control should be ended, but a period of five years after enactment should be allowed.
4. Where the WA can apply for an order prohibiting certain industrial activities within an area, industry should have the right of appeal and compensation.
5. While the CBI opposed advertisements of applications for consents which would expose decision-making to public pressures, public access should be accorded to the analyses of surface and underground waters and samples of effluent as well as to the register of consents, although review of consents on application by a riparian owner was opposed.
6. Consent conditions may be varied by a WA if the dischargers are allowed the right of appeal and time to conform.
7. The CBI asserted that a damaged person should be able to collect compensation from a polluter even if he meets the consent conditions set by the WA because, if the WA were to be entirely responsible, the WA would tend to be too cautious in setting consent conditions.

The British Waterworks Association generally welcomed the proposed legislation for water pollution control which would be a boon to the protection of water supplies. Particular attention should be given to pollution resulting from accidents and the transportation of materials. The Institution of Public Health Engineers added that consideration be given to pollution from aerial spraying and from tanker traffic on roads.

The Institution of Water Pollution Control agreed that the system of calculating charges for trade effluents discharging to sewers might be on a national basis, but charges for effluents in different areas of the country need not be identical. It can be expected to cost much more to treat a trade effluent discharging into a trout stream than into a sea outfall. Charging for the trade effluents is not simply a matter of raising money but can be a convenient method of controlling the quality and quantity of discharges to sewers and full account of this incentive should be considered.

Summary comments

The general opposition to the reorganization was largely muted by the issuance of the series of individual consultation papers which focused objections on individual elements of the reorganization. Respondents often preceded their comments by repeating their objections to the context in which each consultation paper was issued; that is, the assumption that there would be major reorganization leading to multipurpose authorities. The effect was virtually to assure that a reorganization bill would be prepared but with modifications in the government's original proposals to reflect some of the reservations raised.

Almost all the respondents voiced objections to the following proposals set forth in the consultation papers:

1. The retention of the statutory water companies.
2. The very short timetable for implementation.
3. The insufficiency of local government representation on the WAs.
4. The appointment of the chairman of a WA by the Minister, as contrasted with his election from amongst the members of the WA.
5. The failure to include a chief technical officer along with the chief executive and finance officer in the early appointments to the WAs.
6. The unsatisfactory proposals with regard to handling of local sewerage.
7. The failure of the proposals to indicate what replacement there would be for the rate support grants for water services.
8. The creation of a weak central authority, the National Water Council, without executive responsibilities of any consequence, thereby leaving the ultimate responsibility for national policy in the hands of the DoE.

In addition, some limited objections were expressed to the following proposals:

9. Authorization of metering of residential water services, primarily on the basis that it would be far more expensive than the Government had indicated.
10. The implied change in the financing of water services from taxation as a public health service to the market approach, treating water service as a utility.
11. Recruiting candidates for the highest staff positions from outside the 'ring fence', as being a slur on and a threat to the professionals in the industry.

Some reservations were expressed about the shifting of responsibility for the amenity use of water courses from existing agencies and particularly from the British Waterways Board. Even those favoring multipurpose authorities supported continuance of the BWB. Otherwise, the strong feeling was that all water-related services should be included among the responsibilities of the WAs.

The proposals for reorganization were met with a wide disparity of responses. Some greeted the proposals with enthusiasm, congratulating the government for being progressive, farsighted and bold; some claimed that the reorganization was not sufficiently radical; while many others claimed that it went far beyond what was necessary to deal with the existing problems.

As was to be expected, the associations representing the local authorities were seriously disturbed by the government's proposals because of the local authorities' loss of important responsibilities. Many proposed the establishment of a powerful national body to coordinate local government services, with operating responsibilities at the local level. The sense of the local government reorganization was that responsibilites of the local authorities be increased.

To suggestions that the WAs be the basis of regional government, the government was of the opinion that the management of water and other local government functions were not compatible. Hydrologic boundaries and political boundaries do not coincide. Local authorities, on the other hand, were concerned that unless the government modified its proposals to make the newly projected local authorities and the successful water undertakings responsible for the water services, then the entire water industry and the housing and industrial developments which depend on them will undergo chaos leading only to further reorganization.

The dissolution of the Water Resources Board came as a great surprise to many, as the WRB had been receiving only encomiums. Some believed that the WRB had not been given sufficient power. Were the WRB to have the powers that were to be granted to the proposed National Water Council, the WRB would serve satisfactorily. On the other hand, others believed that the proposed NWC would be even less powerful than the WRB and was being introduced as a way of preserving power for the government.

Most of the outcries resulted from the projected removal of responsibility from local authorities to authorities that would be some distance, both literally and figuratively, from the consumers they serve. However, of all public services, consumers are least interested in day-to-day phases of water management unless service falters. If the new arrangements would provide better service, complaints of the consumers would reach Whitehall and Westminster regardless of the nature of the organization.

The stream of consultation papers had almost saturated the opposition by allowing little time for comment and little real dialogue. The government position seemed to have hardened and even the concessions made to the associations representing the local authorities did not appear significant. Banks summarized by pointing out that the WAs '... will suffer from fundamental defects in being too large for this small and varied country; in lacking the checks and balances of independent authorities; in being monopolies with obligations to show returns on capital employed (as do other state corporations) and whose spending will be influenced primarily by the needs of the water cycle rather than the consumer; in divorcing the provision of the essential services from the provision of housing; and in setting standards and seeing to their achievement.

'They will however benefit from the emphasis of dedicated officers in the water services whose efforts and good will undoubtedly ensure that those defects are minimized and that the new WAs are the envy of the world.'[14]

The government's response

The four local authority associations sent a deputation to Peter Walker, then Secretary of State for the Environment, backed up by a call for a boycott of the working parties, seeking greater local authority responsibility. The consultative council idea should be scrapped and local authority representatives should form a majority on all WA management committees and the committees, not the Minister, should appoint their chairmen.

Walker responded in August 1972 promising local authorities a substantial role in the control of the water services. He stated: 'Our problem is how to secure vital public interests and to associate local government with the solution.

'On the other hand, the logic of the situation obliges one to allot to the regional water authorities extensive powers over river management, water supply and sewerage and sewage disposal. They must own the assets and be responsible for finance (revenue and capital); regional water authorities must necessarily have to make the effective decisions on investment programs of water supply, sewerage and sewage disposal, both as to size and timing, subject to the local authorities development plan.

'On the other hand, we do believe that the elected local member has an essential part to play in the operation of these functions.'[15]

Walker concluded that he was impressed by the force with which the case for local authority representation on the WAs was presented. His main concessions were that:

1. The new district councils would be the local authorities for sewerage under the control of the WAs but with a substantial field of local discretion.

2. Local authorities would have a statutory responsibility for overseeing the environmental health aspects of sewerage, sewage disposal and rivers in their areas.

3. There would be greater local authority representation on the WAs (an implied promise).

4. The chief executive would not be an *ex officio* member of his WA.

5. The regional consultative councils would be abandoned in favor of the proposed joint consultative committees for public participation, which would be built around the new local authorities.

6. He confirmed that the WAs would be statutorily obliged to prepare action plans and assessment programs with regard to the plans of local authorities.

Upon quelling the local authority uprising through making some concessions, the government was on its way to the new multipurpose regionalization for water management.

CHAPTER 4

The Water Bill in Parliament

The government planned to submit the Water Bill to parliament in the late summer of 1972. The organizations that had expressed opposition to the reorganization, particularly the associations representing the local authorities, had hoped to delay the introduction of the Bill and kill it by inaction. The Secretary of State for the Environment had made some concessions in the Bill, but these apparently had not been enough to mollify the opposition. With no important constituency pushing hard for reorganization, delay seemed politically acceptable. The pressing business of government and a full parliament agenda were ample reasons for postponing consideration of a Bill which, after all, responded to no great crisis. In fact, local authorities through their representatives in parliament might very well have characterized the Bill as unpopular.

Parliamentary leaders were not anxious to initiate consideration of such a major reorganization bill, which was likely to take considerable time and be rather tedious and, more important, was not likely to satisfy any important political need. Had there not been some considerable pressure from interested quarters, the legislation might not have come up and, had it not, it would not be considered again for at least five years.

However, the professionals and those in the Civil Service who had been at the heart of the planning for reorganization were not content to lose the momentum generated by the proposals, the consultation papers, and the Secretary of State for the Environment. Stepping into the breech was the Royal Commission on Environmental Pollution which, as its chairman, Lord Ashby averred, has no statutory power but some political influence. In November 1972, when the Water Bill appeared to languish, Lord Ashby wrote the Department of the Environment that failure to act expeditiously on the Water Bill would be detrimental to the environment, as the many authorities and individuals concerned would be left in a most uncertain position. The reorganization must be acted upon one way or another without delay. The change in the Secretary of State for the Environment, with Geoffrey Rippon replacing Peter Walker, facilitated compromise that would allow the Bill to be introduced.

The Bill as submitted to parliament on 23 January 1973 did meet some of the major objections raised by both opponents and supporters of the legislation. The first major concession was that each water authority have a majority of local authority members. With this, the regional consultative councils were abandoned. Second, the British Waterways Board would be left intact. Third, local authorities would be given the responsibility to act as agents for the WAs for sewerage, with the WAs obliged to show regard in their own plans for the development plans of the local authorities.

Also, in interest of time and because it was not essential to the reorganization, the government did not include in the Bill provisions for controlling water pollution more effectively. Such legislation, which had little opposition, was to become the Control of Pollution Act 1974.

The public press acknowledged that 'The Bill goes a long way to redeem objections of local councils, although they are still opposed to losing their powers as water suppliers and sewerage authorities.'[1] Despite his earlier statements, Lord Nugent of Guildford, president of the Association of River Authorities, gave the Bill a general welcome. The tide on the Bill had turned.

THE WATER BILL AS INTRODUCED

'An Act to make provision for a national policy for water, for the conferring and discharge of functions as to water (including sewerage and sewage disposal, fisheries and land drainage) and as to recreation and amenity in connection with water, for the making of charges by water authorities and other statutory water undertakers, and for connected purposes.'

Part I defined the powers and responsibilities of the Secretary of State for the Environment and the Minister of Agriculture, Fisheries and Food with regard to promoting a national policy in England and Wales and, through the bodies established by the Act, to secure the effective execution of these policies. The WAs were defined and their constitutions established together with the areas that they were to cover.

Each WA was to consist of a chairman appointed by the Secretary of State, two or three members appointed by the Minister of Agriculture, Fisheries, and Food, a number appointed by the Secretary of State, and members to be appointed by local authorities, with the requirement that the total number of members appointed by the Secretary of State and the Minister be less than the number of those appointed by the local authorities.

A National Water Council would be established, which would consist of a chairman appointed by the Secretary of State, the ten chairmen of the WAs and not more than ten others appointed by the Secretary of State and the Minister, who should have special knowledge of matters relative to the functions of the WAs. The NWC was to advise the government on matters relating to national water policy, to promote and assist the WAs in the efficient performance of their responsibilities, particularly relating to research, establish a scheme for the testing and approval of water fittings and prepare a scheme for training and education.

Part II provided for the transfer of relevant functions to the WAs, including the functions of the river authorities, responsibilities for water conservation, water supply, sewerage and sewage disposal, control of river pollution, fisheries, land drainage, recreation, and nature conservation and amenity. Provision was made for the discharge of the WAs' duties with regard to water supply by existing statutory water companies under agency agreements.

Similarly, provision was made for the discharge of sewerage functions by local authorities as agents on behalf of the WAs. Sewage disposal facilities and all facilities operated by joint sewerage boards, main drainage authorities, or the Greater London Council were not to be subject to agency agreements. The discharge of land drainage functions was to be executed through a regional and local land drainage committee on each WA. The Greater London Council's responsibilities for land drainage in the London area were preserved. WAs were to provide sewerage for existing premises, or for proposed new development.

Provision was made for the establishment of a Water Space Amenity Commission for the purpose of advising the Secretary of State, the NWC and the WAs on the discharge of their functions in relation to recreation and amenity in England. The Welsh National Water Development Authority was to have specific functions in relation to recreation in Wales.

Part III contained general financial provisions for the WAs and the NWC and the necessary powers for the WAs to levy charges for the services they perform and the facilities they provide. Their revenue is to be sufficient to meet their costs and they may be directed to achieve a specified rate of return on the value of their assets.

The Bill provided for the net cost of all water services, except land drainage, to be met by charges, replacing the existing system whereby expenditures on sewerage, sewage disposal and the prevention of pollution were met from general rates. The cost of land drainage would continue to be met by precepts on local authorities and internal drainage boards and by charges on agricultural land.

Exchequer grants would be paid to WAs instead of to river authorities in respect of land drainage and to WAs instead of to local authorities or joint boards for the first-time provision for piped water and sewerage in rural localities.

The WAs were to be empowered to install water meters in residential premises. The Secretary of State might make regulations with respect to metering and which would be subject to annulment in either House of Parliament.

Part IV abolished certain existing bodies such as the Water Resources Board, the Central Advisory Water Committee, all the river authorities, all the joint water and sewerage boards and the Water Supply Industry Training Board.

Because of the majority given to local authority representatives on the WAs, the proposal for the establishment of regional consumer councils was dropped from the Bill. Also, the government gave up, under considerable pressure, incorporating the British Waterways Board in the reorganization.

With the potentially most troublesome element in the reorganization, namely, the constitution of the WAs, providing for a majority of local authority members, and with political opposition focusing on only minor elements of the legislation, passage through parliament might have been expected to be rather smooth. The government's strategy of focusing on elements of the reorganization, rather than on the reorganization as a whole, had not given opponents much opportunity to address the larger issue. Much of the resentment and opposition began to reveal itself through members of parliament when the Bill was introduced.

INTRODUCTION OF THE BILL IN PARLIAMENT

In the United Kingdom, a Bill, generally prepared by government, may be introduced either in the House of Commons or in the House of Lords. It is managed in parliament by parliamentary officers who are in the government as well as being members of parliament. Parliament has no committees that prepare legislation nor that have available to them staff that could help both the majority and minority members with technical information concerning the legislation. Neither parliament nor its committees holds public hearings. Members of the party in power depend upon the government to provide them with the background on government-sponsored legislation, while both they and the opposition depend upon interested professional and trade organizations to furnish them with technical information on the legislation.

For example, the British Waterworks Association arranged to have its views put forward in Parliament by four MPs, two from the Labour and two from the Conservative Party. The two Labour Party representatives, Denis Howell and Nigel Spearing, were particularly influential, being members of Standing Committee D, which gave the Bill detailed review. Representations were made on behalf of the BWA with regard to concern for concentrating the powers in the water industry in the hands of the Secretary of State for the Environment, the need to provide for the WAs and the NWC to elect their own chairmen, the need for the agency concept to be extended beyond the statutory water companies to include local authorities responsible for water supply undertakings, and for the NWC to be strengthened to provide for planning, advisory and coordinating functions as well as for research and development, amenity and recreation, and executive powers for initiation and construction of major new works. The BWA was not successful as is clear in the pages that follow.

After two readings in the House of Commons, its first *pro forma* introduction, the legislation may be turned over to a committee. Following committee deliberations, a report stage and a final third reading take place in the House of Commons, after which the legislation moves to the House of Lords, which sits as a committee of the whole. After consideration in the House of Lords, such amendments as are there introduced are considered by the House of Commons, and the Bill is voted upon. Upon passage it receives Royal Assent. In parliamentary proceedings, legislation introduced by the government and sponsored by the party in power is seldom defeated, as each vote, except for minor issues or issues specifically declared not to be so, is considered a vote of confidence in the government and defeat would challenge the government and possibly call for a national election.

The first reading of the Water Bill on 23 January 1973, its formal introduction to parliament, was presented by Geoffrey Rippon, on his behalf and that of Peter Thomas, Secretary of State for Wales. The purposes of the Bill were water conservation (water resources development), water supply, sewerage and sewage disposal, prevention of river pollution, promotion of fisheries, land drainage, and recreation. The reorganization to accomplish these purposes was to take place alongside the reorganization of local government and the health services. With the introduction there was submitted to parliament the publication, *A Background to Water Reorganization in England and Wales*, in which it was stated that the Government's policy is designed to achieve the following major objectives:[2]

'1. To secure an ample supply of water of appropriate quality to meet the growing demands of the people, industry, and agriculture—while at the same time assuring that it is not wasted.

2. To provide adequate sewerage and sewage disposal facilities to cope with the natural increase in water use with new housing, industrial and agricultural developments.

3. To ensure that the vital contribution of land drainage and flood protection to both urban and agricultural areas alike is maintained and, where appropriate, expanded.

4. To achieve a massive clean-up of the country's rivers and estuaries by the early 1980s.

5. To make the widest use of water space for other purposes, including recreation and amenity and, where appropriate, the protection and development of salmon and fresh-water fisheries and provision of water needed for navigation.

6. To protect the interest of those who may be affected by proposals for the development of water resources in any of these respects.'

The highlights of the debates on the second reading are presented below, but the more detailed debate took place in Standing Committee D and is discussed in the next section.

Finance

The opposition focused on the government's statement that the WAs would, like the nationalized industries, require target rates of return on capital employed raising the spectre that the water undertakings would behave like private undertakings.

The government's response was that, inasmuch as each WA would comprise a majority of local authority representatives, this should assure that there would be no drastic changes in the way the water undertakings are managed, or in the charges levied. The government was often to fall back upon the accountability allegedly afforded by the majority of local authority members on each WA. Had the government not given way on the issue of local authority representation, its defense of many elements of the Bill would have had to have been far more substantive.

Local authority representation

Howell (Labour, to become Parliamentary Under Secretary of State in the DoE with the change in government) stated that the country used to have a Ministry of Housing and Local Government that ensured that houses were built and that local government was based on local democracy:[3] 'We now have the Department of the Environment. It builds fewer houses and is busily engaged in desecration of local democracy.' In giving more and more power to the Ministry, he saw '... another step towards the destruction of local government'. In decrying the slender majority of local authority representation on the proposed WAs, he added 'If ever there was an opportunity for packing these bodies with blue-eyed boys representing a political philosophical ideology of the government of the day, it is present in this Bill'.

John Hunt (Con.) reminded his colleagues of the 1970 General Election Manifesto *New Style of Government* proposing that government power will be ordered so that more decisions will be made locally. This explains why so many are unhappy about the Bill. Instead of having directly elected councillors controlling these services, there shall be 'faceless men of the new regional water authority—unelected, undemocratic and remote'.[4]

The government in response asserted that the main reason that the Secretary of State should make appointments to the WAs is that he is the one charged with developing and implementing the national water policy. As the WAs are to be crucial in carrying through the policy, it is necessary that the Secretary make appointments to them.

National Water Council

Conservative and Labour MPs alike supported retention of the Water Resources Board so that its success could be exploited. Spearing (Lab.) stated that the government had not given a good reason for dispensing with the WRB. The Secretary of State for the Environment had made speeches at Stockholm advising the countries of the world to organize their water programs on a national basis. When he returned home, he smashed the WRB. He quoted the Confederation of British Industry, an organization whose views on government reorganization would generally not be in harmony with his own, as also regretting the passing of the WRB, a body independent of the government.

The government's response was that the WRB was no more independent than the proposed NWC as all of its members were appointed by the Secretary of State. Specifically, the WRB's very success had led the government to the conclusion that rather different arrangements were now needed. The WRB was required when there were some 200 statutory water undertakers and 29 river authorities. With the much smaller number of all-purpose authorities, the WRB was no longer needed, although its planning arm would be kept as an independent source of advice for the Secretary of State and the NWC. The NWC was not seen as a replacement of the WRB.

Statutory water companies

As was to be expected, the recommendation for retention of the statutory water companies raised strong opposition, particularly on the Labour side. Also, this proposal led to recommendations that the publicly owned water undertakings also continue to serve as agents for the WAs. Lena Jeger (Lab.) affirmed that the Labour Party, if elected, would take over the private water companies. In general, the government did not feel obliged to respond, depending upon the philosophy of the Conservative Party with regard to nationalization to carry the issue.

Metering

The Labour Party zeroed in on the proposals to authorize the WAs to introduce residential metering of water. They rejected metering as being against the public interest and against the interest of large families and characterized the proposal as classic Conservative Party policy. Jeger spoke against metering because of the waste of labor and in principle because she was against metering a natural resource. Metering would seriously increase the cost of water. David Stoddard (Lab.) identified the real problem, that metering would change the emphasis on water supply from a social service to a profit-making enterprise. The government's response was that metering was not its policy, but that the WAs ought to be permitted to use metering if they found it to be effective.

Wales

The City of Birmingham had built the dams for the reservoirs in Wales which provide the City with a supply of pure and soft water which is not surpassed in quality anywhere else in the British Isles. Julius Silverman (Lab.) representing Birmingham, feared that these water sources would be lost to the city and would pass to the WNWDA despite the fact that they exist only through the considerable foresight of the people of Birmingham. The Welsh members suggested that the Welsh, from whose area the waters were derived, should gain the benefit. Silverman responded that the water came from heaven and that the reservoirs in Wales proved to be of benefit to the people of Wales through the payment of taxes on the property as well as by providing employment.

The Welsh Members claimed a Welsh right to Welsh water. The Severn Trent Water Authority would have to come to Wales to make arrangements for its use. The establishment of an unelected body that would have a right to take water from Wales or to construct reservoirs that would flood land in Wales was unthinkable. If the WNWDA were to be responsible to the Welsh people, it should be elected. 'The truth is that the Ministers are taking power away from the Welsh people. Transferring it to the bureaucrats and the new water authority would be unrepresentative and therefore untrusted and remote from our people.'[5]

General

The opposition agreed with the ends of the Bill but not with its means. The government had gone out of its way to make the subject of water more political than it should have been. That there was no green paper or even a white paper and that there was limited time between publication of the Bill and its second reading, only 13 days, was troublesome. The opposition believed that water should be regarded in the same way as the health services and education. They are not services that people are free to use or not to use, as all members of the community derive equal benefits. The proposals of the government represent very clearly the Tory philosophy, especially on the metering of water.

Eldon Griffiths, Parliamentary Under Secretary of State for the Environment, in response for the government, stated that the re-organization of the water services was a third pillar with the reorganizations of local government and the health services in the modernization of the machinery of government.

The need was great in that the future supply of water was giving rise to serious concern. Most of the rain falls in the north and west while demands for water were growing in the east and south. About 50 gallons (230 liters) of water *per capita* were used daily for domestic purposes, and the demands were expected to double within 20 years. The current reliable yield available to water undertakers was about 4000 million gallons (18 million cubic meters) per day with an estimated demand within about 20 years of 6000 million gallons (28 million cubic meters) per day, leaving a deficit of almost 2000 million gallons (10 million cubic meters) per day.

One approach to this problem was the consideration of rivers not as drains or sewers but as water mains capable of transporting large volumes of water over long distances. Because one-third of all the water taken from rivers in one stage or another had received large quantities of sewage and industrial wastes, the important objective was to plan together all aspects of water development. The government's policy recognized that political boundaries could not be the basis for water management. The boundaries of the WAs were selected primarily on a hydrologic basis.

In response to comments that the government's proposals do not have 'a friend in the world', he listed the following organizations that supported the Bill:[6] The Institute of Water Pollution Control, the Society of Chemical Industry, and the Society of Water Treatment and Examination amongst the technical societies; the Society of Clerks and Treasurers of the Water Authorities, the Association of River Authorities, the Confederation of British Industry, the Central Electricity Generating Board, the trades unions, including the National Union of Water Works Employees and the Association of Water Boards Officers amongst the administrative bodies; and the Royal Commission on Environmental Pollution, the Committee for Environmental Conservation and the Salmon and Trout Association among environmental organizations. Among those missing were the associations representing the local authorities.

The Bill passed the second reading on a party line vote, 220–210. The rather narrow majority of only 10 presaged a somewhat more turbulent passage through the committee stage than had been expected.

COMMITTEE DEBATE

The Bill was considered by Standing Committee D of the House of Commons in 19 half-day sittings from 20 February thru 12 April 1973. Standing Committee D comprised 21 Members of Parliament representing a wide range of interests. R. Graham Page, Minister of Local Government and Development, David Gibson-Watt, Minister of State for Welsh affairs, and Paul Hawkins, Lord of the Treasury, were members of the committee. In all, the Conservative–Labour distribution in the committee was 12 to 9. In addition to the Conservative Welsh Minister, two Labour members from Wales were also on the committee. London was represented by a Conservative and a Labour member and Birmingham by a Labour member. Most of the controversial views were well represented by interested parties on the committee.

James Allason (Con.) proposed that, amongst the responsibilities of the Secretary of State to secure effective execution of policy relating to the use of inland waters for recreation, the language be extended to include 'conservation and improvement of the environment of rivers', in which the environment of the river rather than the water itself is of concern.[7] Page, for the government, agreed that the environment of rivers, particularly in industrial areas, could do with a great deal of improvement. However, he agreed with the opposition in feeling that this would extend into the responsibilities of local planning authorities. The government required that in formulating proposals relating to the functions of the WAs, local authorities should have regard to the 'desirability of preserving natural beauty'.[8] This would encourage WAs to go to local planning authorities in connection with such matters. However, Page did agree with Howell's (Lab.) amendment that including 'amenity' in the Bill would be an improvement.[9]

London

An amendment that would establish a separate London Water Authority accountable to the people of London was introduced by John Hunt (Con.) of London.[10] The Greater London Council was established in 1964 and has had great success. It has provided main drainage services to 7·5 million people over an area of 630 square miles (1630 square kilometers), with 700 miles (1100 kilometers) of main sewers and it has treated 50 million gallons (230 000 cubic meters) of wastewater every day. 'Even the serried ranks of the hydrologists and technologists which appear to be cramming the corridors of power in the Department of Environment have been unable to fault the performance of the Greater London Council in all of these spheres'.[11] Why should GLC be deprived of these responsibilities? The government cannot make an exception of London, but London is already exceptional.

Howell stated that the opposition was completely convinced that the government was moving '... further and further away from the people, moving further and further away from the democratic content of local government'.[12] Therefore, the opposition proposed a half-way stage so as not to pre-empt in the future the right to move to full control of the water service by directly elected local authority bodies, with emergence of some form of regionalism and regional government.[13] The opposition could not understand the government's '... absolute mania, in the fear of local government, for smashing up things which happen to be working well. ... There has never been a bigger bunch of revolutionaries sitting on the government benches that there are at present. The only difference between this government and Karl Marx is that he knew what he was doing'.[14]

The population to be served by the proposed London Water Authority would be larger than the population served by several of the projected WAs. Howell, although not a Londoner, felt he could say without serious contradiction that London was the best governed capital city in the world. It had done its planning exceedingly well.[15]

William Whitlock (Lab.) was torn by the dilemma. He believed in the need to involve people in democratic government above all else. However, he also believed in the need to base water management on the natural water regimes of river catchments. These two concepts are difficult to rationalize. Bigness can mean remoteness. The new local governments as well as the WAs would be remote from ordinary people. '. . . people turn taps, throw switches, pull levers, yank chains without the slightest conception of the vast amount of human endeavor and the enormous capital investment which lie behind the convenient resource. Most people do not care how they get their water or electricity or gas as long as they get it when they need it. It is only when it is not there that they demand to know who is responsible'.[16]

Whitlock felt it would be odd to say that for the rest of England and Wales the boundaries would be based on natural catchments but that London should pretend that the laws of gravity, nature and river engineering must be suspended. London might be a special case but breaking away from the catchment area concept might be a bad precedent.

Griffiths (Con.), in responding, disagreed that the government had any intention to smash local government and he did not believe that the issue was a question between technology and democracy. To meet the incipient shortage of water, all-purpose management of water services appeared to be necessary. Had the Greater London Council been a creditable unit for integrated water management, the government would have found a way for accomplishing this. However, this could not be done successfully in a case such as London any more than in the case of Manchester, Liverpool or other large conurbations. The GLC was not responsible for sewerage within the whole of London. The GLC land drainage area did not coincide with the GLC's own boundaries. The Thames and Lee Conservancies looked after London's water resources, the Metropolitan Water Board looked after the water that Londoners drank, and the Port of London Authority and the Conservancies were the main pollution control authorities in most of the tidal river. All of these were to be placed into one authority, the Thames Water Authority. The Port of London Authority and the Thames Conservancy agreed with this change.[17] The government proposals were far better for democracy as well as hydrology. The local authorities would have a clear and absolute majority on the TWA. The GLC and the London boroughs would have a clear majority of that majority. The position of the local authorities on the TWA would be strengthened and improved.

Where London had had no influence, democratic or otherwise, on that part of the Thames which provided potential supplies for the future, now for the first time, the democratically elected local authorities in London would have power to make decisions and influence the policy of the whole Thames, stretching right back to Oxford and beyond.

In summing up the debate on London, Howell quoted from a song, *Old Father Thames:* 'Kingdoms may come, kingdoms may go; whatever the end may be, Old Father Thames keeps rolling along, down to the mighty sea'.[18] This kingdom would soon go and if it is gone—if not this year, next year, another kingdom will come which would correct the abuses of the democratic process which were enshrined in this Bill.

On the division, establishment of a London Water Authority was defeated 9 to 8.

The Welsh National Water Development Authority

An amendment was proposed by the opposition to include within the Welsh National Water Development Authority that part of the upper Severn River Basin which is within Wales.[19] The pride of London is the Thames. This had been recognized by allowing the Greater London Council responsibility for amenity and recreation in the portion of the Thames that passed through the city. The Welsh also loved their rivers, and the Severn was a Welsh river. It rose in Wales, and like most Welsh people, it sojourned for a while in England, but it came home.

Gibson-Watt, for the government, stated that to bring a portion of the upper Severn River basin into the WNWDA would contradict a statement made by George Thomas (Lab.) of Wales, a supporter of the amendment, who had declared that it was not feasible to talk about Welsh water nor to try to deal with Anglo-Welsh rivers in two parts. If total water management were to be achieved on the Severn, it would not be feasible to have any of these responsibilities become a part of the WNWDA merely because the political boundary crosses the river.[20]

The amendment was defeated 11 to 8.

Authority areas

In a discussion of the large size of some of the WAs, particularly the proposed Anglian Water Authority, the largest in land area, Howell pointed out that it would be difficult to get local authority members to participate. The Minister '... will choose in the first place as many Conservative ladies as he can who will be bound to give up the time because even Conservative businessmen are finding it increasingly difficult to attend local authority committees'.[21] There were physical difficulties in getting democratically elected people to serve on an authority of this size. The Labour side had the added disability of their people getting time off from work. On the other side was the difficulty of businessmen being able to take time from their businesses. Furthermore, how would local authority representatives know the very large area well enough? It would be an administrative monstrosity.[22]

Griffiths in response pointed out that most of the operating functions within the authority would be carried out at local levels. The prospective provisional management units or divisions would be based upon existing water systems and committees would deal with problems within these local areas.

Chairmen of the Water Authorities

The method for selection of the chairmen of the WAs was a most contentious issue, the only issue with which the opposition had success in Standing Committee D. The British Waterworks Association and the Association of Municipal Corporations offered an amendment through Howells and Spearing that the members of the WAs should select their chairmen from amongst their numbers. This would afford greater democratization of the WAs and go a long way toward removing the objections to the constitution of the National Water Council, which would otherwise have its entire membership appointed by the Government. Opposing the amendment, Griffiths stated that the Secretary of State would be in an untenable position if he was unable to appoint men in whom he had confidence, as he had ultimate responsibility for the WAs. The chairmen would have to be people with experience and demonstrated ability to rule large organizations with enormous investment programs.

After extensive debate, the government lost, 11 to 5, the only vote it lost in Standing Committee D. The government was taken by surprise and it was widely predicted that this decision was almost certain to be reversed during the Bill's report stage in the House of Commons.

The National Water Council

The opposition characterized the approach of the government to the National Water Council as political vandalism in destroying the Water Resources Board which had done invaluable work and had probably put Britain ahead of every other nation regarding water development and research.[23] Three different units were to be established for planning, research and data collection. Although the object of the Bill was to formulate a national water policy, Gordon Oakes (Lab.) noted that no mention was made of the NWC responsibility with regard to national water policy. To link the ample water in the west to the heavy population in the east should be a function of the NWC. Some of the schemes anticipated in the future would be immense, requiring resources beyond those likely to be available even in the large WAs. Such national schemes should be considered within the framework of a national policy for water under the aegis of the NWC.

A feature of the second reading debate was that everyone deplored the breakup of the WRB.† The British Waterworks Association had advocated

† A comment on the acclaim accorded the WRB was that, when one is dying or deceased, only words of praise are heard. As the WRB's demise seemed imminent approval could be expressed like the encomiums heaped on former Prime Minister Heath after he had resigned.

for almost 30 years the need for a strong independent but responsible national body to bring together the planning, advisory, and coordinating functions to look to the country's water services.[24]

The government did not want policy to be settled by any national body. When the Labour government faced a similar situation in the case of gas and electricity, they nationalized. This government was instead trying to form a partnership between local authorities and expert management. The Conservative government did not support nationalization and for that reason the government did not wish to give the NWC full powers to run the water industry such as the National Gas Board and the Central Electricity Generating Board had in their industries. The WAs, supported heavily by the local authorities, should be the executive arm of the water industry. If there were conflict, it would be the Secretary of State who was responsible to Parliament. The WAs would not, in their executive functions, be under the management or control of the NWC. In providing the NWC with access to the information it needed to give advice to.the Government, it would need considerable influence over the Central Water Planning Unit, the Data Collection Unit and the Water Research Centre. For that purpose the Government proposed that the chairman of the Steering Committee of the CWPU be the chairman of the NWC. The membership of the WRC, although it was not to be a statutory body, should be largely drawn from the NWC and the WAs. Therefore, the NWC and the WAs would be able to steer these two bodies.[25]

An amendment to give the NWC executive responsibility was defeated 7 to 6. Similar efforts at greater centralization were also defeated.

Grants

The rate support grants to local authorities in 1973–74 from the exchequer were about £482 million, of which about 60 percent was allocated for meeting the sewerage and sewage disposal responsibilities of the local authorities. The proposed legislation was vague as to how this very important annual contribution was to be made up in the new proposal for financing. Arthur Jones (Con.) proposed an amendment to obtain assurance from the government about the availability of the existing grants. The amendment would require that the Secretary of State pay at least a comparable amount in grants to each WA, the amounts being those that would be payable if the WA were a local authority.[26]

In responding, Page pointed out that much of the basis for the rate support grant was not applicable to water. Also, because water supply had long been regarded, in principle, as a trading service and therefore excluded from expenditures on which the rate support grant was based, it was difficult to include the rate support grant within the legislation. The government would have to replace money lost from the rate support grant but would not want the same formula. In principle, the government was against making any provisions for a generalized grant. In making a decision about the appropriate level of exchequer grant after reorganization, the government would take full account, not only of local government expenditure, but also of the fact that the ratepayer of the future would be paying directly for water services that were at present paid for from rates and rate support grants.[27]

Statutory water companies

The opposition attacked the Bill for continuing the privately-owned statutory water companies to serve as agents of the WAs. Not the quality of their performance but strictly party political considerations were the issues as contrasted with the more ethical political considerations that otherwise divide the opposition from the government.

W. E. Garret (Lab.), while not the principal spokesman for the opposition, stated that '... when we win the next election we shall nationalize the industry'.[28] Gordon Oakes, the spokesman of the Labour Party in the committee did not categorically commit the party to nationalizing the privately-owned water companies under a future Labour government, but stated, 'It is certainly one of the matters that will be looked at very closely by a future Labour government, with a view to the full rationalization of water supply'.[29]

In response to the government's interpretation that the Labour Party would 'nationalize the lot', Howell asserted that, although the Labour Party believed in the public ownership of water and a strong water authority, it also believed passionately in local development and democracy. Local authorities should retain control of the water received, its distribution and quality and its disposal back into the river system. Regional authorities should act as wholesalers for water and be in charge of the river systems. At some future date they would hope to ensure that these authorities would be able to transfer their functions to new, elected regional authorities which they hoped to see eventually created.

The government's response was that the exchequer would need to find £250 million to pay off the shareholders to take these privately owned water companies into the public sector, an unwarranted expenditure. Finally, Griffiths indicated that it would be much wiser to continue the work being done by these companies without cost to the British taxpayers than to carry out a moral obligation which would not bring one additional drop of water.[30]

Sewerage and sewage disposal

The stripping of responsibilities for sewerage and sewage disposal from local authorities under this legislation raised exceedingly strong objections both from the Labour Party and from some members of the Conservative Party. Jones (Con.) indicated that, with the reorganization of local government, local authorities would be larger and in a far better position to exercise their responsibilities for sewerage and sewage disposal in proper fashion. Transferring these responsibilities to the WAs would reduce engineers' responsibilities in local authorities and would leave the local authority with no potential for developing qualified engineering services to discharge their other obligations. More important, local authorities were responsible for development and for providing the facilities that would permit development, and they should have control over the local sewerage which was a necessary facility for development.

In the long and contentious debate, the government responded in principle that the responsibility for managing wastewater must be with the WAs if a rational water management program were to be developed in the future. The Bill called for mutually acceptable agency agreements with the local authorities to discharge the sewerage function under the direction of the WAs.

The Committee voted 10 to 9 against an amendment that would retain local authority responsibility for sewerage and sewage disposal with Jones (Con.) abstaining and the other votes along party lines.[31]

Feelings were mixed about the outcome of the lengthy discussions between the government and the four associations representing the local authorities that led to the compromise which allowed the local authorities to serve as agents for the WAs for the sewerage function. Complete rationalization would incorporate local sewerage into the operations of the WAs, just as the water distribution system was so incorporated. To mollify local authorities in the face of the reorganization, the government had been willing to compromise; possibly because had it not made some concessions, the opposition in parliament might have been stronger on behalf of the local authorities.

Recreation

The government and the opposition were in harmony on the subject of developing the water resources of the nation for recreation.[32]

Research

The government's proposal on research was buried in one paragraph of the Bill indicating that the WAs '... may make arrangements for the carrying out of research and related activities in respect of such matters by subscribing or otherwise financially contributing to an organization formed for that purpose'. This was a veiled reference to the proposed Water Research Centre which was to comprise the Water Research Association, the Water Pollution Research Laboratory, and the research components of the Water Resources Board. Questions were raised in committee as to why this research center should not be responsible to the NWC. The government's response was that the responsibilities of the WRC would be broader geographically in its membership than only the WAs in England and Wales. For example, it would serve Scotland and Northern Ireland, and would have membership from among consultants, manufacturers, and universities. The NWC and the WAs would be dominant in the control of the program of the WRC so that there would be no danger that their needs would be overlooked.

The government pointed out that the WAs were not obliged to look to only the WRC for their research needs. They might perform research themselves, or they might look for specialized information to other public and private research organizations.[33]

Finance

The Bill proposed that the Secretary of State have the power to direct the WAs to secure a rate of return on the value of their assets. This approach had had ample precedence in the nationalized industries. The opposition contended that water services were not services that a customer could choose to take or not to take, like the services of the nationalized industries.[34] The government did indicate that the people's interests, as represented in Parliament, were safeguarded, in that reports of the WAs and the directions that WAs would get from government were to be made regularly to each House of Parliament. Members of Parliament would have the obligation to exercise influence on the Ministers in regard to serving the public's interests.[35]

Metering

Jones (Con.) introduced an amendment which, in effect, would prohibit residential metering. From an economic standpoint, wide use of metering for domestic purposes could not be justified.[36] The opposition pointed out that the British Waterworks Association also did not want metering, alleging that metering is not necessary to obtain economy in the domestic sector. The government was obliged to justify introducing powers to initiate residential metering.[37]

In response, Page indicated that the Bill called for providing permissive power for almost any form of charging. Considerations were to be given to the best way of providing water and charging for it. One might treat it as a completely free social service only restricted in quantity, quantity not being restricted at present. However, it might be necessary to restrict it in some form in the future and CAWC did state that water should be treated as a commercial commodity and that its supply should not be completely unrestricted.[38]

The government desired to promote a transition from a rateable value basis for sewerage whether one has the service or not, which is the current system, to payment for service, similar to charges for gas and electricity. A mixed charge might be adopted, such as a basic payment and beyond a certain volume, payment by volume. The government was considering these alternatives and all that the legislation called for was permissive power for the WAs to choose their own schemes for charging.

Admission to WA meetings

Both the government and the opposition were in full accord that the meetings of the WAs as well as its committees should be fully open to the public and the press and it was on this note of harmony that the hearings before Standing Committee D were terminated.

REPORT STAGE AND THIRD READING IN THE HOUSE OF COMMONS

The report stage of the Water Bill in the House of Commons was taken on 1 and 2 May and the Bill received its third reading on 2 May 1973.[39]

One of the principal measures introduced in the report stage by the government was a clause whereby WAs might be required to supply sewers for domestic purposes, similar to provisions in the Water Act 1945 for the requisitioning of domestic water supplies, to which the WAs would also be subject. Local authorities had been obliged to provide sewerage and sewage disposal only in parts of their service areas where occupied premises existed, and this had acted as constraint on development. This clause would overcome that constraint and was also consistent with the government's White Paper on housing where it recommended that developers should contribute towards the cost of providing the infrastructure for housing developments. A prospective developer, whether a local authority or a private person, would be able to requisition sewers on the condition that he made up each year, for up to twelve years, the amount by which the capital costs exceeded the annual charges paid in respect to the property served.[40]

Members on both sides of the House joined in an effort to retain the Water Resources Board and to increase its powers. If the opposition failed to retain the WRB, they hoped to convert the NWC to its equivalent by bringing to it responsibilities now being proposed to be distributed amongst the Water Research Centre, the Water Data Unit, and the Central Water Planning Unit.[41]

The government's view was that, in 1963, when the WRB was authorized, conservation was a rather new function. The conspicuous success of the WRB in organizing regional and national water conservation planning meant that the new WAs would not be starting from scratch. Also, as the areas of the WAs were much larger than the river authority areas, much of the coordinating work required of the WRB would be internal within the WAs. In addition, all aspects of water quality and water quantity control would be united in the WA for each region, so that need for coordination was diminished. The WAs would be much larger and stronger in resources and in expertise than the separate agencies that had existed previously and would have less need to turn to a national agency for technical assistance. National planning would be carried out by the Central Water Planning Unit. While this unit would be within the Civil Service in the DoE, it should be no less independent than the staff of the WRB.[42]

The third reading of the Bill went over the London controversy in considerable detail. The government did accede to the dissidents to the extent that the Greater London Council would be given responsibility for recreation and amenity on the Thames as it flows through London.[43]

The issue of the privately owned statutory water companies surfaced once again as a symbolic issue between the Labour and Conservative Parties. After pointing out the 'municipal socialism' of the public water authorities, Howell asserted that the issue had been brought up in the cabinet and taking over the private water companies was identified as 'socialist'. In order to prove that the water reorganization legislation was not socialist, this exemption had to be made.[44]

On a division, the proposal to nationalize the privately owned water companies was defeated, 174 to 145.

Chairmen of the WAs

The one change that had been made by Standing Committee D, that the chairmen of the WAs be selected from amongst their number, was brought to the full House by the government. It would be wrong and illogical to require of the Secretary of State that he should procure policy and its execution and at the same time to say that he should not have the decision on the principal instruments of that policy, namely, the chairmen of the WAs.[45]

Under division, the House approved over-ruling the Committee change, to restore to the Secretary of State the power to appoint the chairmen of the WAs, by 157 to 139.

The constitution of the WAs

The major issue upon which the government had yielded in submitting the Bill, namely, that local authority representatives constitute a majority of each WA, did not satisfy the opposition and an amendment was introduced requiring that two-thirds of the membership of each of the WAs be from local authorities.

Griffiths summarized the government's dilemma in regard to the size of the authorities. The government wanted relatively compact executive bodies and at the same time wanted to include wider representation from local authorities and the many other entities concerned. CAWC, CBI, the Association of River Authorities, the professional societies; all wanted to have a small executive authority without elected personnel. On the other hand, the local authorities associations and many of the Members of Parliament proposed that there should be substantial local government majorities.[46] In the end the government sought balance between the democratically-elected element and the compelling need to have executive people with wide experience.

In a division, the House rejected the proposal for two-thirds elected representation, 138 to 115.

Metering

The last flurry of opposition centered on metering, with the opposition proposing an amendment which would exempt domestic premises. What would the government do in the event that a water bill was not paid? Would it cut off the water supply? What would be the public health significance of this approach? Water is an essential necessity of life. If metering were to control wastage, this could be done in more economical ways. The government claimed only to allow the WAs to introduce metering where appropriate, but these essentially undemocratic WAs were not the agencies for making this type of decision.

The government responded that the Bill only allowed the WAs to introduce metering should they find, by study, that this would be an appropriate way of charging. The present system was unfair in that those who used little water were paying the same as those who used large quantities if they resided in properties of equal value. The poor elderly are obliged to pay the same as a large family in the same general economic condition, and this is patently unfair.[47]

Unmetered consumption, mainly by domestic users, accounted for nearly two-thirds of the total water supplied by public undertakings and even a small percentage saving on the future increase in use would be significant. Wastage from household leaks, from careless use in the home, and a variety of other reasons was estimated at 15 percent of the total use for domestic purposes. The government believed it was time to recognize that water was becoming too expensive to be wantonly wasted or polluted. When the question was put, a division went with the government, 228 to 210.

In the third reading of the Bill, the Bill was adopted by the House of Commons 224 to 201 and was then sent to the House of Lords.

HOUSE OF LORDS

Earl Jellicoe introduced the Water Bill in the House of Lords on 21 May 1973 in the same vein as it had been introduced in the House of Commons.[48] Except for identifying two of the issues which had raised serious objections to the House of Commons, namely the removal of functions from local authorities and the retention of the statutory water companies, the treatment of the Bill was similar.

Baroness White (Lab.) led the opposition both on behalf of the Labour Party and on behalf of Welsh interests. On the latter issue, she stated that the fact that the Welsh National Water Development Authority would have some jurisdiction in parts of Cheshire and Hertfordshire '. . . will not make up for the fact that the heart land of mid-Wales, the upper Severn catchment, is to be torn out and added to the powerful Trent Authority to form a combined Severn Trent territory stretching across the whole width of both England and Wales . . . which . . . no self-respecting Welshman or Welshwoman can accept without at least some modification'.[49]

Baroness White believed that the Bill was not likely to offer either the advantages of a centralized administration nor those of true local control. The local authority representatives were to serve on the WAs for one purpose—communication—rather than with any direct responsibility to their constituents. Therefore '. . . the principle of overall numerical superiority is surely something of a gimmick; it is a bit of bogus democracy, a bit of a window dressing to cover up the fact that even the enlarged new local authorities are being further deprived by this government of genuine functions'.[50] Among the other points raised were the defense of the Water Resources Board as contrasted with its replacement by an assortment of centralized authorities, and the matter of metering.

Upon conclusion of the second reading of the Water Bill in the House of Lords, the Lords engaged in debate on the Bill sitting as a Committee of the Whole. The debates covered much of the same ground that had been covered in the House of Commons. A sampling of the divisions indicated the following:

On the creation of a London Water Authority: contents, 41; not contents, 100.†

On a proposal to permit authority members to elect their chairmen from among their numbers: contents 48; not contents 76.

The report on the Water Bill was received in the House of Lords on 2 July. Divisions were taken during the report stage including, for example, an attempt by the opposition to extend the responsibilities of National Water Council by adding to its duties planning and research, particularly in relation to national water policy. On division this was defeated: contents 56; not contents 70.

After the third reading on 9 July, the Bill passed the House of Lords and was returned to the House of Commons. In the mutual extensions of courtesies between Baroness Young for the government and Baroness White for the opposition, the latter stated that she could '. . . only wish that

---

† 'Content' indicates support for a proposal and 'not content' indicates opposition.

the courtesy of the government front bench had been matched by a willingness to accept amendments from the opposition because I do not think a single amendment has been accepted from our side. This is a little discouraging. We have put forward some very constructive suggestions, but not one of them of substance has found favor with the government. So in my mind, courtesy has hardly been matched by depth of thought.'[51]

In summarizing, Baroness White discussed reservations of the opposition with the whole problem of the central organization for water. She hoped that Lord Nugent of Guildford might be listening and that, in the view of the opposition, unless the NWC really exerts itself, particularly in research and planning, it would not fulfil the expectations which the Government has for its success. Finally, she referred to the '. . . country of Wales, where water is still one of the most "inflammable" substances there is'.[52]

FINAL HOUSE OF COMMONS CONSIDERATION OF THE WATER BILL

The House of Commons met on 17 July to consider the amendments to the Water Bill made in the House of Lords, none of which was controversial. The NWC was to have the duty to promote and assist the efficient performance by the WAs of their functions, including planning, not as a take-over of WA responsibilities but just as assistance to them. Further, the government endorsed, with the concurrence of the opposition, an amendment that would require that a Minister generally should consult the NWC before giving policy directions to the WAs.

The addition of the word 'amenities' to 'natural beauty' introduced by the House of Lords was fully acceptable as a means of covering urban as well as rural situations.

The government supported the Lords' amendment that the Secretary of State, after consultation with the NWC, give all or any of the WAs directions as to the criteria to be applied for charging but not the charges themselves. The opposition felt that this would have the government setting policy and giving orders as well. The WAs, unless they toed the line with regard to government policy, would seem to be subject to direction from the Secretary of State. In response, the government stated that what was hoped for was a partnership in considering the criteria for charges amongst the WAs, the NWC and the Secretary of State. Any direction given by the Secretary of State would merely confirm the results of these discussions.

As originally drafted, the Bill appeared to give the WAs wide discretion in deciding whether to comply with directions from the Secretary of State. The government felt that compliance should be mandatory. The opposition expressed concern in that this represents a whittling away of local authority.

Howell for the opposition expressed sorrow that the government had taken this last step backwards at the last moment. Page for the government explained that the amendment merely tidied up what was already in the Bill and he was candid in stating clearly the mandatory powers of the Secretary of State.

With final approval of the Bill in the House of Commons, on the next day, 18 July 1973, the Bill received the Royal Assent.

COMMENTARY

Despite the 19 sittings of Standing Committee D of almost 3 hours each, and extensive debate on many issues ranging from the important to the trivial and from the national to the local, the impact on the Bill in committee was small. The extensive debates in the House of Commons and in the House of Lords also effected relatively little change in the Bill.

With the very strong party discipline that characterizes parliamentary issues, it was not unreasonable to expect that the Bill would go through with relatively minor changes. The extensive debate serves mainly to provide a background to the legislative history of the Act to be used in its implementation. By far the greatest impact on the government's original intentions was made through the less formal and less politically partisan representations following the issuance of the consultation papers.

Had the Labour Party been in power when the Bill was being prepared, the Bill might never have actually reached parliament. If it had, and had there been a sufficient head of steam built up to enlist the support of the Labour Party behind it, many of the details might have been quite different. For example, the majority of local authority members on the WAs might have been greater and the WAs might well have been made up entirely of local authority members, the chairmen might have been selected by the WA membership rather than by Ministerial appointment, and London, with its Labour Party government, might have succeeded in establishing its own water authority.

Certainly, the statutory water companies would have been absorbed into the WAs and a stronger central body than the NWC would have been created. With the Labour Party ascension before the Act was implemented, the new government's review of the reorganization after it had been in operation some 18 months did propose take-over of the water companies and the creation of a stronger National Water Authority, as discussed in detail in Chapter 11.

If the extensive and expensive debates in parliament effected relatively minor changes in the Water Bill, the deliberations may be credited (or debited) with affecting the aftermath of passage of the Bill in two significant ways, one positive and one negative.

The negative contribution of the deliberations derived from the successful, if brief, revolution in Standing Committee D which reversed the government's proposals for the appointment of the WA chairmen by the government. With the government clearly dedicated to reversing this change, a considerable amount of time was required to be devoted to this issue thereby delaying the final passage of the legislation by several months and seriously foreshortening an already tight schedule of implementation. With only nine months between enactment of the Bill and the date of assumption of responsibilities by the WAs, additional months, weeks and even days of time for preparation would have been gratefully accepted by all in the industry.

The positive outgrowth of the deliberations was the much greater familiarity with the legislation that was afforded the Members of Parliament, the public, and those in the water industry than would have been the case had there been swift passage with little debate. Thus, at the time of Royal Assent and immediately thereafter, the Act generated, if not euphoria with respect to the future of water management, at least some considerable enthusiasm for the legislation and a confidence in it that flowed from the knowledge that there had been ample debate and that many of the problems that were to be faced in the reorganization had had an opportunity to surface and to be well aired by those who were to be involved. Even the Labour Party, despite objections to specific issues in the Bill, often expressed support of its principles. With the change in government that took place in February 1974, when on 1 April following the legislation was to be implemented, this commitment of the Labour Party to the reorganization was exceedingly important.

CHAPTER 5

Towards 1 April 1974

Even before the Water Bill received Royal Assent, preparation for implementation of the Act had begun. The attitude of most in the water industry was that the reorganization had to be made to work. The presidential address of Leonard W. F. Millis to the 64-year old British Waterworks Association, the last such address, was typical.[1] Millis had for 34 years been director and secretary of the BWA, which was composed of the nation's waterworks undertakings and was to cease its existence with the incorporation of their constituent undertakings into the new water authorities.

'We have claimed and rightly so that we have provided water supply for virtually every home in the country; that it is unlimited in quantity and unequaled in quality and that this has been done at a price which makes virtually no impact upon the budget of the poorest people of the land. That is a proud boast. But it is true and we are right to be proud of our achievements.

'It is not to be wondered at therefore that the Government in its wisdom is using this highly successful water supply industry as the basis upon which to bring about an improvement in other relevant services. I am sure we can undertake that burden. I am sure that the comprehensive industry will reach the highest standards that we have set, are setting and will in the future continue to set.'

This promise of leadership was fulfilled as a large percentage of the management and the highest professional positions in the WAs were to be filled by individuals who had been in executive positions in the water supply side of the industry. The large water supply undertakings created by regrouping required the development of management personnel of high calibre who were well suited to the new WAs. In the highly fragmented sewerage field, the responsibility for management was often at a low level within the local authority. Even where highly qualified engineers had that responsibility in local government, their time had to be shared with other local authority functions so that their professional expertise tended to be diluted. Outstanding exceptions were the personnel serving the relatively few large conurbations and main drainage boards.

In contrast to the note of affirmation during the BWA annual meeting, the Institute of Water Pollution Control members at their annual conference expressed grave concern over the reorganization and prophesied that few from among their number would be given leadership positions in the new organizations and that their collective views would not be important in the reorganization.[2] Perhaps this prophecy would be self-fulfilling!

Differences in attitude toward the reorganization were identified between those at the executive level, who were involved in planning at an early stage, and the greater mass of individuals in the industry for whom uncertainty was the hallmark of the period. While the cooperation of both groups was necessary, the key to getting off the mark was the acceptance of the reorganization on the part of those who had fought it bitterly. Exemplifying this latter category were Peter Black, chairman of the Thames Water Authority and Alex Morrison, its chief executive. Black had been a member of both the Thames Conservancy and the Metropolitan Water Board, which were to disappear. Morrison had been on the staff of the Greater London Council which was to lose much of its powers. Both had had leadership roles in formulating opposition to the reorganization and, when reorganization seemed inevitable, in seeking a special role for London. Now that reorganization was an accomplished fact and they had been selected for leading roles in it, they were determined to make the Thames Water Authority and the entire reorganization successful.

THE CONSTITUTION OF THE 'SHADOW' AUTHORITIES AND THE NATIONAL WATER COUNCIL

The government's intention in trying to move the legislation through Parliament as quickly as possible was to have it become effective on 1 April 1974, simultaneous with implementation of the local government reorganization. Competition for local authority personnel was inevitable. Were the local authorities to have had an extended lead in establishing their own organizations, they would have been in a strong position with personnel who might otherwise have been recruited to the water industry. As it was, enactment of the local authority reorganization in 1972, well ahead of the water reorganization, made problems in the recruitment of key individuals to the WAs.

Anticipating passage of the Bill, the government announced on 10 July 1973 that, if parliament were to pass the Water Bill, certain designated individuals would be appointed as chairmen of the WAs. These chairmen, including the chairman of the National Water Council, were to be the individuals with by far the greatest authority of any in the water industry. The appointments were reassuring to the water industry in that almost all had had considerable experience in some phase of the water industry: five had been associated with river authorities, three with water undertakings, five with county councils, one with industry, and only one had had no identifiable experience in water or water-related activities. Eight of the 11 chairmen had been primarily involved in private enterprise, business, industry or farming.

The WAs were to be created in 'shadow' form as soon as possible so that they might begin to appoint staff, organize into committees, make budgets and in all ways be so organized as to be 'off and running' on 1 April 1974. This practice of establishing shadow organizations, perhaps peculiar to Great Britain, follows from the organization of the opposition in parliament, where a shadow cabinet is established, ready to take responsibility immediately upon a change in government. With so massive a reorganization anticipated, and with the necessity of keeping essential operations functioning during the 'lame duck' period of the existing organizations, anything less could not have been satisfactory.

The ten water authorities were established by statutory orders during the period 26 July thru 14 August, while the National Water Council was brought into existence on 23 August. The first meetings of all the WAs were held in August 1973.

Of a total of 238 WA members excluding the chairmen and the Welsh National Water Development Authority, 99 were appointed by the Secretary of State for the Environment and the Minister of Agriculture, Fisheries and Food, and 139 were nominated by district and county councils. In the Thames Water Authority, the local authority members dominated with 36 as against 16 appointed, while in some of the smaller authorities, such as the Wessex and the South West Water Authorities, local authority members were a majority of one. Table 5.1 indicates the initial distribution of members of the WAs.

TABLE 5.1
Proposed Composition of Water Authorities

WA	Local authority appointees	Ministerial appointees	Total	Authority members per million population
North West	14	13	27	3·9
Northumbrian	10	9	19	7·0
Severn Trent	22	16	38	4·5
Yorkshire	13	12	25	5·6
Anglian	18	16	34	8·3
Thames	36	16	52	4·3
Southern	10	9	19	5·1
Wessex	8	7	15	7·5
South West	8	7	15	11·5
WNWDA	20	15	35	12·1
TOTAL	159	120	279	5·7

Among the members appointed by the government, about 40 percent represented private industry with 60 percent representing some element of public life, including the nationalized industries, agricultural and environmental groups, and local authorities. The composition of the WAs represented a far different mix from what had been intended by the government in its original proposal for a small number of selected appointees.

The ten members of the NWC, in addition to the WA chairmen, were appointed primarily for their experience and competence in a field related to water. They included an economist, a geology professor, and representatives of industrial,agricultural, amenity, fisheries, and water-works interests, the last being Mr Millis. However, the WA chairmen were to be the strong nucleus of the NWC and, with its staff, should be important to its functioning. Having been characterized as a weak central body as compared with even the defunct Water Resources Board, which had no power but did have strong technical resources, the constitution of the NWC of itself did not indicate its direction or posture. Much would depend upon the role that the WA chairmen wish to play.

THE APPOINTMENT OF WA OFFICERS

The DoE listed priorities for the WAs as shown in Table 5.2.[3] After the establishment of temporary headquarters, the highest priority task was the selection and appointment of chief executives and directors of operations and finance. Because of the lack of WA staff to make the necessary arrangements, and to avoid a situation whereby applicants might be called to two or more interviews on the same day, the Water Supply Staff Advisory Committee marshalled the application forms, sought the references to help prepare a short list of candidates, arranged an orderly program of interviews in London and undertook the mechanics of the appointment exercise. They played no part in the selection for short listing or interviewing of candidates, which were the exclusive responsibilities of WA members.

In announcing the procedures to be followed in filling the first of the top appointments in the WAs, the WSSAC stated:

'For these posts it is essential to insure that the new WAs are in a position to choose the best from a wide field of candidates. The post of chief executive is regarded as having a greater responsibility and being more complex and wide ranging than any existing post in the water services. Reorganization will create an entirely new concept of regional control of water services and each new WA will have a greater responsibility in these matters both geographically and functionally than ever held before by a single authority. The applicants will need to possess outstanding executive ability and the capacity to lead a team which must respond to the challenge

TABLE 5.2
Immediate Administrative and Technical Tasks for the WAs

1	Establish temporary headquarters.
2	Examine applications for Water Authority top posts and interview applicants.
3	Decide on Water Authority committee structure and headquarters organization.
4	Carry out preliminary examination of Working Party Reports in order to identify matters requiring action. These include making good deficiencies revealed by the Reports, e.g. by devising arrangements whereby one divisional unit can help another (water supply and river management divisions helping sewage disposal divisions). A start can also be made on devising divisional organizations based on the Working Parties' recommendations.
5	Assess the need for agency arrangements with local authorities under 'Section 7(2) of the Act' and initiate discussions with local authorities for this purpose.
6	Prepare and send to water companies, local authorities, and development corporations, drafts of the arrangements for water supply by companies and the discharge of the sewerage function by local authorities and development corporations.
7	Determine arrangements for delegation to divisions.
8	Determine staff complements for HQ and divisions.
9	Ascertain the retirement intentions of existing chief officers and deputies.
10	Designate managers/chief officers in water supply and river management divisions.
11	Appoint managers of sewage disposal divisions.
12	Advertise and interview staff for vacant posts.
13	Consult with local authorities on transfer of staff.
14	Consult with staff associations and trade unions on all staff matters (continuous process).
15	Consult with local authorities on transfer of property.
16	Establish accommodation for divisions.
17	Coordinate communication systems and reporting structures.
18	Establish information service to public and public relations system.

of the new WA concept within a new framework of financial self-sufficiency and to work in harmony with the new authority. The salary accordingly will be higher than those of existing posts within the water services. The committee has therefore concluded that the field of recruitment for the chief executive posts should be unrestricted.'

The directors of finance and the directors of operations also fell into this category and the field of recruitment for these posts was also unrestricted. In the event of all other factors being equal, the preference would be given to candidates with experience in public service.

Competition for these positions was expected, as the starting salaries ranged from £12 000 to £14 000 in the larger authorities to £10 000 to

£12 000 in the smaller, not including perquisites such as chauffered automobiles and reduced house mortgages.

NALGO (the National Association of Local Government Officers) was much troubled by the way staff matters were being handled during the reorganization and they sent a deputation to the DoE. Their greatest complaint centered on the WSSAC's refusal to 'ring fence' the top WA positions, in order to restrict these positions to candidates from within the water industry. NALGO claimed that the WSSAC had made little or no attempt to consult with the various unions involved. If the DoE would not reconsider, NALGO threatened to withdraw completely from the reorganization scene. NALGO was concerned that the recruitment of outsiders would not only prejudice the core structure of senior water officers, but could well disrupt staffing at middle managerial levels at a time when securing the confidence and cooperation of staff was vital to successful reorganization. Resentment was felt because the WSSAC, whose sole purpose was the protection of staff interests during the changeover, had never given reasons for favoring unrestricted recruitment.

The government explained that not only should the best man for the job be appointed, but the best man must be seen to be appointed, and the public must not feel that only insiders had access to these positions.

Part of the difficulty lay in the very restricted timetable which did not allow opportunities for adequate consultation or adequate negotiation of pay scales through the National Pay Board. The government assured NALGO that the chairmen of the WAs would meet with the unions thereafter in connection with the other WA positions.

After the WAs had selected their short lists of five individuals for each position the personal interviews with these individuals were held in the mornings of ten successive working days, one day per WA, over a two-week period. Upon conclusion of their interviews, the candidates were requested to wait, the personnel committee of the WA met and made their selection and the successful candidate was advised that afternoon, and asked to accept the position then and there. Because many of the applicants were candidates for positions with several WAs, the interviews were scheduled in descending order of WA size, the larger WAs with their higher salaries coming earlier, with the expectation that an applicant would prefer the higher salary and the greater challenge, and would thus accept the first position offered.

That this was all a very trying experience for these candidates can readily be understood. In all, more than 300 applications were filed for the 11 chief executive positions (including the director general of the NWC). Some of the candidates, who had applied for several of the chief executive positions, suffered disappointment on the first but made the last. Some who were not successful for any of these were then applicants for one or another of the directorates.

If these applications and interviews were not an adequate test of technical and managerial competence, they were certainly a test of personal fortitude under pressure, perhaps the most important requirement for the top officers of the WAs.

Within the water industry, questions arose concerning the qualifications of those likely to be selected as chief executives. For example, a leader (editorial) in *Municipal Engineering* asked:[4] 'How many of the chief executive officers of the new regional authorities will be engineers? Not so very long ago the question was not how many but *will any* of the WA chief executive officers be engineers? And more recently the question had ceased to be asked at all, it being generally assumed that all ... would go to clerks with a treasurer or two thrown in for good measure. .... It was cynically suggested ... that the chief executive could come from any professional discipline provided that he was a lawyer.'

As it turned out, of the 11 chief executives initially appointed, 7 were engineers and all but 2, who were recruited from the Greater London Council for the National Water Council and the Thames Water Authority, were from within some element of the water industry, 4 being from river authorities and 3 from water supply undertakings.

Despite the relatively small number of river authorities and executives serving them as compared with the other services absorbed into the WAs, the river authorities supplied a good many of the top executives of the reorganized water industry. In Britain, water supply engineering had always been professionally distinct from sewerage and sewage disposal, which flies under the title of *public health engineering*. Individuals were seldom members of both the Institution of Water Engineers and the Institution of Public Health Engineers or the Institute of Water Pollution Control. The water supply and sewage disposal undertakings themselves had always been under quite separate management without any of the combined water and sewer departments so common in other parts of the world. Even consulting engineers tended to specialize in one or the other activity. As river authorities had responsibility for pollution control and for providing souces for water supply, only those associated with the river authorities had any occasion to come in contact with both the clean and dirty water phases of the industry. This, added to the experience they had in regional enterprises, made them prime candidates for top positions in the new WAs.

The backgrounds of the individuals appointed to the top management positions in the WAs affirms that the regrouping of water supply undertakings had created opportunities for engineers from the water supply field to occupy positions of high technical and management responsibility, not open to personnel from the highly fragmented sewerage and sewage disposal phase of the industry. For example, among the members of the corporate management team of the WAs, of the ten directors of operations, eight were members of the Institution of Water Engineers, two of the Institution of

Municipal Engineers and only one, also a member of the Institution of Water Engineers, was a member of the Institute of Water Pollution Control. Similarly, among the ten directors of resource planning, eight were drawn from the water supply industry, all being members of the Institution of Water Engineers.

Thus, amongst the 30 executives responsible for both water supply and sewerage and sewage disposal, including the chief executives, the directors of operations, and the directors of resource planning, almost all were drawn from the water supply phase of the industry, and only two could be identified with sewerage and sewage disposal in their previous professional employment.

Individuals drawn from the sewerage and sewage disposal field, as represented by membership in the Institution of Public Health Engineers or the Institute of Water Pollution Control, did fill almost all the posts of directors of scientific services. Pollution control had required more chemists and biologists than water supply, and the competence of people from this field in the area of analysis and pollution assessment was evidenced by their selection almost without exception for the scientific services which, in most instances, carried responsibilities for monitoring for pollution control.

The dominance of the water supply engineers in the hierarchy of the WAs continued even into the lower posts. Of some 70 positions as assistant directors or division managers, where the responsibilities were broader than for water supply alone or for sewerage and sewage disposal alone, some 80 percent were drawn from among members of the Institution of Water Engineers, with some 10 percent from the Institution of Municipal Engineers and 10 percent from the Institution of Public Health Engineers and the Institute of Water Pollution Control together. Of all the instances where a division was responsible for operations in sewerage and sewage disposal plus water supply or river management, in only one or two cases had the manager been selected from the field of sewerage and sewage disposal. In almost all the other instances the managers were drawn from water supply undertakings or from the river authorities.

Whether the WAs will suffer from inadequate staff in sewerage and sewage disposal, the field which is to require the greatest capital expenditures during the early years, remains to be seen. However, this outcome seemed to justify the fears of the engineers responsible for sewerage and sewage disposal who had urged that the reorganization be delayed until after the reorganization of local government, allowing regrouping in the sewerage and sewage disposal field so as to give comparable experience in that field.

Any dissatisfaction on the part of the water industry officers with the posts that they were likely to get under the reorganization was ameliorated to a considerable extent by the policy established both for the local government and water reorganizations. Officers who would have reached the age of 50 by 1 April 1974, and who would have had five years of service in the industry, were permitted to retire with all benefits accruing to them from retirement as if they had retired at age 65. This 'golden handshake' did encourage many to take positions in other fields, in private enterprise, or to retire. One important beneficial effect appears to have been that, during the early days of the WAs, when morale was likely to be at low ebb because of uncertainties, a nucleus of possibly disaffected officers in high positions was largely eliminated. Those who were eligible for early retirement but who elected to remain were likely to be the officers with an enthusiasm for the new opportunities open to them.

If NALGO was not successful in placing a 'ring fence' around the three top jobs in each WA, it did succeed in influencing the Water Services Staff Advisory Committee to place 'ring fences' around all the other positions.

In its announcements for appointments to the remainder of the headquarters staff of the WAs and of those divisions where the managers were not designated *pro forma* from among the chief officers of the existing organizations that were to form the divisions, the WSSAC advised that applications would be invited in the first instance from officers employed in the existing water industry in England and Wales. The industry was defined as comprising the river authorities, water boards, joint sewerage boards, local governments where staff had a significant experience in the function to be served by the new WAs, new town development corporations, again where staff had significant appropriate experience, statutory water companies, DoE and Water Resources Board professional staff, Water Pollution Research Laboratory, Water Research Association, Port of London Authority pollution control staff, Water Supply Industry Training Board, British Waterworks Association, and the Association of River Authorities.

The prediction that positions would be available for all who had been employed in the water industry was proved correct when the 'ring fence' on recruitment to the WAs and the NWC was dropped as of 1 August 1974 with little objection.

THE ROLE OF THE WATER AUTHORITIES

With less than nine months for gestation of the WAs, the government felt obliged to provide them with considerable assistance during this period. Precedents for the organization and operation of the WAs did not exist. Never before in Britain nor anywhere else in the world had there been established such water authorities, comprehensive both in scale and in breadth of their responsibilities. Large regional organizations had been created elsewhere, but their responsibilities were generally limited to one or at most a few of the services and regulatory responsibilities to be within the purview of the WAs. Even the *genossenschaften* in the Ruhr area in Germany are not responsible for sewerage or water distribution.

Accordingly, the Government inaugurated a number of activities intended to help the WAs in getting organized and beginning to function. 'The water authorities are a new type of body. They are not local authorities or joint boards, or river authorities writ large; nor are they area boards of a nationalized industry. They are a new type of regional authority responsible for a number of individual functions, but overall for the effective management of water.'[5] The government concluded that, subject to the Act and related earlier legislation that it inherited, the WAs are not bound to accept the procedures, attitudes, and structures of any other body in Great Britain. The Water Act 1973 called for a new structure and a new approach to management.

The relationship between the government and the Water Authorities

In setting out guidelines for the WAs, the government was quite conscious of the responsibilities that it had retained. The accountability of the WAs to the Secretary of State for the Environment, the Secretary of State for Wales and the Minister of Agriculture, Fisheries and Food and through them to the parliament were spelled out in the Water Act 1973.

Section 1 places on the Ministers the duty to promote a national policy for water and to secure its effective execution.

Section 3 provides that the chairman of each WA shall be appointed by the appropriate Secretary of State.

Section 5 empowers the Secretaries of State and the Minister to give WAs direction of a general character.

Section 24 requires WAs to secure the approval of the appropriate Minister for their capital expenditure programs.

Section 29 empowers the Secretary of State to direct a WA to achieve a specified rate of return or to place them under any other financial obligation.

Section 30 empowers the Secretary of State to direct WAs as to the criteria or the system to be adopted by them for fixing their charges.

Schedule 3 requires the WAs to submit to the Ministers a statement of their accounts and annual reports which the Ministers are obliged to lay before parliament.

The government regarded their powers of direction as reserve powers and would conduct their business with the WAs on the basis of consultation and exchange of views as far as possible, using their direction-giving powers very sparingly and only as a last resort. In keeping with the new organization, the DoE reorganized its own house.[5]

The government undertook to assist and guide the WAs during their formative days through the establishment of: local working parties in

March 1972; a committee, to be known as the Ogden Committee, to give guidance on WA management structure in June 1972; a working party to prepare advice on the principles to be followed in preparing annual estimates and accounts, under the chairmanship of J. B. Woodham in September 1972; a Water Services Staff Advisory Committee in February 1973; and a steering group, to be known as the Jukes Committee, in March 1973, to advise on economic and financial policies that should be adopted by the WAs. All of these were created before the Water Bill was enacted into law.

Relationship between the local authorities and the Water Authorities

Within a month of the Water Act 1973 becoming law, the DoE advised the chairmen of the WAs and the clerks of county councils, county borough councils, county district councils, statutory water undertakers, joint sewerage boards, river authorities and other agencies such as the newly created local authorities, of the impact that the Water Act would have on the local authorities and the necessary cooperation required between the local authorities and the new WAs.[6] Among the salient points were the following.

Transfer of property and staff. The ownership of all public sewers, all sewage disposal works and all water undertakings owned by local authorities or joint boards of local authorities to be transferred to the new WAs on 1 April 1974, together with other physical property associated with transfer of function, as the outstanding liabilities relating to the property transfer, and the staff employed on these functions.

Sewerage. While the statutory responsibility for sewerage and sewage disposal will be transferred to the WAs, Section 15 of the Act contains provision for district and the London borough councils to discharge sewerage functions on behalf of the appropriate WAs. Accordingly, these local authorities will retain such staff as is necessary to discharge these agency functions on behalf of and with financial support of the WAs. Specifically excluded from these agency arrangements is any permission for the WAs to delegate to the local authority their responsibility for sewage disposal, trade effluent control, and the maintenance and operation of any sewer which before 1 April 1974 was vested in a joint sewerage board.

Modifications to the Public Health Act 1936. The Water Act 1973 gives owners and occupiers, local authorities, and developers the right to requisition the provision of sewerage for domestic purposes, subject to certain specified conditions which correspond to the rights that are already theirs in relation to water supply under the Public Health Act and under the Water Act 1945.

Environmental health. Local authorities (district and London borough councils) are to continue to discharge their responsibilities for environmental health and, in particular, they are to retain their function of taking from time to time such steps as may be necessary for ascertaining the sufficiency and wholesomeness of water supplies within their areas. The district councils have a duty to notify their WA of any insufficiency or unwholesomeness in the water supplies within their area. Exchequer grants will continue for the time being to be available under the Rural Water Supply and Sewerage Act for rural water supply and sewerage schemes, with payment to be made to the WAs.

Land drainage. Local authorities will retain their functions under the Land Drainage Act 1961. Surface water sewerage will form part of the sewerage function of the WAs. Each WA will establish a regional land drainage committee and area land drainage committees to discharge the land drainage functions of the WA, except the making of drainage charges, the levying of precepts and the borrowing of mony for land drainage works, which are the responsibility of the WA.

Forward planning. WAs are required to prepare estimates of the demand for the use of water over the next 20 years and to prepare plans of action to meet the demand. They are obliged to send a copy of their report to every local authority in their area. Section 24 of the Act places a specific obligation on the WAs to consult local authorities in formulating their plans and programs.

Financing of water services. With the exception of exchequer grants for rural services and funds for their land drainage functions, the WAs are to derive their revenues from charges for the services they provide. The general rate or taxes against property, which was the basis for financing sewerage and sewage disposal in the local authorities, is transferred as from 1 April 1974 to a charging basis. The general rate is not to bear the cost of pollution control which had been financed by precept against local authorities and the general rate is no longer used to meet deficits on water supply and fisheries accounts. The system of charges, while initially to be based upon property values similar to the rates, may take the form of separate charges for separate services, facilities or rights, or of combined charges. WAs, if justification for it can be demonstrated, may introduce metering for domestic consumers. WAs may levy a combined charge on each household for water supply, sewerage and sewage disposal, and pollution control. The government recognized that initially there would be many changes in the levels of rates and charges partly as a result of local government reorganization and partly as a result of water reorganization. In taking a decision about the appropriate level of exchequer rate support grants to local authorities after reorganization, the government would take full account of the fact that, in the future, rate payers will be paying directly for some water services that were previously paid for by local authorities from the general support grant.

Local advisory committees. It was envisaged that the WAs would have an extensive divisional organization with officers at local points of contact for convenience to the consumers. It may well be desirable for an additional channel of communication to be established between the WAs and local communities. This might take the form of advisory committees covering all of the functions of the WA other than land drainage and fisheries for which committees are specified in the Act.

DIVISIONAL WORKING PARTIES

The government believed that initially, to facilitate the orderly transfer of responsibilities for ongoing services, arrangements might be made for the transfer of functions in already operating units to be made to *provisional management units* or *divisions*. Separate local working parties covering rivers, water supply, and sewerage and sewage disposal functions had been established in 1972. Because of the relatively small number of river authorities and water undertakings taken over into the WAs, the management of these functions in the WAs would be simple with the transfer of facilities and personnel being relatively orderly.

However, with the very large number of separate sewerage and sewage disposal operations, generally responsible to and interwoven with other local authority functions, the orderly transfer of these responsibilities was considered to be far more difficult, and the structure and conduct of the working parties for sewerage and sewage disposal were far more complex. Such difficulties and delays that were to occur with the working parties occurred almost exclusively with the working parties for sewerage and sewage disposal. The complications resulting from trying to unify a great many small, often poorly organized, sewerage and sewage disposal services into comprehensive management units in a matter of months, as compared with the regrouping for water supply which took place over almost 30 years, led to many delays. These delays were further aggravated by the slow-down initiated by the associations representing the local authorities who were dissatisfied with the government's response to their views of the reorganization and who consequently encouraged local authority personnel to hang back on these working parties. The slow-down was easily established, as the chairmen of many of the working parties believed that members of working parties who were seconded from the local authorities should have been paid some nominal amount as they were caught in the middle between unpaid responsibilities to the working party, and their continuing responsibilities to their employers.

The working parties were concerned with the coordination of sewerage and sewage disposal functions so as to ensure that the existing units continued to function in the period immediately after 1 April 1974. (The contents of the reports that were to be submitted by the working parties is indicated in Table 3.3.)

THE WA MANAGEMENT AND STRUCTURE (OGDEN COMMITTEE REPORT)

The opportunity to create *de novo* a group of massive organizations seldom appears. The challenge is particularly great when these organizations are to employ some 65 000 individuals, spend hundreds of millions of pounds annually, and affect the lives of every individual in the nation in some way.

The Ogden Committee was charged in 1972 to consider possible forms of management structure with the view to producing guidance on this matter for the WAs. One year later their report, *The New Water Industry Management and Structure*, was issued.[7]

With everyone in the water industry in England and Wales likely to be affected by the structures recommended, the appearance of the Ogden Committee report stimulated considerable discussion and argument. Because there had been no prior experience with a comprehensive system of water management upon which to draw, the committee did not follow the customary practice of issuing a general invitation to interested bodies to present evidence. The committee itself was drawn from a wide range of disciplines and from all the various types of bodies that would be affected by the water reorganization and it felt that its own views would be reasonably representative.

The committee was made up of its chairman, Sir George Ogden, Town Clerk of Manchester, and 13 other appointed members, 6 departmental assessors from the government and a secretariat from the DoE. The disciplines represented included administrators, four drawn from water supply undertakings, three drawn from sewerage and sewage disposal agencies and the Under Secretary of the DoE.

The government envisaged that the divisional structure of the WAs for the first few years would be based upon the existing river authorities as river divisions, existing statutory water undertakers as water supply divisions and 88 newly formed sewage disposal divisions that would 'regroup' the almost 1400 separate local authorities and joint sewerage boards that were still in existence. The committee felt obliged to accept this preparatory work as the shortness of time would not permit the building of an integrated structure at the local level by 1 April 1974.

However, the committee emphasized that a multifunctional, multidisciplinary approach to management was essential and that a start should be made immediately at headquarters.

While the overall planning process must be determined at the regional level, the committee recommended that responsibility for the different water functions should be delegated to divisions to the fullest possible extent, consistent with efficiency and economy, in part on the basis that such decentralization would encourage staff involvement.

The committee recommended against the establishment of any

intermediate organization such as area headquarters, between the regional headquarters and the divisions, primarily because of the great need to strengthen the divisions. The scarcity of personnel to man the sewage disposal divisions properly also militated against intermediate area-based structures. The hope was to strengthen the sense of responsibility of each of the divisions. Should in the fullness of time some intermediate organizations be found to be necessary, they would be easier to create then, than to first create an organization and then dissolve it.

With regard to the operation of the WAs themselves, the committee hoped the members of the WAs would adopt a corporate approach and not pursue local constituency or special interests. A committee structure was suggested (Fig. 5.1) to carry out most of the activities of the WA, with membership as small as possible but with each member serving on at least one committee. The policy and resources committee would be the central committee of the WA and the chairman of the WA would serve as its chairman. Its responsibilities would include the corporate planning of water resources; priority objectives in planning; the formulation of water quality control policy; control and allocation of financial resources; levying charges, preparing annual estimates and capital investment programs; agency arrangements; and relationships with the NWC and local authorities.

A quality advisory panel would act as the WA's internal check on water quality. To provide the necessary degree of independence, this panel must derive its power directly from the WA and not from one of its committees. It would be responsible for providing reports on water quality, not only on the performance of outside bodies such as those making discharges to the WA's rivers, but also on the WA's own performance as water supplier, sewage treatment authority, and custodian of the rivers.

The water management committee would be responsible for operations and new works in relation to water conservation, water supply, sewerage and sewage disposal and pollution prevention and the oversight of relationships with the water companies, local authorities and new town development corporations that operate as agents of the WAs. This committee would embrace the whole of the water cycle reflecting the need for unified management.

A fisheries committee is required by statute. It would also be desirable for the WAs to establish a committee responsible for amenity and recreation which might be combined with the fisheries committee. This area is one that would be particularly sensitive to local knowledge and advice and local advisory committees might very well facilitate an exchange of views between the WA and the populace with interests in these matters. Regional and area land drainage committees are also statutory requirement in the Act.

Once the WAs have laid down policy guidelines, they should then delegate most of their responsibilities to their officers.

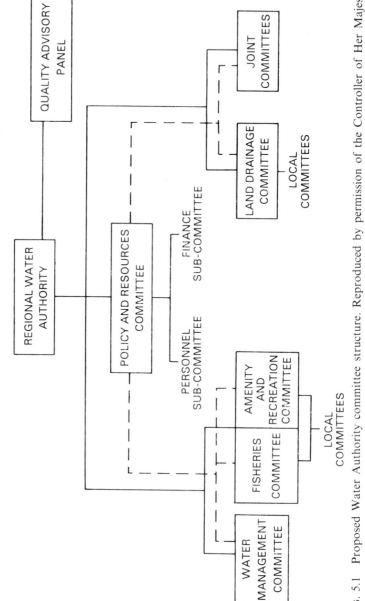

Fig. 5.1 Proposed Water Authority committee structure. Reproduced by permission of the Controller of Her Majesty's Stationery Office.

In order to consider the water cycle as a whole and to adopt a corporate approach to management, the committee recommended management at the regional level by a corporate management team. This team should be as small as possible and should be led by a chief executive who would be the main link between the WA and its officers and be the WA's principal adviser on policy. The team should include up to five directors, according to the size of the WA, one of whom would be a director of finance.

A single director of operations should serve to coordinate the operation of the existing services of water supply, sewerage and sewage disposal and river management. Separate directors for each of these services was specifically rejected.

Resource planning was considered of such importance that a separate director with a place on the management team was recommended. Directors of scientific services and administration might serve on the management team in the larger WAs but possibly not in the smaller ones (Fig. 5.2).

The director, or should he be an assistant director, of scientific services would have special responsibility directly to the WA and to the public on water quality matters. When he is not a director in his own right, he should be located in the directorate of resource planning with a direct line to the chief executive and through him to the WA.

A suggested scheme for the delegation of functions to the divisions to be used initially, was an appendix in the report. Divisions would report to the WA corporate management team and would have a direct line of command from the director of operations. On issues of considerable importance, designated senior officers at division level would feel free to refer decisions taken by the divisions to their functional chief at headquarters, but this should not be done frequently.

WAs need a strong legal department with direct access to the corporate management team, an estates officer to administer their land holdings and an officer in charge of public relations. Consumer relations would be a function for the divisions.

MANAGEMENT AT THE DIVISION LEVEL

While the steering committees and working parties were intended to alleviate some of the problems of the short transition period, it had become clear that for a considerable period, possibly three years, the operating units, the divisions would have to carry on as far as possible under procedures which they knew and understood, although the responsible authority would no longer be a local authority or a local water board, but a more distant WA.

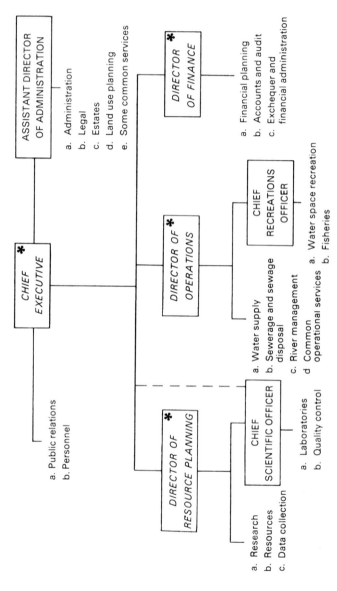

REGIONAL CORPORATE MANAGEMENT TEAM — SMALL AUTHORITY

* *MEMBERS OF MANAGEMENT TEAM*

FIG. 5.2 Proposed Water Authority corporate management teams. Reproduced by permission of the Controller of Her Majesty's Stationery Office.

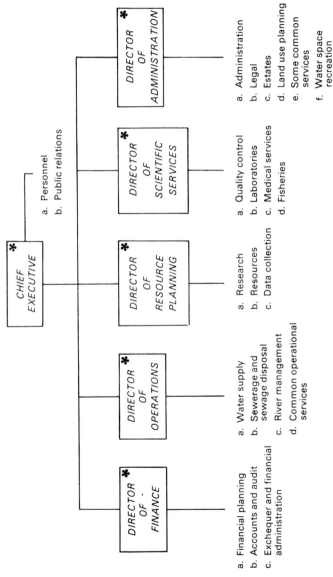

REGIONAL CORPORATE MANAGEMENT TEAM – LARGE AUTHORITY

CHIEF EXECUTIVE *

a. Personnel
b. Public relations

DIRECTOR OF FINANCE *

a. Financial planning
b. Accounts and audit
c. Exchequer and financial administration

DIRECTOR OF OPERATIONS *

a. Water supply
b. Sewerage and sewage disposal
c. River management
d. Common operational services

DIRECTOR OF RESOURCE PLANNING *

a. Research
b. Resources
c. Data collection

DIRECTOR OF SCIENTIFIC SERVICES *

a. Quality control
b. Laboratories
c. Medical services
d. Fisheries

DIRECTOR OF ADMINISTRATION *

a. Administration
b. Legal
c. Estates
d. Land use planning
e. Some common services
f. Water space recreation

* *MEMBERS OF MANAGEMENT TEAM*

Fig. 5.2—*contd.*

The aim of the Ogden Committee in establishing a scheme of delegation of responsibility was to provide only a suggested framework, with each WA deciding itself how best to manage its own affairs. The major objective in setting forth a scheme was to assure continuation of essential services. In no way was it intended to determine the long term pattern of the industry.

The report outlined a scheme for delegation of certain special functions to the divisions which would not require reference to regional headquarters and others that might need reference. The extent of the delegation was to vary according to the size of the division: *Group A*—those serving a population of over one million; *Group B*—over 500 000; and *Group C*—the remainder. For example, the authority for a division to incur expenditures without reference to WA headquarters varied from £60 000 for the larger divisions down to £10 000 for the smaller.

The biggest challenge would be in the establishment of some 88 sewerage and sewage disposal divisions out of a total of 1393 separate local authorities previously responsible for these functions, while at the same time setting up agency agreements with the district councils, many of them also newly created, to exercise the sewerage function.

Visits to several prospective division headquarters revealed some of the problems that were being faced at the operating level during the transitional period. For example, the Vales Division of the Thames Water Authority, which was to have the responsibility for water supply, sewerage and sewage disposal, and river management, was built largely on the Oxfordshire and District Water Board, which had been created by regrouping in 1967. The chief engineer of the Board had prepared the report on regrouping of the water undertakings in that area in 1958, but the objections of one or two local authorities, including Banbury, delayed regrouping until 1967. The regrouping of 14 undertakings into the one board had been quite successful, as many of the smaller authorities had not had the resources to provide good service. Following the regrouping, personnel to address problems in these smaller authorities were obtained by borrowing from Oxford. For example, Banbury had had a severe series of water shortages accompanied by water rationing, but after regrouping, the Board had resolved these problems. The improved efficiency or economies attributable to regrouping were difficult to assess, as after regrouping more investments had been made and better service had been provided. The people of Oxford were required to pay higher rates after regrouping, presumably to help improve the services in the outlying areas. No objections to these increases in rates were raised because the people of Oxford had always received good service and had been educated to understand their obligations for water service in the area.

One important 'plus' attributed to the regrouped water supply system was in the provision of 'belt and braces', stand-by facilities for emergency. One of the river intakes of the Board needed to be closed because of a high level of cyanide in the river. This could be done because the Board had alternative groundwater sources that could be used. This would not have been possible prior to the regrouping.

Integration of all water services in one authority created a problem that might portend difficulties. There had been a history of labor difficulties, often resulting in strikes, at sewage treatment works, with potential serious effects on rivers used as sources of water supply. With the unification of all operations in the WAs, a single union might serve the entire industry so that industrial actions would be far more detrimental than when the industry was fragmented.

A foretaste of the significance of integration of all water services in the WAs was provided by the recently introduced effluent charges for discharges into the Oxford sewerage system. The combination of the effluent charges with higher water supply charges caused a substantial reduction in industrial water use which resulted in a delay in approaching the design capacity of the water supply system.

While the personnel to be responsible for the Vales Division were well aware of the problems they would face, these did not appear to be singularly pressing, perhaps because the Division was to have a nucleus of a strong water board, a well-operated sewerage and sewage disposal facility serving the bulk of the population in the area, and a former Thames Conservancy river management office already located near division headquarters.

The situation was substantially different in what was to become the West Kent Drainage Division in the Southern Water Authority. Just ten days before 1 April 1974, the division manager stated that his major problem was the number of fitters and truck drivers he would be able to have transferred from the local authorities. The local authorities had the first choice on those who had been working for them. They would pick the best. The head start that the local authorities had had in their reorganization was far more important with regard to the skilled labor staff than with professional staff. However, even with professional staff, as of 1 April only 4 engineers were expected to be available for a total of 12 positions.

At one of the sewage treatment plants, the chief chemist pointed out that, after reorganization, substantial expenditure would be needed for laboratories and equipment, because the local authorities, knowing they were losing responsibility for these facilities, had not made any investments in the year prior to the reorganization.

The headquarters of the West Kent Drainage Divisions were to be in Maidstone as were the headquarters of the separate Kent River and Water Division, although both would have quite different responsibilities. However, this new drainage division, without nearly the extensive resources of the Kent River and Water Division which was based on the Kent River Authority and Medway Water Board headquarters, would utilize maintenance and other facilities of the latter in order to avoid duplication.

This extensive close cooperation and joint use of services would provide the basis for integrated divisions in the future.

A visit to the East Sussex Water and Drainage Division in the Southern Water Authority affirmed most of the problems found in the other divisions. An additional statistic causing concern was that the average age of sewage and water works operators in the division was 59 and 49 years respectively.[8] An important obligation of the divisions, and the WAs, would be in establishing a recruiting program and in making career opportunities in the WA attractive to assist in recruiting younger personnel.

Consulting services

Among the least enthusiastic with regard to the reorganization were the private consulting engineers in Britain. While most of the larger authorities and joint boards had had their own design organizations, the many smaller authorities utilized consulting engineers, and consulting engineers in turn depend upon design work for these local authorities for a substantial portion of their work in Britain. The consulting engineers feared, as was the case with regrouping of water supplies, that the large WAs, with their relatively large divisions, would be able to provide their own design services.†

Most British consulting engineering organizations are quite active in providing their services to developing countries abroad, particularly, but not exclusively, in the countries of the Commonwealth. The consultants claimed that, if they did not continue to get substantial design opportunities from the WAs, they would not be in a position to maintain the quality of staff required to conduct their consulting services abroad, and Britain would lose an important export industry. Consequently, the DoE has requested that the WAs make use of consultants.[9]

How consultants will fare in the face of the ambitions of division managers to develop their own design capabilities remains to be seen. The consulting firms could initiate measures during the formative years of the WAs that would make careers in their organizations attractive, because of their far greater flexibility in establishing pay scales and conditions for employment than is the case in the WAs. The consulting engineering firms could corner the market on design capability and limit the development of design offices in the WAs. However, their main concern was that the WAs would recruit their personnel rather than with taking advantage of

---

† In the United States, even the largest local authorities, such as the cities of New York, Chicago, and Detroit, utilize the services of consulting engineers for the design of their facilities. They only maintain an engineering capability adequate to deal with consulting engineers, but not the large staffs required for preparation of the engineering reports and detailed designs and specifications.

uncertainties during the reorganization period to recruit actively themselves.

The consultants can always expect to be called upon for the unusual and difficult projects such as, for example, the design of sea outfalls, where up to now there had been no local authorities with sufficient experience to establish competence. However, where WAs have extensive coastlines, such as the South West, Southern and Anglian Water Authorities, they may develop their own expertise because of the very many outfalls for which they will be responsible, and may find it less necessary to call upon consultants for even this type of work.

One of the difficulties in the use of consulting engineers by the local authorities in the past had been that the consultants had not been supplied with proper briefs because of limitations in technical staff in the local authorities. Staff of the new WAs, on the other hand, expressed the view that they would continue to use consultants in varying degrees, but they would be certain to prepare the terms of reference for each project most carefully. Under the reorganization, the professional competence would exist at WA headquarters or at the division level to assure that consultants were wisely used.

Agency agreements

While the statutory responsibility for sewerage and sewage disposal was transferred to the WAs, the Water Act 1973 contains specific provision for district councils to discharge sewerage functions on behalf of the WAs. Sewerage programs are required to be prepared with WA guidance and submitted annually to the WAs. The district councils are to carry out the program using the relevant powers of the WA.

The government, in conjunction with the local authorities associations, developed model agreements, the intention being that the local authorities should retain a substantial degree of discretion in relation to the maintenance and operation of sewers, and should also have discretion in formulating the program of future capital expenditure for approval by the WAs.

If a WA and a local authority agree, the responsibility for sewerage can revert to the WA. A number of the agency agreements were expected to be defaulted with time. The smaller district councils would tend to yield their sewerage responsibilities to the WAs, leaving the stronger local authorities to continue this dichotomy.

Local authorities under these arrangements will have more power than they might have hoped for initially, including the valuable power of requisitioning sewerage facilities for domestic purposes. The nature of the agency agreements between the WAs and local authorities is likely to vary significantly from one local authority to another, but is worthy of follow-up as it may be a source of substantial continuing difficulty.

THE WATER INDUSTRY RESPONSE TO THE PROPOSED STRUCTURE

The Ogden Committee recommendations were generally well received. The need for managerial capability at divisional and regional levels was endorsed with the view that the size and scope of the WAs would undoubtedly attract some of the best professional talent in the nation. Beddoe affirmed that the new structure would provide great scope for engineers within the corporate management team as well as throughout the industry.[10] Reorganization would provide new opportunities to engineers and scientists who would want to move from their specialties into water management.

While support was expressed for the decision to integrate the three technical services at WA headquarters within the responsibilities of a single director of operations,[11] one negative reaction might have been predicted. A member of the committee had made a strong plea for separate directorates for water supply, sewage disposal, and rivers. This was elaborated upon outside the committee at the annual conference of the Institute of Water Pollution Control in September 1973.[12]

'The sewage function should not be carried out by one officer responsible to another officer, whose primary discipline may be one of the other two functions; water supply or the river. No man can do justice to all three functions; there will inevitably be a conflict of loyalties and there is plenty of precedent in local government on this important subject.

'The whole matter of providing an adequate sewage treatment organization is far too important a matter for such a policy, and one must not lose sight of the fact that only by achieving an effective and efficient sewage and industrial waste treatment function can we in turn achieve the desired improvement in water quality in the river, in turn necessary to produce a better quality water for public supply.

'The sewage and industrial waste treatment function is the heart of the whole hydrological cycle, and should be treated as such!'†

A panel at the conference discussed the Water Act 1973.[13] Strong feelings of anxiety were expressed as much at the uncertainties of the structuring as at the proposed structure. Richard Wood, then chief engineer of the West Hertfordshire Main Drainage Authority and to become President of the Institute, expressed the feeling that, for those in the sewerage and sewage disposal field, reorganization was a great 'con'. The comment that '... morale ... could scarcely be lower' elicited loud applause from the

† A similar issue in 1940 had been argued at the first Annual Conference of the Sewage Works Federation (now the Water Pollution Control Federation) in the United States in 1940, when Professor Abel Wolman stated that the world did not turn upon a sewage treatment axis; 'Must it (sewage treatment) always have priority number 1?'

audience. Those who had been working on sewerage and sewage disposal in local authorities were vulnerable and worried and did not know whether they would end up with local government or with the WAs.

Charles Simeons, then a Conservative member of parliament and a member of Standing Committee D, indicated that reorganizations of the type being faced by the water industry had been happening in private industry for years. Such reorganizations, until positions are allocated, do create initial problems, but most such reorganizations, and in particular the water reorganization, promised expansion of acitivies rather than contraction.

An individual on the staff of a local authority, who indicated he had never spoken before at such a meeting, explained that he felt he must speak then because he might not get another opportunity to attend such a meeting after the reorganization. Initially there was lots of enthusiasm for the reorganization. The people in charge were 'their own kind'. But the DoE 'missed the boat' by failing to exploit the enthusiasm of the grass roots personnel who wanted to be allowed to participate in the planning of the reorganization. He attributed the problem to a lack of communication between those at the Ministry and executive level, involved on a continuing basis with the reorganization, and those in the field who were largely in the dark. This problem was to continue for a considerable time, even after the WAs were created and operating.

The Water Industry General Management Program

A Water Industry General Management Program was sponsored by the Water Supply Industry Training Board at the Administrative Staff College at Henley-on-Thames in October 1973.[14] At the urging of David Kinnersley, then executive secretary of the Association of River Authorities, representatives of the local authorities responsible for sewerage and sewage disposal and of the river authorities were invited, the first extensive exchange amongst officials of the three types of water agencies that were to come together in the new WAs, a unique experience in Great Britain.

The first plenary session was devoted to a presentation by Sir George Ogden on the Ogden Committee report, which he described as a 'do-it-yourself kit', from which the WAs might take pieces to guide their own structures. The most important concept in the report was the acceptance of a multidisciplinary approach to the water management structure. The chief executive of each of the WAs was to become one of the most responsible officials in the program. He would need to have considerable initiative and develop a special relationship with the chairman of his authority and with the public. The director of operations would have to be an unusual individual as being the first multidisciplinary type, including within his purview water supply, sewerage and sewage disposal, and river management. The sewerage and sewage disposal professionals were quite concerned that directors of operations would be chosen from fields other than their own (as in fact occurred, with only one of the ten directors of operations coming from the field of sewerage and sewage disposal). Nevertheless, to have separated the operations functions in headquarters would have defeated the very purpose of the reorganization.

The director of resource planning was to have responsibility for planning policies in the region. His major role would be selling planning schemes to the local authorities and to industry. Sir George believed that engineers would be more likely than administrative officers to bring creative skills to these posts. As it developed, almost all the directors of resource planning are, in fact, engineers.

The director of scientific services occupies a special place in the WA structure, being responsible to both the corporate management team and to the WA, advising on the WA's own discharges and on the treatment to be provided and being responsible for the monitoring of water quality throughout the region. The public must have confidence in the director who would be the principal representative of the public's interest and who protects the WA from seeming to be in conflict as both 'poacher' and 'gamekeeper'.

While the Water Act 1973 continues to endow local authorities with the responsibility for attesting to the wholesomeness of the drinking water, the WAs have this responsibility with regard to the quality of water for all other purposes. Their role is clear when it comes to protecting their waters from agricultural and industrial discharges and other discharges emanating from sources under the jurisdiction of others than the WAs themselves. On the other hand, a major source of pollution in all the WAs are the discharges from the wastewater treatment plants to be owned and operated by the WAs themselves. The director of scientific services must call attention to WA operations that have a detrimental effect on water quality, being thereby in conflict with the director of operations. The director of scientific services, therefore, is to have direct access to the chief executive and to the WA, most likely through advice to the WA quality advisory panel. The public must have confidence that the director of scientific services will in fact represent the public interest within the WA.

The discussion that followed revealed an air of considerable uncertainty, with many misgivings being expressed. Some of these misgivings might well have arisen because most of those in attendance did not know what their own positions would be under the reorganization. Still, many expressed concern that too much authority would be concentrated at headquarters and not enough in the divisions.

The other concerns expressed were about the relationships between the 'clean' and 'dirty' water personnel. Some of the water supply personnel at the meeting expressed fear that contact with the engineers from the sewerage and sewage disposal field would 'contaminate' them. Typhoid fever might be carried from the sewerage personnel to the water pipes as both these services would be within the same organization. In general, the feelings at this first multidisciplinary session were negative, with reservations articulated about the likely success of the reorganization.

At the last plenary session, at the end of a week of meetings, the subject again was the Ogden Committee report, with the discussion being led by a group of seven panelists, six of whom had been members of the Ogden Committee. During the week between these two plenary sessions, the participants had been members of syndicates, or working groups, made up of individuals from the water supply, sewerage and river management fields. The entire air of the second session was quite different from that of the first. At the earlier meeting, the Ogden Committee report waɔ being attacked for having moved too quickly to multifunctional operations at headquarters. At the later meeting, after a week of multifunctional personal relationships, the first question was why had there not been consideration given to establishing multifunctional divisions immediately, rather than separate divisions for water supply, for sewerage and sewage disposal, and for river management. Beddoe responded that the Committee did not believe that it could move that quickly to multifunctional divisions, and in fact, it had to take a stand on creating a multifunctional director of operations. Further, the WAs are not likely to follow the Ogden Committee report faithfully. Signs were already evident that some of the WAs would create multifunctional divisions immediately.

If a deliberate effort is made to go multifunctional, how far down into the organization should multifunctional units be created? The fears expressed about multifunctional operations were represented as a head of household who might resent seeing the same individual come into a home to rod a sewer and then replace a washer in a water faucet. The response of the panel was clear: the intention was not to make the man in the trench multifunctional, but to make the management multifunctional.

With regard to timing, the first few months were critical and should be used for all major changes. Changes not initiated in the early days of the reorganization might be much more difficult to initiate later.

The principal concern, as at the opening session, was with the extent of delegation of responsibilities not specifically set out in the Ogden Committee report as, for example, the design function. If the design function were not kept within the divisions, the divisions would be emasculated. The panel responded that new works would not likely be centralized unless they were unusual in size or in concept. In general, the amount and kinds of delegations to the divisions would vary amongst the WAs and within the WAs in accordance with how the divisions were established.

The role of laboratories within each regional water authority came under scrutiny. Some laboratories were intended to serve the functioning unit and, therefore, should be the responsibility of the director of operations, while other laboratory functions were responsible primarily to the director of scientific services in attesting to water quality. No organizational pattern had yet been developed.

One prescient set of comments concerned the importance of a public relations officer who would be needed to explain to the public why charges would be much higher as of 1 April 1974.

All in all, the Administrative Staff College program demonstrated the value of communication among the various disciplines and among the various echelons in the water industry in raising morale and enhancing the likelihood of success of the reorganization.

Accountability

Few comments were made publicly concerning the organization of the WA membership itself and the role that individual members would play. The general approach that the Ogden Committee had taken to WA membership was that, once appointed to a WA, the member would be divested of his origins and would assume responsibility to the WA as a whole. He would not serve as a representative of his employer or the government, if appointed by the government, or of his local authority if appointed from a local authority.

Some months after implementation of the reorganization, J. B. Hender, chief executive of the West Midlands County Council, at the Institute of Water Pollution Control annual conference in September 1974, expressed surprise '... that Ogden suggests that complaints should be taken up through the chief executive officer rather than through the local government member ... members, particularly those from local government, will wish to feel involved.[15] This view was echoed by C. E. Jarvis, a member of both the West Midlands County and the Severn Trent Water Authority.

Propinquity and familiarity might encourage complainants to contact WA members whom they know. In general, however, the WAs had not intended to provide a regularized opportunity for the flow of information or complaints through their local authority members. The Yorkshire Water Authority did request that its members, whether local authority or government appointees, become familiar with YWA staff in the areas in which they resided and thereby, through their familiarity with the area, be of assistance in interpreting YWA policies and procedures to the people.

In the fullness of time, criticism of the role of the 'corporate management team' began to be heard. Hender again decried the emphasis on 'labeled boxes', indicating that far more attention should have been given to the process of management rather than the structure, and he faulted the Ogden Committee report for this lack. Sir William Dugdale, chairman of the Severn Trent Water Authority summarized the general approach to the management structure by calling corporate management 'a weapon against departmentalization' and not an aim in itself. 'The corporate management team was just like a board of members—verbose, discursive and in most cases fairly irrelevant—but it had the great advantage of letting everyone know everybody else's business.'[15]

The Ogden Committee report certainly served an eminently useful purpose in helping the shadow WAs get started. Without such guidelines, or even with less thoughtful assistance, considerably more time might well have been required for the sheer creation of the organizations necessary to continue the water services, let alone to begin to accomplish the integrative purposes of the Act. That departures from the suggested structures began to be made within most of the WAs is only added testimony to the value of the guidelines which provided a point of departure and allowed adjustments in structure to meet local circumstances.

The report represented the philosophy of the new approach to water management as well as full appreciation of the pragmatic considerations involved in the massive reorganization. This approach, if not the substantive recommendations which are after all peculiar to the situation in England and Wales, might serve very usefully as a model for other major reorganizations.

FINANCIAL CONSIDERATIONS

The report to the Secretary of State for the Environment, *The Water Services: Economic and Financial Policies,*[16] the so-called Jukes Committee report, offered the shadow WAs financial guidelines as the Ogden Committee report had offered management guidelines. For the first two years, charges would be levied as far as possible on the basis which would have existed in the absence of reorganization. Attempting to introduce new charging systems would be difficult during the transition period. WAs were to levy a charge on the new district councils together with, but as a separate item from, the general rate. In the long term, the charging policies would be influenced by the aim to make consumers aware of the real costs of the services.

Apart from exchequer grants for specific purposes, such as rural facilities, the revenue to enable the WAs to discharge their main functions should come from charges for the services they provide. Statutory safeguards would be necessary to ensure that the costs of WA operations were distributed equitably among the various categories of water users. A transitional period to 1 April 1981 was proposed in order to make the necessary adjustments in the charging schemes to achieve this objective. The government would not concern itself with detailed levels of charges, but would retain control over matters of major policy such as methods of pricing, the extent of self-financing, and investment programs. The raising of revenue and the expenditure of funds for non-capital items would be entirely within the purview of the WAs. Reports would be issued by the government from time to time to provide guidance in implementing the principles under which the financing is to be accomplished.

In making plans and charging decisions, the WAs are to consider real alternatives and demonstrate that they have done so. For example, increased expenditure on preventing leakage from water distribution systems might be an economic alternative to increased expenditure on new water sources and treatment. The same principle should apply to plans for meeting river quality objectives.

As a general principle for charging policy, water services should be provided only when their value to the user is greater than their cost to the community. And the value of services is best indicated by the user's willingness to pay for them. In the case of any conflict between this principle and public health needs, public health should be given priority.

Application of these principles might mean that some present demands for water services, to which users attach low value, may not be met in the future. It will not always be possible to determine realistically the willingness of the users to pay for water services. The concept of costs and benefits to the community requires wide ranging examination in relation to the financial objectives of the WAs and the national policy of the government.

In the case of the standards which the WAs will lay down for effluents discharged directly to river systems, improvements in river quality must be recognized as a public good as well as a direct benefit to river users. Decisions on standards of river quality and effluent discharges must be on the technical factors involved and the desired uses of the river systems as well as on the costs imposed on dischargers.

The financial issues of the transitional period

The report affirmed that there would be little scope for changing the existing systems of charging during the transitional period nor should there be any moves to equalize charges within a region, although of course, this does not mean that existing levels of charges and the relationships between charges would remain unchanged. A substantial equalization of sewerage and sewage disposal charges would result from the creation of more extensive rating areas in consequence of local government reorganization. The WAs should not initiate further equalization of such charges.

In order to implement the principle of minimum change in charging methods during the 1974–76 period, each WA would calculate a uniform percentage of increase in revenue expenditure for each main group of services over that for the previous year, and add this element to the estimated expenditure of the previous year as a basis for fixing charges. Consumers within each division should bear the full weight of any differences (and benefit from any carry-over surpluses) inherited from the existing authorities in their areas.

While most of the charges would continue as in earlier years, some new charges would be created by the formation of the WAs. For example, the central administrative expenses to be incurred in establishing and maintaining a headquarters organization is to be divided among the rivers management, public water supply, and sewerage and sewage disposal services in proportion to the revenue expenditure on each, with appropriate increases and charges to cover these expenses. Furthermore, the WAs will be obliged to make contributions toward the upkeep of the National Water Council and to pay subscriptions to the Water Research Centre. These will be apportioned amongst the WAs according to population, and the costs involved should be spread over all the water services. The main problem will be in replacing funds made available to local authorities in rate support grants which were applicable for a wide range of purposes, including to a large measure, sewerage and sewage disposal. These would not be available to the WAs, but the government has indicated that it will seek to take full account of this fact through some transitional adjustments.

The cost of new capital schemes is to be spread throughout the water authority areas from the beginning, thus taking full advantage of the optimization potential of regionalization from the outset even though the general principle of minimum change in charging methods during the transitional period is maintained.

There was not nearly the response to the Jukes Committee report that the Ogden Committee report generated, principally because it was not seen to affect each individual in the water industry as the Ogden report would, and because the staffing for budget making and the budget making itself was still some months off. The full significance of the new charges, even though the changes in the methods of charging were minimized, was to come when the first budgets were being prepared and when the magnitude of the increase in the new water bills, both for the residential consumers and for industries, would be fully recognized.

Initial budget making

Financial officers in the water industry had long recognized a need for revising the basic principles upon which accounting practices should be based, and the reorganization offered an excellent opportunity for this. Because of the limited lead time for the first budget, the DoE established a working party with J. B. Woodham as chairman, to advise on the general principles to be followed by the WAs in the preparation of their estimates and accounts.[17] The Woodham report proposed that estimates and accounts (1) be related to WA objectives and economic and financial obligations, and (2) form part of an integrated management purpose.

The making of these first budgets suffered from many difficulties:[18] they were to be prepared much earlier than usual; they were to be prepared largely by officers who would not necessarily be responsible for the control of the expenditures; and inflation was running at historically high levels.

The rules about borrowing had been changed, but the effects of the new rules were not yet known. With the chairman of the WAs being appointed in July, the WAs themselves being organized in August and the estimates needing to be completed and returned in September, before the directors of finance had taken up their positions, the preparation of these budgets was particularly difficult. Also, they were coming from many sources. For example, the budget estimates for sewerage and sewage disposal were prepared by the local authorities, who would have little interest in them thereafter.

Another problem was that the local authorities themselves were being reorganized and personnel who would ordinarily have been familiar with the budgets might have already departed for other positions.

The estimated expenditures of one of the WAs for each of the services, shown in Table 5.3, gives some idea of the distribution of inherited obligations and the allocation of funds amongst the various services.[18]

TABLE 5.3
Estimated Annual Expenditures for a Typical Water Authority

Service	Loan charges £000	%	Other expenditure £000	%	Total £000
Sewerage	6 615	82	1 467	18	8 082
Sewage disposal	4 140	40	6 086	60	10 226
Water supply	2 601	39	4 117	61	6 718
Water resources	39	11	306	89	345
Land drainage	356	19	1 514	81	1 870
Pollution prevention	5	1	415	99	420
Fisheries	3	2	133	98	136
	13 759	49	14 038	51	27 797

The Woodham report was critical of the practice of earmarking revenue contributions to capital and recommended the setting up of a capital reserve account to be credited with all resources set aside from revenue to meet capital expenditures. It is to be expected that the WAs will in time be required to finance their capital expenditures from internally generated funds in this way rather than from external sources.

A comment in summary:[18] 'Everyone has difficulties and if those engaged in water finance appear to believe that they have got more than their fair share, humour them, for they have not fully recovered from the traumatic experience of Woodham, after Jukes, after Ogden, and already Jukes II and III are on the way.

'There are going to be major changes in the financial approach adopted in the water industry and those with strong constitutions welcome the opportunity to break new ground.'

Charges

If any one matter created difficulty during the transitional period, it was the level of charges that was set by the WAs as discussed in Chapter 9. These represented substantial increases and were particularly troublesome in Wales where the increase in domestic charges in one area was to exceed 400 percent, with an average of 165 percent.

In the North West Water Authority area, largely industrialized, the percentage increase of the water rate charged domestic customers ranged to 48 percent with an average increase of close to 33 percent.

Similar increases were anticipated in all of the WAs and were attributed by Beddoe to:[19]

1. An increase in the price of water which would have occurred without reorganization, as there had been a 2-year backlog in raising the charges,
2. exhaustion of balances that had accumulated in the local authorities and water boards,
3. the fact that the new sewerage charges are not comparable to the figures on the rate demand slips when sewerage and sewage disposal was being paid from rates,
4. inevitable increases in costs because of rapid expansion in the water services over the last few years,
5. added overhead for the WAs, which will be providing a new service, and
6. a somewhat larger structure than absolutely necessary initially, in order not to dismiss staff.

The reorganization was being launched at a most difficult time from an economic standpoint, with Great Britain undergoing rampant inflation and with considerable pressure from unions for substantial increases in salaries and wages.

The responses of the individual WAs to the rates that they would have to initiate varied somewhat. The Thames Water Authority, in presenting its budget to the public, drew attention to two interesting statistics: (1) headquarters costs have been kept below one percent of the revenue expenditure; and (2) the cost to the public of all the services to be provided by TWA would be less than 25 pence per week *per capita*. In presenting the TWA budget, estimated at about £45 million for 1974–75, three figures were highlighted: £350 000 for the National Water Council; £752 000 for the Water Research Centre; and £308 000 for training. These elements of the budget were highlighted, not because they had a significant impact on the budget, being less than one percent of the total expenditure, but because they represented expenditures over which TWA had no control and regarding which there appeared to be some resentment.

Much of the heat on the WAs with regard to their charges was fermented by the calling of a national election in February 1974, the disbanding of parliament and the taking of office of a new Labour government at the time that the WAs assumed their responsibilities. That charges were still of major concern was evidenced in the first *Bulletin* of the National Water Council.[20] Of 20 questions in parliament related to the water industry, seven related to rates and charges, with particular emphasis on Wales.

In responding to the queries about the high water charges, the Labour government characterized the burden as 'part of the inheritance that we received from the last government'.

The new Labour government was quite harried about the charges in Wales, with C. E. Roderick (Lab.) complaining that his '... constituents are extremely angry to find that their water charges are five times as high as the charges made to people who live in Birmingham who receive water from the same source . . . That water is carried 80 miles and yet is charged at only one-fifth of the rate charged locally.'[21] In response, the Under Secretary of State for Wales, Edward Rowlands, indicated that these charges are a direct and inevitable consequence of the Water Act 1973 which was passed by the Conservative government. He did indicate that the chairman of the Welsh National Water Development Authority had promised to review the charges in light of experiences during its first year.

In response to specific questions on rate rebates, Denis Howell, Under Secretary of State for the Environment, explained that water and sewerage services would be paid for through charges rather than rates (even though they might be computed on the same basis for the time being). While the rate relief program is to be applied to the general rates or taxes, and would be increased to offset somewhat the impact of increased water charges, there were no proposals to extend the scope of the rebate scheme to recover charges for the water services.

To a question raised in parliament concerning Southern Water Authority rates, Howell explained that the government had no power to intervene and that the rates did not require ministerial approval.[22] The Southern Water Authority took account of the advice provided by the previous administration whose policies were responsible for the increases. This response of the government can be interpreted in several ways: as absolving the Southern Water Authority for its rates because it followed the government's advice and guidelines in their establishment; or as an indictment of the previous government; or both.

The general posture of the new Labour government was to help interpret the new rates even though they were a legacy from the previous government. For example, in explaining the increases of more than 100 percent in the water charges in North Devon and East Cornwall, Howell pointed out that prior to the reorganization, the water boards had covered a substantial part of their expenditure by precepting on the general rates.[23] This was no longer possible, so that with the increase in water charges, there should be a corresponding decrease in the tax rates.

Continued questions were raised with respect to the government's assistance to local authorities in the matters of water and sewerage charges, with the government continually responding that the Water Act 1973 made these responsibilities those of the WAs and not the local authorities. It is no longer the role of government to authorize funds for sewerage projects required for serving new housing programs. In the future, the water services would be self-supporting. They could no longer depend upon general taxation to meet deficiencies.

R-DAY—1 APRIL 1974

Most of the activity in preparing for reorganization day, 1 April 1974, and for the period beyond was concentrated within the WAs. In the very abbreviated time interval between their formation and the date that they would assume full responsibility for hundreds of millions of pounds worth of facilities, the employment of some 65000 personnel, and service to almost 50 million people, the WAs were required to organize themselves, employ officers, staff, and workers, establish their headquarters and those of their divisions, prepare budgets and assess charges and collect moneys, all in the context of an agency that was unique in the annals of the British experience as well as the experience anywhere else in the world.

The date, 1 April 1974, that had hung like a sword of Damocles over all in the water industry, was viewed with expectancy and anticipation by some and with foreboding and apprehension by others. So far as the general public was concerned, 1 April came and went scarcely noticed.

The WAs themselves, frantic to arm themselves with the tools they needed to assume their responsibilities, hardly had time to observe the date. Only the Thames Water Authority, with the help of its public relations consultants, conducted a formal press conference on 1 April at its New River headquarters, complete with the requirements for toasting the birth that are traditional at such occasions.

An editorial commemoration of 1 April 1974 was arranged by the *Surveyor* which had called for contributions to an issue concentrating on reorganization and the day on which it was to occur, All Fools Day.[24] The responses were characterized as generally gloomy, and the published contributions had the air of the condemned whistling on the way to the guillotine.

While the date of 1 April 1974 might not, like many other historic events, have been celebrated at the time, it will certainly be marked by the historians and professionals in the water field far into the future. Whether this was the greatest reorganization ever 'perpetrated', a characterization of the reorganization rendered by the chairman of the NWC, Lord Nugent,[25] will be left for history to judge.

CHAPTER 6

The Water Authorities

This chapter describes each of the ten new water authorities. Some of the trials and tribulations of the organizational period for the Southern and Thames Water Authorities are recounted in some detail, as being indicative of how all the WAs were occupied during their early days.

Despite the guidelines from the government in their many circulars and memoranda issued from 2 Marsham Street, the headquarters of the Department of the Environment, and the reports of the Ogden and Jukes Committees, as well as the promulgations of the National Water Council, the Water Services Staff Commission and the other central agencies, the individual WAs did exhibit, perhaps more than might have been anticipated, considerable independence in how they organized themselves. Very quickly, each WA displayed a character and style of operation uniquely its own. The WAs vary extensively in area and population served, in water resources availability, and in the nature of the problems they face. Potential regional organizations in the United States and elsewhere may find that one of these WAs might serve as a useful model.

The author did not visit all the WAs, but was privileged to attend the first 11 meetings of the Southern Water Authority, from August 1973 thru June 1974, and several meetings of the Thames Water Authority and its committees, thereby becoming more familiar with these WAs. He attended one meeting of the Severn Trent Water Authority, visited the offices of the North West Water Authority and visited several divisions. This chapter also draws from a report made by the *Surveyor* one month before the WAs were to step out of the shadow and assume their responsibilities,[1] and from the WA's first annual reports.

The Ogden Committee had provided a series of guidelines which were influential in guiding the WAs in the structure of their management teams and committees.[2] Although constrained to recommend a single-purpose divisional structure, the Ogden Committee's proposals for eventual creation of multifunctional divisions were put into practice earlier than they had believed possible. The creation of multifunctional divisions during the 'shadow' period prior to reorganization was not expected because of the necessity for assuring that the services would be operating properly over the transition period.

The DoE had anticipated that there would be a total of some 260 provisional management units or divisions including 29 river divisions and 143 water supply divisions, both categories in general taking over from existing operating units, and 88 new divisions for sewerage and sewage disposal that would be constituted from the almost 1400 local authorities and main drainage boards that had been in existence (Table 6.1). Within three months of the creation of the shadow WAs, the *New Civil Engineer* headlined an editorial 'RWAs go their different ways'.[3]

TABLE 6.1
Divisions Proposed by Department of the Environment

WA	River divisions	Water supply divisions	Sewage disposal divisions	Total
North West	3	24	14	41
Northumbrian	1	5	4	10
Severn Trent	2	23	13	38
Yorkshire	1	20	11	32
Anglian	5	18	13	36
Thames	2	10	9	21
Southern	4	10	6	20
Wessex	3	7	6	16
South West	2	8	5	15
WNWDA	6	18	7	31
TOTALS	29	143	88	260

Key factors identified in the planning of many of the WAs, and this was apparent in the Southern Water Authority, were the future career decisions of the chief officers of the water boards, the river authorities, the sewerage boards and the local authority undertakings to be incorporated within the WAs. Where a chief division officer was contemplating early retirement, the way was seen open to combining his division with others at an early date. Accordingly, in many of the WAs, a philosophy for organization was replaced by expedience with regard to both the departure and the availability of key personnel.

Several WAs, such as the Yorkshire and Thames Water Authorities, indicated almost immediately that they would begin largely with multifunctional divisions. The Welsh National Water Development Authority, on the other hand, looked towards a gradual restructuring over a ten-year period.

As of reorganization day, of the ten WAs, three planned to begin with their divisions as multifunctional entities, three hoped to approach multifunctionalism gradually, one viewed multifunctional operations skeptically and one had not yet determined, on principle, how it would move. Two of the largest, the Severn Trent and Thames Water Authorities, appeared to be prevented from going completely multifunctional by large monolithic bodies, such as the Upper Tame Main Drainage Authority and the Birmingham City Water Department in the STWA, and the Greater London Council, the Metropolitan Water Board, and the Thames Conservancy in the TWA, that they had inherited. Accordingly, on reorganization day only 152, instead of 260, divisions were created, representing all combinations of functions, as shown in Table 6.2.

TABLE 6.2
Divisions in the Water Authorities

Functions	Recommended by government	Adopted by WAs as of 1 April 1974
R	29	21
WS	143	62
SSD	88	41
R + WS		4
R + SSD		1
WS + SSD		12
R + WS + SSD		11
	260	152

R = River management
WS = Water supply
SSD = Sewerage and sewage disposal

Although the concept of area administrations intervening between the divisions and the WA was specifically rejected by the Ogden Committee, this approach was chosen by the Northumbrian Water Authority.

The *Surveyor* summarized:[1] 'If it is possible to draw any conclusions from such a diverse set of structures, the main one must be that, whatever their ideas on multifunctionalism and philosophies about the water cycle, all the top men see reorganization as improving efficiency. The drastic pruning of the number of authorities responsible for water supply and sewage disposal is welcomed, everybody expecting to see immediate benefits from the reduction of duplication of effort and improved coordination of the two ends of the cycle. Shared services are generally looked forward to, while better resource planning and spending of capital in these penny pinching times is seen as a major advantage.

'The time scale for reorganization has been short and the pressures on the men at the top have been great. Almost without exception, however, the chief executives have said that they would not have wanted things to have been done any slower, nor would they have preferred water reorganization to have been embarked upon after local government had settled down.'

SOUTHERN WATER AUTHORITY

Covering the southern counties extending from the Isle of Wight and Hampshire in the west along the channel coast eastward to the North Sea including Sussex and Kent, the Southern Water Authority serves some 3·7 million people. While it is sixth among the WAs in the size of the population served, it is fourth in estimated rateable value. One of the most affluent areas of England, it is the site of many second and country homes of Londoners. Whereas some of the WAs have a natural geographic or hydrologic integrity, SWA is made up of four separate river authority areas, with only their propinquity serving to bind them together. In fact the first four meetings of SWA were held in London, outside the SWA area, because of the easier travel arrangements for SWA members.

All meetings were publicized and were open to the public. Perhaps because its meetings were held outside its area, the author constituted the entire 'public' representation at the first four meetings, and attendance by representatives of the local press only began when the controversial issue of water charges surfaced.

SWA members, ten appointed by local authorities and nine, including the chairman, appointed by the Secretary of State and the Minister of Agriculture, Fisheries and Food were strangers to one another, because they had had little occasion for any cooperative enterprise. Accordingly, the chairman, A. H. M. Smyth, as the only SWA member with any experience and knowledge of the obligations of the authority, led the discussions throughout the early meetings. At the first meeting, officers had not yet been appointed, and the SWA staff consisted only of the chairman and temporary staff recruited on a part-time basis from neighboring local and river authorities.

The chairman opened the first meeting by reporting upon the progress made in the establishment of SWA. He outlined the immediate tasks with emphasis on relationships with existing river authorities, local authorities, water companies and other statutory bodies with whom it would be necessary to establish transfer arrangements and formal 'agency' arrangements. One problem was delineating the northern boundaries of SWA, as initially five different northern boundaries each defined an area encompassing a single function. To ease the WAs' initial operations, the government had prepared a comprehensive Technical Brief for SWA,[4] as it did for each WA, which provided the data concerning the WA area.

The first major responsibility of each WA, after recruitment and appointment of the chief executive and the directors of operation and finance, was the establishment of divisions and the appointment of their managers. Such managers were likely to be immediately available for water supply and river divisions. However, there had been no equivalent organization of sufficient size to accomplish a direct transfer of responsibility in the case of sewerage and sewage disposal.

Another major responsibility was the preparation of a budget for the first year of operation, 1974-75. The fiscal year in Great Britain runs from 1 April, which coincides with the date of inauguration of the WAs. The 'shadow' staff would have to make contact with approximately 150 authorities in the SWA area, whose anticipated needs, to become the needs of the SWA, would form the basis for this first budget.

A considerable amount of time was spent defining the position of chief executive, the key officer of the authority, and particularly his perquisites. The chief executive would be involved in the appointment of all of the other officers.

Observation of the participation and behaviour of individual members of the SWA was far easier than for the larger WAs where the conduct of the meetings was far more formal and where there was not likely to be active participation by all members in attendance. No sign of a caucus of local authority members appeared to develop. The level of participation was more a function of the individual. The more articulate during the initial meetings were about equally divided amongst local authority members and government-appointed members, although the latter tended to hold back to allow more voice to those from the local authorities. When land drainage or fisheries was discussed, the Ministerial appointees for these areas did play a major role.

Two of the local authority representatives initially made a point of being elected representatives and having to account to their authorities. In the instance of one of these, this banner did continue to be waved, particularly when the matter of rates became an issue. In general, however, the SWA gradually came to assume the character of an independent organization with relatively little recognition or attribution to the origins of the members. The SWA members were charged with responsibilities to SWA without regard as to how they were appointed. While some could not divest themselves of their origins, frequent reiteration of the role of the authority member did serve to establish, during the initial period of the life of the SWA at any rate, that distinctions were not being made upon the basis of the origins of the authority members.

In minor controversies local authority members often did hang together, but seldom all at one time on any one issue so they did not generally succeed in carrying the day. For example, in deciding on whether or not the SWA should employ a full-time director of public relations, the only objectors were local authority members, but they were defeated 10 to 3. Similarly, in discussions of personnel, the local authority representatives objected to the SWA's personnel committee, made up entirely of SWA members, having powers delegated to them by the SWA. They feared that the authority would then be by-passed. In the vote, the local authority members again stuck together, but lost 9 to 6.

Scientific services

An issue, identified as the 'poacher–gamekeeper' conflict in Chapter 9, arose concerning the chain of command of the chief scientific officer. Brian Thorpe, chief executive, attending his first meeting, had recommended that, because of its size, SWA did not necessarily need to have a director of scientific services. The Ogden Committee had recommended for smaller WAs that the chief scientific officer be placed within the orbit of the director of resource planning. E. J. Pipe, an official of the Central Electricity Generating Board, nominated to the SWA by the government, believed that the scientific capabilities of the SWA should not be dispersed. Inasmuch as scientific capabilities were required for operations, the scientific officer might just as well report to the director of operations.

After considerable discussion, eight voted to have the scientific officer report to the director of operations and seven voted to have him report to the director of resource planning. The chairman then voted, as provided for in British practice, and created a tie. Pipe suggested that, with so close a vote, the decision should wait on a position paper on the subject by the chief executive for consideration at the next meeting.

The position paper is worthy of examination because this issue was to arise in other WAs. The requirements for scientific services are three-fold: (1) the provision of impartial and detailed advice on the consequence of future plans; (2) advice on the efficiency of existing operations; and (3) public reporting on the performance and progress of the authority in maintaining and restoring water quality and in maintaining the wholesomeness of public water supplies.

In order to accomplish these tasks the chief scientific officer must have freedom to select the sites and frequency and timing of his measurements and the parameters to be measured. Water quality monitoring requires expert staff and expensive laboratory resources. Considerable expertise and facilities already exist within the SWA, as each of the river authorities and the larger water undertakings employ scientific staff, with a total of some 80 biologists, chemists and other professionals. Laboratories are scattered throughout the area and a reduced number of well-equipped laboratories capable of dealing with the major analytical work can be established, supplemented by small field laboratories located at or near the sites of inidividual works.

Inasmuch as the WA would have regulatory as well as operating responsibility, the Ogden Committee considered objectivity of first importance. The director of operations is responsible for the management of divisions and one measure of the effectiveness of these divisions will be the quality of their effluents to the rivers. To place the surveillance of water quality in the hands of those responsible for the discharges raises the question as to 'whether justice is manifestly being seen to be done'. In the larger WAs this problem is being met by the appointment of separate directors of scientific services. In the smaller authorities a separate directorate may not be required, but the function should be kept separate from that of operations.

Accordingly, the position paper carried the recommendation which the authority adopted, that the scientific staff, headed by an assistant director of scientific services, be responsible to the director of resource planning and that they serve the SWA's requirements for scientific services as well as necessary advice in fulfilling their regulatory role.

The formation of divisions

The naming of the divisions occupied the SWA in its formative days. Early on, the division titles were to indicate both the area and function served. By virtue of withdrawals and retirements of potential division officers, the SWA seized the opportunity to create larger multifunctional divisions. In the interest of shortening their titles, the 'main' was deleted from 'main drainage', the term for sewerage, leaving the term 'drainage' to stand for sewerage and sewage disposal.

While no one in the SWA seemed to be concerned that the word 'drainage' hardly identified the sewerage and sewage treatment and disposal functions, the member appointed to be the land drainage expert on the SWA insisted that the word 'river' be included in the title of any division where river management, including land drainage functions, was to be included. (On the other hand, in the Severn Trent Water Authority, where sewage treatment and disposal are among the most important functions of the authority, and where the director of operations came from a main drainage board, the initial description in division titles for the responsibility for sewerage and sewage disposal was 'water reclamation'. Other WAs used 'effluent treatment', 'recovery', 'sewage' and 'water pollution control'.) The SWA ended up with one water division, three drainage divisions, four river and water divisions, and two water and drainage divisions.

The budget and water charges

A major problem that haunted SWA during its shadow existence, and was to haunt it thereafter as well, was the matter of the charges they were to impose upon the consumers within their area, charges, according to the chairman, that 'don't bear thinking of'.

The SWA budget for 1974–75 amounted to £48·1 million, an increase of 129 percent over the estimated net expenditures for 1973–74 of £21 million.

In actuality, making adjustments in the 1973–74 expenditures for inflation and loan repayment, the true comparison should be betweeen £48·1 million and £29·5 million, a still substantial increase of 63 percent.

In presenting the budget to the authority, the chairman pointed out that neither parliament nor the DoE would have direct control of the level of charges to be instituted by the SWA. Income and expenditures need to be balanced, and contributions need to be made to the National Water Council, both for its own operation and for its training function, and to the Water Research Centre.

The need to increase charges substantially led to a stimulating discussion with representatives of the local authorities complaining that they would have to carry this unhappy message to their constituents. K. M. Hepburn, a Ministerial appointee, suggested that the SWA hold a conference to which representatives of all the constituent local authorities and the press be invited, during which the budget issues would be explained, removing the burden of explanation from the shoulders of the local authority members of the SWA. This suggestion was adopted.

This conference, held in Worthing on 14 February 1974, was the only such meeting conducted by a WA. About 200 representatives of local authorities, including council members and officers, as well as a number of the local press were present. The chairman and his officers sat on the dais, while members of the authority sat in the front row, joined by the author, invited perhaps to add visible strength.

The chairman's opening remarks explained that the water reorganization legislation was initiated in the halcyon days of 1971 to 1973; while there can have hardly been a worse time in recent history for reorganization of local government, health services and water, it was too late to draw back.

The timetable for inaugurating SWA was short and the chairmen thanked the local authorities for releasing personnel to help get SWA started. With only some four months to prepare the budget with a skeleton staff, and with the constituent authorities slow in getting their estimates into SWA, time had been an important constraint. The budget, prepared in late 1973, had been based on prices and conditions as of 1 July 1973, 21 months before the end of the budget period 1 April 1975, beginning with an eight-month period during which inflation had never been higher.

SWA staff were not in a position to evaluate the many local authority budget proposals, and accepted them. In subsequent years, the estimates would be made by SWA staff, and estimates would only be needed from the local authorities for operation of the sewerage function under the agency agreements.

The chairman listed the factors that led to the high budget:

1.   The high inherited debt.
2.   New SWA headquarters and some new division headquarters.

3.   The inclusion of depreciation.
4.   The low level of balances inherited from the local authorities.
5.   The cost of operation of the SWA during its shadow period.
6.   Allowances, recommended by government, for contingencies for up to 35 percent inflation; and a reserve to be built up to 10 percent in three years.
7.   The rate support grants, which had been available to local authorities from the exchequer, not being available to the WAs.

The government had promised to provide relief to the domestic ratepayer so that overall increases would be limited to nine percent, but regardless of its impact, SWA was obliged to approve its budget because it had the responsibility of assuring that the services are provided as of 1 April 1974.

The questions from the floor were trenchant and vigorous. Their main thrust was that this was a time of stringency and therefore the increase in local authority rates was limited to two or three percent. The SWA budget is far too generous in its reserve fund, in its contingency allowance and in the very high allowance for inflation. It also seemed to be an appropriate year to introduce changes in the method of capital finance. The budget of the SWA did not recognize the financial crisis. The local authorities were allowed a 37 percent increase over two years while the SWA had run up a budget representing a much higher increase in one year.

In answer to a question about the motor cars made available to the chairman and officers, the chairman replied that he presumed that everyone knew the answer, because it had been well reported in the newspapers. The audience cried out 'No! no!' Answer: 'The chairman and the four officers had been provided with Rovers.' Audience: 'Disgraceful!'

The SWA was putting its constituent local authorities under intolerable conditions in collecting charges on its behalf. Words from the audience included 'irresponsible', 'prodigal', 'reckless', 'shocking', 'luxurious' and 'scandalous'. The salaries of SWA staff, which were said to be higher than local authorities can bestow, provoked resentment but they had been agreed to by the national Pay Board.

Several asked the purpose of the meeting. Was it just for letting off steam? Was it possible for the meeting to send a deputation to the SWA or even to the DoE? Was it to pass on the budget introduced by the chairman? The chairman indicated that the budget was not being presented. He and the members of the SWA attending the meeting would report the sense of the discussion back to the full SWA meeting to be held the following week.

The meeting was adjourned for tea. Immediately upon its conclusion a rump session was held at which it was agreed with a show of hands of about 30 or 40 that a telegram be sent to the government and to the three party leaders, then running in the election, asking for inquiries into the SWA budget.

The meeting at Worthing was the first to attract significant newspaper attention to SWA. A banner headline, 'FIRST BUDGET IS CALLED "PRODIGAL"', was followed by a quote from a member of a district council:[5] 'At present the average ratepayer in Seaford pays about £2 in his rates bill for sewerage; you are going to ask us to collect for you £12, a 600 percent increase. How am I going to explain that to a ratepayer who wants to know why such an increase is being levied?'

In defending the budget, the chairman emphasized that the SWA would provide an essential service and would not be thanked if water was not provided or if the SWA were to go bankrupt. In response to the charge that the SWA is a remote bureaucratic body, it was pointed out that a majority of the 19 members represented local government. With almost 4 million people in the area, it was not feasible to contact every constituent local authority in preparing the budget. There had not been a rise in the charges for two years, the reserves had been eaten away, and inflation had taken its toll. The SWA had reduced the requests for capital expenditures from the local authorities by over half.

Letters of complaint were received by the SWA from eight local authorities. The chairman indicated at the next meeting of the SWA that the complaints that were received were expected. Had there not been a public meeting, more letters would have been received. The tenor of the comments at the meeting and the letters was that the budget should be redrawn with substantial reductions. The chairman pointed out that the local authorities bear no responsibility for the rate except that they are only asked to include the charges for water service in their rate documents.

Two days after the Worthing meeting, the government reported the sharpest increase in the cost of living in history. The chairman believed that the next range of wage increases would undoubtedly reflect this change and that the estimated inflation figure might turn out to be too low, rather than too high.

A. B. Haworth-Booth, appointed from the West Sessex County Council, a most vociferous member of the STWA, congratulated the chairman but pointed out that the local authority members were exposed to expressions of 'no confidence' by their local authorities. He felt somewhat responsible for not seeking the establishment of a finance committee which, with a majority of local authority members, might have taken some of the heat off the SWA by coming in with a more responsible budget. He proposed to call on the local authority members of the SWA to use their majority to work for a finance committee in the future. This represented the first overt attempt to create a caucus of local authority members and distinguish them from the others.

Haworth-Booth believed that £5 million could be cut from the budget, an opinion shared by several other local authority members, who suggested that if a bit were knocked off, the budget might be well received. However, others were concerned about an under-estimate of inflation which would require the SWA to borrow at a much higher rate of interest in the future.

Another local authority member objected to this expression of a different set of responsibilities for appointed and elected members of the SWA. The authority should have confidence in its officers; the budget was provident and modest. The SWA should not go into debt before it began operations.

The appointed members then began to express their opinions, first by indicating that there should be no distinction in the responsibilities of members of the SWA. A very bad precedent would be established if the budget were changed at the request of the local authorities. The local authority members should defend the SWA and its decisions. The Worthing meeting was worthwhile, but the budget should be kept. Should the budget turn out to be too high, charges might be reduced in the future.

Haworth-Booth stated that he had tried to reduce the budget at the time it was originally presented and that he defended the SWA at his local authority meetings. He then moved a reduction of £2 million to demonstrate the sensitivity of the SWA to the local authorities, while he recognized that it would have little effect on the charges.

Four members of the SWA voted in favor of reducing the budget. The vote was not recorded and members were advised that they were free to have their names recorded if they so wished. None so wished.

THAMES WATER AUTHORITY

Being the largest of the WAs in population and resources, and because it includes London, the Thames Water Authority occupies a special place in the reorganization. TWA serves a population of some 12·1 million, about 25 percent of the total population of England and Wales, and embodies several old and prestigious organizations: the Thames Conservancy, created in 1857, and the Metropolitan Water Board, created in London in 1903. With its headquarters in London, the TWA is bound to be the cynosure for all who may be interested in water management throughout the world.

A three-day retreat for the corporate management team, division managers and certain committee chairmen was held in January 1974 at Tadley Court, the administrative center of the Water Supply Industry Training Board. Alex Morrison, chief executive, described the organizational structure of the nine divisions. Except for the Metropolitan Water Division, formed from the Metropolitan Water Board, the Metropolitan Public Health Division formed from the Public Health Engineering Division of the Greater London Council, and the Thames Conservancy Division, all the divisions are multifunctional, based in general on serving all three functions. The only exception is the Lea Division where river management was inherited from the Lea Conservancy and the sewerage and sewage disposal within that area incorporated into it. With multifunctional divisions as the ultimate objective, the officers found no advantage in establishing temporary single-purpose divisions. The pain of re-organization might as well be sustained all at one time.

Considerable discussion ensued concerning the management of the divisions. Morrison indicated that directions would come from any director at headquarters to the division managers and not functionally from a director to a member of division staff in his functional area. For example, if the director of scientific services has a request for some action on the part of a laboratory director of a division, the instruction regarding this would be passed through the division manager. Hugh Fish, director of scientific services, disagreed. Inasmuch as division managers are accountable to the director of operations, the director of scientific services would be forced to go through the director of operations to have his request filled.

Dr C. S. Sinnott, director of resource planning, asserted that planning should not need to go through the director of operations to communicate with division managers. Nevertheless, division personnel would be responsible to division managers who in turn would be responsible to the director of operations. Some flexibility in administrative arrangements would be necessary.

E. J. Gilliland, director of finance, discussed the financial problems facing the TWA. While capital investments are limited by the government as a mechanism for controlling the economy, operational expenditures are not controlled, and leasing would not require the approval of government. Thus, leasing might be employed for some facilities which generally are purchased from capital funds, such as computers, vehicles, space and the like. However, as the WAs will have to derive all their funds from revenue, shifting capital investments into revenue may not be advantageous.

Eric Reed, director of operations, indicated that the top priority for the TWA was keeping the operation going, and therefore the transfer of staff to the divisions was highly important. Other than two assistant directors of operations, each looking after three divisions, the directorate of operations did not have professional staff, looking to the division managers for all technical input. New works projects were the responsibility of the divisions. Contract tenders were to go out from the division managers, with contract evaluation to be in headquarters.

The directorate of scientific services had assistant directors for pollution control and for divisional services. The divisions handled pollution control on the river within their areas with their own scientific services, except that the Metropolitan Water Division was served by the TWA Center for Scientific Services at New River Head.

With the overwhelming population of TWA being within the London metropolitan area, the location of headquarters in London was virtually mandated by parliament. Because of the high cost of commercial space in London, TWA headquarters were located at New River Head, former headquarters for the Metropolitan Water Board, an historic location marking the first distribution center for public water supply for London, established almost 300 years earlier.

The TWA, virtually alone amongst the WAs, made a valiant attempt to inform its public. Immediately upon its creation, it employed the services of a commercial press information organization, which issued frequent news releases to catch the attention of the public.

The initial staff of the TWA, before any permanent officers were appointed, included six officers seconded from the Metropolitan Water Board, the Thames Conservancy, and the Greater London Council. This utilization of personnel from these three massive agencies was to continue with the selection of permanent officers. The chairman of the TWA had been a member of all of these agencies, the chief executive and the director of resource planning were from the Greater London Council, the director of operations from the Metropolitan Water Board and the directors of finance and scientific services from the Thames Conservancy.

Because of the large size of the TWA, a steering committee of nine including the chairman was appointed. Of the nine, five were from among those appointed by the government and four represented London. The steering committee had no representation from the county councils or district councils outside London, who constituted 16 of the 36 local authority representatives on TWA. Peter Black, chairman of the TWA, nevertheless affirmed that the members were considered as individuals and not as designated and delegated representatives.

A meeting of the TWA on 22 January 1974 indicated something of its style of operation. Two reports were presented. A water management committee report indicated that water was short and there was a need for rain: it would be too bad if restrictions needed to be imposed during the first year of operation of the TWA. A second report, that of the finance committee, explained the budget. A member asked how TWA could be asked to take action on a budget with the figures in hand only one day. Pressure on the staff had been great as the timetable was short. Pruning the budget prudently in the time available would be quite difficult. The local authority representatives must accept this procedure as an interim step as it was important to get the budget information to the press. With a shaking of heads, the budget was approved.

The TWAs meetings take something well under two hours, while the much smaller SWA requires some six to seven hours for each of its more frequent meetings. The TWA, with 36 elected members and 16, later increased to 22, appointed members, operates largely through its committees with considerable dependence on its officers.

Altogether the TWA fared well during the first year of reorganization, with lower charges and lower increases than the other authorities. The inheritance of the soundly organized London agencies and the Thames and Lea conservancies undoubtedly helped. Black concluded that the first year was altogether 'splendid'. 'Despite the biggest reorganization of the water industry ever to take place in this country, we have established a successful enterprise. Notwithstanding inflation, the accounts show a modest surplus of income over expenditure.'[6]

ANGLIAN WATER AUTHORITY

'The new Anglian Water Authority covers a slab of eastern England from the Humber estuary to the Thames. This terrain is afflicted with just about every sort of problem which makes a water engineer's life difficult.

'Rainfall is low, the lowest in the country, and the East Anglian acres have no equal for rapid evaporation of what they do get. Water has to be brought long distances—and it has to be reused more often than most. Which makes it expensive and ratepayers angry.'[7]

Many problems have resulted from expanding towns in the midst of the AWA area and from the very heavily developed rural areas, often without either water supply or sewerage. The rivers of the area are slow moving and easily polluted. Petrochemical plants pose a problem in one area while mangel wurzels (a variety of beet used as cattle feed) pose problems in the other. Water management is important; the land in the Fens has to be drained by pumping up to the rivers.

The AWA covers the largest land area of any of the WAs although its population is fifth largest, 4·1 million. Management of the area is made difficult because of the very large number of entities that were absorbed into it: five river authorities, 25 water undertakings including four water companies, and 196 sewage disposal authorities.

The AWA was the one WA that did not adopt the concept of multifunctionalism in the operation of its divisions. However, it did reduce the number of units recommended by the DoE from 18 water supply units to ten divisions and from 13 sewerage and sewage disposal units to seven, retaining the five river authorities as river divisions. After one year, except for combining three water divisions, the AWA appeared satisfied with its divisional structure, particularly in that the status of the new sewage divisions resulting from the regrouping of the highly fragmented organizations in the local authorities resulted in high morale and enthusiasm.[8]

Because of the larger number of small communities and the shortage of water in the region, the reuse of water by abstraction from rivers that receive wastewaters probably has greater potential in the AWA than in any other WA, and would seem to augur well for a multifunctional approach to management. While not attributing much value to the multifunctional approach at the grass roots level, the advantages of reorganization are seen primarily as a rationalization of the administration of water services at the national level and the better coordination of the water and sewage phases of the cycle at WA headquarters.

The AWA has adopted the recommendations of the Ogden Committee for the organization of headquarters almost without modification. Despite their relatively small size, design and construction will be relegated to the divisions, which will enjoy a high degree of autonomy.

In its committee structure, the AWA did not establish an independent water quality panel. Peter Bray, the chief executive, considered such a panel an illusion, because the panel would be largely dependent on reports from AWA officers. He is depending upon the independence of the director of scientific services, who has a straight line to the AWA, for avoiding the appearance of conflicts arising from the 'poacher–gamekeeper' relationship. If an independent check is essential, it should be carried out by the DoE.

NORTHUMBRIAN WATER AUTHORITY

The Northumbrian Water Authority, in the northernmost corner of England, with an extensive border along the North Sea coast and bordering Scotland, is one of the smaller WAs, serving a population of about 2·7 million, and occupying an area formerly served by the Northumbrian River Authority. The NWA has under its jurisdiction about one-third of the polluted estuaries of England and Wales, with a heavy industrial conurbation centered on Newcastle-upon-Tyne.

The NWA, composed of 19 members, is organized into committees following in general the Ogden Committee report, with a policy committee including the chairman of the NWA and the chairmen of the three other committees: the water management committee, the fisheries and recreation committee, and the public and public relations committee. The policy committee would see to it that the NWAs policy is implemented and would report to the authority how their programs were proceeding. It would have direct responsibility for finance, the appointment of personnel, and the acquisition, disposal and maintenance of all of the assets of the NWA. The water management committee would control all the water supply and sewage treatment activities and would look after river control and water quality monitoring. Because of its massive responsibilities it would be subdivided into three subcommittees: water supply, sewerage and sewage disposal; resources; and river control and monitoring. The fisheries and recreation committee would be concerned with activities under the general responsibility of the Ministry of Agriculture, Fisheries and Food, namely fisheries and land drainage, together with recreation, and would have three subcommittees, one for each of these subject areas. The public and personnel relations committee would be responsible for relationships with outside bodies, the public, and with NWA staff.

The main departure in this committee structure is that the NWA would not have an independent quality advisory panel as recommended in the Ogden Committee report. The matter of independence with regard to pollution monitoring, representing the general public interest, appears to be obscured throughout the NWA organization.

The headquarters structure follows closely upon the Ogden Committee report recommendations for the smaller authorities with directors of finance, operations and new works, planning and scientific services, and administration, all of these being part of the corporate management team (Fig. 6.1). This last directorate departs somewhat from Ogden, and is charged with administration, public relations, personnel and training. The assistant director of scientific and fishery services in the directorate of planning and scientific services is to have a direct line to the chief executive to report on water quality.

The NWA is readily divisible into three catchment areas: the Tyne and Northumberland, the Wear, and the Tees, each of which is served by a multifunctional division with a divisional director at division headquarters and managers for water supply and for sewerage and sewage disposal within each division. Finance and administration for the divisions are being handled within each of the divisions.

The theory was that the same logic that led to the creation of multifunctional WAs should lead to the formation of multifunctional divisions to take charge of all the day-to-day operational work which can be more effectively carried out by a smaller unit located close to the customers it serves and the staff and installations it controls. Also, the driving concept behind the formation of the WAs compelled the NWA to minimize functional subdivisions within any discipline to avoid creating a structure which encourages specialization.

In considering the time element, the clear consensus was that the multifunctional divisions be established as soon as possible. There was strong support for an early decision and the announcement of that decision to prevent deterioration in staff morale and loss of staff.

The NWA, when it came into being, had to assume responsibility for two major projects together costing about £100 million: the building of the controversial Kielder water scheme; and the major cleanup of the river Tyne which was started in 1972 and which drains much of the NWA industrial area.[9]

The Kielder project involves a reservoir on the upper Tyne and a 25-mile pipeline from the Tyne below the reservoir to the middle of the rivers Wear and Tees. This system would provide the NWA with all the water it

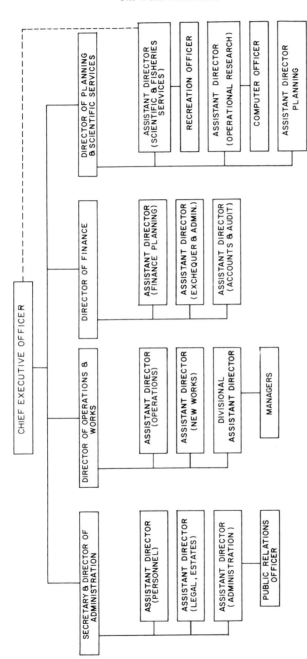

Fig. 6.1   Northumbrian Water Authority structure.

would need until the end of the century. For much of that period, the NWA would have an excess supply which it might make available to the Yorkshire Water Authority to the south.

A side effect of the Kielder scheme is that clean water will be available to be added to the flows of the Tyne, Wear and Tees. On the Tyne, a Tyneside Joint Sewerage Board was established in 1966, comprising 17 local authorities. The first stage of the scheme adopted by the Board, and now the responsibility of the NWA, includes the construction of interceptors along both banks of the Tyne carrying the wastewaters to primary treatment plants before being discharged into the river.

On the river Tees, where the major problem is industrial pollution, industrialists have agreed to reduce their pollution by 50 percent over a period of five years. The economics department of the University of Newcastle has inaugurated a study on behalf of the DoE to produce a mathematical model for the Tees with the aim of providing a pricing policy for charges for effluents being discharged into the river.

Chief executive A. S. Robertson summed up:[1] 'There are tremendous opportunities for increasing efficiency—by running our inherited plants better; by improving our designing and our buying. We have a hotch-potch of an organization at the present time. It might take us four or five years to end up with something that we can see as a unit, operating as a unit—an efficient unit to do the job as well as it possibly can be done.'

NORTH WEST WATER AUTHORITY

One of the largest of the WAs, serving some 7 million people with an amount of water second only to that of the Thames Water Authority, the North West Water Authority occupies the northwest of England along the Irish Sea extending from Scotland in the north to Wales in the south. It is highly varied in character, with the scenic Lake District in the north and the highly industrialized areas of Manchester and Liverpool in the south. With responsibility for absorbing the functions of 231 separate authorities, more than were obliged to be taken over by any other authority, the NWWA faced perhaps the most difficult task of organization of all.

The NWWA adopted a corporate structure virtually identical with that recommended by the Ogden Committee for the larger authorities. Also, in its divisional structure, the NWWA initially deviated least of all the WAs from the divisions or provisional management units proposed by the DoE. In fact, because of its early uncertainty as to what its divisional structure should be, these operating entities were titled 'units'. As contrasted with the 41 units recommended by the DoE, the NWWA had only reduced these to 35 as of R-day, more divisions than any other WA and with only one a dual-purpose unit. The only innovation was in naming the sewerage and sewage disposal division 'effluent treatment units'.

As contrasted with many of the other WAs, the NWWA decided that amalgamation of unit functions would not be influenced by the retirement plans of unit officers.

After examining many options, including a bulk water supply division to manage the water drawn from the Lake District, the NWWA reorganized as of 1 April 1975 into seven area dual-purpose divisions, each to handle water supply and sewerage and sewage disposal while an eighth river division would be made up of the three river units that had taken over from the three river authorities incorporated within the NWWA. The rivers division manager, like the other division managers, would report to the director of operations.

For the first several months following its formation, the NWWA met at a hotel 'The Tickled Trout'.[10] After occupying temporary offices, the NWWA found that among its assests was a fine new building recently completed by the Mersey and Weaver River Authority which it could occupy 'free, freehold, and free of debt'.

The NWWA settled on the establishment of a strong policy and resources committee and a small water quality panel, the latter vital to the critical monitoring role it is required to develop. Peter Liddell, the NWWA chairman, characterized the problems that the NWWA was to face on 1 April 1974 '. . . when many of the worst pollution dischargers become our property. Unless we so arrange matters that critical assessment of our own perfomance is on a level footing with our critical assessment of the performance of others whom we have power to prosecute, we cannot expect to be trusted.'[10]

The tight timetable for reorganization precluded many of the activities which, in normal conditions, a chairman and his authority might carry out from the start: frequent visits to units being drawn into the new organization; meetings with staff representatives and trade unions; the chairman's participation at occasions throughout the region where he would have helped make the authority and its purposes better known and understood; and the establishment of a wider understanding with the many agencies, both public and voluntary, with which the authority will need to work. That this perception, particularly as it affected personnel within the NWWA, was accurate, was affirmed by staff and potential staff in the field who were heard often to complain that they were not privy to the events taking place at headquarters and were in the dark as to their own role in the future development of the NWWA.

As much or more than any of the other WAs, the NWWA devoted considerable time and attention to characterizing the role of each of the members of the corporate team and the organization of each of the departments at headquarters. Because the NWWA organizational structure is modeled closely after the Ogden Committee recommendations, its organization typifies WA organization generally, although departures from this in the other WAs are to be expected as, in the fullness of time, adjustments within the NWWA itself would be made.

The five departments at headquarters are operations, finance, administration, resource planning, and scientific services.

Operations

The directorate of operations is to ensure that all the works of the NWWA are operated in such a manner as to fulfill its statutory obligations. Four assistant directors in the third tier handle common services, water supply, sewerage and sewage disposal, and river management. The organization of the offices of each of the assistant directors varies. For example, the assistant director in charge of water supply has three principal water supply engineers responsible for new works, for head works, and for distribution. The assistant director for common services provides common technical services, such as mechanical and electrical engineering, for all the operations.

As an example of fourth tier organization, the principal water supply engineer for new works is responsible for the preparation of standards for the design, construction and supervision of projects, for the preparation of contract documents, and for the provision of materials. He has overall supervision and integration of the design of regional projects where the actual design is to be carried out at the division level, although larger projects would be executed at the NWWA headquarters. He would be responsible for investigating capital program proposals submitted from the field, review the proposals from consultants and assess their performance.

Administration

The director of administration has responsibilities for administrative services for the authority and all its committees, including housekeeping, legal services, estates management, computer services, management services including operational research and project coordination, and purchasing and contract procedures.

Resource planning

J. G. Lloyd, originally director of resource planning and then to become chief executive, prepared a comprehensive statement on the role of the directorate of resource planning:[11]

'Planning should be a continuous circulatory process, starting from forecast of demand related to the aims and objectives for each water function, considering the available supplies, calculating the deficits, giving full attention to optimal management of the existing developed resources to minimize or defer the deficits, suggesting and appraising the alternative means for satisfying the deficits by environmentally acceptable and (preferably) multifunctional schemes and strategies, arranging programs carefully so as to match the proposals for action with the timing of forecast deficits, then continuing through capital investment plans, manpower plans and expenditure plans to revenue plans and charges scheme plans; with a feedback from there to the beginning of a process in order to take into account the probable effects of the charges policy upon demand and consequentially, upon the whole of the Authority's policy.'

Lloyd laid out three different structures, all based upon the principle of secondment of staff in the middle and lower grades from the other directorates and divisions and the principle of interdepartmental and interdisciplinary officers' committees or joint working parties with the resource planning directorate providing the chairman and the secretariat. The organization adopted, as shown in Fig. 6.2, includes assistant directors for corporate planning, water and sewage planning, and river and aquifer management planning.

Scientific services

The responsibilities of the directorate of scientific services include:

1. adequate scientific support to the operational units, including advice on the treatment of water and sewage, and the control of industrial effluents,
2. fisheries, conservation and development,
3. research into methods of treatment in association with directorates of operations and of resource planning,
4. advice on environmental and public health aspects of the NWWA functions,
5. recommendations of standards, and ensuring these are complied with,
6. independent quality monitoring,
7. development of automatic quality monitoring methods,
8. provision of 'troubleshooter' capability to deal with emergencies, and
9. general liaison with other directorates in the fields of public relations, recreation and resources.

Laboratory resources are organized so that process control is performed at the water and sewage treatment works, while the river unit laboratories are devoted primarily to monitoring. In addition, the river laboratories, which would generally be larger and provided with more sophisticated equipment, would provide support on advanced analyses and analytical troubleshooting for all the units where these facilities are not readily available within the divisions.

Three assistant directors would be appointed for analytical services, water quality, and operational services. The assistant director for water quality would be responsible for monitoring and for protecting the interests

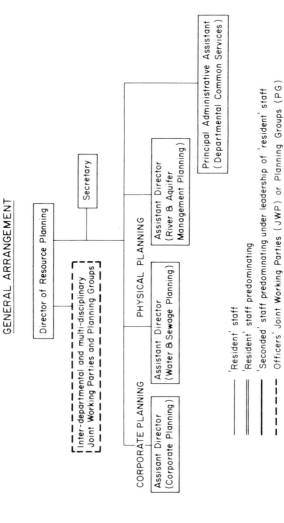

Fig. 6.2 North West Water Authority—organization of the directorate of resource planning (April 1974).

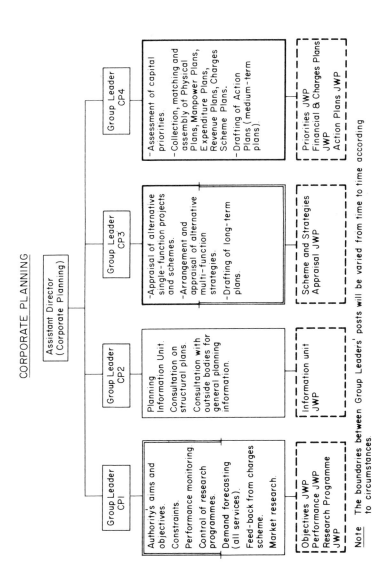

Fig. 6.2—*contd.*

of the general public. Gerald Ainsworth, director of scientific services, stated that the assistant director for water quality should provide the conscience of the NWWA, acting as assessor on behalf of the general public on the standard of water quality achieved by the NWWA in its own operations as well as by those regulated by it.

Such monitoring of river water quality and sewage works effluents as would be performed by staff of the rivers division, which is responsible to the director of operations, should still permit that staff to be in a position to maintain a posture of independence, provided there is an acceptable direct line of reporting to and control by the directorate of scientific services, which must be involved in the planning of the sampling programs, the setting of standards, and the policy related to the granting of consents for discharge to or abstraction from the rivers.

Finance

The director of finance, R. C. Jenking, set up the directorate somewhat differently from that recommended by the Ogden Committee, in that the audit function is separated from the accountancy function within the directorate. Assistant directors for the exchequer and for planning complete the directorate.

The assistant director for financial planning and research would be responsible for project appraisal, including cost-benefit analyses, as well as the seven-year estimates required by the government, the regional long-term financial plans, program budgeting, and the establishment of prices and charges, as well as the development of research projects. Research in financing methodology can be expected from the NWWA, as Jenking had been responsible for the only modern comprehensive study of metering in England, and had early on initiated a study of effluent charges for the NWWA.

SEVERN TRENT WATER AUTHORITY

The second largest of the WAs, both in population and area, the Severn Trent Water Authority is unusual in that it combines the drainage areas of the river Severn which drains west into the Atlantic Ocean and the river Trent which drains east into the North Sea. A substantial part of the drainage area of the upper Severn within the STWA is in Wales. The Severn is the source of ample quantities of high quality water that will undoubtedly be eyed by other WAs, while the Trent, with Birmingham at its head, has been heavily polluted as it serves as a drain for the industrial midlands.

Because the STWA serves a highly industrialized area, its labor and industry members exert a somewhat greater role than might be the case in other WAs. Local authority members appear to serve more as representatives of their authorities than is the case in the other WAs. For example, the STWA, while in its shadow form, was obliged to make its views known with regard to a reservoir that had been recommended by the Trent River Authority and approved by the Water Resources Board. In private discussions, one member from the area involved revealed that he supported the reservoir project but he declined to give his approval at the meeting, because he had not yet contacted his constituents.

Organization of the headquarters of the STWA initially followed the guidelines set out by the Ogden Committee. The STWA division structure was organized in accordance with Ogden, with divisions for the separate functions: water supply, water reclamation (sewerage and sewage disposal) and rivers. However, two of the areas had no 'growth points' for an adequately manned water reclamation division, and accordingly for these two areas, Montgomeryshire and Shropshire, dual-function divisions were established for water supply and water reclamation. Where the DoE had recommended a total of 38 divisions, the STWA succeeded in reducing the number initially to 28.

The late Marshall Nixon, the STWA's first chief executive, saw the initial period in the life of the authority as being devoted primarily to meeting R-day, 1 April 1974, with the maximum delegation to the operational units. However, as a member of the Ogden Committee, he indicated that the STWA would be examining very closely the two dual-purpose divisions, as their structure would be truly multifunctional, with four key individuals in each division being concerned with chemistry, operations, new works and finance, all on a dual-function basis. The success of these divisions would affect the speed with which the remainder of the STWA moves towards dual-function operation. Each of the two rivers would be managed by separate divisions, with basin-wide management programs for monitoring and optimization. The river management division for the Trent would provide a useful vehicle for implementing some of the ideas emanating from the Trent Research Programme.

Unfortunately, Nixon died before the STWA had become operational, the first 'casualty' of the reorganization. He had played an important role in the reorganization throughout England and Wales as well as in the STWA. J. E. Beddoe, who had been Under Secretary in the DoE, and characterized as the 'architect' of the water reorganization, was appointed chief executive on 25 April 1974. As he had been intimately involved in the reorganization from its initial emergence as a possibility through its most difficult periods, as a member of the Ogden Committee, and behind the scenes in many of the government's activities with regard to the reorganization, professionals in the industry would follow with interest the impact that he would make on the STWA.

They did not have long to wait. In October 1974 the STWA announced that it would, as of 1 April 1975, operate on a completely multifunctional basis with eight all-purpose divisions replacing the previously organized divisions (Fig. 6.3), 26 of which had been single-purpose. Included among these new divisions was to be one which would include the Birmingham Water Supply Division and the Upper Tame Water Reclamation Division, entities that incorporated what had been the two largest agencies taken over by the STWA. The two river divisions were abandoned and their responsibilities distributed amongst the eight new multipurpose divisions which were assigned areas, in general based upon hydrologic considerations, incorporating river sub-basins or river reaches and their tributary areas.

FIG. 6.3 Divisions of the Severn Trent Water Authority as of 1 April 1975.

This latest reorganization was the subject of considerable adverse criticism, particularly from those associated with the river divisions, who felt that their jobs were being threatened by the new organization. NALGO's national organizer for the water industry indicated that the union had yet to be convinced that the reorganization was necessary at all. The new changes would disband what had proved to be an experienced and successful team in managing the Severn, and many river officers believed that the STWA's two catchments, the Trent and the Severn, should continue to be managed by separate divisions. A division with its own budget and powers to control pollution, license abstractions, manage land drainage and fisheries over the entire catchment was felt to be the only effective way of safeguarding the river.

In *STREAM*, the house organ of STWA, Beddoe gave the following explanation, characterized by the *Surveyor*[12] as 'jargon-clad': '... we must look forward and consider how the pioneering work of the former river authorities has led the way to this present recognition of the need for the primary functions to be organized on a broader basis'. This praise preceding a summary execution was reminiscent of the approbation extended to the Water Resources Board by the government that indicated that the WRB's very success was responsible for its demise.

Asserting that the STWA reorganization was only accelerating a process that had been planned, D. A. D. Reeve, director of operations, pointed out that integration of river management with the rest of the STWA's responsibility was a natural corollary of the Water Act, bringing all water functions under a single control. All functions would be coordinated at headquarters and those responsible for river management would report to the director of scientific services rather than the director of operations, moving the dual role of 'gamekeeper' and 'poacher' one step higher in the management pyramid. Reeve was convinced that the decision to speed up the introduction of multipurpose divisions reflected the wishes of most of the staff to minimize the evolutionary period, and in opting for the more revolutionary change 'there has to be some blood spilled on the way'.

Officers indicated that the STWA divisional reorganization should not be interpreted simply as a 'Beddoe broom' sweeping clean. The new structure was arrived at by the whole corporate management team in consultation with the STWA's various committees and the regional joint council consisting of the STWA members and trade union and staff representatives.

Blood was also spilled at the STWA headquarters, which initially had been organized, following the Ogden Committee's guidelines, with five directors. In the summer of 1976, Beddoe proposed and the STWA endorsed the elimination of the directorate of resource planning and its replacement by a small central planning unit reporting to an assistant director with dispersion of its staff to the other directorates. That the STWA is the only WA abandoning its directorate of resource planning gives credence to the view that the issue was one of personalities rather than principle. The director had been Barry Rydz, formerly deputy director of the Water Resources Board and a strong advocate of its strategy, particularly the commitment to the enlarged Craig Goch scheme, tying the STWA to Wales.

SOUTH WEST WATER AUTHORITY

The South West Water Authority, serving the extreme southwest corner of England, with its touristically important counties of Devon and Cornwall, and extending to Land's End, with extensive coastlines on the English Channel and the Atlantic Ocean, is the smallest of the WAs in terms of population served.

From the very beginning, the SWWA had decided to be multifunctional. The DoE had recommended 18 single-purpose divisions which would have slowed down multifunctionalism considerably and would have required another reorganization later. Instead, the SWWA created an organization comprising three divisions, each multifunctional, and each divided into two areas.

Initially, each division was to have two division managers, one for water supply and the other for sewerage and sewage disposal, with the intention of gradually shifting these into multifunctional responsibilities. Actually, as of 1 April 1974, one of the divisions was already divided along area lines with each area manager being responsible for all functions. The other two divisions followed suit shortly thereafter.

According to the managing director (chief executive) of the SWWA, the multifunctional approach provided a saving of £100 000 per year on salaries alone against the structure recommended by the DoE. Although each of the three regional directors came from different backgrounds in the water industry, each is responsible for all the functions within his division. (The division manager drawn from the sewerage and sewage disposal field was one of the few such to be given responsibility over activities in water supply and river management.)

The SWWA management structure follows closely the Ogden Committee report for small authorities except that a director of administration is part of the corporate team. The chief scientific officer on the staff of the director of resource planning is completely divorced from operations, with a reporting link directly to the managing director to assure independence in water quality assessments.

The SWWA carefully delineated delegation of authority to the divisions, specifying in detail the divisions' responsibilities with regard to tendering and purchasing procedures for contracts, land and property transactions, exercise of regulatory functions, personnel, public relations, hospitality and the like. Functions of a regulatory nature (e.g. action in respect of the control of discharges of trade effluent to public sewers) are exercised by the division in accordance with arrangements made by headquarters. Abstracting licenses and consents to discharge to rivers are dealt with by the director of resource planning.

A decision to keep the new works program within headquarters, rather than at division level, flowed from the small size of the SWWA, the level of activity being insufficient to maintain a design staff at division level. A fair amount of design work would still fall to the divisions: water distribution mains, service reservoirs, pumping stations, and similar works.

THE WELSH NATIONAL WATER DEVELOPMENT AUTHORITY

Embroiled in controversy from the outset, the Welsh National Water Development Authority continued to be a focus of contention long after the reorganization. With part of Wales being consigned to the Severn Trent Water Authority and with Wales being the source of water for much of England and with the prospect that Welsh water will be continued to be developed to serve England, the WNWDA had become a target for Welsh Nationalists.

The annual precipitation in Wales ranges from 40 to more than 100 inches (1000 to more than 2500 millimeters) per year as contrasted with annual precipitation of well under 30 inches (750 millimeters) per year in southeastern England, where the population is concentrated. In the 19th century, the industrial cities of Liverpool and Birmingham developed water sources in Wales.

With the reorganization, and an attempt to make the charges for water services reflect the true cost, the sharp increase in charges in Wales had led the Welsh members of parliament into pressing the government to investigate the anomaly that Welsh water is cheaper in Birmingham and Liverpool to which it is exported than in Wales itself. This issue is discussed at some length in Chapter 9, as it was to become a real threat to the principles upon which the reorganization was based.

The WNWDA structure follows the Ogden Committee recommendations for a large WA. Services in Wales had been highly fragmented prior to reorganization. For a population of 2·9 million, the area had been served by six river authorities, 29 water undertakings, and 174 sewage disposal authorities. Of all of the WAs, the WNWDA proceeded most conventionally in its initial divisional organization, with 25 single-purpose divisions for river management, water supply, and sewerage and sewage disposal, much in the way that had been initially recommended by the DoE. According to chief executive Dr Harry H. Crann, the WNWDA's main concern was to effect a smooth change-over on reorganization day, with eventual multifunctional operation envisaged. Initially the combination of the existing divisions was to depend largely on the retirement plans of the division managers, but it soon adopted a policy of programmed integration.[13]

WESSEX WATER AUTHORITY

The Wessex Water Authority is one of the two smallest, serving some 2 million people within its area directly to the west of the Thames and Southern Water Authority areas. Based upon the areas covered by three previous river authorities, the Bristol Avon, Avon and Dorset, and Somerset, the divisions were structured to keep these hydrologic boundaries intact, being convenient dividing lines for management purposes. Initially three water supply divisions, three water recovery divisions and three river divisions were based upon these areas, nine in all, many fewer than the DoE recommended. With pay levels established by the government's Pay Board generally based *inter alia* on the population being served, reducing the number of divisions and increasing their size made the division manager posts desirable enough to attract high caliber applicants.

Although the initial organization was based upon separate functions to ease the transition, their geographical distribution is such that these functions can be readily combined into three multifunctional divisions on a catchment area basis. The outlook had been clearly multifunctional in that the three assistant directors of operations are not single-purpose men assigned to water supply, sewerage and sewage disposal and rivers, but multifunctional with each responsible for all services within a hydrologic area. By the end of 1975, the WWA had established a fully multifunctional divisional structure with three divisions based on hydrologic areas.

In the WWA area, fishing and fisheries are of prime importance, not only for recreation but as a business.[15] The area affords first-class game and coarse fishing as well as exceptional lake fishing and the management of this resource could not be relegated to a second-class status. As a consequence, this phase of water management was made a direct responsibility of the chief executive, as is the case in the South West Water Authority. In trying to decide whether the chief executive should have line responsibility for any of the functions, Wessex took the view that it was unrealistic for the chief executive to sit remote. Accordingly, not only does he have responsibilities for fisheries and recreation, he also has direct responsibility for personnel and public relations.

In recognizing that the major accusation against the reorganization was that the WAs are unrepresentative, despite the fact that in every instance the majority of WA members are representatives of local authorities, the WWA established three advisory committees, one in each area, with representatives from each district council and from such bodies as the National Farmers Union, Country Landowners Association, the Sports Council, the Confederation of British Industry and so forth. The WWA hopes that these advisory committees will play an important role in helping formulate policies by commenting on proposals before the decision making stage.

YORKSHIRE WATER AUTHORITY

Of all of the WAs, the Yorkshire Water Authority attracted the most attention during the pre-reorganization period. First, the selection of the chairman of the YWA, J. C. Brown, a life-long industrialist with Imperial Chemical Industries who was alleged to assert that perhaps too much attention was being paid to pollution control, aroused those who thought that the new authorities would be soft on polluters. This view was supported when the pollution control officer of the Yorkshire River Authority, who had established a reputation as being a strong pollution control regulator, was not continued as a chief scientific officer or pollution control officer in the YWA. Even though the YWA is the fourth largest in population served, it opted for a structure recommended by the Ogden Committee for the smaller authorities. The Ogden Committee recommended that the chief scientific officer, if he was not to head a directorate, be placed in the directorate of resource planning. In the YWA, an assistant director for scientific services, under whom the chief pollution officer would be located, was placed in the directorate of operations. In the management structure charts prepared by the YWA, no lines were drawn from the assistant director for scientific services or the chief pollution officer directly to the chief executive or the authority (Fig. 6.4). To avoid the appearance of a conflict of interest, most WAs identified a direct line for those responsible for water quality control to either the chief executive or the authority. To have the officer responsible for monitoring water quality report through the director of operations, who is responsible for the quality of effluent produced, creates an apparent conflict of interest, the 'poacher–gamekeeper' problem.

In addition to the controversies stirred by its posture in pollution control, the YWA also attracted attention because it was the first to announce and to implement a multifunctional division structure.[16] The rivers of Yorkshire drain to the Humber estuary roughly as the ribs of a fan converge to its handle. It was therefore convenient to divide the YWA's area by boundaries drawn along the watersheds of the six natural tributary basins in the area. Each of these areas is approximately wedge-shaped, with its point at the outlet to the estuary. The seventh geographical division was formed around

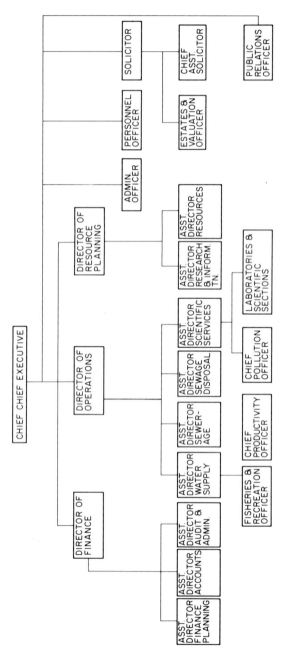

Fig. 6.4　Yorkshire Water Authority structure.

the confluence of the tributaries with the upstream boundary approximately at the tidal limit. While the Control of Pollution Act 1974 obliterates the differences in law in respect of discharges into tidal and non-tidal waters, this boundary separates the area where initially little attention had been given to pollution control and where the work involved in raising the quality of water would be different from the task in the non-tidal rivers. Also, this seventh division would have the responsibility for working with the Severn Trent and Anglian Water Authorities which also have discharges into the Humber. Thus, each valley in Yorkshire has its own division director who is responsible for the totality of the management of water in that valley as a natural resource.

The division director has three functionaries: a water supply manager, a water pollution control manager, and a division finance officer. The two managers share common services in the division for design and construction, productivity, pollution control of discharges to rivers and to sewers and the scientific arm. The success of the water pollution control effort will be monitored in the tributary that constitutes the division as it leaves the division. The divisons are titled according to their geographic location within the Authority area, by the points of the compass.

On the pollution control side, each division is to have a trade effluent officer and, according to size, up to four area water pollution control managers. Hopefully, this would increase coordination and cooperation with industry.

The new pollution control officers in the divisions are able to offer advice on pollution management at the source, as contrasted with the pollution control officers of the river authorities who had been merely policemen, useful but not very creative. Pollution control officers report directly to the quality advisory panel of the YWA. A director of scientific services may be appointed in the future, but this role is seen as 'professorial', a fountain of knowledge on scientific services and pollution control, rather than as a 'super policeman'.

The YWA is constituted of 12 members, including the chairman, appointed by the government and 13 members appointed from local government. Their approach has been to act as a board of directors rather than as a council reviewing the activities of committees. They have given themselves the task of taking charge of the overall management of the YWA, and so have not created a separate water management committee.

Members of the YWA have been asked to take particular interest in the activities of the division in which they reside and make formal contact with the division directors. Rather than have advisory committees, the Authority has decided to utilize, on an *ad hoc* basis, members of the YWA to meet with local authorities and representatives of organizations that have an interest in water services. Any identifiable pressure group is to be met by a group of members appropriate to the occasion.

In an attempt to shed the image of an authority with little concern for water pollution, the YWA organized a series of symposia on the rivers within the YWA area. The second of these, concerning the Rivers Don and Rother, was chaired by W. M. Jollans, director of operations, although the chairman of the YWA and its chief executive were present. To those representing the Conservation Society and the angling interests, who had been fearful that the departure of the 'scourge of polluters' from Yorkshire meant that the YWA would give short shrift to pollution control, it came as a surprise to learn from the chairman that the rate of prosecutions for pollution was about the same as it had been. With more than 300 people in attendance, representing a wide range of interests, the YWA image was enhanced by the symposium.

The main theme of the symposium was the heavy pollution of the Don and Rother. Colin Watson, scientific officer of the Southern Division of YWA presented the situation: steel, coal and people have contributed to the deterioration of these streams, with the pollution created equally by industrial and domestic wastewaters. J. B. Rhoades, the YWA chief pollution prevention officer, pointed out that 90 miles (150 kilometers) of south Yorkshire's rivers were class 4, grossly polluted. While it was acknowledged that 'the rivers can and must be made pleasant', the chairman of the YWA was quick to point out that upgrading these streams would cost millions of pounds and he wondered whether the ratepayers would suffer such expenses gladly.

A. B. Baldwin, chief executive and an accomplished sculptor in his spare time, time which is not likely to be available during the early years of reorganization, spoke eloquently of the Water Act as the 'finest piece of legislation in the world—quite brilliant'. He was convinced that the new organization would provide an opportunity for the provision of water services at lower costs than otherwise possible.

CHAPTER 7

The National Agencies

The Water Act 1973 did not change the relationship between the government and those responsible for providing the water services, now the water authorities. The Secretaries of State for the Environment and for Wales and the Minister of Agriculture, Fisheries and Food continue to have the duty to promote jointly a national policy for water in England and Wales.

The Act did bring about certain minor changes in the relationship between the government and the WAs:

1. the WAs have greater freedom in the control of charges for water service,
2. the WAs are required to plan on a river basin scale, and
3. the WAs are obliged to consider recreation on inland waters.

Even initially, the newly created WAs were to have much greater freedom of action and relief from detailed control as contrasted with the predecessor authorities. Nevertheless, the government still retains important functions in directing national policy and in assisting the WAs with problems common to all of them. For meeting these purposes, several new national agencies were created: the National Water Council and the Water Space Amenity Commission are statutory bodies established under the Water Act 1973; the Water Research Centre is established as a company (like one of its predecessors, the Water Research Association); and the Central Water Planning Unit and the Water Data Unit are part of the Department of the Environment.

THE DEPARTMENT OF THE ENVIRONMENT

The Secretary of State for the Environment and several of his Ministers, including the Minister of Housing and Local Government, and several Parliamentary Under Secretaries, as well as the Minister of Agriculture, Fisheries and Food, are members of parliament and of the party in power. The Conservative government had taken the initiative in drafting, promoting and passing the Water Act, but with the change in government in

February 1974, the Labour government was in power at the time of implementation. Denis Howell, the key Parliamentary Under Secretary in the new government, who was amongst the most articulate opponents of elements of the legislation, during the debates in the House of Commons, found himself leading its implementation.

Lending continuity in the DoE are the senior civil servants. During the period of the reorganization, J. A. Jukes, Deputy Secretary (Environmental Protection), had been'the senior official responsible for the reorganization. He was then responsible for five directorates within the DoE, three of which were involved in the environment, including the Directorate of Water which was responsible for the Water Bill and which, following the reorganization, became responsible for DoE relationships with the WAs. Jukes did become well identified with the water reorganization, serving as chairman of the steering group on economic and financial policies, with three important reports identified with his name. The echelon below the Deputy Secretary includes the Under Secretaries, with J. E. Beddoe, the 'architect' of the reorganization, having been one such.

Reorganization of the DoE in 1974 resulted in Jukes' replacement by Trevor P. Hughes, who had been Director General Water Engineering and was now to hold this position as well as serving as Deputy Secretary (Environmental Protection), including all of the water services. Thus, Hughes had become, during the critical period of the reorganization, the single most important civil servant in the government with reponsibilities in the water field.

The DoE modified its procedures following reorganization, abolishing a requirement that it give consent to applications for loans. WAs are now free to borrow within an overall capital ceiling, with the DoE determining these ceilings (subject to Treasury control). Ceilings are based upon a compromise between the requirements of the WAs and the national needs for capital in other fields. Even this control may cease to be critical, as the cost of capital financing may itself deter capital spending by many of the WAs. The other major responsibility of the DoE is to be in the surveillance of the corporate planning responsibilities of the WAs, including long term plans and estimates of future demands for water over a 20-year period.

The government's policy to decentralize the water industry was seen by many as a scheme of the senior civil servants to maintain tight control in Whitehall. Whether the government will maintain control of the WAs will be determined only in the fullness of time. The WAs have had strong leadership and have appeared quite independent in responding to the government advice on organization and on economic and financial policies. Organizations may be structured, but the people who make them work are not. The reorganization has created opportunities for strong individuals to exert considerable influence within the WAs, resulting in more decentralization of power than had been anticipated.

THE NATIONAL WATER COUNCIL

The National Water Council is not like any other central water organization previously existent in Britain or elsewhere. It is not a successor to the Water Resources Board although they are similar in their advisory functions to government. However, as it includes all the chairmen of the WAs, the NWC's potential is much greater than that of the WRB, which had no constituency with any commitment to follow its advice. More important, the NWC is not constrained by the limited mandate of the WRB, which was concerned only with water resources quantity and was specifically excluded from responsibility for water quality.

According to Section 9(5) of the Water Act 1973, it shall be the duty of the NWC:

1. to consider, and advise the government on any matter relating to the national policy for water,
2. to promote and assist the efficient performance by WAs of their functions,
3. to advise on any matter brought to the NWC by a Minister,
4. with a view to the establishment of a scheme for the testing and approval of water fittings, to consult with water agencies and other interested parties throughout the United Kingdom, and
5. to prepare a scheme for training and education in connection with water services provided in the United Kingdom.

The responsibilities of the NWC, other than the statutory powers for the testing and approval of water fittings and the training of personnel, are by sufferance of the government or the WAs. The NWC was seen at its creation as facing in two directions, to government and to the WAs, with little to offer but advice and with no obligation on the part of either to accept this advice, although two or more WAs may authorize the NWC to act in matters of common interest.

For such an ostensibly weak body, the NWC is handsomely endowed both in its membership and in its staff. The strength of the NWC lies in its permanent *ex officio* membership, the ten WA chairmen, who can be expected to dominate the NWC, because the other appointed members have a less continuous interest. The appointed members represent such specialized interests as labor, amenities, economics, science, local authorities, training, and the like. It cannot be expected that they will master the overall problems of the water industry as will the chairmen. Furthermore, the chairmen have been selected for their demonstrated leadership qualities and they are all highly articulate. The other appointed members, while some may be leaders in their own fields, cannot be expected to make as forceful and sustained representations in the NWC as the WA chairmen.

In the early days, a member described NWC meetings as being concerned with everything but water, but this was to be expected during its formative stages. Nevertheless, the character of the NWC will be that character which the chairmen of the WAs are prepared to establish. To note that the chairmen occasionally meet as chairmen without the other members, and that they tend to dominate the NWC, is not to disparage their integrity. It is just that they have a continuing consuming concern for the performance of their WAs that cannot be expected of the other members.

The NWC also initiated meetings of chief executives, and directors and other officers of the WAs. In some of these, the director-general of the NWC takes the chair and representatives of government are present. In others, the meetings are limited to the WA personnel.

As the WAs built upon the agencies whose responsibilities they assumed, so too the NWC was fortunate in having the British Waterworks Association and the Water Supply Industry Training Board upon which to draw to meet their statutory obligations and to help establish their administrative facilities. Also important to the initial operations of the NWC were the assets, and some of the personnel, of the Association of River Authorities.

The BWA was an incorporated organization including in its membership virtually every water undertaking in England, Wales, Scotland and Northern Ireland, some 233 in all. The BWA represented the employers' side in all staff relationships with personnel. The BWA also tested and approved fittings and established many committees that worked with government, with water undertakings and with others with any interest in the water supply industry. It had provided the secretariat for the International Water Supply Association.

The former long-time director of the BWA, Leonard Millis, became a member of the NWC. His successor as director and secretary from 1 June 1973, John R. Buckenham, became the secretary of the NWC, and the headquarters of the BWA provided the first headquarters of the NWC.

The BWA influenced the activities of the NWC in other ways as well. Its *Gazette*, with a record of all activities of interest to the water industry including pertinent parliamentary debates, formed the basis for the weekly NWC *Bulletin*. The NWC journal, *Water*, followed after a similar BWA journal. The NWC also advises WA information officers on the establishment and operation of their own regional information services. The computer capability inherited by the individual WAs varied considerably, and NWC proposed a computer strategy for the industry.[1]

In accordance with the statutory authority given to the NWC to provide services that two or more WAs desire, handling employee relations in the industry became a prime obligation of NWC through its manpower division.[2] Four joint negotiating bodies were established to deal with some 46 000 manual employees, 24 000 staff, and 65 chief officers.

The NWC manpower division works closely with the WA personnel officers and with the Water Companies Association, and serves the employers' side in joint negotiations. The NWC provides a forum for discussion of industrial relations and other personnel matters of common interest, an important service to the water industry, which has become more vulnerable because of 'nationalization' of workers who previously had been fragmented in local organizations.

Training

The most important statutory obligation of the NWC is for the training and education of the 65 000 employees in the water industry in England and Wales and an additional 15 000 in Northern Ireland and Scotland. A training committee responsible to the NWC was established to supervise the work of the Training Division with Anne Yates, a member of the NWC, serving as chairman. Employers, trades union representatives, and educators are represented on the committee. The NWC's inheritance of the staff and assets of the former Water Supply Industry Training Board provided a flying start.

The Industrial Training Act 1964 requires companies to undertake programs of training and education for their employees, and encourages companies to take part via their appropriate Training Boards, which collect an obligatory levy proportionate to their payrolls. In turn, companies may receive grants related to the quality and quantity of training carried out. The WSITB was created in 1966 to serve the United Kingdom, with four residential training centers in England and one in Scotland, with a capacity to house 180 trainees. Some 1·6 percent of the payroll of the water supply industry went into the formal training budget; 40 percent of this was assigned to the WSITB, while the remainder was used for in-service training or formal training grants to individuals. While a similar training establishment for local authority personnel existed, it had not focused on sewerage and sewage disposal, so that up to the time of reorganization the water supply phase of the water industry had been far better served than any other. To meet the greater obligations after reorganization, the Training Division was authorized to increase the number of residential places to 252 by April 1975. In the summer of 1975, the Training Division offered 37 separate management courses, some 60 courses in administrative and technical subjects, 17 courses in supervision, and 34 courses for operators and technicians. Its program is the best on a national scale anywhere in the world.

An interesting dimension of the Water Act 1973, is that Section 4(9) gives power to the NWC to '... furnish to any person or body for the benefit of any country or territory outside the United Kingdom technical assistance in connection with training and education in relation to any services corresponding to those provided in England and Wales by water authorities'. While the WSITB had been giving some assistance to the World Health Organization and bilateral assistance to other countries in training for water supply, this had not been explicitly authorized. Such activities will likely increase substantially and provide a vehicle for the dissemination of technical information and the institutional aspects of water management, hopefully stimulating integrated regional organizations for the water industry in the less-developed countries where that approach is appropriate.

The future of the NWC

The ambivalent nature of the NWC was aptly characterized in the title of an article reviewing the first year of operation of the new water industry, 'Watchdog or Lapdog'.[3] Members of the NWC were identified to include three former Conservative Ministers, a merchant banker, a farmer and chartered surveyor, four company directors and a major landowner. Of the 19 male members, six had attended Eton, three had been in the Guards and one in the Hussars, two have been office holders in the Country Landowners Association, and one is a Master of Fox Hounds. The NWC membership was not seen to reflect a representative view of the industry.

In its statutory responsibilities, the NWC is neither 'watchdog' nor 'lapdog'. Training and testing of fittings are essential to the industry, but do not of themselves require a highly placed, highly qualified, and elegantly housed centralized agency. The test will be in how well the NWC provides advice to the government and to the WAs and how well this advice is heeded. Two main areas of challenge face the NWC: first, an evaluation of the national water strategy proposed by the Water Resources Board; and second, the resolution of problems arising between two WAs, as illustrated by the issue of exporting water from Wales to England. The leadership provided by the NWC in resolving these issues will go a long way towards indicating its future role. As Peter Stott, director-general of the NWC, said with regard to the WRB proposals: 'There couldn't have been a much larger issue with which to launch the NWC because the report deals with matters of water supply . . . So when somebody produces a report which talks about spending so much on water supply, our first question must be: "How does this affect any needs we might have to spend on other parts of the system, such as pollution prevention, sewerage and sewage treatment?" We now see it in a much larger context than the people who write it.'[4]

The commentary throughout the industry concerning the role of the NWC had been that government, i.e. the DoE, purposefully created the NWC with few direct responsibilities so as to keep the reins of control in its own hands. Some sense of a limited role for the NWC was discerned in an interview with Stott prior to implementation of the Water Act.[5] He averred that among the many issues facing the people of England, water was not 'hot'. There are a few instances of serious water pollution and even where they exist they are less important than the environment within the urban centers. The major task was to be in establishing the new organizations and in seeing to it that the responsibilities of the water industry to the public were met. Such a posture would not challenge the government in its desire to maintain control over a water industry with ten centers of power.

An issue at the constant boil is the matter of accountability of the WAs to the local authorities and to their customers. The NWC, with no local authority representation, was not inclined to be sympathetic to such a view. This was reflected by Stott:[3] 'It is interesting that anyone should suggest local government was an effective forum on these issues. A look at the Severn Trent "Domesday Book", the water quality report which elaborates on the poor inheritance from the local authorities [discussed in Chapter 8], is enough tc damn the local forum forever.'

The NWC itself has not done much to wrestle with the matter of accountability, particularly with regard to the public response to the increased WA charges. Nor has the government. These battles were left almost entirely to the individual WAs. Nevertheless, the NWC began to play a bigger role than had originally been anticipated.

Whether or not Stott believed that a low profile was initially necessary, it became clear that his initiatives grew stronger than might have been suggested by his stance during the shadow existence of the NWC. One measure of the enlarged view of the NWC's role was the selection of David Walker as assistant director-general. An engineer with experience in the water industry, he came from the Electricity Council where he was responsible for advice on pricing policy. That Stott saw an enlarged role for NWC seemed clear from his contention in September 1975 that national water resource planning can no longer be left to a body without executive functions.[6] That this became the government's view is clear from the recommendations for a stronger National Water Authority following its review of the industry as discussed in Chapter 11. Another measure of NWC initiative was in the mounting of the first National Water Conference at Bournemouth in March 1975, when there was little enthusiasm for it within the WAs or government.[7]

THE WATER SPACE AMENITY COMMISSION

An important additional dimension on the water scene brought about by the Water Act 1973 was the provision for the WAs to have a special duty in the discharge of their functions with regard to:

1.   the preservation of natural beauty,
2.   conservation of flora, fauna and geological and physiographical features of special interest,

3.   protection of buildings and other objects of architectural or historic interest, and
4.   preservation of public rights of access.

In addition, the WAs are empowered to take steps to secure the use of water, and land associated with water, for recreation. While the Countryside Commission, the Nature Conservancy and the Sports Council all have an interest in the amenity value of water, the Act provided for the establishment of a Water Space Amenity Commission with the task of advising the Secretary of State on the formulation, promotion and execution of national water policy for recreation and amenity in England, and to advise the NWC and the WAs on their duties as regards recreation and amenity. In Wales, these responsibilities fall to the Welsh National Water Development Authority.

The Commission is made up of ten appointed members from the major amenity societies and statutory bodies in England, together with the ten chairmen of the WAs, with the chairman of the Commission being a member of the NWC. The headquarters of the WSAC are located in the NWC headquarters, and the Commission publishes a new quarterly, *Water Space*, devoted to the recreational uses of the waters of England.

Fears were expressed that, with the primary concern of the WAs for water supply, the recreational uses of water, other than for fishing, would get little attention.[8] Initially, recreation had not enjoyed priority, not because it posed a threat to water supply, but because the WAs had inherited many problems requiring immediate solution. Not the least of these was the need to get many poorly operated sewage treatment plants into good operational order which would improve opportunities for recreation.

The WSAC's greatest test will be its ability to persuade the WAs to make their water space available for recreation by the greatest number of people, which requires a policy other than merely letting facilities to private sailing and angling clubs. The general public is still not assured that reservoirs enhance recreational opportunities, because reservoirs eliminate some facilities for hiking, nature study and the like on the lands they flood.

THE WATER RESEARCH CENTRE

The Water Act 1973 addresses research in only two ways: 'Each water authority shall make arrangements for the carrying out of research and related activities (whether by the authority or by others) in respect of matters affecting the authority's functions, and in particular, . . . may make arrangements for the carrying out of research and related activities in respect of such matters by subscribing or otherwise financially contributing to an organization formed for that purpose'; and 'It shall be the duty of the [National Water] Council to promote and assist the efficient performance by water authorities of ... their functions relating to research ...'

'The organization formed for that purpose' is the Water Research Centre which comprises what previously had been the Water Research Association, the Water Pollution Research Laboratory, and the technology division of the Water Resources Board. The organization of the Water Research Centre follows on the structure of the Water Research Association, typical of industrial research associations in the United Kingdom. This type of organization is made up of members who contribute funds on the basis of some formula, and the government contributes as well. Such organizations do contract research for members and others. In addition to the WAs, the WRC serves Scotland, Northern Ireland, the private sector and other members, such as the University of North Carolina at Chapel Hill. By takeover of existing activities, principally in the Water Research Association laboratories at Medmenham and the Water Pollution Research Laboratory at Stevenage, the WRC began business with a total staff of some 435 and a budget of approximately £4·0 million of which members provided £2·5 million and the DoE supplied £1·5 million by making contracts for specific projects and by making selective grants for research in areas in which the DoE and the water industry have a common interest.

The original structure called for the WRC to be governed by a Council drawn from the members, while a Research Advisory Committee composed largely of professionals and scientists was to advise on the formulation and conduct of the research program.

The new WRC ran into early difficulties, stemming in part from the London authorities' historic coolness towards national research organizations and in part from the WAs' reluctance to contribute to an organization over whose performance they would have little control. The London Metropolitan Water Board had not been a member of the Water Research Association. The large London organizations believed that they could do their own research and that their research would be better attuned to their needs than that which could be done on their behalf by centralized research organizations. Accordingly, when the time came for joining the WRC, and payment of their membership fee for the first year, £752 000, the Thames Water Authority balked.

A compromise settlement was reached well into the first year of operation. The first year's payment by the TWA was reduced, although thereafter they would pay according to the formula for the WAs based on revenue operating expenditure. Other members would have other membership formulae or minima.

The key element in the TWA compromise was a revision in the method of administration of the WRC. The Water Research Council was not much changed, being made up of 27 members including ten from the WAs, five from the DoE, two from the water companies, two from Scotland, and one from Ireland, one from industry and so on. There continued to be a Research Advisory Committee with some 30 members including representatives of all the WAs. The major change was the creation of a strong 13-member management committee chaired by J. C. Brown, chairman of the Yorkshire Water Authority, made up of members of four of the WAs, a member of the NWC, a representative of the DoE, and representatives from Scotland and Northern Ireland.

In addition, there is a Water Authorities Panel with each of the ten WAs represented by technical personnel and including Scotland and Northern Ireland, with Stott as chairman. The WAs believe that this new structure will give the WAs considerably tighter control over the operation of the WRC.

That the WAs have had the greatest stake in the WRC though providing the bulk of the funds and having the greatest need for the results of research, left little doubt that the Water Authorities Panel would take the lead in defining the role of the WRC, which it did.[9]

The priorities for research identified by the panel demonstrated a somewhat different emphasis from that previously pursued by the WRC as the WAs explored their own needs with a shift from technological research to emphasis on problem-solving and dissemination of information. 'Pure' research and the role of universities in the research effort are virtually ignored. And without a strong relationship with universities, the potential for recruiting highly qualified personnel will be neglected. Actually, the individual WAs are actively involving universities in their programs, the Southern Water Authority having arrangements with four institutions in their second year of operation.

A small group devoted to operations research and the economics of water had been formed in the Water Research Association. In general, however, the research efforts of the WRC can be expected to be primarily in the area of so-called 'wet' research. It is not foreseen that the WRC will expand to include economic and institutional research on a large scale. Such research is important for the water industry at this crucial juncture in its history and perhaps it will be established under one of the other central units, although no particular locus appears to be promising. In any event, as discussed in Chapter 11, the government's review of the water industry recommended bringing the WRC into the projected NWA.

THE CENTRAL WATER PLANNING UNIT

While not specifically called for in the Water Act, the DoE established, under its own aegis, a Central Water Planning Unit. Of all of the elements of the reorganization, the role and function of this CWPU is the most difficult to understand. The responsibility of the CWPU is the national planning needed over and above regional plans for multipurpose river basin water management, including:

1. endorsement of programs of the WAs to assure that they are compatible with one another, particularly considering alternative trans-regional schemes, and
2. formation of a general policy to provide framework for regional and national planning such as inter-regional schemes, and the several approaches to augmenting water resources.

The CWPU was to be responsible for advising the Ministers and the WAs. The provision of this advice has been and probably always will be the subject of much controversy as the NWC is also responsible for providing advice to government. At any rate, the ambivalence of the position of this agency was recognized by government and, as noted in Chapter 11, following its review of the water industry the recommendation was that the CWPU be encompassed in the projected NWA.

THE WATER DATA UNIT

Another central unit not called for in the Water Act is the Water Data Unit in the DoE, which takes over responsibilities of the WRB for hydrologic data; of the Directorate General of Water Engineering for water quality and river pollution surveys; and of the DoE for data from local authorities and water undertakings, such as surveys of expenditures, construction. In addition, the WDU will collect other data as may be necessary. The WDU is to provide information on a national basis for the WAs and the government, and take on such tasks as:

1. advising on the standardization of data collection among the WAs,
2. ensuring that the WAs include in their own data-gathering systems the data required for national needs,
3. collecting and processing national information into a form suitable for each national body,
4. publishing national data and providing an information service,
5. advising the WAs, the NWC and other central authorities on data collection and processing methods, and
6. advising the WRC on research needs for information purposes.

The government's review contained no comment about the future of this agency, as presumably the collection and dissemination of data is a useful and non-threatening service.

CONCLUSION

The fragmentation of responsibility at the center amongst the DoE, the NWC, the WSAC, the WRC, the CWPU, and the WDU does not augur well for the future. If changes are to be made by the government after the first two years of operation, it may very well be in the direction of a reordering of the central units for the purpose of strengthening them, perhaps under a stronger National Water Council as was in fact recommended by government in its consultative document *Review of the Water Industry in England and Wales*, 1976, which is discussed in Chapter 11.

CHAPTER 8

Water Quality Management

The pressure for reorganization centered in good measure on problems of water quality management: inflexibility and conflicts in the development of new water supply sources; the promotion of large schemes that would make optimal use of all resources; and most importantly, the inadequate level of wastewater treatment resulting in the pollution of rivers, estuaries, and the sea. Of the six items of policy in Section 1 of the Water Act 1973, only one, concerned with navigation, is little related to water quality. This chapter deals with the management of the quality of water supplies and water pollution control, including water reuse, and the significance of the Control of Pollution Act 1974.

WATER SUPPLY DEVELOPMENT IN BRITAIN

The earliest water supplies in Britain were organized by the more important towns, generally drawing upon underground sources or nearby surface sources. By the mid-19th century, however, only few communities possessed water supply systems and even in these, only a small portion of the population had piped services into their homes, which were generally restricted to a small section of the town—the commercial and high quality residential areas.

The 'Great Sanitary Awakening' of the mid-19th century saw full appreciation of the hygienic significance of water supplies brought to the attention of civic authorities through the pioneering epidemiological work of Dr John Snow in associating cholera with water supply from a contaminated well, the Broad Street pump, and from the Thames. Sir Edwin Chadwick found that only six of some 50 towns had an adequate water supply and only one a proper drainage system.[1]

The private water companies serving London were prohibited from drawing water from the tidal Thames and were obliged to go above Teddington Weir by the Metropolis Water Act of 1852. At about the same time the Manchester Corporation initiated the first of the large upland impounding schemes with the Manchester and Salford Waterworks Company being authorized to construct impounding works on the River

Ethrow some 15 miles east of Manchester, where over a period of some 30 years seven reservoirs were constructed to bring water to Manchester through gravity aqueducts.[2]

The trend of development of upland sources of high quality water for public water supplies became widespread during the latter part of the 19th century. With the industrial rise of Lancashire and Yorkshire, the Pennines became the first major upland source to be exploited. These moorlands have retained their importance for water supply to the present although, as demands grew, cities began to look further afield as nearby dam and reservoir sites had been taken for earlier development of water supply, railroads, industry, or housing. In the 1880s the Liverpool Corporation obtained a large supply from the Vyrnwy Valley, North Wales; 10 years later Birmingham began reservoir construction in the Elan Valley in Central Wales, 75 miles to the west. When Manchester's demand exceeded the capacity of its Elthrow River valley supply, parliament in 1879 authorized the use of the natural storage afforded by Lake Thirlmere, some 100 miles north in the Lake District.

These schemes had much in common. They were dependent upon direct supply reservoirs capable of storing ample supplies of soft high-quality water draining from extensive catchment areas which could be conveyed by gravity to treatment works on the outskirts of the communities they served. To safeguard the purity of the supplies, most of the authorities purchased the gathering grounds around the reservoirs and thereby prohibited public access to large areas of upland Britain. Farming in these catchment areas was strictly controlled to the extent that many hill farms were eventually abandoned. Later on, in the mid-20th century, public access was authorized on these reservoirs under controlled conditions to permit some recreational activity.

Even the rural areas profited from this type of development as aqueducts carried over long distances were permitted to be tapped for use by smaller communities along the way. Regional endeavors were exemplified by the Derwent Valley Water Board, created in 1899 by the amalgamation of five constituent local authorities, Leicester, Sheffield, Derby, Nottingham, and Derbyshire County, to permit joint development of a large upland resource in the Derwent to provide supplies over a large area of the northern midlands.

Water supply for London—a brief history

London was virtually alone among the major urban areas throughout England and Wales that departed from this policy of developing upland supplies.[3] The Thames, ' the noblest river in Europe', has supplied London with water from 1581 until now.

From 1827, when a concern for water quality in the Thames resulted in the creation of a Royal Commission, to 1903 when the several privately owned water companies serving London were incorporated into the Metropolitan Water Board, frequent studies were made of water supply for London.[4] Despite eloquent proposals for developing sources in Wales for London,† the so-called 'progressive' scheme was adopted by the MWB and remains the basis for water supply for London to this day. This scheme depends upon abstractions from the Thames above Teddington Weir just above London, with regulating storage in large off-channel reservoirs prior to treatment.

While the Thames has gained international renown with the return of salmon and rainbow trout to the estuary, the quality in the non-tidal Thames used as a source of water supply has become more critical. Levels of nitrogen at the London intakes have begun to approach the limits set by the World Health Organization, and concentrations of phosphorous have grown from 0·3 mg/l in 1960 to 1·0 mg/l in 1972.[5] While phosphorous itself is not hazardous, it is an indicator of high levels of wastewaters discharged into the rivers with comcomitant concentrations of other contaminants.

POTABLE WATER QUALITY STANDARDS

Legally enforceable standards of water purity have been adopted in many countries and that such standards should be used in Britain has been suggested from time to time. River authorities in particular had had occasion to refer to foreign water quality standards and criteria guidelines and found them to be useful. 'In this country the absence of formal standards laid down by regulation has been regarded as being advantageous. The results of new research indicating the significance of the concentration of any particular constituent in water can be considered and implemented without having to wait for the revision of a Statutory Instrument. Furthermore the circumstances of the individual supplies may sometimes have to be taken into account in determining a practical solution. There is inevitably a large arbitrary element in the setting of any standards since the determination of border line cases between the concentrations which have no effect, those which might have an effect and those which have a demonstrable effect is a difficult medical problem and adequate evidence is frequently not available.'[6]

† 'No one acting for himself personally with regard to a water supply to his country house would allow the small difference in cost to determine whether he should go to a pure spring or to a stream into which some other house drained. ... It appears to us that in coming to a decision upon so vital and irrevocable a question as additional water supply of water to London for a long series of years, the safe course would be to act for future generations as our instinctive and deeply rooted feelings in favor of pure water would lead us to act for ourselves.'

—From an engineering report by Sir Benjamin Baker and George F. Deacon to the London County Council in 1897.

Because of the difficulties associated with deciding upon appropriate levels to be included in publications of standards, the practice in the United Kingdom has been to rely on the description of 'wholesome'.

'While the word "wholesome" is not defined in the Water Act it has been taken to imply clear, palatable and safe and the final decision as to the wholesomeness of any particular water supply would rest ultimately in the hands of a court of law. In practice, however, ... authorities have utilized published works of reference including in particular the World Health Organization's European Water Standards ...'[6]

Previous usage and experience have shown this to be a satisfactory solution for acutely toxic contaminants when linked with the generally applied maxim that '... the best quality source of water should be used in preference to any other, based on the known histories of the sources of the water, their analyses and lack of risk of possible contaminations'.[6] However, an easy selection of supply is seldom possible because of the limited availability of unpolluted sources.

To provide guidance as to bacteriological quality, the Departments of the Environment and of Health and Social Services have recommended standards for micro-organisms in potable waters. Some WAs use these standards while others have adopted a somewhat different approach to achieving the same level of quality.

International standards for chemical quality are generally used as guidelines, with some WAs using the recommendations of the European Committee of the World Health Organization which take the form of levels of impurities above which difficulties attributable to water quality may arise. With lead, arsenic, selenium, cadmium and cyanide, absolute tolerance limits are defined. Other standards are adopted only if they appear to be appropriate in specific situations and ignored if they appear to be of little health consequence. Each WA is free to use these standards as guides as it wishes and to apply them differently within their own areas.

The problem of setting standards for organic chemical contaminants is not nearly so tractable, as the uncertainty as to threshold value for many of them has not been resolved. The polynuclear aromatic hydrocarbons (PAH) offer one example for which the WHO has established a maximum recommended concentration of $0\cdot2\,\mu g/l$, although '... the slightest exposure to carcinogenic PAH will cause irreversible effects (on health) and that, unlike some toxic agents, no safe level exists.'[7] In the waters of the polluted Trent, PAH values were above $0\cdot5\,\mu g/l$, with tributaries containing more than $2\,\mu g/l$, while the cleaner Severn showed substantially lower concentrations.[8] Fortunately, PAH is associated with suspended solids and much of its is readily removed in water treatment, which is not the case with many other synthetic organic chemicals.

One tactic often used is the dilution of water that fails to meet standards with water from a purer source so that the final distributed product meets the standards. As the areas served by a single authority become larger, such flexibility becomes greater.

WATER SUPPLY PLANNING IN BRITAIN

As the most easily developed upland sources of water were developed, and as demands increased, several options were available to water purveyors in Britain. Many of the early upland developments did not require full development of a watershed, so that the sizes and numbers of reservoirs on some upland catchments were increased to try to meet the need. A second course of action has been the development of ground waters, although for large centers of populations, these cannot be expected to meet more than a small portion of the total requirement. The most obvious source of additional water is from the lower reaches of rivers, where the catchment areas are large and the minimum flows are great. Where pollution might be heavy, consideration has been given to upland storage for augmenting low flows and diluting pollutants.

Most water supply engineers have continued to show a decided preference for either ground waters or further development of upland supplies, particularly in the densely populated industrial areas of the north, the midlands, and south Wales. All together, three-quarters of all upland waters so collected are used away from the source area. The regrouping of water supplies promoted this approach, as large undertakings can better afford to go longer distances to acquire good sources of water supply.

However, in time, uplands resources inevitably became more limited, with fewer convenient sites for reservoirs and greater opposition by environmentalists because of the loss of land that would result from reservoir construction, and because of the stringent limitations on the use of the reservoirs themselves for recreation. This led to the consideration of downstream abstractions, with the obvious advantage offered by using the rivers instead of expensive pipelines for aqueducts. Also, by abstracting water downstream, the much larger catchment areas permit the same yield to be developed with smaller reservoirs that would be required at an upstream location providing a direct supply.

With the passage of the Water Resources Act 1963 and under the general leadership of the Water Resources Board, such river regulation approaches have tended to become the major philosophy of water conservation and development. In the meanwhile, one of the first British rivers to be regulated was the Dee which drains part of northeast Wales before reaching the Irish sea.

The water resources of the River Dee were first utilized on a large scale by the construction of a direct supply reservoir in 1907. The next development, in 1950, involved abstractions downstream in the river in return for financial assistance in construction of Lake Bala upstream as a regulating reservoir, as this would improve low flow conditions sufficient to support the proposed downstream withdrawals.[9]

The River Tees in northeast England was the second river to be regulated. Initially this had been developed solely for water supply by the Tees Valley and Cleveland Water Board around the beginning of the century.[10] By 1965 the Water Board delivered 77 percent of its total supply to industry. When it became apparent that the Board would be unable to meet demands with conventional water supplies, a separate industrial water supply was developed by pumping raw water from the lower reaches of the river. Abstractions could only be supported by river regulation, and Balderhead Reservoir, initially proposed as a direct supply reservoir, was operated on a river regulating basis. For direct supply it would have provided 12 million gallons per day (mgd) ($55\,000\,m^3$ per day) but operated to improve the reliable flow in the lower Tees it provided an increment of 24 mgd ($110\,000\,m^3$ per day).

The efficacy of river regulation for sustaining flows for industrial water supply abstractions downstream cannot be gainsaid. But such a strategy for potable water supply nationwide deserves more detailed examination.

THE WATER RESOURCES BOARD STRATEGY

As its culminating action, the Water Resources Board issued its report *Water Resources in England and Wales*.[11] Based upon three earlier regional reports and other related studies, this report on a water strategy for the remainder of the 20th century is inextricably woven into the reorganization. While largely prepared prior to an appreciation that major reorganization would take place, the final report recognized that the Water Act 1973 would, in fact, become law. Accordingly, sections of the report concerning water quality management and the water reorganization are dealt with here in some depth.

The WRB recognized that there is no intrinsic shortage of water in England and Wales. The total annual rainfall is ample to meet all demands for the foreseeable future, taking into account problems arising from the uneven distribution of available water over both time and place, and irregularity between wet and dry seasons requiring use of some type of storage. The imbalance of resources between one part of the country and another makes it sensible to provide for the transfer of water from areas of surplus to areas of shortage. The report was mainly concerned with parts of the country that cannot easily be served by the additional development of local sources.

The WRB adopted the general principle that storage, either on the surface or underground, would be used to regulate rivers wherever practical and the rivers used to convey water to where it is needed.

The 'Summary and Recommendations' of the report as they bear upon the reorganization, are presented below:

'Water can be stored in inland surface reservoirs, in estuaries and underground in aquifers.

'Inland reservoirs are the most important category of storage. There are advantages in using reservoirs to regulate rivers rather than for direct supply by aqueduct. There is scope for enlarging some existing reservoirs and converting them to use for river regulation.

'The effective and economical management of resources will require sources to be developed and operated in an increasingly integrated way. This will involve the use of rivers for conveying water from sources to demand, the regulation of rivers, transfers between river basins, the combined use of different types of source, the artificial recharge of aquifers and the successive use and reuse of water and effluents.

'The quality of water in rivers used for potable supplies must be maintained and in many cases improved. Water authorities will need to make decisions on reuse of effluents and on the treatment necessary for discharges into and abstractions from rivers and the quality standards required. The reorganization of water services will provide the framework within which effluent treatment and disposal can be planned to produce the maximum benefit to water quality.

'Over the longer term there is a range of possibilities between virtually complete dependence on inland sources at one extreme and virtually complete dependence on estuary storage at the other; and between exploiting fully the advantages of an integrated strategy of development and concentrating on the self-sufficiency of Regional Water Authority areas.

'We rule out a strategy based on regional self-sufficiency because of the proliferation of sources required, the high costs and the lack of flexibility afforded in deploying sources to demands.

'The solution we favour is an integrated strategy based on a mixture of inland and estuary sources. It makes the maximum possible use of groundwater; and includes the enlargement and redeployment of existing sources. It is based on flexible allocation of sources to demands, and exploits the advantages of moving water from the wetter areas to the dryer by river to river transfer. The reclamation of the river Trent and the artificial recharge of the London Basin could contribute if they prove capable of development on the necessary scale.

'We recommend investigation of a number of other projects from which choices may be made later. This includes in particular further research and development on the reclamation of the river Trent as a source of *potable* water ...' (Italics mine.)

In early 1974, the government supported the WRB in its assessment that the giant £80 million Dee estuary scheme should be built by the end of the 1980s. The Secretary of State for Wales, Peter Thomas, advised the House of Commons that, while the scheme was not needed until the 1980s, there was a 'strong probability' that it would have a significant role to play in the water resources of the country in the early 1990s, and that planning should therefore forthwith proceed.[12] Of the estuaries considered for water supply, the Dee is probably the least polluted and least likely to be polluted.

Initiated long before the reorganization and before the release of the WRB strategy statement, the Kielder water scheme in Northumbria represents in essence the strategy that is being recommended. This project, already under construction, incorporates the largest man-made reservoir in the country at the upper end of the river Tyne. Water from this reservoir will be released into the river and withdrawn at a lower point in the river Tyne for transfer to the upstream end of two other rivers to the south—the rivers Wear and Tees.[13] While the general water quality in the area would benefit from the scheme, the existing water quality at the proposed points of major abstractions is not now unsatisfactory.

National Water Council review of the Water Resources Board strategy

One of the early charges to the National Water Council was review of the WRB strategy.[14] The WAs and the NWC were pleased to have the WRB report as a basis for their initial consideration of water resource development in England and Wales. Their first response acknowledged that the report represented the first overall assessment of water resources for most of England and Wales and it provided a welcome appraisal of a wide range of technological alternatives. However, the NWC pointed out that the report was mainly concerned with bulk water storage and transmission and not the whole of the water supply for which the new WAs are now responsible. 'Important aspects of river quality, local distribution, water utilization and effluent treatment were touched upon only indirectly by the WRB.'

The NWC and the WAs furthermore do not assume that past trends of water use will necessarily continue and they are considering the possible effect of pricing policies on water demands. Also, better forecasts of direct industrial demand require more detailed analysis on each river than the WRB was able to undertake.

The effect on industrial water use of increased charges for metered water supplies and for direct abstractions from rivers (recognizing that the charges for direct abstractions have up to now been only trivial), and the indirect effect of more rigorous effluent standards and trade effluent charges, are being kept under review.

The NWC and the WAs endorsed the following conclusions of the report:

'(a) There are advantages to using reservoirs to regulate rivers rather than for direct supply by aqueduct provided the quality of water in rivers can be maintained or improved.

'(b) Groundwater resources may be deployed more effectively by using them intermittently for river regulation or in conjunctive use with surface water sources.

'(c) Estuary storage is best provided by embanked reservoirs filled by pumping from rivers...

'(d) The use of sea water by distillation or other methods of desalination is unlikely to contribute substantially to water resources in this century.

'(e) The costs involved make any large scale transfer of water from Scotland into England too expensive for present consideration.'

However, they added this important proviso: 'Although the NWC and the WAs find it persuasive that reservoirs should be used for river regulation as opposed to direct supply, they emphasize that this must be subject to the quality considerations discussed below.' These quality considerations are, *inter alia*, the following:

In adopting the principle that storage should be used to regulate rivers and that rivers be used to convey water where it is needed, the WRB report emphasized that this strategy will only be practicable if the quality of waters in these rivers is satisfactory. 'At present, the safety of British water supplies is second to none, and the WAs intend to make sure that this remains the case.

'Present treatment practices enable public supplies to be provided with virtual certainty that they are free from harmful bacteria ... While maintaining these standards, WAs are also concerned to avoid the presence of substances which could be harmful in water abstracted for treatment. As explained in the First and Second Reports of the Steering Committee on Water Quality, further work is needed in this field...

'The NWC and the WAs acknowledge that the WRB strategy of increased river use is persuasive. It ... depends on certain working provisos e.g. adequate investment in treatment works, knowledge of harmful substances, rigorous control of effluents into rivers used for potable supplies and protection against accidental contamination. WAs will now wish to examine this strategy in their own particular areas and may wish to provide special protection for rivers used for potable supplies...

'They have also investigated, and will continue to investigate, the possibility of developing previously polluted rivers (such as the Trent) for water supplies, but this presently appears more likely for industrial use than for potable supplies.'

The reorganization has given new scope to considerations of water strategy. For example, the prospects for integrating present supplies within the new WA area will enable certain schemes to be deferred; increased attention to water demand management on the part of the WAs will enable better use to be made of existing resources; and unless water use *per capita* grows faster than previously expected, and subject to the changing pattern of industrial water use (possibly influenced by charging schemes), the reduction in demand may affect the choice of planning strategies.

The WAs themselves face difficult decisions in determining priorities. Heavy capital expenditures are required for servicing new housing developments and for essential replacements to existing facilities. Increased use of rivers for potable water supplies is not feasible if sufficient capital is not available for adequate upstream effluent treatment. Restraints on capital expenditure and the impact of increasing householders' bills for water services may affect the potential for using downstream sources for potable water supplies.

The NWC document included the critiques prepared by the WAs. Typical is that of the Severn Trent Water Authority: 'We are also specifically concerned, as our predecessors were not, with the balance of expenditure between the various sectors of water management and this will have a bearing on the use we make of the Board's advice'.

A critique of the Water Resources Board strategy

The proposed water strategy is discussed at length not because it is inherently an interesting problem, which it is, but because alternative strategies, not adequately considered by the WRB, show greater promise because of the reorganization. Many elements of the national water strategy might have been considered differently had there been full appreciation of the nature of the reorganization, where each of the new WAs would have complete responsibility not only for water supply but for water quality management as well.

The following critique of WRB strategy will have been anticipated by the reader of Chapter 2, who will have discerned criticism of the WRB's failure to address water quality adequately. In its summary report, the WRB stated:[15] 'The effluent from a sewage works or a factory may help to meet a demand for additional water farther downstream, as already happens, notably on the Thames. But this is only possible if the quantity [*sic*, quality] of the effluent is high enough to enable the river water to be treated to produce drinking water.'

The WRB strategy rests largely upon the economies that would result from having smaller reservoirs and using rivers as aqueducts under the assumption that the downstream quality problems are tractable. England and Wales are to follow London. Current technology is and has been for years adequate to render polluted water bacteriologically safe and to monitor that safety.[16] However, the chemical revolution of the mid-20th century no longer permits us to be sanguine that a water supply is indeed wholesome if it is drawn from a polluted source.

Hundreds of new chemical compounds are being formulated and introduced into the environment annually. Some 469 organic chemicals have been reported in freshwater of which 66 were identified, with some of these having been shown to be carcinogenic, teratogenic, or mutagenic, at least in laboratory animals.[17] Of 120 compounds examined for carcinogenicity in animals, 22·5 percent were positive; of 32 compounds examined for teratogenicity, 62·5 percent were positive; of 29 compounds examined for mutagenicity, all were found to be positive. The Genetic Study Section of the US National Institutes of Health pointed out that special attention should be given to low concentrations of mutagenic compounds that are brought into contact with large populations because the total of deleterious mutations that could be induced in the whole population over an extended period of time, as would be the case with public water supply, might be significant.[18]

In a comprehensive paper on cancer hazards from water pollutants, Hueper stated:[19] 'It is obvious that with the rapidly increasing urbanization and industrialization of the country and the greatly increased demand placed on the present resources of water from lakes, rivers and underground reservoirs, the danger of cancer hazards from the consumption of contaminated drinking water will grow considerably within the foreseeable future'.

Unfortunately, the significance of the long term ingestion of low levels of pollutants of water is difficult to ascertain because their effects are insidious and are often screened by aging or other chronic diseases with similar effects. However, some studies have been made and more are currently under way. About 15 percent of London's population obtain an unpolluted water supply from Kent chalks underground, while the rest of London obtains water from the highly polluted Thames and Lea. In 1947, Stocks noted that people in southeast London had lower cancer mortalities than those who obtained their water supplies from the rivers.[20] And this was prior to the revolution in synthetic organic chemicals. More extensive studies of London are now under way (1977).

Studies made in Holland show that municipalities receiving their drinking water from polluted rivers had higher cancer death rates than those taking their water from pure underground sources and that those served by public systems had lower cancer death rates than others.[21]

Data collected in 1950 by the US Public Health Service revealed that the bladder cancer rate in New Orleans, which draws its water supply from the lower end of the Mississippi River which drains much of the United States, was three times higher than in other similar cities.[22] A more recent and somewhat more sophisticated epidemiological study was conducted in 1974 by Talbot and Harris who analyzed the relationship between cancer mortality and water supply in the parishes (counties) of Louisiana.[23] They concluded that there is a correlation between the source of water and cancer death rates and that a parish that switched from 100 percent river water to 100 percent groundwater would reduce its cancer death rate in white males by 33 per 100 000 population. These studies are not considered conclusive, and certainly not sufficiently definitive to require that New Orleans take immediate measures to modify either its source of water or its method of treatment.

However, whether or not such epidemiological data on health effects are developed within the next several decades, when the chemical revolution can expect to have its greatest impact, prudence dictates that these concerns be placed in the balance in weighing the options available in selecting a water management strategy that will influence structures to be built over the next 25 years and which will still be operating a century hence.

When it was proposed that there might indeed be chemicals in the wastewaters discharged into the Thames, the Metropolitan Water Board responded as follows:[24]

'There is no evidence of increase in traces of toxic metals or organic pollutants in the Thames river...

'The laboratories of the Metropolitan Water Board carry out special comprehensive analytical surveys of the water abstracted for London's water supply to measure the level of metallic and organic pollutants. And as far as organic matter is concerned, looking back at past records, there has been no significant increase during the past 100 years.'

The amount of organic chemicals in the water drawn from the Thames and Lea may have decreased, but the number and diversity of chemicals present *must* have increased. A strategy that is predicated upon a policy of using rivers for aqueducts seems to lack the prudence necessary to assure that waters drawn from protected sources will continue to be protected as they flow down a river that receives wastewaters.

The Steering Committee on Water Quality in its first report in 1971 put the problem of the non-degradable organics in water courses succinctly:[25] 'A portion, at least, of this organic matter is not removed ... during passage down the river or treatment of the water before supply. Little is known either about the composition of these persistent residues or of any effect they may have upon the health of the population consuming the water.'

This was followed up in the committee's second report:[6] 'We need more information on the occurrence and identification of specific organic groups which might be physiologically significant ... Because of the long periods of time involved in this study approaching the life span of a human being, it is difficult to be able to state categorically that the presence of such a concentration of a particular substance might be harmful. As the quality of life improves ... epidemiological studies ... can demonstrate possible trends in certain areas which might be associated with the known presence of some substance in the water supply of the area.'

The committee concluded: '*Although the securing of suitable sources of water relatively free from pollution as the raw water sources for potable supply is of prime importance*, in considering guidelines of water quality due regard must be made also to other users of water resources.' (Italics theirs.)

Hugh Fish, director of scientific services for the Thames Water Authority stated:[26] 'It is becoming increasingly difficult for any water authority drawing supplies from a developed river to demonstrate convincingly that the supplies it delivers are wholly safe in chemical quality for long-term consumption.'

In the keynote paper of the NWC's first National Water Conference, J. C. Brown, chairman of the Yorkshire Water Authority, voiced concern for a strategy that depended on polluted sources for water supply:[27]

'The Thames catchment area has been protected by national legislation, augmented by local bye-laws which had been effectively administered. . . . major industry which had previously settled around the lower regions of the Thames moved north to the coal fields and, in order to maintain and improve the Thames water cycle, new industries with different effluent problems have not since been encouraged to settle there without stringent safeguards. . .

'Until recently, [the north] was so rich in water that our predecessors were able to operate simple systems with no recycling. Numerous reservoirs were built in the Pennines to supply raw water for drinking purposes and industrial use and the lower stretches of many rivers were used as the conduits for liquid effluents of industry, humanity, and agriculture to the sea . . . Pressure to protect the environment has resulted in public opinion hardening against building further reservoirs and in calls for improvement in the quality of grossly polluted sections of our rivers . . . How large are these problems and can they be resolved?'

Brown pointed out the one major problem which is perhaps sufficient to give pause in adopting, without further examination, the proposed strategy: '[The] combined system of oxidation at a sewerage works, followed by filtration and chlorination in the waterworks, may have been good enough for the recycling of water 10 or 20 years ago, but is it good enough today? I very much doubt it.

'. . . many new organic based products are now available and are widely used . . . on a scale unimaginable before the war. Are all the residues from these products treatable by the classical sewage works biological system, or do some components pass through unchanged? If they do pass through unchanged, do they also pass through the treatment works unchanged or, worse still, are they changed by the chlorination process into compounds with physiological significance? Furthermore, are there any synergistic effects when two or more are mixed in our rivers?

'Can we continue to expand still further recycling operations, rather than draw more upon fresh waters, until we have a better understanding of what might be happening? . . .'

At the same session, Frank Shaw, director of finance of the Severn Trent Water Authority, also made reference to this problem: 'Mr Brown is rightly concerned about the longer term health hazards that may possibly arise from the consumption of recycled water. Is it not time that we looked much more closely at the economic aspects of obtaining a far greater proportion of our water supplies from new reservoirs in the west of the country? I have never tried to put money values to this concept but is it really so unrealistic to store much water in the mountains and pipe it to consumption points throughout the country rather than use our rivers for conveyance? I wonder whether from the aspects of both health and costs it might not be a more attractive proposition than raising the standards of our rivers to a level where we can recycle water for potable purposes.'[28] Rydz, formerly of the WRB and director of resource planning for the STWA responded that direct supplies would be twice as costly. Shaw did not know which strategy was in fact cheaper, but studies were required with regard to both cost and health significance. Colin Spens, past-president of the Institution of Water Engineers and Scientists called into question the philosophy of the reuse of water in rivers for potable supplies.[29]

If the strategy is to use rivers as aqueducts, with waters drawn for drinking from their lower reaches, then all upstream wastewaters will need to be treated to an exceedingly high degree to permit the water supply facilities a reasonable chance of removing the residual synthetic chemicals to render the drinking water safe. If, on the other hand, waters for potable supply are drawn only from protected upstream sources or from underground, wastewater treatment requirements will not be nearly so rigorous.

This approach is supported by a new thrust in water quality management:[30] 'The NWC and the WAs are working together on a proposal to scrap the principle that all rivers should be improved as far as possible. Its replacement would be a scheme whereby river pollution control would be carried out on the basis of the intended use of the river.'

The impetus for this changed approach came from the top Government official in the water field, Trevor Hughes, Under Secretary and chief water engineer in the DoE, who challenged each WA to consider its objectives, river by river, and the uses to which the river is put.[31] 'What quality of water is necessary for these purposes? . . . What strategy would make the best use of the resources available?'

One outcome of this challenge was the creation of a WA working party to address these questions. The key principle that would guide the new strategy was stated by David Walker, assistant director general of the NWC:[32] '. . . consent conditions should be related to the use to which a river is put'. Thus, if a river is used in its lower reaches as a source of water for potable purposes, the consent conditions would require much greater expenditures for wastewater treatment than if water supplies are abstracted from upstream impoundments and the use of the river as an aqueduct may not be economical. In any event, this approach to pollution control opens options for water management that were not considered by the WRB in developing its national strategy.

Monitoring

A strategy depending upon high river water quality in turn depends on the quality of the monitoring program. The DoE initiated a comprehensive survey of environmental monitoring programs before reorganization, when efforts at monitoring were limited both in frequency and in location, as well as in the nature of the parameters studied.[33] Some attention is being given to the identification of heavy metals and organo-chlorines, pesticides and PCBs, but responsibility for examination for these substances has been fragmented.

Except for investigation into the relationship between cardiovascular disease and water hardness, few epidemiological studies on the health effects of contaminants in water supplies have been mounted. Monitoring of public water supplies should be linked by the WAs to the work of health agencies to help identify relationships between water supplies and health. While some liaison has existed in the past in connection with bacteriological monitoring, this has not at all been adequate on the chemical side.

The low priority given to health effects was revealed in a symposium on 'Pollution Detection' organized by the Society for Water Treatment and Examination.[34] The emphasis was on more effective methods for determining the classical pollution parameters with virtually no mention of monitoring for protecting health when polluted waters are used for potable purposes. The most hopeful sign of increasing attention to this problem is in the appointment by the larger WAs of medical officers to their directorates of scientific services.

The division of responsibility in Britain between the DoE with its concern for the environment and the Department of Health and Social Services with its concern for health has not produced as much cooperation between these agencies as might have been expected. With the reorganization of the health services taking place simultaneously with the reorganization of the water services, and with primary missions of these agencies not related to one another, the monitoring required to assess health significance of contaminants in drinking water is still to be worked out. On the other hand, the impact of pollution on fisheries, with statutory committees established within the WAs, can be expected to be kept well in hand.

AN ALTERNATIVE STRATEGY—DUAL WATER SUPPLIES

Three strategies are available for protecting the public from exposure to potentially toxic substances in water sources:

1. Eliminate these substances at the source. This approach, enacted into law in the United States, through the goal of eliminating the discharge of pollutants, is hardly realistic. Pollutants emanate from many sources in an industrial society: from industrial operations directly through sewers and stacks; from households that use a wide variety of chemicals; and from agricultural and public enterprises that apply chemicals to the land and its vegetation. As soon as one hazardous chemical is eliminated, two others arise in its place. Containing all these substances so as to prevent them from reaching rivers that drain large areas seems hardly feasible.

2. Granted that these chemicals will find their way into surface waters, they might be monitored and removed in water treatment. However, the technology for the routine monitoring of these chemicals is a long way from being available, and the instrumentation and personnel required to perform the monitoring would be extraordinarily expensive. Further, the treatment processes are not now designed for the removal of these contaminants. The installation of facilities to assure their removal, to operate these facilities properly and to monitor their operation through continuing analytical surveillance is not now technically feasible not is it likely soon to be economically feasible.

3. The last option is to use unpolluted sources for potable supplies. However, groundwaters and protected upland sources may not be adequate to meet future demands if they are used indiscriminately for all purposes. If the run-of-river polluted sources, or even reclaimed wastewaters, can be used for non-potable purposes, then the more limited protected upland sources or groundwaters can be conserved for potable supplies. In many cases this would mean that dual water supply systems would be required. Where polluted sources are used for non-potable purposes, the quality of this second supply would be little different from the quality of waters now often used where supplies are drawn from polluted sources. The only difference between the two would be in the presence of synthetic organic chemicals in the non-potable supply.

This third option may not necessarily be the most feasible or the most economical solution, but it deserves evaluation with the many other options in any national water strategy adopted for the long term.

A philosophy for planned water reuse that might lead to a hierarchy of water quality, including dual supplies, was stated by the United Nations Economic and Social Council in 1958:[35] 'No higher quality water, unless there is a surplus of it, should be used for a purpose that can tolerate a lower grade.'

In his presidential address to the Institution of Water Engineers, J. W. Seddon pointed out that some undertakings already use dual supplies, the domestic supply being of the highest quality and industry accepting a quality no better than necessary.[36] What will be the eventual significance of drinking waters containing residues of hormones, antibiotics, and the 'pill'? People, if made truly aware of the alternatives, would be prepared to accept increased costs to secure the best possible quality of potable water in sufficient quantity to meet every need and eventuality. In a detailed study of twelve hypothetical configurations, Deb and Ives concluded that, if the potable portion is less than about 25 percent of the total water utilized, a dual system is more economical than a conventional system where extensive treatment is required to assure potability.[37]

The Trent Research Programme report, *Dual Water Supply Systems*, offers a useful model for water quality management in highly industrialized areas where rivers, particularly the downstream reaches, would tend to be highly polluted.[38] The implementation of such a program may be technically feasible under almost any system of management but it is particularly adaptable under the aegis of the new regional WAs.

Trent dual supply system study

Prior to water reorganization, with each local authority responsible for its own water supply and for disposing of its own wastewaters, comprehensive river basin water management, based upon some optimum economic model might have seemed attractive on paper, but could hardly have been expected to be readily implemented because of institutional problems. However, the Trent model, with all its elements within what is now the STWA, can readily be implemented should any element of that program give promise of being feasible. The study was directed towards the extent to which non-potable water might be used as a part of dual supply systems for selected industrial premises.[38] While essentially a desk study, the project included a comprehensive survey of the potential for non-potable supplies within the Trent river basin and neighboring areas and an outline design and economic appraisal of non-potable supply schemes as part of a dual system. While the obligation of the WAs is to afford wholesome water for domestic purposes and this continues to be their prime concern, under Section 27 of The Water Act 1945, they are obliged to provide water for purposes other than domestic. In 1967, 42 of 278 English and Welsh water supply systems were providing non-potable supplies, two-thirds of which were less than about one mgd (4500 m^3 per day).

The study indicated that about 90 percent of the large potable metered demands in the study area, with metered supplies being only for non-residential consumers, could be met by water of lower than potable quality. In quantitative terms, the indigenous resources of the Trent catchment are substantial, with an average of 1500 mgd (7 million m^3 per day) runoff. Unfortunately, most of the water is only available in polluted rivers, as the headwaters of the main river system have been polluted by industrial development for many years. The potable waters for the large municipalities in the Trent river basin are drawn from protected supplies outside the basin, in part from Wales. The forecast is that public water supply deficiencies would be substantial. Other studies have considered methods by which water supply in the Trent river basin can be augmented by imports from the west and by the augmentation of some local sources. The study of dual systems was just one additional option which upon completion was largely ignored.

The quality of the Trent river water is akin to that of wastewater treatment plant effluent. For purposes of the study, the non-potable quality water was considered that which could be obtained from the polluted Trent river system after so-called 'tertiary' treatment: clarification, foaming or flotation, coagulation, rapid filtration, and chlorination. Although total dissolved solids, chlorides, nitrates, sulfates, and hardness would be undiminished, there could be significant reductions in BOD, suspended solids, ammonia, phosphates, detergents, and color. There would of course be no significant impact on the presence of the non-degradable synthetic organic chemicals.

In initiating the study, the assistance of the Confederation of British Industry yielded data from industries which revealed that up to 65 mgd ($300\,000\,m^3$ per day) of current public water supplies in the area, now of potable quality, could be replaced by non-potable water if this were available at an attractive price, with an increase of about 150 percent by the year 2000.

Dual supplies are unnecessary where ample supplies of low-cost, high quality water are available, so they were considered only where they could be economically justified because a reduction in supply costs would offset increased distribution costs.

The conclusions of the study were:

1. Non-potable supplies could be introduced at no significant extra cost, and possibly some saving, to reduce the quantity of potable water otherwise required.

2. Non-potable water could meet current demands of about 40 mgd ($185\,000\,m^3$ per day) increasing to 100 mgd ($450\,000\,m^3$ per day) by the end of the century.

3. The economic advantages of these non-potable schemes is estimated to range between about plus or minus 2 pence per thousand gallons (£5 per thousand cubic meters).

4. The decision for or against the development of non-potable supplies may well turn on considerations other than those of strictly economic advantage.

The advantages of developing non-potable schemes were that:

1. They might be introduced on a local basis within the framework of a wider water resources development plan.

2. Flooding of land for water resources development would be minimized.
3. Non-potable waters could be used to meet certain domestic water requirements, e.g. toilet flushing in large housing blocks.
4. They could overcome the problem of differing water quality requirements of domestic and industrial users.

The disadvantages of non-potable schemes were:

1. The possible hazard to health from cross-connections or inadvertent use.
2. The increased congestion of services in built-up areas.
3. Less flexible operation than extending the potable distribution systems.

To the merits might be added the elimination of downstream abstractions for potable supplies where such waters would contain pollutants of uncertain composition, concentration, and health significance. The preservation of the protected sources for potable purposes exclusively would assure the population of long-term protection against chemicals which are now or may in the future be introduced into the environment.

The hazards resulting from cross-connections or inadvertent consumption of non-potable water would be mitigated if the non-potable waters were adequately disinfected. The danger from the non-potable waters derives from the life-long ingestion of the chemical contaminants they contain.

The congestion of services in built-up areas need pose no problems in new communities or in redeveloped areas of old communities. The number of services in urban areas is being increased at a prodigious rate, with a wide variety of communication links, umbilical cords between home and community. In high-density communities underground utility tunnels or 'utilidors' may well be used for the many services now being provided or which may need to be provided at some time in the future.

The Humberside scheme

One of the more imaginative schemes for providing non-potable water for industrial supply was developed for Humberside.[39] The planning for this project was begun in 1964 as a simple search for water supply by a water board facing the full exploitation of its groundwater resources but developed into a major inter-river transport scheme. The project is under the aegis of the Anglian Water Authority, with arrangements for abstractions of non-potable water from the Trent, which the STWA is anxious to provide.

The project is designed to augment the flow in the river Ancholme which flows into the Humber river estuary, firstly by transfer from the Witham and secondly by transfer from the lower Trent River via a canal and the Witham. Water supplies had been obtained from groundwater sources exclusively and industries in the area were accustomed to using these high-quality public water supplies for their industrial purposes. The proposal involves replacing much of the industrial demand with surface water from the Ancholme supplemented by water of poorer quality from the Witham and Trent, thereby preserving the high-quality groundwater resources for potable supplies. Furthermore, this dual system approach permitted the abandonment of a reservoir project that would have involved the loss of good agricultural land in Lincolnshire.

While it is unlikely that initially Trent water would amount to more than 15 percent of the total supplied by the system, under severe drought conditions, 100 percent of the water supplied to industry might be of Trent river origin.

The project was commended at a meeting of the Institution of Water Engineers because of the proposed use of polluted water from the Trent, a major source that might otherwise go untapped.[40] Health hazards resulting from cross-connections were thought to be 'over-played': '. . . one cup of tea made from Trent water would not have disastrous effects'. While the project might well be the forerunner of other industrial water supply projects, early testing of industrial acceptance is unlikely because of the financial recession that reduced the rate of growth in the area.

Another option might have been feasible had the reorganization taken place before the project had been conceived, namely, the diversion of surplus water from Empingham Reservoir, which was formerly not available but is now part of the Anglian Water Authority and available to be used to regulate the Witham. The reduction in the number of separate authorities involved in a scheme makes its planning and implementation far simpler.

Acceptance of dual systems

Dual systems are now being found feasible in more and more locations throughout the world. As shortages of potable water begin to grow, dual systems should become part of the armamentarium of the water engineer and not be dismissed out of hand because of either the 'hazards' of cross-connections or because of the anticipation of excessive costs without cost studies actually being made.

When the presentation on dual water systems for the Trent river basin was made at the meeting of the Institution of Water Engineers, the response was surprisingly favorable.[40] C. H. Spens '. . . had felt for a long time that the possibility of introducing dual supplies in appropriate districts in order to effect economies in water treatment had been neglected'. Where non-potable supplies became available for industrial use, potable waters usually used by industry could be made available for domestic use. The economic advantages emphasized in the Trent study were not the only criteria to be considered. In the past, when water at the source was not a scarce commodity, water engineers had given too little consideration to the possibility of dual supplies; it was generally cheaper to lay only one distribution network of mains. Now, however, it is not unusual for a new town such as those in North Lancashire, or even an old town, to be planned with a compact industrial estate set as a unit outside that town; such a setting often presented an attractive layout for a dual system.

Professor K. J. Ives pointed out that there were important opportunities for dual supplies in residential water supply systems: 'Of household water, only two percent was used for drinking and two percent for cooking. About 35 percent was used for toilet flushing, ten percent for laundering, and six percent for general cleaning. The remainder was for personal hygiene and dishwashing. Consequently at least 50 percent, and more likely 90 percent, household use was indifferent to levels of dissolved solids, including chlorides and other contaminants which would cause objection if ingested. Because of the cost of removing dissolved salts, or certain organic compounds, some sources were being rejected as potential domestic water supplies. However, assuming some small fraction only (e.g. 15%) was required to be of drinking water quality, the volume to be treated by sophisticated technical processes would be small enough to warrant economic re-appraisal. The larger volume of domestic (non-drinking) water could have much cheaper processes.'

John T. Calvert questioned whether the possible hazard to health was exaggerated: '... any non-potable supply would undoutedly be sterilized and would, therefore, be a safe water ... in Aden, a sea water supply had been provided for flushing toilets and it had never been suggested that this represented a health danger.' One of the best known of such sea water supplies for toilet flushing is in Hong Kong.

L. E. Taylor (of the WRB) considered that the time had come in some areas, and that the Trent would appear to be one of them, for a reappraisal of the licensing of groundwater for abstraction by industry. As Jackson pointed out in response, the case for restrictions on the use of groundwaters for non-potable purposes would be much strengthened if alternatives, such as non-potable waters of good quality as replacements, were available.

At the first National Water Conference in Bournemouth, J. G. Lloyd, of the North West Water Authority, indicated that WAs, with the cooperation of industry and local planning authorities, should be able to move towards the planned reuse of water in river systems for industrial purposes, greatly to the advantage of the nation through more economical use of water, land, and money.[41] 'The principle involved is the encouragement of direct industrial abstractions and effluent discharges in controlled schemes in order to reduce, as far as practicable, the need for placing further burdens unnecessarily on the high quality piped public supply systems. The plans could be conceived and brought into effect only through an imaginative attitude towards the location of water-using industries and through wholehearted cooperation between the water authority planners, the local authority planners, the river managers, the water supply managers, the sewerage and sewage treatment managers, and industrial planners and managers.' Herein lies the promise of the reorganization.

In a summary of the conference, Appleton stated that:[42] '... resistance (to developing a non-potable network) is beginning to falter in the face of the increasing costs of providing "wholesome" water for industrial processes, and the WAs are actually seeking ways of persuading industry to accept lower grade water. It is unlikely that we will see the complete reversal of WRB recommended strategy that Dan Okun advocates, but an increasing amount of reuse of sewage effluent by industry could be an important step in reducing the contaminating load on drinking water rivers.'

An extensive bibliography has developed on dual water supplies describing where such approaches have been successful and where they are now being studied.[43] In 1975, the American Water Works Association established a committee on dual distribution systems, and a full-day seminar was devoted to this subject in 1976.[44]

The WRB summary of the Trent Research Programme makes brief mention of the conclusions from the study on dual supply systems:[45] 'The DoE's study has concluded that there is potential for introducing dual supply systems in both Birmingham and South Staffordshire and that other areas are worthy of consideration. But there may be doubt about the practicability of such systems except where introduced from the outset in connection with extensive new development. The introduction of a dual system into an existing built-up area would involve major upheavals in local factories and in streets and there could be some risk to health from errors in the cross-connection of mains. Such a system could not be recommended unless all the local implications had been thoroughly explored, as well as the costs involved.'

These two objections, health hazards from cross-connections and cost, have traditionally been advanced wherever dual supply systems have been suggested.

Dual water systems in the past, where one system delivered potable water and the other furnished unsafe water for emergency use only, have led to serious water-borne disease outbreaks in many parts of the world. However, in the dual systems here discussed, the non-potable supply would be adequately treated and disinfected. Inadvertent ingestion would create no problem even if not discovered for weeks or months. In any event, proper plumbing codes and supervision of construction should minimize this danger.

The matter of cost, on the other hand, does deserve considerable exploration. The vision of tearing up urban centers for the installation of a second water supply pipeline is not one that would give promise of being reasonable in cost. However, with so much new construction, both urban and industrial, being contemplated, consideration might very well be given to dual systems. Britain is amongst the leaders in new town construction, and the introduction of promising strategies for water quality management are appropriate in these situations. At the very least, such approaches should be among the options considered.

WATER POLLUTION CONTROL

One of the proud achievements of modern water pollution control was pictorially flashed around the world shortly after the reorganization, as Peter Black, chairman of Thames Water Authority, held up the first salmon caught in the Thames estuary in more than a century. From the mid-19th century, when a headline of the day read: 'India is in Revolt and the Thames Stinks' and the draperies of the Houses of Parliament needed to be soaked in chloride of lime to mitigate the stench from the polluted river, the Thames had become continuously more heavily polluted.

At about the turn of the century, when the first measurements of dissolved oxygen were made, the 'sag', the point of lowest DO in the estuary, about 30 percent of saturation, was about 12 miles below London Bridge. The DO dropped steadily, reaching zero over a stretch of some 5 miles at half-tide in the 1950s. Recovery ensued until the present, with virtually no periods of anaerobiasis today.[46] The recovery of the Thames estuary has given hope to those responsible for cleansing polluted streams and estuaries throughout the world.

The recovery of the Thames is a tale of slow but steady accomplishment, which the interested reader is encouraged to explore but which is outside the scope of this volume. The initial step, recommended by Sir Joseph Bazalgette, involved the construction of large intercepting sewers along the Thames to conduct London's wastewaters to the lower estuary for greater dilution in combination with the construction of the Thames Embankment, and indicated that, even a century ago, the joint enterprise of local authorities was required to address problems of this magnitude.

Water pollution control standards

A concern for pollution of the other waters of Britain was evidenced by the creation of the Royal Commission on Sewage Disposal, whose eighth report, in 1912, provided guidelines which have proven valuable not only in Britain but throughout the world. The Royal Commission standards for sewage treatment plant effluents to be discharged to inland waters were based upon the assumption that if the biochemical oxygen demand (BOD) in a receiving stream does not exceed 4 mg/l, adverse effects would not result. Clean river water was characterized as having a BOD not exceeding 2 mg/l. Accordingly, the Royal Commission established a BOD effluent standard of 20 mg/l, assuming a minimum of 8-fold dilution during periods of low summer flow. Thus, one part of effluent of 20 mg/l plus 8 parts of river of 2 mg/l would yield a receiving stream with 4 mg/l. Because the cost of conventional biological 'secondary' treatment facilities to meet this standard was not regarded as unreasonable, local authorities had the burden of justifying a more relaxed consent condition. Where the dilution is not available, where the quality of the diluting water was not satisfactory, or where the use to which the water was to be put required a stream of exceedingly high quality, the proof for a more stringent standard was on the regulatory authority. The adoption of the 30 mg/l standard for suspended solids was based upon its being readily accomplished while reaching the 20 mg/l BOD effluent.

The Ministry of Housing and Local Government in 1966 argued that the river authorities should give regard to the factors that vary from river to river, including such matters as gradient, depth, flow, weirs, and the use to which the river is or may be put, with individual standards for individual discharges.[47] Requirements for 10/10 effluents would generally only be imposed on rivers used directly for sources of potable water supply or rivers with high amenity value. Even a 10/10 standard was recognized to be inadequate in some circumstances, e.g. industrial Luton, which discharges with little dilution into the river Lea, a source of potable water for London. On the other hand, in some circumstances, the river authorities did not require compliance with the 30/20 standard.

The British preferred in practice not to be inflexible in establishing treatment requirements as the river to be protected might be far more seriously affected by other factors such as overflows from combined sewer systems or by non-point sources from agricultural runoff. Under these circumstances rigid effluent control would be ineffective and needlessly costly.

River standards

In its classification of rivers, the DoE established four quality classes.[48]

Class 1—Rivers unpolluted and recovered from pollution
Includes rivers that are known to have received no significant polluting discharges or, though receiving some pollution, have a BOD of less than 3 mg/l and are well oxygenated.

Class 2—Rivers of doubtful quality and needing improvement
Includes rivers not in Class 1 on the basis of BOD and which have a substantially reduced DO level at normal dry summer flows or regularly at

other times; or which irrespective of BOD, are known to have received significant toxic discharges which cannot be proved to have had harmful effects.

Class 3—Rivers of poor quality requiring improvement as a matter of some urgency

Includes rivers not in class 4 on BOD grounds, and which have below 50 percent DO saturation for lengthy periods; or which contain substances which are suspected of being actively toxic at times; or which have been affected by the discharge of solids in suspension; and which have been the subject of serious complaints.

Class 4—Grossly polluted rivers

Rivers having a BOD of 12 mg/l or more under average conditions; known to be incapable of supporting fish life; which are completely deoxygenated at any time, apart from times of exceptional drought; which are sources of offensive odors; and which have an offensive appearance.

The classes represent a practical compromise of several characteristics which collectively meet the general concepts of river pollution, but the intention has been that all streams would eventually be brought to Class 1 status.

While the Yorkshire Water Authority was the first to introduce a classification according to use, establishing a Class 0 for rivers intended for potable water supply, as noted earlier, the WAs are examining the possibility of classifying all rivers according to use.

Consent conditions

Until implementation of the Control of Pollution Act 1974, discharges of effluents to water courses are subject to the Rivers Acts 1951 and 1961. Discharges are permitted by consent, subject to prescribed conditions of maximum flow rate and minimum quality aimed at insuring that effluents do not cause an unacceptable depreciation in the quality of the receiving streams. If the quality of the stream is not satisfactory below the point of discharge, while remaining satisfactory upstream, then either compliance with consent conditions has been unsatisfactory and remedial action at the works is needed, or the consent conditions themselves require modification.

Each WA has inherited consent conditions established under a wide range of criteria and it has become necessary to re-examine all consent conditions to establish a common quantitative philosophy. Such an exercise will determine those discharges whose quality needs to be improved and those discharges for which the consent conditions are unnecessarily stringent. Policy decisions will need to be made for those streams in industrialized areas which have become largely effluent carriers and which would require a disproportionate share of the capital budget to bring them up to Class 1 status.

Pollution control by a typical river authority has been described as comprising four steps:[49]

1. assessment of water quality at key points throughout a river system,
2. assessment of pollution loads discharged to the river system,
3. prevention of the deterioration of river water quality, and
4. securing remedial action as appropriate.

The latter two steps fall within the context of this discussion. The prevention of the deterioration of river water quality requires that the river authorities exercise surveillance over the treatment plants to insure that the installations are being properly operated and maintained. In addition, outfalls need regular inspection to insure that combined sewer overflows are not operating improperly and industrial facilities, where effluents are supposed to be discharged into public sewerage systems, need to be checked regularly to verify that unauthorized discharges to a river are not taking place.

An important factor in preventing deterioration of river quality is the action taken by the river authority in dealing with applications for new or increased discharges of effluents. Most river authorities have a series of established standards to apply to new municipal discharges, but industrial effluent standards are tailored to suit the individual circumstances, necessitating the participation of senior personnel. Liaison with planning authorities concerning proposals for new domestic or industrial developments might indicate that a particular development be deferred pending the provision of the necessary sewerage and/or treatment facilities.

With regard to securing remedial action, the initial approach was to secure significant improvements in water quality by persuasion. However, with the 1961 Act giving the river authorities important new powers to control pre-1951 discharges, the authorities began to be somewhat more resolute. The main emphasis continued to be on discussions and negotiations with the local authorities, as well as industrialists, towards diverting effluents to sewers where practicable, or providing treatment facilities on site. River authorities were often required to take the initiative toward securing the centralization of sewage treatment or the closure of inefficient and/or inadequately staffed plants and their connection to larger and more modern works.

Government and the river authorities had power to force regrouping of sewerage and treatment facilities, but little regrouping was actually accomplished, except for a few large main drainage boards, which became exemplary by their high quality of performance, applying modern technology far more successfully than the smaller authorities.[50] The Institute of Water Pollution Control gave evidence to the Royal

Commission on Local Government advocating that sewage treatment and disposal should be controlled by regional authorities.[51]

State of the nation's waters

Despite limitations in the law, the fragmentation of responsibility amongst many local authorities, the exclusion of many effluents from control, and a reluctance to call upon the law to enforce pollution control, a steady improvement in the state of the rivers occurred over the years.

The DoE undertook water pollution surveys of England and Wales early in the 1970s, assessing the changes in the quality of waters in England and Wales between 1958 and 1973.[48] These studies also helped establish quality levels for waters not previously studied, particularly tidal rivers and estuaries.

Rivers were classified according to the criteria described earlier. Tables 8.1 and 8.2 indicate something of the changes that have taken place between

TABLE 8.1
Non-Tidal Rivers: Comparison of Mileages by Chemical Classification
(England and Wales)

Class	1958		1970		1972		1973	
	Miles	%	Miles	%	Miles	%	Miles	%
1	14 603	72·9	17 000	76·2	17 279	77·4	17 449	78·1
2	2 865	14·3	3 290	14·7	3 267	14·7	3 151	14·1
3	1 279	6·4	1 071	4·8	939	4·2	935	4·2
4	1 278	6·4	952	4·3	832	3·7	794	3·6
Total	20 025	100·0	22 313	100·0	22 317	100·0	22 329	100·0

1958 and 1973, during which the river boards and then the river authorities were responsible for pollution control programs in the non-tidal inland waters, which were under legislative edict. Control of tidal rivers or estuaries was required to be primarily by persuasion as relatively few orders were issued.

Rivers included in the table are of stretches with a low flow of at least one mgd (4500 m^3 per day), thus bringing most rivers or their tributaries into the survey to within a few miles of their source.

From these tables, several conclusions can be drawn: some 75 percent of the length of inland rivers, the rivers under control, have been classified over the 14-year period as being unpolluted. As much of this mileage is in upland tributaries, they are not readily subject to pollution. The tidal rivers are not nearly as good, with about 50 percent being classified as unpolluted. Their geographic location would naturally preclude their being unpolluted in the first place, and stringent efforts would be required to effect significant change.

Similarly, the percentage of grossly polluted mileage was substantially greater in the tidal rivers as compared with the inland waters.

The polluted inland non-tidal rivers moved into unpolluted Class 1 at a rate of about 200 miles per year, and out of the grossly polluted status at a

TABLE 8.2
Tidal Rivers: Comparison of Mileages by Chemical Classification
(England and Wales)

Class	1958		1970		1972		1973	
	Miles	%	*Miles*	%	*Miles*	%	*Miles*	%
1	720	40·7	862	48·1	880	49·4	903	50·7
2	580	32·8	419	23·4	414	23·2	397	22·3
3	250	14·1	301	16·8	253	14·2	261	14·6
4	220	12·4	209	11·7	236	13·2	221	12·4
Total	1 770	100·0	1 791	100·0	1 783	100·0	1 782	100·0

rate of about 32 miles per year. Figure 8.1 indicates that most of the Class 3 and 4 waters are in the industrial midlands and near the coast. Inasmuch as the surveys were carried out in terms of mileages, they do distort the assessment of the volume of water pollution, because it is the lower reaches of the rivers, with their larger flows, where the worst pollution occurs. The Royal Commission on Environmental Pollution pointed out that classifying a one-mgd river as unpolluted is not very significant, as it is not much in the way of an amenity, yet it counts as much in the Table as the Thames.

Approximately 56 percent of the total lengths of rivers in Classes 1 and 2 is unsuitable for abstraction because of insufficient quantity, so that the fact that 92 percent of the total length of these rivers is in these higher classes is of relatively little significance.

All in all, the general quality of inland waters of England and Wales has been improving at a slow but steady rate. If the rate is not increased substantially in the near future, many miles of rivers will remain in poor quality and grossly polluted for many years to come.

On the other hand, the situation with regard to tidal rivers, with almost no legal constraints, is that there has been some slight improvement in the mileage of unpolluted waters, but almost none in the polluted category. Discharges to estuaries and coastal waters are virtually untreated, while

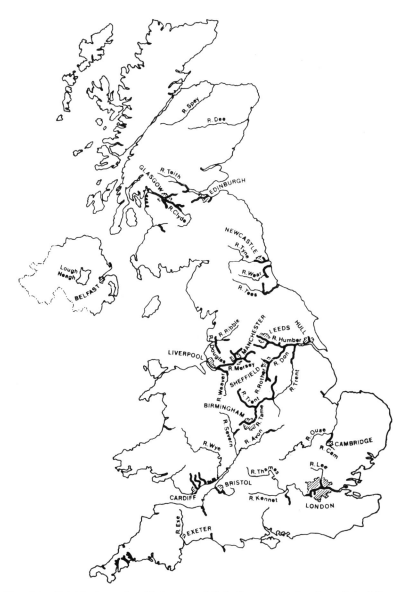

FIG. 8.1   British rivers classified as 'poor' (light lines) or 'seriously polluted' (heavy lines). Reproduced by permission of the Controller of Her Majesty's Stationery Office.

more than 90 percent of discharges to inland rivers, whether measured by population served, number of installations, or volume treated, are served by treatment facilities.

Which?, the British consumer publication, studied the condition created by sea outfalls in 1973 and again in 1975.[52] The basic objectives to be attained were that: (1) sewage should always be mechanically treated to remove solids and (2) discharge should be far enough out to sea to prevent sewage from reaching bathing areas. Of 200 coastal sewage outfalls found unsatisfactory in 1973, not including outfalls in estuaries, only 18 were improved sufficiently to meet the basic conditions. Some 95 places, including popular holiday resorts, are near 'blackspots'. Because outfalls have generally had a low priority in investments by local authorities, and because such a low priority is likely to continue in the water authorities, public efforts, such as those of *Which?*, will need to provide the spur to action.

A working party report on the pollution of Swansea Bay, in Wales, adopted a 'consumer' approach to its task, interviewing local people and parties of visitors with regard to their views on pollution of the beaches.[53] Only five percent of the parties gave pollution as a reason for not bathing. Of those interviewed, 57 percent claimed to have seen some type of pollution on the beaches, and some 16 percent claimed to have seen sewage. Bathing in polluted sea waters allegedly constitutes little health hazard, while the aesthetic effects are most significant.[54] The Swansea survey reporting that 75 percent of all households interviewed gave 'a clean beach' as a major factor influencing their decision to visit a particular beach, so that visual appearance should help establish priorities for requirements for sea disposal.

The Royal Commission elaborated on pollution of estuaries in its third report,[55] and helped focus on this problem, so important to an island nation, by commissioning a study of the problems of four of the more heavily-polluted estuaries.[56] The reorganization has simplified the administrative arrangements for the control of the pollution of estuaries with only two of the major estuaries, the Humber and Severn, the joint responsibility of more than one WA.

With about 94 percent of the total population of England and Wales being served by public sewerage (a proportion higher than in any other country in the world) and its long history of treatment designed to meet Royal Commission standards, why is the pollution control record, even in inland waters, still so relatively poor? Two causes predominate: overflows from combined sewerage systems and inadequate operation of those facilities that have been built.

Combined sewer overflows

The first sewers built in Britain in the 19th century were to carry away storm runoff to protect commercial areas in urban centers. The development and rapid adoption of water closets, ending dependence upon house-to-house scavengers with 'honey buckets' to remove offal, led to the use of storm sewers for collecting their discharges. This resulted in what has since been called the *combined* sewer that carries both storm runoff and household wastewaters or foul sewage.

Originally, the storm sewers were designed to take the shortest route to the rivers. The addition of the human wastewaters to these sewers, particularly during dry periods when much of this material would remain in the sewers to be flushed into the rivers at the first rain, led to exceedingly noisome conditions near sewer manholes, sewer outlets and in the rivers during dry periods. These difficulties led eventually to collection of these wastewaters for treatment. Conventional practice in Britain had been to size combined sewers to carry six-fold greater than the average dry weather flow (DWF). Inevitably rainfall would occur with intensities greater than could be handled by the interceptors and overflows were built to allow the excess to be discharged directly to the rivers. (Combined sewer overflows are a far more serious problem in the United States, where rainfall intensity is greater than in England, and interceptors are generally designed to carry no more than the peak DWF so that almost every rain triggers an overflow.)

Each overflow involves untreated sewage being discharged directly to the river. Devices that might segregate the cleaner from the dirtier water have been developed but these do not offer any great potential for success and none has been adopted. Thus, the impact of combined sewer overflows on the condition of the inland rivers will continue to be a problem for many years into the future.

While some local authorities had continued to construct combined sewerage, the WAs are now committed to providing *separate* sewerage systems, where domestic and industrial wastewaters go to treatment and storm waters flow to the nearest water course. The installation of separate sewers in existing systems is exceedingly costly. Thus, depending upon the nature of the domestic wastewaters, and the proportion of industrial effluents they contain, pollution from overflows will be a continuing impediment to upgrading many reaches of rivers in England and Wales. Further, combined sewer overflows threaten any strategy that depends upon abstracting for potable water supplies downstream from such overflows.

The operation of treatment facilities

Britain has an excellent record in the construction of wastewater treatment facilities providing 'secondary', biological treatment, for the protection of inland waters. However, a good measure of difficulty has resulted from the fact that about 60 percent of the local sewage treatment plant effluents failed to meet proper standards.[57,58] For example, Table 8.3

TABLE 8.3
Classification of Treatment Facilities to Non-Tidal Waters in the Mersey and Weaver River Authority (1969)

Discharges	*Satisfactory*	*Borderline*	*Unsatisfactory*	*Bad*	*Total*
Sewage works	111	66	70	8	255
Trade premises	39	35	92	12	178
Totals	150	101	162	20	433

illustrates the status of treatment in the Mersey and Weaver River Authority in 1969.

Many of these treatment facilities were built years ago and have not been maintained or enlarged to keep pace with growth. Smaller authorities lacked specialized staff to deal with such problems as trade effluent control. As working conditions were often unpleasant, they could not recruit capable operators and consequently works were not properly manned. The quality of the inheritance in facilities handed down to the WAs is discussed more fully in the next section.

THE WATER AUTHORITIES' INHERITANCE

The WAs took over all the facilities within their areas for providing water supply (excepting the water companies), wastewater collection disposal, and river management. Little need be said about the legacy of the river authorities. They had little in the way of major capital investments, and were generally satisfactorily staffed.

Annual reports of the Chartered Institute of Public Finance and Accountancy, which prepares statistical publications for a wide range of public activities such as crematoria, education, housing, police, libraries, rates (or taxes), deaths, as well as water and sewage purification and disposal, reveals something of the different quality of these services.[59] The ability of the Institute to extract data from the authorities is an interesting measure of the quality of their operations. In the publication on water statistics for 1972–73, data were available from 40 local authorities, 95 water boards and 22 water companies in England and Wales, or 84 percent of a total of 187 undertakings. On the other hand, the Institute was able to obtain data for its 1972–73 sewage disposal report from only 2 boards, 100 boroughs, 55 districts and the Greater London Council, about 11 percent of the total of 1393 authorities.

The awful truth, however, did not begin to dawn upon the WAs until they began to take inventory of the facilities that they had inherited. The technical journals reported almost no criticism of the quality of the water supply facilities inherited, but they were replete with revelations concerning the sewage treatment facilities.[60] 'The hypocrisy behind many voices of local authority protest [at loss of facilities to the WAs] has now been revealed. While a lot of councils were undoubtedly very conscientious, inquiries ... in three WAs reveal large numbers of sewage works which have been allowed to deteriorate over a period of several years, while staff to run them were either badly trained or allowed to drift away without being replaced.'

While each WA has its own list of 'horrors', those of the Severn Trent and Yorkshire were most thoroughly documented and are illustrative of the others.

The Severn Trent Water Authority inheritance

In examining their inheritance, the Severn Trent Water Authority studied the quality of water supply systems of 25 water supply undertakings, the wastewater collection and disposal facilities of 210 local authorities and two drainage boards and the quality of industrial effluents discharged to rivers. They prepared a report to serve as a baseline for the assessment of the future performance of the STWA.[61]

The report noted with satisfaction that all the water supplies in the area met the overall public health requirement of being 'wholesome'. The standards recommended by the European Committee of the WHO in relation to chemical quality and the DoE in regard to bacteriological quality were met in almost every instance. The few failures to conform to the bacteriological standards were traced to local defects which were promptly rectified or found satisfactory upon immediate resampling.

The only exception in the chemical samples were cases of lead, nitrates and fluorides. Lead was found to be high in some instances because of lead service piping with soft waters from upland sources, and replacement of these services enjoys a high priority. Nitrates exceeding $11 \cdot 3 \, mg/l$, the WHO limit, were found in several wells, and this has been rectified by blending these waters with waters low in nitrates before distribution. Where one source contained a higher concentration of natural fluorides than the $1 \cdot 5 \, mg/l$ recommended by the WHO, it was blended with other waters to bring it within limits. The regionalization of water supplies simplified the implementation of such blending schemes.

'In contrast ... the overall quality of sewage effluents discharged to rivers was appalling. Nearly 300 of the 700 sewage works produced unsatisfactory effluents based on the conditions of consent given by the former river authorities and more than 25 percent of the 436 mgd ($2 \, M \, m^3$ per day) of sewage effluent discharged was unsatisfactory in quality.' If the requirements of the receiving stream were being considered, 43 percent of the treatment facilities discharging 66 percent of the daily volume of effluent would be classified as unsatisfactory.

While most industrial effluents, other than cooling and mine waters, are discharged to the municipal sewerage systems, the industrial effluents that do discharge to rivers exhibited a picture not dissimilar from that for municipal effluents and discharges. Some 43 percent of 210 industrial discharges were found to be unsatisfactory, constituting 17 percent of the 200 mgd (0·9 M m³ per day) flow. These unsatisfactory effluents caused tributaries of the Severn and Trent to be so polluted as to be incapable of supporting fish life. Thus, even where they had legislative authority on inland waters and enjoyed an 'adversary' relationship with those being regulated, the river authorities for a wide variety of reasons did not make a strong record.

Yorkshire Water Authority inheritance

The Yorkshire Water Authority study of its inheritance revealed that about one to three percent of samples from its 21 water supply undertakings were of unsatisfactory bacteriological quality.[62] Almost 20 percent of the samples were rated as unsatisfactory against the WHO's standards on a volume-weighted basis, generally due to such characteristics as pH, color, iron and mangenese. In virtually no cases had all the tests mentioned in the WHO standards been carried out. For example, no authorities determined cadmium, mercury, selenium, PAH or pesticides. Arsenic and cyanide were determined on a small percentage of samples and lead on a few more. While the supplies are generally satisfactory, far more attention needs to be given to surveillance for the protection of potable water quality, a function more readily discharged by the YWA than by the individual undertakings.

The YWA had taken control of 624 separate sewage treatment facilities, varying in size from those treating 1000 gpd (5 m³ per day) to the largest works treating 36 mgd (160 000 m³ per day). With only six months to assemble the data, the YWA recognized that this might well not be the total number and, in fact, within several months 21 additional plants had been located.

Some 40 percent of the works produced unsatisfactory effluents, representing 50 percent of the total effluent flow. The YWA considers a facility satisfactory if it produces an effluent which complies with its consent condition 80 percent of the year. In some cases effluents were satisfactory only because the treatment facilities did not receive all the flow originally destined for the plant, some of which overflowed untreated to the river because of inadequate sewerage.

One facility, which had been extensively rebuilt just months before takeover by the YWA, had completely collapsed, easing the problem of the YWA which combined this facility with a larger works nearby, which previously had been the responsibility of a separate local authority. The smaller local authorities could not justify full time attendance at their facilities and workmen were often engaged in other activities of the authority, leading to discontinuity of effort and apathy towards what should have been an important task. The YWA exhibits a concern for such facilities, not evident when the works were under a local authority which had 'much more important problems'. Operators now feel a greater sense of responsibility and see some future in moving ahead in the organization.

'The YWA has changed the rules. From now on nothing will be done manually. If necessary, we will take portable diesel engines around to work scrapers and so on. There will be no reason for a man to get into a tank.'[60] YWA's aim is to make the work less noxious and thus attract a better quality of personnel to the facilities.

The YWA inherited discharges from 510 industrial premises, excluding cooling and mine water. Of about 180 mgd (0.8 M m^3 per day) of industrial effluents discharged to Yorkshire rivers some 41 percent, from 33 percent of the industrial establishments, was of unsatisfactory quality. These unsatisfactory effluents resulted from the inadequacy or lack of on-site facilities, antiquated drainage systems on industrial sites, lack of space for treatment, and lack of capacity in the municipal sewerage system or treatment facility to handle the industrial wastes with or without pretreatment, and lastly an apathy of some industrialists towards minimizing the impact of their effluents.

Prior to reorganization, sewers were considered separately from rivers. The industrial effluent disposal inspectors, who controlled discharges to sewerage systems, were the responsibility of the local authorities. River authority inspectors, who had powers to control most discharges to surface waters, had no jurisdiction over effluents discharged to municipal sewers despite the fact that, if a sewer were not of adequate size, it might overflow directly into a river. The YWA, and the other WAs, inherited a situation where some local authorities charged industry realistically while others subsidized industry by making token or no charges for effluents discharged into their sewerage systems. Local Acts often gave these industries a free license to use municipal sewers as a means of attracting industry to the area. The YWA believes that a great opportunity is open to minimize costs and maximize benefits in solving these inherited problems.

THE 'POACHER–GAMEKEEPER' RELATIONSHIP

The one substantive question about the Water Act itself was raised at the outset by David H. A. Price, then of the Directorate General of Water Engineering in the DoE. Would problems arise from the fact that the WAs would be responsible for discharges from their own sewerage systems as well as being responsible for these discharges complying with standards that the WAs themselves would establish? Would the WA be both polluter and regulator, poacher and gamekeeper?

Local authorities would continue to be responsible for seeing to the wholesomeness of potable water supplied by the WAs, a division of responsibility that would no longer exist for water pollution control.

The response was that such conflicts had a habit of working themselves out; that expressions of concern about conflicts of interest tended to impugn the professional integrity of individuals involved; that internal structures created by the WAs would see to the independence of those within the authority responsible for checking on water quality.

At the time of the reorganization, J. E. Beddoe, then Under Secretary in the DoE, averred that those who would condemn the WAs as being both judge and jury were thoroughly 'old-fashioned'. Splitting these responsibilities was like trying to split an indivisible process. 'You might as well split water treatment and supply.' One of the most common complaints about the Water Resources Act 1963, he pointed out, was the division of responsibility between the river authorities' functions in water resources development and the responsibilities of water supply undertakings for water supply.[63]

The 'poacher–gamekeeper' controversy did not let up after the reorganization despite the data presented that the 'gamekeeper' without responsibility for the treatment facility, had not been exactly 'successful' as evidenced by the legacy left to the WAs. The failure of the adversary relationship may be attributed to the fragmentation of sewerage and sewage disposal in England and Wales, and '... double standards of control [of most river authorities], pursuing industrialists in the courts while turning a blind eye to the local authorities, or, more probably, prosecuting only in those cases where failure to reach consent standards caused serious pollution of the receiving waters'.[64]

Recognizing the problem, WAs have established water quality advisory panels or something similar in an attempt to assure the public of their dedication to pollution control. In introducing the STWA report, the chairman of the water quality advisory panel stated that the report '... records in quality terms the past performance of the Authority's predecessors and will form the base line for the assessment of the future performance of STWA by the water quality advisory panel and by the *public at large*'.[65] (Italics mine.)

In addition, the WAs have an officer responsible for water pollution control who is free to report directly to the water quality panel and thus directly to the authority. In general, he is either the director of scientific services where such a directorate exists, or in the directorate of resource planning, neither of which is responsible for operations. This arrangement has been adopted in all but the YWA.

The river authorities, because a majority of their members were representatives of the local authorities, were often reluctant to put pressure on them because the costs would be borne by the local authorities. Now, however, the local authority members on the WA are interested in having the WA do whatever is necessary to serve their own local constituencies, as the cost is likely to be borne by the population of the entire authority.

With the WA members and staff responsible for maintaining water quality well identified, the public now has a place to focus pressures for corrective measures. The zeal of public interest groups might be tempered by their recognition that the WAs have responsibilities other than pollution control alone, responsibilities in which these public interest groups also have a stake, such as providing sewerage for highly needed housing developments, or water supply, or fisheries.

The continuing concern for this issue was revealed in *Sewage Disposal*, a special supplement of *Municipal Engineering*,[66] which began with a lead responding to the author's statement in the first issue of *Water*,[67] that '. . . not only will WAs have to be responsive to pollution problems, they will have to appear to the public to be responsive'. Prior to reorganization, the larger treatment facilities collected their own so-called 'control' samples, often over 24 hours, as a basis for managing the works.[67] At smaller facilities, often no such samples were ever collected. As the regulators, the river authorities exercised their statutory functions by collecting so-called 'snap' or 'grab' samples (now referred to as 'audit' samples) of all discharges to establish whether or not they were complying with consent conditions. In the case of the larger facilities, the audit samples were many fewer than the control samples, while in the case of the smaller facilities these might often be the only samples collected. Seldom were audit and control samples comparable, because they were collected in different ways under different circumstances.

The Thames Water Authority, with responsibility for collecting both the control and audit samples, have established the separation of functions in the directorate of scientific services by having the assistant director (division services) take responsibility for providing the scientific support for operation of the facilities, the so-called control samples, generally at division level but augmented when necessary from headquarters. For the regulatory function another assistant director (pollution control) has responsibility for the collection of audit samples from all works, including those owned by the TWA as well as industrial and other discharges. In response to the view that stream standards should be the main or even the sole method of assessing the performance of facilities discharging into the stream, the experience of most regulatory authorities has been that both effluent and stream samples are essential to permit a precise picture of the situation to be assessed and finally judged by the public.

Concern for assuring the public of WA integrity are ever present. Hugh Fish, director of scientific services for the TWA and an acknowledged spokesman for the scientific and river quality community in the water industry, had defended the WA's role in serving as its own regulator.[68]

While recognizing that the regulating function and the provision of unbiased information to the public should be performed by agencies completely outside the WAs, he believed that this would not be economically practicable because of the wasteful duplication of effort and resources. Furthermore, a 'watchdog' agency would never be content simply to monitor and it would soon insist that it would need to have knowledge and responsibility in decisions on the prevention of pollution. Conflicts in the exercise of power and responsibility would multiply, particularly as the WA would feel obliged to duplicate all the measurements made by the watchdog agency.

Nevertheless, Fish did make a formal proposal to the TWA water quality advisory panel that it retain a firm of consultants as 'gamekeepers' to keep check on water quality quarterly audits.[69] The proposal was rejected by the TWA water quality panel, giving assurance to the public that the TWA has confidence in its own professional staff and believes that the public, which it represents, would share that confidence.

The Royal Commission on Environmental Pollution, in its first report after the reorganization, did not address the reorganizational aspects of water pollution control other than to describe them briefly.[70] However, in reporting on the decision in Scotland to maintain separate river purification boards while leaving the responsibility for sewage disposal with local authorities, the Commission by implication criticized the dual role of the WAs as both polluter and regulator.

Lord Ashby had emphasized the importance of fisheries—on any given Saturday more people are fishing than watching football. Despite the poacher–gamekeeper roles of the WAs there might be some natural checks on the quality of inland waters, but he was concerned that, without the sea fisheries committees, no pressures would exist to help shift WA priorities in the direction of protecting the coastal waters.[71]

With the clear concern of the Royal Commission, and the sensitivity of the WAs to their anomalous position, progress of this unusual internalized approach to water pollution abatement will be observed with interest. Some signs have already begun to appear. A case of pollution attributable to the Wessex Water Authority (albeit an inherited problem) brought about a wave of local criticism. In order to demonstrate that the matter was not being 'swept under the carpet' the WA water quality panel carried out an investigation and made recommendations to the authority which were accepted and publicized.

THE CONTROL OF POLLUTION ACT 1974

Part II of the Control of Pollution Act 1974 '. . . complements the Water Act 1973 to provide a fairly radical reform of the control of pollution of waters.

It brings a wider class of waters under control, and gives increased rights to the individual. The Rivers (Prevention of Pollution) Acts are repealed almost entirely, and most of their provisions re-enacted in amended form.'[73]

The major contribution of this Act is to add statutory control of underground, tidal, and coastal waters (as far as the territorial limits) to the inland waters previously controlled, all termed 'relevant waters'. This extension of control has long been needed and often recommended, particularly by the Royal Commission on Environmental Pollution. Somewhat more controversial is the shift in concern of sea discharges from the sea fisheries committees to the appropriate WAs.

An important element in the Act is that a known discharge of poisonous. noxious or polluting matter to the relevant waters is an offense unless the discharge was authorized by statute, a consent granted under the Dumping at Sea Act 1974. The original Bill would have enjoined riparian owners from taking an injunction against polluters if the pollution had been given consent by a WA. This provision, 'mercifully', does not appear in the Act.[74] Support for this deletion came from widely divergent sources. The Anglers' Cooperative Association, the National Federation of Anglers and others such understandably battled in parliament to retain the power to obtain an injunction against a polluter even if his effluent meets a WA's consent condition. Industry did not seek to immunize itself against such injunctions because, if meeting consent conditions were to protect a polluter from legal redress, the redress would fall upon the consenting WA, which would then be obliged to be far more restrictive in establishing its consent conditions, imposing heavier costs on industry.

Control of discharges

The most important part of the Act is in the extended powers given to the WAs to control discharges of municipal and industrial wastewaters. In addition to adding to the waters brought under control, the discharge of wastewaters without consent by pipeline from land to the sea even beyond the territorial limits becomes an offense. Controls are also extended to discharges of pollutants from all types of sewers and drains, including highway drainage.

The WAs continue to remain liable for industrial effluents discharged into their own sewers which they were obliged to receive, because of pre-organization agreements, or to which they had consented. On the other hand, the WAs are not liable for discharges into their sewers which either had not received consents or had contravened consents.

The consent conditions procedures which had been part of the administrative structure for discharges for many years, are strengthened under the Act. The teeth of the Act apply primarily to industry, as the control of the WA's own discharges will inevitably fall under internal WA regulations. In addition to governing the place of a discharge, the design and construction of the outlet, its nature, composition, temperature, volume and rate of discharge, the consent may also designate the periods during which the discharges may be made. Discharges to tidal waters may be restricted on the flood tide, but permitted on the ebb tide. The WAs are to have the power to require, as part of the consent condition, that the dischargers provide for and operate devices for measuring, sampling and analyzing the rates of discharges and their composition, with these records being submitted to the authority.

Consents are to be subject to review over periods of not less than two years, when changes in the consent conditions can be made. If a WA finds that a change is required earlier, the discharger must be compensated for any extra costs involved. Consents for the WA discharges from its own treatment facilities may be given by the Secretary of State for the Environment, but this is uncertain, as the 'poacher–gamekeeper' relationship of the WAs is not addressed in the Act.

As with authority for metering in the Water Act 1973, the Act authorizes the Secretary of State, after consultation with the NWC, to enable WAs to impose effluent charges on industrial effluents discharged direct to rivers and widens their existing powers to charge for effluents discharged to sewers. These charges would be imposed according to the character and volume of the discharge.

An unusual feature of the Act is the approach to so-called 'non-point sources', e.g. farmland runoff. A farmer will not be accountable if pollution results from sound agricultural practices, but this defense will not be allowed if, upon the application of a WA, the Secretary of State serves on the farmer a notice requesting him to prevent such pollution. While normal farming practices that result in no particular difficulties will not be hindered, farmers will be obliged to change practices not in the general social interest. Considering the political strength of agricultural interests, these controls, although not strong, are an important first step, possibly to be strengthened in the future.

Preventive measures

Primary emphasis on pollution control in the past has been based upon detection of pollution offenses and their punishment, usually with trivial fines, after the damage was done. In time, as pollution control programs develop, a larger percentage of pollution events can be expected to result from accidents or other 'unforeseen' events, and the Act is intended to minimize these threats. The significance of the preventive measures is revealed in a synopsis of the Act by the Confederation of British Industry:[75] 'The Secretary of State may, by regulations, require precautions to be taken by any person who has custody or control of poisonous, noxious, or polluting matter to prevent the matter entering the water course. He may also introduce regulations to restrict or ban the carrying on in a particular area of activities likely to result in water pollution. *These provisions should be fully considered when the siting of industrial premises; the introduction or modification of industrial processes; or the location of storage areas are being determined.*' (Italics theirs.)

The rights of the individual and the public

A major contentious issue before, during, and after passage of the Water Act 1973 is the accountability of the WAs to the people they serve. The Control of Pollution Act 1974 constitutes a virtual 'bill of rights' for the public with regard to water pollution. Almost all information concerning consent conditions and audit samples by the river authorities had constituted privileged information from which the public and even the damaged individuals were excluded. For example, a downstream riparian owner had no rights to object to a consent or to acquire information about the nature of the application unless the applicant for that consent agreed. The 1974 Act constitutes a right-about-face as the WAs are to publish notices of applications for consents and to inform the appropriate district councils and, for tidal water or sea discharges, the Minister of Agriculture, Fisheries, and Food. Public notification is not necessary if the WA considers that the discharge will have no appreciable effect. Any person, even if not personally affected, may make written representation and the WA is obliged to consider such representation and to inform the complainant if the consent is to be granted; he may then personally request the Secretary of State to direct that application be remitted to the Secretary for determination. Thus, the way is open for public interest groups to intercede for the public at large, as the new Act permits private prosecutions without restriction and the WAs as well as those given consent may both be subject to prosecution.

Information on water pollution control activities of the WAs is to be made freely available. Where publicity might prejudice to an unreasonable degree private interests by disclosing information about trade secrets, or otherwise be contrary to the public interest, application for protecting such information may be made to the Secretary of State.

The control samples that the WAs require both for their own operations and the operations of others are not obliged, perhaps because of oversight, to be made public, thereby excluding the public from a significant volume of pertinent information. However, in the interest of satisfying the public with regard to their 'poacher–gamekeeper' status the WAs will likely make all their monitoring data freely available.

The combination of availability of information and the right of class actions might result in a spate of prosecutions by those who have felt restrained over the past decade. The frequency of such prosecutions may be seen as a measure of the success the new WAs attain.

A critique of the Act

The control of coastal waters is now to be divided between the MAFF, which will license dumpings from ships and aircraft under the Dumping at Sea Act 1974, and the WAs which, under the Control of Pollution Act 1974, will control discharges from pipelines to the sea. While the WAs have inherited no expertise on the hydrobiology or the fisheries of coastal waters, the WAs include appointees of the MAFF, which has advised the DoE on such matters. MAFF appointees have taken leadership in most WAs with regard to inland fisheries, and in the next round of appointments, marine experts will likely be appointed to the WAs.

Industrialists have criticized dependence upon what McLoughlin terms '. . . a single primitive method—watching the end of a pipeline and insisting upon what must not come out'.[73] River authorities had realized this and had sent their officers into factories. The Alkali Inspectorate, responsible for air pollution control in Britain, has the legal power to require specific types of treatment facilities to be installed. The two-pronged approach, specification of the quality of the effluent to meet a prescribed stream standard and a specification of the treatment that might be used to achieve this, might well be appropriate.

Accepting in general the Control of Pollution Act 1974, the Confederation of British Industry expressed reservations about requirements for the release of information and is categorically opposed to the initiation of 'effluent charges' for direct discharges to waters, and to some of the requirements for compensation.

Early impact of the Act

The first noteworthy impact of the passage of the 1974 Act was the notoriety given to the publication of the Severn Trent Water Authority's report on its inheritance.[61] Anticipating the Act, the report 'named names', which were picked up in an article in the popular weekly, *New Scientist*.[76] The author of that article, Jon Tinker, had three years earlier in the same journal excoriated the existing laws which made it a criminal offense (punishable with up to 3 years in prison) for a pollution officer to disclose any information about a consent or an effluent sample, as prescribed in the Rivers (Prevention of Pollution) Act 1961.

Because the Control of Pollution Act 1974 and its freedom of information clauses had not yet been implemented, the STWA used the fact that disclosure had been permitted under the old law if the discharger gave permission. Information on effluents from its own facilities inherited from local authorities created no problems and these data were amply reported. With industry, on the other hand, the STWA requested formal permission to disclose the nature of their consents and the results of analyses of their effluents. Whether the STWA would have sought such disclosures without the 1974 Act is conjectural. A better response could be expected from industry with implementation on the horizon.

Of 103 companies solicited, 40 companies, the 'furtive forty', did not authorize publication. Among these were not only industries representing the private sector but also nationalized industries such as the National Coal Board and the Central Electricity Generating Board. The article then identified the 'dirty dozen'—companies discharging strongly polluting effluents, which were significantly exceeding the standards laid down by the river authorities. Continuing with its alliteration, the article listed also the 'exceptional eleven', industries to which river authorities had laid down no consent conditions, and then the 'nasty nineteen', those local authorities, since taken over by the STWA, that were generally not meeting their consent conditions. Tinker extolled the STWA for its courageous unlocking of the secret files, despite the implied criticism of former river and local authorities, many officers of which are now on the staff of the STWA. Tinker concluded that exposure of data to the public is the beginning of improvement.

The Confederation of British Industry felt that the *New Scientist* article was unscrupulous and justified industry's fear of the publicity the new law calls for, as data are often published out of context.[77] For example, the *New Scientist* intimated that the 'furtive forty' were reluctant to publicize the data, whereas many had submitted their acquiescence too late for publication in the report, while others were afraid of misuse of the data which, they feel, did in fact occur.

The STWA published a similar report for its second year of operation,[78] and because Part II of the Control of Pollution Act 1974 had still not been implemented, the permission of industry was still required for publication of pollution data. This time only 32 firms refused consent, with 87 percent of those approached agreeing to disclosure. The STWA example was lauded by the DoE, and the Yorkshire and North West Water Authorities may well follow suit.[79]

Implementation of the 1974 Act

With the passage of the 1974 Act during the depth of economic crisis, and with the WAs already facing serious limitations on expenditures for which they were already responsible prior to the passage of the Act, the government was understandably slow in initiating implementation. The first order with regard to pollution of water was that those industries that had 'ancient rights', or 'grandfather rights', for discharges into inland waters would have to obtain consent prior to 30 January 1975 for their discharges.

In February 1975, the DoE gave notice as to its plans for the long-term implementation of the Act, beginning by pointing out the need to restrict increases in local authority expenditures.[80] The government's aim was to implement the Act in two interrelated steps: activating the consent system, and making the discharge of effluents without consent an offense. This second step would give the WAs control of all discharges into tidal and coastal waters up to the three-mile limit. The government did not propose, without extensive consultation with NWC, to implement the provision that authorizes the WAs to institute effluent charges for discharges directly to rivers.

If fully implemented, the Act would put the WAs in jeopardy because of the facilities they had inherited. The requirements for heavy investment in capital improvements did not permit them to correct the situation immediately, and the public would have the right to prosecute the WAs under the Act. Accordingly, a working party of the NWC on behalf of the WAs recommended that the DoE provide a three-year delay in implementing the provision of the Act that authorizes the public to prosecute.[81] How such a delay would affect the posture of the WAs in their pursuit of offending industrial polluters was not discussed.

Pressure for pollution control did come from the Royal Commission on Environmental Pollution.[70] In introducing its fourth report the chairman, Sir Brian Flowers, said: 'We are extremely anxious to see the Control of Pollution Act put into practice as soon as possible, bearing in mind the present economic circumstances ...'[82] Sir Brian went on to assert: '... expenditures sooner rather than later on the needs of the environment may be wise economics as well as socially desirable'.[83]

Responding, Anthony Crosland, Secretary of State for the Environment, expressed concern for the government's ability to cope with the new responsibilities brought by the Act and concurred in the Royal Commission's disappointment that '... because of limitations of resources some environmental improvements are taking longer to achieve than we had hoped: I think particularly of the cleaning up of our major estuaries ...'[84] The government went on to show how it had responded or was planning to respond to each of the recommendations made by the Royal Commission in its four reports, asserting that the Control of Pollution Act 1974 is the answer. If implemented, it will be the answer.

As the economic climate in Britain worsened thru 1975, the government did pull back. In a letter to Lord Nugent, chairman of the NWC, Denis Howell, Under Secretary of the DoE, stated:[85] '... [the government] had reluctantly concluded that, in view of the current economic situation, the introduction of the major provisions in Part II of the Act would have to be deferred'. Provisions that would not involve significant additional expenditures, such as those relating to the control of discharges of trade effluents to sewers, would be implemented within months, but the control of discharges to tidal estuaries and coastal waters would be delayed. The WAs and industries were expected to cooperate in joint studies of problems affecting these waters in preparation for the long-term plans for the management of these waters. Knowing that implementation will not be far off, industries can be expected to make plans and initiate changes as opportunities for changes arise. While the freedom of information provisions of the Act also would not be implemented immediately, the government hoped that the WAs and industry in cooperation with the WAs would make more information available to the public in the spirit of the Act.

The economic situation will oblige the WAs to establish priorities so that they obtain the greatest yield per unit of such investments as they are able to make. It may very well be that by beginning in such straitened circumstances, a pattern for budgeting in the future will be established that will continue to exact strong justification for every commitment of funds, even when funds cease to be scarce.

CHAPTER 9

Finance

'Money is indeed the most important thing in the world; and all sound and successful, personal and national morality should have this fact for its basis.'[1] The problems of finance, rates, and charges have been among the trials of reorganization. Even if not exacerbated by the dire economic situation at the time of the reorganization, the problem of money would still have weighed heavily.

While funds for water supply have been relatively easy to obtain, the opposite has been true for wastewater treatment, largely because the benefits are less important and they generally accrue to others than those who pay. Consequently, wastewater treatment financing has been inadequate and largely in the form of subsidies, which hide the true costs from those receiving the services.

Against such a background, the new economic philosophy of the reorganization is nothing less than revolutionary. Water service financing is to be shaped by the application of two principles: that the services must pay for themselves, and that a service should be offered only if its benefit exceeds its cost. The effects of this new approach are seen in the requirement that any subsidy 'for the public good' be rendered explicit, so that all might know its cost.

Few of those involved realized just how long and painful the transition, still incomplete, from subsidy to solvency and from expediency to optimality would be. The inheritance of inadequate and outdated facilities, combined with heavy debt service charges and rampant inflation, resulted in large charge increases not only in the first jolt of 1 April 1974 but also in the presentation of the subsequent annual budgets of the WAs. Public resistance to the new charges, much of which the public had already been unwittingly paying, focused on charges levied against properties not connected to sewerage systems. Elimination of the rate support grants also hurt those regions that could afford the costs of self-sufficiency the least, for they had been the heaviest recipients of aid. In particular the sharp increases of water rates in Wales resulted in a political imbroglio that was to threaten the future of the reorganization and the economic principles behind much of its promise.

228

HISTORICAL BACKGROUND

In general, both in the United States and in Britain, money for water supply has never been a serious problem, except in rural areas and, in the United States, in very small communities. Water supply service had grown to be considered a utility from its earliest days, as in both countries the first public water supplies were provided by private water companies. When these were taken over by public bodies, the philosophy of finance of the facilities changed little. On the other hand, sewerage has its origins in the installation of storm drains to protect the commercial areas of cities, installed as a municipality's responsibility to its citizens, and financed along with streets, police and fire protection and other public services. When the storm sewers began to be utilized for the collection of household wastewaters, the method of financing went unchanged. The costs of sewers that were then built solely for the purpose of collecting wastewaters from homes, commercial establishments and industry, and the costs of treatment facilities, continued to be met from local authority tax revenues. The first deviation from this approach appeared when charges for the use of public sewerage systems for industrial wastes were instituted although, in many communities, in the United States and Britain, industries still pay for sewerage and treatment through their general *ad valorem* taxes, or rates.

Services to accompany growth in local government could be met with only normal stress on the local government exchequer. However, requirements for sewage treatment, a public service not previously required, suddenly imposed a major new financial burden on local authorities. Also, because the benefits from such treatment generally redounded to the residents of other communities, local authorities had little incentive to provide adequate sewage treatment, particularly when these facilities competed with other public services for limited funds.

In Britain, increasing costs for sewage treatment were met from rates on property, and many communities were not in a position to afford the facilities required. The British response was the 'rate support grant' which was a contribution from the national to the local authority exchequer in accordance with local needs, but with the funds undesignated for any specific purpose. The amount of the rate support varied considerably from community to community, with the highest grants in the most impoverished areas such as Wales. These grants hid from the public the true costs of sewerage and sewage treatment, a problem that was to plague the WAs on reorganization.

PRIOR FINANCIAL ARRANGEMENTS

Each of the agencies taken over by the WAs was financed in its own way prior to the reorganization:

Water supply. Public water supply undertakings, whether operated by local authorities, water boards, or private water companies, charged residential and most commercial customers for water service on the basis of property valuations. Except for Malvern and Fylde, the latter only for study purposes, residential water supplies in England and Wales are not metered. Houses with hose connections for lawn sprinkling might pay a fixed surcharge. Industries and other large users of water are metered, with charges varying considerably from place to place depending upon the historical costs of water. Communities that had made substantial investments in water supply early in their history exacted modest charges, while other communities required higher charges for similar service. In some instances, particularly in Wales, rate support grants from government for local authorities were tapped for water supply to keep the charges low. In general, however, most water supply charges were intended to meet all the costs involved, including debt amortization.

Sewerage and sewage disposal. Costs were met from local authority rates which were assessed to include all local services. The rate statement received by the homeowner would indicate the distribution of the rate among the various services, but these were only illustrative. Rate support grants from the exchequer went a long way to keep the rates low, particularly in the more impoverished communities. Wet industries, in addition to paying the rates, were generally charged for the acceptance of industrial effluents in the sewerage system and for their treatment. The charges were related to disposal costs by means of formulae incorporating the costs of administration, conveyance to the treatment facility, and treatment. About 70 percent of all industrial process water is disposed of through publicly-owned sewerage systems.[2]

River management. The river authorities levied charges on licensed abstractions, these charges being related to the quantity of water, its quality, the season of abstraction, and the volume and quality of the wastewater returned to the resource. As noted in Chapter 2, most of these charges had been nominal, meeting the requirements for administration of the river authority but not usually the investment required to assure sufficient water for abstraction. The water pollution control function of the river authorities was financed by levies, so called 'precepts', on the local authorities. In 1970, for example, with local authority expenditures on sewerage and wastewater disposal amounting to £110 million for capital construction, and £50 million for operation and maintenance, only £1·5 million was collected for regulation.

Land drainage. Land drainage and flood protection had been financed by precepts on local authorities and on internal drainage boards. In some instances drainage charges were imposed on certain large landowners. Government grants were usually available to meet capital costs for land drainage and sea defense schemes.

Fisheries. These were financed mainly by angling license fees with deficits being made up by precepts on local authorities.

Research. Members of the Water Research Association paid an annual fee, in accordance with their size, while research conducted by the Water Pollution Research Laboratory and other government agencies was funded mainly from the exchequer.

Estimates and accounts

A Working Party on Estimates and Accounts was established by the DoE in September 1972, under the chairmanship of J. B. Woodham, to advise on WA budgeting.[3] The estimates and accounts of the WAs should be related to their objectives:

Water resources development.
Water supply.
Sewerage and sewage treatment and disposal.
Pollution prevention and environmental improvement.
Water space.
Fisheries.
Land drainage and flood protection.

An important policy recommendation was that relief given to customers by the government or by the WAs in providing services below cost should be clearly identified and publicized. In particular, any subsidy of one group of consumers by another, or between geographical areas within a region or between different regions, should be forthright. Although the government was reluctant to move towards equalization rapidly, any subsidy associated with equalization should identify the true cost of providing the services. Externalities, defined as 'social benefits conferred on, or amenities made available to those who may not be immediate consumers of the services', and the benefits and costs arising from WA activities should be clearly defined and taken into account in planning and in assessment of performance.[4]

Relief from paying the full costs of a service may be justified by the social value of the benefits conferred. While water should not be the device for righting social ills nor for the amelioration of maldistribution of income, some such uses of public services are almost inevitable. Recognizing this, the Woodham committee stressed that such social functions be clearly identified.

FINANCIAL IMPLICATIONS OF THE WATER ACT 1973

'It shall be the duty of every water authority so to discharge their functions as to secure that, taking one year with another, their revenue is not less than sufficient to meet their total outgoings properly chargeable to revenue account.'

This first paragraph in Part III of the Water Act 1973 embodies the radical change in the system of financing of the water services associated with the reorganization. The income to be received is to be sufficient to meet all the costs of providing the services, with no dependence upon grants from the exchequer other than continuation of grants to stimulate provision of services in rural areas or perhaps to stimulate employment. While the Act does empower the Secretary of State for the Environment, subject to exchequer approval, to make grants to WAs 'as he thinks fit', and some land drainage is financed by grants and precepts against the local authorities, the intention was that the WAs be entirely self-supporting.

In anticipation of this radically different scheme of finance, the DoE established a Steering Group on Water Authority Economic and Financial Objectives, chaired by J. A. Jukes, the DoE Deputy Secretary (Environmental Protection), four months before the Act became law, to advise on the economic and financial policies that should be adopted by the WAs. Its first report included recommendations concerning the two-year transitional period, although the need to consider the long-term economic and financial objectives was emphasized.[5] Policies were recommended not only to meet the requirement to cover expenditures, but also to make consumers aware of the real costs of the services provided.

The prime policy statement was that water service should be provided only when its value to the user is greater than its cost to the community. The value of services to the user was believed to be best indicated by his willingness to pay for them, and only in the case of public health needs would services be justified that would not be paid for directly by the user.

In order to facilitate the transition, little change in methods of charging during the first two years was foreseen. Specific recommendations were made against any moves to equalize charges within the regions during the first two-year period, although some equalization was expected resulting from the creation of more extensive rating areas as a result of local government reorganization. Many of the prior authorities had resorted to a number of financial expedients, such as expending their balances or incurring deficits to meet their expenditures during the last year prior to the reorganization. To assure that consumers were treated equitably, they were expected to bear the full weight of any inherited deficits or the benefit from any inherited surpluses. In establishing the charges for the first year following reorganization, the estimated increases in expenditure over the charges rendered by the previous authorities were recommended to be allocated on a uniform percentage basis to each division. The charges were to be adequate not only to cover estimated revenue expenditures, but also sufficient to contribute to building up a reasonable reserve (ten percent of annual revenue) over the first three years.

Each WA would receive funds from: abstraction charges; precepts for land drainage; public water supply; the general service charge which would include sewerage and sewage disposal, pollution control, and all the other functions not otherwise provided for; and trade effluent charges.

Grants made available from the exchequer under the Rural Water Supplies and Sewerage Acts, which had been matched by county council contributions, would henceforth be matched by the WAs by proportionally increasing charges throughout the areas.

Because of the elimination of rate support for water services, the government gave assurances that the rate support grant for the other local services would be increased to ameliorate the effect of sudden large scale increases in water charges to residential consumers. Unfortunately, consumers would fail to see the connection between their higher water bills and their rates which were held in check by increased rate support. Also unanticipated by the Jukes Committee were the severe economic blows that would descend on Britain, with interest rates doubling and inflation exceeding 20 percent per year.

IMPACT OF REORGANIZATION

The outcries resulting from the increased charges imposed by the WAs after the reorganization led the DoE to push on with recommendations for financing the second year of the reorganization, as well as considerations of long term policy.[6] Of the total of £649·3 million of annual expenditure of all the WAs, debt charges inherited from the previous authorities accounted

TABLE 9.1
Financial Condition of Authorities in the First Year

WA	Inherited surplus/deficit 1 April 1974 (£ million)	Gross revenue expenditure 1974–75 (£ million)	Estimated surplus/deficit 31 March 1975 (£ million)	Population (millions)
North West	−0·1	96·1	+0·6	7·0
Northumbrian	+0·4	22·2	+1·0	2·7
Severn Trent	+2·7	107·5	−2·5	8·5
Yorkshire	+1·0	60·4	+2·2	4·5
Anglian	+1·4	76·7	+4·9	4·1
Thames	+1·9	139·3	+6·7	12·1
Southern	+0·4	50·2	+2·1	3·7
Wessex	+0·8	26·7	−0·1	2·0
South West	+0·4	21·4	+1·0	1·3
WNWDA	+1·5	8·8	+0·3	2·9
TOTALS	+10·4	649·3	+16·1	48·8

TABLE 9.2
Debt Liabilities and Charges on Capital Expenditure

WA	Outstanding inherited debt 1 April 1974 (£ million)	Estimated new borrowing (£ million)	Budget for debt redemption (£ million)	Debt on capital expenditure (£ million)	Debt redemption gross revenue expenditure (%)
North West	330	57	9	3·3	9·7
Northumbrian	83	23	2	1·2	9·6
Severn Trent	318	69	16	3·9	14·9
Yorkshire	184	32	7	2·4	12·3
Anglian	343	59	10	2·6	13·1
Thames	398	48	15	3·5	10·4
Southern	180	23	8	2·7	14·9
Wessex	106	18	3	1·4	12·5
South West	80	15	3	1·1	12·8
WNWDA	178	40	6	3·1	11·5
TOTALS	2 200	284	79	25·2	12·1

TABLE 9.3
Revenue Expenditures—All Authorities (1974–75)
(Based on £649·3 million)

Labor, material and debt charges	
Labor, material, overhead	55·7%
Interest charges	32·2
Debt redemption	12·1
	100·0%
Total debt charges	44·3%
Services	
Water conservation and development	1·6%
Water treatment and supply	40·1
Sewerage, sewage treatment and disposal	52·8
Land drainage	4·1
Pollution prevention and other services	1·4
	100·0%

for nearly half, with about three percent of the outstanding debts being redeemed each year. Also, during the first year following the reorganization, a total capital expenditure of £394 million was anticipated, nearly all to be financed by new borrowing. Tables 9.1–9.6 indicate the range of financial data that was revealed during the first year following reorganization for each of the WAs.

Sewerage and sewage disposal service accounted for about half the revenue expenditure and two-thirds of the capital expenditure, with water supply and treatment accountable for the bulk of the remainder. The revenue was obtained during the first year about equally from domestic and nondomestic consumers. Only 20 to 30 percent of the total was derived from

TABLE 9.4
Capital Expenditures—All Authorities (1974–75)
(Based on £394 million)

Water conservation and development	5·3%
Water treatment and supply	25·0
Sewerage, sewage treatment and disposal	65·7
Land drainage	3·7
Pollution prevention and other services	0·3
	100·0%

measured services such as meters for water supply and effluent charges for industrial effluents discharged into sewerage systems, with nearly all the rest coming from charges assessed according to rateable values.

The small surpluses inherited were hardly adequate to provide much financial assistance. The high inflation rate, greater than allowed for in their initial budgets which had been considered generous, was to place some WAs in deficit by the end of their first year. Local authorities, whose facilities were to be taken over, had exacerbated the situation by holding back normal investments for maintenance and repair, supplies and the like, putting a bigger burden on the new WAs.

TABLE 9.5
Income of the Water Authorities (1974–75)

Public water supply		
Unmetered	22·6 %	
Metered	14·8	
Bulk supplies & other income	2·8	
Total water supply charges		40·2 %
Direct abstraction		1·4
Sewerage, sewage treatment & disposal		
Domestic	26·4	
Non-domestic	24·2	
Total rateable value charges	50·6	
Trade effluent charges	1·5	
Other	2·0	
Total sewerage and disposal charges		54·1
Land drainage		3·6
Fisheries		0·1
Other		0·4
		99·8 %

The cost of reorganization itself was only about 2 percent of the gross revenue expenditure and some WAs were able, even in the first year of operation, to offset these new administrative costs by savings resulting from the integration of services and functions.

The inaugural charges of the WAs represented a 41 percent increase over the charges of the prior authorities, as compared with a retail price increase of about 20 percent over the same one-year period.[7] Increased charges resulted from: changes in structure; the shift in meeting costs away from

TABLE 9.6
Water Supply and Service Charges (1974–75)

WA	Water rates p/£[a]		Metered water p/1000 gal[b]		General service charges (incl. sewerage) p/£[a]	
	Range	Average	Range	Average	Range	Average
North West	2·1–9·6	5·3	16–36	26	2·9–9·5	5·1
Northumbrian	3·0–7·5	5·8	17–30	28	1·7–14·6	4·4
Severn Trent	2·9–8·4	5·1	17–46	26	2·2–17·5	5·5
Yorkshire	4·5–10·4	7·0	12–39	30	3·8–11·6	6·4
Anglian	3·0–8·4	5·8	18–50	31	2·7–12·5	6·9
Thames	1·9–6·0	3·1	17–35	29	1·7–10·8	3·1
Southern	2·6–8·6	5·0	20–54	31	1·4–14·7	7·0
Wessex	2·1–7·0	5·4	22–43	28	3·1–10·1	6·4
South West	5·0–11·5	7·4	24–51	34	3·1–19·1	7·5
WNWDA	6·8–20·0	11·5	17–50	38	3·0–17·7	7·8
	1·9–20	4·9	12–54	29	1·4–19·1	5·3

[a] Pence in the pound of rateable value = percent of rateable value. (One penny per pound is approximately equivalent to 5 cents per $100 valuation in the US if the rateable value is taken as 5 % of the property value.) Accordingly, 5p/£ is equivalent to $50 per annum on a $20 000 property. In 1975–76, the average charge was about 25p per week each for water supply and general services, the latter including sewerage and sewage disposal.

[b] One penny per 1000 gallons is equal to about 2 cents per 1000 US gallons.

rate support grants to full charging for services rendered; the increased services, including a commitment to improving the quality of sewage treatment and disposal; and an increased effort in promoting the amenity use of waters. Also, some WAs used their first year's charges to inflict upon the consumer the new costs at one fell swoop, with charges presumably large enough to include a generous allowance for inflation, a reserve fund, and in some instances the establishment of a depreciation fund. The expectation had been that the second year of reorganization would see only minor adjustments in the charges and the furor associated with the reorganization would then be expected to have abated.

However, because of the effect of exceptionally high interest rates (reaching over 17 percent at one stage) in this capital-intensive industry with its heavy burden of inherited debt, the need for new capital investment for restoration of facilities that had been allowed to deteriorate, the need to meet other urgent demands that had been neglected prior to the reorganization, and because of the increasing rate of inflation and interest rates, the budget projected for the second year offered no relief to the WAs in facing their several publics. Table 9.7 indicates something of the level of increases in water supply charges and general services charges (which include sewerage, sewage treatment and disposal, pollution control and other services) for the second year. Increases of more than 40 percent in water supply charges and the general service charges were being required by many WAs. The disparities in charges among the WAs were accentuated. The

TABLE 9.7
Increases in Charges for the Second Year of Reorganization

WA	Water supply % increase 1975–76 over 1974–75	General service charge	
		% increase 1975–76 over 1974–75	1975–76 p/£
North West	56	41	7·2
Northumbrian	50	50	6·6
Severn Trent	51	40	7·7
Yorkshire	45	50	9·6
Anglian	30	35	9·3
Thames	25	25	3·9
Southern	36	36	9·5
Wessex	35	50	9·6
South West	38	42	10·7
WNWDA	41	90	14·8

Thames Water Authority, with the lowest charges, also required the lowest increases in charges, about 25 percent. At the other extreme, the Welsh National Water Development Authority, with the highest charges, exhibited the highest rate of increase, amounting to 90 percent in general service charges.

In appreciation of the philosophy that charges for all of the water services should be sufficient to meet the costs, the Conservative government had promised relief to householders through increased rate support grants. In January 1974, the government predicted that the increase in domestic rate burdens could be kept to a maximum of about 9 percent. The actual situation turned out to be far more serious. On 27 June 1974, Anthony Crosland, the new Labour Secretary of State for the Environment, announced the details of the rates for 255 local authorities, and in only ten of these was the average increase within the maximum nine percent predicted, and the average national increase was more nearly 30 percent.[9]

The Labour government charged that the Conservative government had been unheedful when '. . . they took water and sewerage off the rates and out of local democratic control, and substituted a system of direct charges'. They conceded that it was too late to go back on the reorganization, but the government would conduct a thorough examination of water services financing after two years of reorganization.

The ratepayers 'revolt' was only subdued by the introduction of a new government rate relief formula, which would subsidize any increases over 20 percent in the sum of both charges and rates as a special measure for 1974–75 only. The storm eventually abated but not before the officers of the WAs had been effectively diverted from implementing reorganization by being forced to spend many evenings on 'whistle stop' tours attending protest meetings.

The further increase in the rate support grant to be paid to local authorities in the second year of the reorganization placed the WA charges in an even more unfavorable light in the eyes of the public, as their unsubsidized charges increased substantially, while the general rates, being subsidized, increased far less.

Charges for 'non-service'

Prior to the reorganization, every ratepayer paid a portion of his rates, incorporated in the general property tax structure, for sewerage and sewage treatment and disposal services whether or not his 'hereditament' was connected to the sewerage system. This was no different from the situation with regard to rates for education being paid by those who have no children in the schools.

In the transitional period following the reorganization little change was effected in the system of charging, and the general services charge, which included as a major item the sewerage and sewage disposal service, was automatically continued.

'Few could have anticipated the cacophony of criticism which arose . . . over the general services charge which was often wrongly described as a sewerage charge. Clearly separated from the insulating effect of other charges on a general rate demand, this charge stood out in isolation, literally inviting protest from persons not on main drainage who realized for the first time that they were partly paying for a service which they did not receive.'[10]

The popular press and television waxed indignant. The WAs were not able to respond because most local authorities from whom they had inherited the sewerage systems had no information as to which properties were and were not connected to the sewerage service, as this distinction had never been significant.

Immediate public pressure was put on the WAs to take inventory of the households without service with the intention that all of their service charges would be eliminated. In the WAs' response, little attempt was made to explain the historic reason for this situation, namely that the provision of sewerage had been considered a public health function chargeable with the general rates rather than a charge for service. The protection of a community against noisome conditions benefits not only the sewered householder, but the community at large. Nevertheless, the WAs found themselves very much on the defensive. They considered providing services for the cleaning of cesspools and septic tanks so that householders would in fact receive a service whether or not they were connected to a sewerage system. The government's response was that those not connected would have their general service charge cut by half.[11] This compromise resulted in part from an appreciation that the general services charge included services other than sewerage, such as pollution prevention and fisheries costs, and that some benefits would accrue to a household whether or not it was connected to the sewerage system.

The WAs did not receive this recommendation with enthusiasm. The South West Water Authority estimated that this change would add about 8·5 percent to the charges of those whose houses are connected to the sewerage system as the proportion of people unconnected in the SWWA, between 15 and 20 percent, is substantially higher than for the rest of England and Wales.

Other WAs objected because the costs of providing cleansing services to the septic tanks and cesspools would often be greater than the cost of providing sewer service. In addition, a property not connected to the sewerage system would generally have a lower rateable value than a similar property that is connected, favoring these unconnected at the expense of those being served.

In May 1975 the courts held that even 50 percent charges against unconnected properties were beyond the legal powers of the WAs. In the case under judgement, *Daymond* v. *Plymouth City Council*, the latter as the local authority collecting agent of the South West Water Authority, the court asserted that the sewerage charges could not lawfully be demanded of a resident with private drainage facilities.[12] Charges under Section 30 of the Act could be exacted only from those for whom services were performed and facilities provided and to whom rights were made available.

The SWWA, in appealing directly to the House of Lords, expressed a concern shared by many of the WAs, that their financial distress would be aggravated if this source of income were denied. The House of Lords dismissed the SWWA appeal, thereby forcing the WAs to refund some £60 million collected from some 900 000 unconnected property owners in England and Wales over the first two years. The NWC estimated that the average charges to customers would have to be increased by about 21 percent in the third year of reorganization, 1976–77, to cover the loss in revenue, with some WAs being hard hit.[13]

Inasmuch as '. . . sewerage and sewage disposal services provided by a WA themselves confer a substantial benefit to the community as a whole in terms of public health and an improved environment . . . regardless of whether . . . properties are connected . . .' the government proposed an amendment to the Water Act 1973 that would permit some part of the costs of the service to be levied against unconnected properties.[14] The Water Charges Act 1976, which divides the general services charge into two parts, one for sewerage to be paid only by connected properties and the other an environmental services charge to be paid by all properties, was given Royal Assent on 25 March 1976. The government estimated that the latter would amount to only two to five percent of the total at this time.[14]

Capital investments

The greatest initial changes in the financing of water services were in capital finance, as the WAs are more akin to the nationalized industries than to the local authorities from whom they inherited the services.[16] While the WAs have the power to allocate their capital resources amongst all the services for which they are responsible, switching their financial resources about as they feel appropriate, the government will be placing a capital ceiling each year on each WA similar to their practice with all nationalized industries. During the first year, the capital requests of the WAs, based upon estimates made by the previous constituent authorities, were considerably in excess of the amount allowed by the government. Even with an initial 40 percent reduction imposed by the government, the financial situation in December 1973 was such that the Chancellor of the Exchequer ordered a further 20 percent cut in capital expenditures, reaching a point where almost all the capital funds were obligated for projects committed by the previous authorities and few new starts could be anticipated. The total new capital expenditure authorized by government, about £284 million for the first year after the reorganization, was about the same order of magnitude as capital expenditures made annually in the years prior to the reorganization.[17]

This control by the government of the capital expenditures of the water authorities was based, as it was for the other nationalized industries, on the need for the government to manage its economy in the face of serious financial strictures. In order to help the government fix these limits, the WAs are required to identify their objectives and prepare long term investment plans. Within this limitation, the WAs are not subject to detailed interference on projects but are able to borrow to the extent necessary to cover their programs after the WA investment program has been approved by the government.

Two other conditions brought the capital program more into line with the nationalized industries than had been the case of the local authorities. Firstly, borrowing for capital purposes would have to be from the National

Loans Fund, the European Investment Bank and other foreign sources subject to Treasury and Bank of England approval. Temporary borrowing from other sources would be permitted only for a short term working capital. Secondly, the WAs are to be set a target rate of return on capital investment.

The limitation on capital investment would not be as much of a restriction as anticipated for some WAs because of the escalating charges they faced on account of inflation and rising interest rates. Gilliland pointed out that, at the prevailing rates, for every £100 spent on capital, £20 had to be provided in financing charges.[18] Such heavy charges were bound to limit the level of capital expenditures. The Jukes Committee's third report emphasized that borrowing was not the best way for the industry to achieve its capital program, with greater emphasis being placed upon raising revenues sufficient to make contributions towards capital investment. However, the financial situation that the WAs inherited precluded beginning large-scale programs of financing of capital investments from revenues, as the charges were already found to be much higher than had been anticipated. The government, which had originally suggested that a ten percent reserve fund be developed over a three-year period, felt obliged in the second year of the reorganization to limit the amounts to be placed in the reserve to two percent of gross revenue, which was to include amounts to be used for capital reserve, signifying that initial capital expenditures would have to be met almost entirely from borrowing.

Eric Gilliland, director of finance for the Thames Water Authority, expressed concern that forcing all capital expenditures to be met from borrowing moved away from the efficient use of resources with the crippling interest rates imposing serious financial handicaps for the WAs early in their existence.

In response to this situation, a working group on economic and financial policies was established with NWC leadership to take over the responsibilities of the Jukes Committee. Peter Stott, the NWC'S director general, served as chairman, with Alex Morrison, the TWA's chief executive, as vice-chairman. Each of the WAs was represented by a director so chosen that all the corporate directorates were represented. The NWC provided the secretariat with observers from the government, the DoE, H. M. Treasury, and the Welsh Office.

The group's first report, *Paying for Water*, issued in April 1976,[19] was intended to be the basis for discussion within the WAs and the government, leading to policy decisions on finance. Without taking a stand, NWC '... noted the very clear implication that the basis of finance which the industry has inherited does not conform with ... Government policy for finance of public corporations. Insufficient allowance is being made for depreciation of assets and consequently the borrowing of the industry is too high.'

It was concluded that the amount charged to consumers ought to be substantially increased (about 20 percent) to reflect their use of the industry's assets. On the basis of current costs, this should yield revenue sufficient to finance about 50 percent of the industry's capital expenditure.

Whether such further increases in charges will be acceptable remains to be seen. The basis for such an increase will need to be explained to the public better than the earlier increases were!

ESTABLISHING CHARGES

In the United States and the United Kingdom the charges for water services have tended to spring from the history of each water undertaking, with little attempt to develop a set of principles and then to apply these principles in fixing charges. A wide variety of rate structures is now used for water supply utilities in the United States in addition to the large variation in charging levels.[20] If other countries are considered, an even wider variety is discernible. The breadth and diversity of charges for sewerage and sewage disposal are even greater, including charges based on property values, on surcharges on water charges, on subsidies from central government, and on combinations of all of these.

With traditional charging schemes based on historic costs being used throughout the world, economists have had difficulty introducing sound principles of finance into these schemes. One such set of principles is that:[21]

1. charges should produce sufficient revenue,
2. charges should be stable and not unnecessarily complex,
3. charges should promote the efficient allocation of resources, and
4. charges should not discriminate amongst classes of customers.

The first three of these principles were explicitly stated by the Jukes Committee in its recommendations, with the condition that the public health be first served.

Gilliland also has provided a set of five general principles upon which long term charging schemes might be based, four of which are identical to those above.[18] Gilliland's fifth principle considered unmetered supplies, not a problem in the United States, where metering is widely used and essential to innovative rate structures currently being proposed.[22] Charging policies available to the WAs are examined below in light of the four common charging principles.

Meeting the revenue requirements

The WAs are explicitly required to meet from charges all of their costs, including operation and maintenance, interest on outstanding debts, depreciation or debt redemption, and a contribution towards a reserve for future capital expenditure. In the water industry, costs rise continuously with time, as additional water resources require going further for their development or as water pollution control requires more extensive treatment. This rising costs situation is exacerbated during periods of inflation, so that the combination requires frequent rate adjustments.

When charges are based upon historic costs, the inherent lag in raising these prices, even if they could be adjusted annually, results in rate levels that are likely to be continually inadequate. This growing gap between revenue and costs seriously affects the financial condition of any public utility and is particularly troublesome to the new WAs which began their existence with large inherited debts. Accordingly, the charging schemes adopted should anticipate and mitigate this problem of lagging charges to the greatest extent possible.

Where charges are computed from measured use, price elasticity may have a moderating effect on the erosion of income. However, when prices are based on historic costs, the price elasticity tends generally to be so low that there is little incentive for modification in water-using practices. One approach often urged by economists, and up to now vigorously rejected by engineers and the water industry generally, both in Britain and in the United States, is the institution of marginal cost pricing. However, where supplies are not metered, and the benefits of price elasticity cannot be realized, marginal cost pricing can be introduced only with difficulty.

These arguments also apply to the imposition of charges for industrial effluents discharged to sewers and for the discharge of industrial effluents to surface and groundwaters, where the utility of these waters would be seriously affected by such discharges.

Simplicity and stability in charging structures

A charging structure should be simple and understood by all customers, so that the customers' options are clear and the savings that they may accrue would not be lost merely by their failure to understand the options available. In addition, if charging structures are to provide any incentives for water conservation, not only must they be simple, but they must be seen to be relatively stable so that commitments made in response to the incentives would be seen to yield returns over a significant period rather than being undone by a new series of rate adjustments.

Residential customers may opt, for example, to use a laundry washing machine that costs somewhat more than a standard model but uses less water, if there is assurance that over a sufficient period of time the difference in water use will be reflected in a difference in water charges that would make this investment worthwhile; or an industry might make costly internal process changes for the purpose of reducing water use and effluent discharge, but only if these large scale investments could be seen to yield a saving over a period of time sufficient to justify them.

Efficient resource utilization

The full value of marginal cost pricing comes into its own in resource allocation and in providing incentives that would optimize the utilization of resources. As indicated in the Jukes Committee's third report,[6] one of the broad objectives of an efficient charging scheme is to produce an appropriate balance between investment in water services and in other sectors of the economy, reaffirming the suggestion in the Committee's first report that it is desirable to provide water services only when their value to the user is at least as great as the cost to the community of providing the services.[5] Furthermore. within the water industry itself or within any of the particular services of the water industry, efficient use of the resources can best be assured by giving the users sufficient incentive to increase or to reduce their demand for these services by ensuring that, as far as practicable, their charges reflect the cost to the WAs of satisfying their demands. Thus, the principle of marginal cost charging: '... that charges AT THE MARGIN of demand should reflect the incremental costs imposed on the system in meeting these demands or the savings which could be made by not meeting them'.[6]

Charges 'at the margin' are concerned with the difference between the cost to the supplier of producing the next unit of service and the benefit to the user of that unit's production, as measured by the price which users are willing to pay for it. The operating rule is a simple one: if the cost to the supplier of providing the next unit is greater than the benefit (as measured by the price which people will pay for it), that unit should not be produced. If the cost to the supplier of producing the next unit is less than the benefit to the consumer of its availability, then it should be produced. This question can be repeated, and the resultant decisions made, until a scale of production is reached where the price people are willing to pay equals the cost of supply of the last unit; at such a point resources are in principle optimally allocated. 'Marginal pricing' of a utility's service, then, consists of setting the price equal to the cost to the utility of supplying either the last unit or the next unit; at such a juncture of supply and demand, society as a whole could only be worse off if more or less were provided than people would buy at such a price, provided that people's willingness to pay for a service is a valid indication of its social benefit. The last point is a major qualification of the optimality of marginal pricing, for it requires that the income distribution of a society be accepted as being equitable, a point that the majority of the British public is hardly about to concede. Economists and professionals in the water field have countered this criticism by arguing that income redistribution, if deemed desirable, should not be an obligation of water authorities, but rather an explicit decision of government, for that is where such responsibility truly lies. Nevertheless, the justifiably strong tradition of public health considerations in both the water supply and wastewater disposal fields might necessitate a modification of the 'willingness to pay' criterion for that level of service considered essential to the public health.

A difficulty in the application of marginal pricing to the water industry is shared with most other utilities: the cost to the utility at the margin may be greater or less than the average cost of production. A fixed service charge can be used to provide for that minimal level of service which is held to be essential for the public health, but it will be at a *higher* rate than the marginal charge, so that the gallon of water for lawn sprinkling at the golf course will be cheaper than the poor man's first gallon. A second fundamental problem in the application of marginal pricing to the water industry lies in the sharply discontinuous nature of investment, and thus in the cost of supply. Any application of textbook marginal pricing soon runs into such practical limitations, not the least difficult being its conflict with the goal that charges be stable and easy to understand.[23]

In light of the practical difficulties in any attempt at marginal pricing, why is so much attention being paid to it? The answer lies in the nature of much of economic reasoning; even where the optimal solution is unattainable in practice, movement towards that solution usually results in greater economic efficiency. The principle that society should be compensated for the cost of the services it provides is a noble goal, and any step, however small, toward such a goal from the *status quo*, where all kinds of hidden subsidies and inequities interfere with economic and efficient resource allocation, is a move in the right direction.

Wastewater treatment

Marginal cost concepts are as appropriate to wastewater treatment as to water supply. The greater the removal of pollutants, the greater the costs of removing any additional unit of pollution. This is readily observed in conventional treatment where primary sedimentation removes at relatively low cost the first 30 percent of BOD or suspended solids. However, after secondary treatment achieves about 85 percent removal, an additional 10 percent removal will cost many times more than removing the first 30 percent. Figure 9.1 illustrates the general relationship between cost and degree of treatment. Depending upon the industry or the pollutant, going from 97 to 99 percent removal may cost as much as the entire effort going from zero to 97 percent.[24] Sharply rising costs accompany higher and higher degrees of pollution control.

Another not unrelated consideration is that the cost of removing a unit of pollution at any level of treatment varies significantly from one industry to another, so that the marginal cost for achieving any given level of quality in receiving streams would vary depending upon which industries were required to institute reductions in their pollutional loads. Uniform requirements, while they might appear to be fair in imposing equal burdens on various industries on a water course, would tend to be uneconomical in total social costs. Similarly, the various formulae established in both Britain and in the United States, such as the Mogden formula, which applies a surcharge on wastewaters in accordance with their strengths and volumes, with little regard for the costs involved in reducing a unit of pollution load, do not provide least cost solutions. If the marginal cost objective were to be met precisely, such formulae would have to be modified according to the industry to which they were applied.

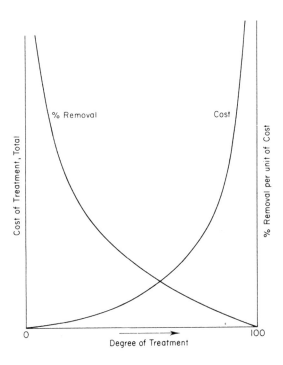

FIG. 9.1 Costs of wastewater treatment as a function of degree of treatment.

The adoption of marginal costs charging tends to violate other sound principles, namely, simplicity and equity amongst different classes of customers. Accordingly the challenge to the WAs in establishing charges for effluent disposal to sewerage systems and eventually, should this be adopted, to receiving waters, is to compromise by establishing charging formulae that are simple but that approach marginal cost objectives. Considering the charging policies inherited, where some industries are not being charged in proportion to their waste loads at all, such adjustments are not likely to be on the agenda for some years.

Peak charging

Another important consideration in marginal cost pricing is the higher cost imposed upon water supply undertakings to meet summertime peak demands for water and upon polluters to meet effluent requirements during periods of low flow in receiving streams. Many of the facilities for a water supply undertaking, including raw water pumps, transmission mains, and treatment facilities, need to be sized for requirements of the maximum day during the year, which would tend to occur over a period of months during summer dry weather periods. Other elements of the system, such as distribution system piping, service storage and highlift pumps, need to be sized for the peak requirement during a maximum day, such as the early morning or late afternoon hours.[25] The marginal costs of providing an additional unit of water during these peak periods is considerably higher than that of providing that same unit of water during off-peak periods. Recognition of these different marginal costs is matter-of-fact in many enterprises, such as the vacation industry. Charges for telephone and electricity services are often reduced during off-peak hours to encourage full use of capital facilities in recognition of the lower marginal cost involved in providing off-peak services. The initiation of variable-charging might be feasible for metered services for water supply and for effluent disposal, but would hardly be feasible where metering is not practiced.

The adoption of varying charges according to seasonal or hourly peaks has only begun to be initiated in the water industry in the United States. The Fairfax County Water Authority in Virginia has adopted a new rate structure that reflects seasonal variations in costs.[26] The authority serves some 84 000 retail customers with some 80 000 housed in individually metered household units. The earlier rate structure was of the conventional declining block variety. The new rate structure has a base rate and a surcharge on all water used in excess of 1·3 times each customer's winter quarter use, '. . . to increase equity by assessing peak users with the extra cost of maintaining capability to meet their peak requirements and to effect water conservation by reducing peak demands.'

Price discrimination amongst customers

The 1973 Act requires that rates charged for water services should not discriminate among classes of customers. When a water service is made available to some consumers at below the marginal cost and to others above, then one group subsidizes the other. The Woodham Committee recommended that any relief given to a group of consumers by providing services below cost, whether subsidized by the government or through cross-subsidization within the industry, should be clearly identified and publicized, intimating that such subsidies are not to be considered government policy.

Subsidies of certain classes of the population have been used by governments to accomplish a wide range of purposes: to low-income segments of the population to assure at least a minimum of the benefits due to all citizens, such as public health, which would require a minimum quantity of wholesome water and means for the sanitary disposal of wastes; or to industries felt to be important either to the local community in which they are to be located or to the nation for accomplishing some public service that cannot be expected to yield a profit immediately. One subsidy that has been widely accepted is the provision of water supply and sewerage services for rural populations under the Rural Water Supplies and Sewerage Acts which provide funds for rural districts from the national exchequer. Such a subsidy is overt and accomplishes a national social purpose which is clearly identified and, as a result the burden is carried by society knowingly.

When water was cheap, hidden subsidies were not considered important, because the amounts involved were trivial. In some instances, particularly in the United States, with water supply service often being the only 'profitable' enterprise of a local authority, it was not uncommon for the income from the water supply department to be diverted, often quite overtly, to other municipal functions.

A far more important, hidden subsidy results from the practice of providing enticements to industry to locate in an area in order to relieve unemployment or to increase the tax base or rateable value, which presumably would then afford the residents of that area opportunities for greater social services from the increased financial resources. The benefits of such subsidies may be illusory, as industries that locate on the basis of financial inducements often end up imposing burdens on the local community that more than offset the increased taxes that they pay. They require roads, additional local health services for new employees, more schools, increased refuse disposal and a wide range of other services. If public policy requires that industry be attracted to an area, and if it is felt that subsidies are warranted, these should be overt and not hidden in water charges, as the water industry has enough difficulty providing the services for which it is responsible with the revenue available to it without being responsible for subsidizing industrial developments.

Implementing a sound pricing policy

The ultimate goals of equity, simplicity, stability, rationality, optimality and sufficiency of both services and financial resources have to be approached gradually, but steadily, and with heavy doses of compromise and expedience.

A charging policy that would combine all of the accepted principles would be ideal but in practice the several principles are rarely compatible with one another.[27] Social, legal and other factors limit the WAs' complete freedom to adopt sound financial policies. The WAs should not use their charging policies to meet social aims, such as the redistribution of income, by varying charges according to the ability to pay. On the other side, the total revenue requirement should not impose such a burden on consumers that financial considerations would induce a domestic consumption below the level necessary to maintain public health standards.

Statutory constraints may also interfere with sound pricing policy. For example, the WAs are prevented from charging for direct abstractions of water for agricultural purposes other than for spray irrigation. Just as agricultural subsidies have dominated water charging policy in western United States, and are slow to be remedied because of the political influence of the agricultural sector, so too in England and Wales, the elimination of this subsidy may be slow to be achieved. However, in humid Britain such subsidies are not nearly as serious as they are in the arid west of the United States.

Another major constraint is the paucity of information upon which to make rational decisions on pricing, including the effect of variations in price on the demands for any one of the services, the various options available for handling presently unmeasured supplies and discharges, and lastly marginal operating and future incremental costs.

Marginal cost pricing faces practical difficulties when the marginal costs vary significantly from place to place within a service area. Traditionally, within the service area of any single water supply undertaking, the charges would be the same whether the customer is located near the treatment plant, requiring small transmission costs, or at considerable distances from the plant and perhaps requiring additional pumping. Charging customers differently in different locations within a single service area is not practical or politically feasible even where differences in the costs of serving various locations are recognized. In the United States, where water supply services are highly fragmented, when one authority sells water outside its own political or service area boundaries to another authority, either wholesale or retail, it not uncommonly charges a higher rate. This practice has been based more upon historic and political differences than on any principle or consideration of marginal costs. Often, the initial costs of the service may have been met in part by general taxation to which the outlying areas had not contributed, making such extra charges reasonable. More often, it is more a matter of monopoly control of a resource with higher charges to those with no right of access to the resource. In Britain, with water supply regrouping, variations in charges within the enlarged service areas have tended to be eliminated. In fact, those in outlying areas may have been subsidized because, with water charges based upon rateable values, rateable values in rural areas tend to be less even though the actual pence on the pound water charges were the same.

METERING

The issue of metering had become a major focus for the Labour party opposition during the debates on the Water Bill. Labour was successful to the extent that any statutory instrument containing regulations for metering would be subject to annulment by parliament. Thus, the Act did not resolve the issue, and the controversy as to the installation of metering for residential customers continues unabated. A sampling of the major papers on metering include those by Rees,[28] Herrington,[29] Smith,[30] Jenking,[31] and lastly a 'for-and-against' pair of articles in *Water*.[32] The controversy is explored below.

The arguments against metering

The cost of metering would be far greater than the savings in water supply costs, so that any investment made for the installation of residential metering would be more productive if made for the development of additional water resources. Dugdale cited the situation in the Severn Trent Water Authority area where the cost of installing meters was estimated to vary between £25 and £35. At current interest rates, about 14 percent, and with the requirements for maintenance, replacement, meter reading and billing, the annual running cost for a domestic water meter was estimated to be between £5 and £8. Against this was set the annual STWA water charge of £13 for the average household with a rateable value of £180. Metering would add an exorbitant charge to achieve a dubious fairness and a questionable reduction in consumption.

Metering would violate the first obligation of a public water supply service, the protection of the public health. Metering would appear to require an ability to pay and would have its greatest impact on the poor.

Opponents of metering claim that charges based upon rateable value are not unfair as those homes with higher rateable values will have more water fixtures and will therefore use more water. Dugdale showed that the average water consumption in the Malvern area increased with rateable value from about 50 gallons (230 liters) per household per day for rateable values of £20 to £80 to more than 100 gallons (450 liters) for values exceeding £180. He concluded that 'water charges based on rateable value are not savagely unfair.'

The arguments for metering

In the early days of water services, metering and billing associated with any sophisticated method of charging might well have cost more than the services themselves, and certainly more than any savings that might have been induced by introducing such business-like measures. However, circumstances have changed in recent years, to the point where the water services have become significant costs to householders and an investment in accounting for the product sold and the services rendered may have become justified. Water has become a big, capital intensive business. Its importance, as related to other industries in the public sector, is revealed in Table 9.8.[33] In the United States, the investment per dollar of revenue for water supply in 1963 was $7·61, as compared with $4·73 and $2·20 for electricity and gas respectively, while the annual revenue per customer was only $71 for water supply as compared with $254 and $209 for the others, respectively.[34]

TABLE 9.8
Comparison of Capital Intensity of Public Utility Industries

Industry	*Capital employed per employee* £	*Annual capital expended as % of gross revenue expended* %	*Annual capital expended per employee* £
Electricity	32 000	21	2 400
Post Office	9 700	38	1 800
British Gas	20 600	13	1 300
Water	40 400	61	7 200

Stott characterized the water industry in Britain as the only public service (1) that is absolutely essential, as it cannot be replaced by some competing service; and (2) where the customer receives a bill over which he had no control. Unless it is metered, the customer cannot reduce his charges by exerting a more prudent use of the water service.[35]

With increasing costs for all water services, the user has begun to be concerned by his helplessness in ameliorating his situation. The costs for water services, as compared to other services, can only rise. Technical 'breakthroughs' that might lower the costs of the water services cannot be expected, while nuclear power, North Sea oil and gas, and electronic number recognition all offer some potential for reducing the rate of increase of the costs of electricity, fuel and postal services respectively. When a product or a service is offered without a charge related to its magnitude, confidence in the enterprise and the quality of the professionals employed suffers. Water service is important and expensive and must be seen to be so by assuring proper accounting of its product.

Price elasticity

A significant issue is whether metering would provide an incentive for water conservation, whether water usage is 'price elastic'. (*Price elasticity of demand* is the percent change in the quantity of a product divided by the percent change in price.) The studies made by British economists have been based upon the American experience, where metering is widespread. In the early days of metering, the conventional wisdom was that 'Meter consciousness depresses domestic use abnormally when meters are first put in, but draft does return eventually to a defendable norm'.[36] Rees does not agree that the demand for water is completely unresponsive to metering[37] and illustrates the issue with the diagram in Fig. 9.2.

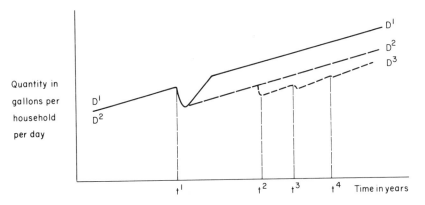

t^1 = the year metering is introduced ; t^{2-4} years in which the unit price is increased.

D^1 = Consumption trend if the impact of metering is only short-lived.

D^2 = Consumption trend line of the initial demand effect is permanent.

D^3 = Consumption trend line if consumers respond to further price rises after metering is introduced.

FIG. 9.2   Impact of metering on water use.

In time-trend studies, Rees reviewed a comprehensive study of the impact of introducing metering in Boulder, Colorado. Between 1955 and 1968, with meters installed in 1962, the internal use within the home was reduced by 36 percent while lawn sprinkling was decreased about 50 percent and did not again increase.[38] In nine communities in the United States where metering was introduced between 1900 and 1963, the consumption fell some 20 to 40 percent.

The National Water Commission (US) affirmed that, depending upon local conditions, water demand is generally responsive to pricing, with price elasticity ranging up to −1·2 (a 12 percent reduction for a ten percent increase in price).[39]

A study in the early 1960s indicated that price elasticity ranged from −0·2 for domestic uses to −1·1 for lawn sprinkling.[40] A cross-sectional study of comparable areas indicated a 33 percent reduction in average annual water use for metered services as compared with flat rate services, with almost all the reduction being accounted for by lawn sprinkling.[41] In a 1954 study of all the communities within the United States, the *per capita* consumption varied with metering as shown in Table 9.9.[42]

From a 1967 unpublished study of 12 large Dutch communities, where conditions are similar to those in the United Kingdom, Rees found domestic consumption varied from 53 gallons (200 liters) *per capita* per day in four communities that were 100 percent metered to about 90 gallons (350 liters) *per capita* per day for three communities without any residential metering. From 13 studies involving several hundred communities in the United States and Canada, during the period 1955 to 1967, price elasticities ranged from a low of -0.05 for some Massachusetts communities to a high of -1.24 for communities in Kansas. In general, the price elasticity of water demand in American cities has ranged from -0.2 to -0.5 but until recently this effect was masked by the effect of increasing affluence.[21]

TABLE 9.9
Water Consumption as a Function of Metering in the US

Percentage of Water production metered	Water consumption gallons per capita per day
0–50	145
50–95	122
95–99	117
over 99	109

Experiences with metering in the United Kingdom would be more useful but residential metering has been limited to Malvern, where metering of domestic consumers has been practiced since 1872, and Fylde, where a special metering study was mounted. Data were collected in Malvern from 1954 to 1969, when Malvern was regrouped with a larger water board and, although metering was continued, pricing practices were changed.[43] Consumption was based upon household usage beyond the meter, while most other data include also losses in the distribution system and other unmeasured public uses.

When the average price charged in Malvern during 1967–68 was 13 to 14 pence per 1000 gallons (4500 liters), the price elasticity for year-round consumption was approximately -0.11. During the summer months it was slightly higher, − 0·14. When the price per unit rose in 1969 to 21 pence per 1000 gallons, the price elasticity rose to − 0·13 for annual consumption and − 0·16 for the summer demands. Adjusting for real prices increases the elasticity somewhat. Malvern residents appeared to be rather more responsive to price during the summer than Americans, who use larger quantities of water during the generally hot dry summer months than are required in Britain. Rees concluded that householders do respond to pricing and it is her contention that the introduction of metering and unit charging would result in an immediate and permanent decline in consumption, amounting to something of the order of 20 percent if the charges were about 20 pence per 1000 gallons. (The charges for metered supplies in 1976 were much higher, ranging from 41·8 to 59·9 pence per 1000 gallons.) In a summary of the impact of metering on consumption in the United States and at Malvern and Fylde, Herrington estimated that metering would reduce total water consumption between three and 12 percent.[46]

When water charges are trivial, or unrelated to use, price elasticity can be expected to be low or even zero. When the true costs of water services are passed on to consumers and the charges are no longer trivial, price elasticity can be expected to increase. When sewerage and sewage disposal charges are added to water supply charges, the higher total price of the water services will further increase price elasticity.

In summary, metering can be justified on a wide variety of bases: the opportunity to introduce the principles of marginal pricing; the provision of incentives for reducing excess water use, thereby postponing major capital investments for additional water supply; providing the consumer with some measure of control over the water bills he is obliged to pay; the introduction of pricing schemes, based on metering, that would tend to be equitable and avoid what appears often to be a subsidy of large water users by the smaller residential users; and lastly, the placing of a major capital intensive industry on a sound, business-like basis where the charges to be made for water services can be defended and can be seen by consumers to be defensible.

Proponents of metering have recommended that metering should be introduced on a trial basis in selected areas, to demonstrate whether or not the potential for savings and equity are in fact realized. Such a trial has been mounted by the Severn Trent Water Authority in Mansfield. Interpreting the results of such demonstrations will not be easy, as the full value of metering will not accrue until metering is widely adopted. For example, water-saving devices will not be introduced on a large scale by plumbing, washing machine and other manufacturers of water-using appliances until a larger and more certain market becomes available. The savings inherent in modern metering technology, such as remote reading, will be available only when residential metering is generally accepted.

The NWC working group concluded that:[19]

1. Alternative bases for charging without metering offer no advantages over rate-based charging, so long as rates are used for other purposes.
2. Residential metering cannot be implemented on a wide-spread basis except over a long period, so it should be adopted selectively to improve the use of existing resources, to reduce losses, or to provide an alternative where existing methods of charging are inequitable.
3. Assistance which may be needed for low income households to achieve welfare goals should be provided through social benefits, rather than through water-charging schemes.

EFFLUENT CHARGES

Charges for the discharge of effluents into receiving streams were authorized in the Control of Pollution Act 1974, although such discharges to sewers have been chargeable since 1937. The Royal Commission on Environmental Pollution explored effluent charges because of its expectation that discharges to estuaries would soon be controlled. Effluent charges might be useful because polluters had not been obliged to take into account the full social costs of pollution in reaching decisions about how much to pollute.[45] The freedom to use the environment as a factor of production without any payment for it or any financial incentives to economize in its use results in a misallocation of resources with 'too much of the scarce resource clean water ... used up in the course of pollution'.

The Royal Commission considered two approaches to controlling pollution. The approach advocated by the Commission was to empower the WAs to give consents, or permits, limiting the quantities and concentrations of effluents, with the duty to prosecute anyone who infringes upon these consents. The other approach considered was a system of charges, under which the WAs, instead of giving consents, would apply a scale of charges according to the quantity and strength of the effluents discharged. Such a system would not preclude the prohibition of certain dangerous substances, and upper limits on these could be imposed. Charges would vary from place to place according to the condition of the receiving body of water and the damage that the pollutants might do. The argument for this approach is that the polluter would have a flexible inducement to reduce his pollution by any means he chose rather than to pay the charge, with the claim being made by its proponents that the overall effect of using such market forces rather than fixed standards would achieve a higher level of pollution abatement. This approach is not novel, as many local authorities have required payment for discharge of industrial effluents into their sewerage systems, although the charges were often based upon meeting the costs of providing the services and were not at a level which offered inducements to reduce the levels of discharges.

Although the Commission did not oppose the use of charges as a means of controlling pollution, they felt that such charges should not be introduced until further studies had been made. Two members of the Commission, Lord Zuckerman of Burnham Thorpe and Professor Wilfred Beckerman, in a minority report, set out a case for the control of pollution by charges with the recommendation that preparations should be made forthwith to introduce effluent charges for the disposal of effluents into all rivers and tidal waters. They stated that a system of control is required which would provide incentive to polluters to reduce pollution up to the point where the costs to them of further pollution abatement would be greater than the marginal damage done to society by the pollution. A price mechanism would provide such an incentive. For example, if a polluter were charged per unit of pollution discharged more than it would cost him to abate that unit of pollution, he would be encouraged to abate it. Beyond that point, where he would have to pay more for pollution abatement than he would save through paying lesser pollution charges, he would opt to make the payment. The charges that he would pay per unit of pollution would of course have to reflect the cost to society of accepting that unit of pollution in the environment. The value of the incentive made irrelevant who received the pollution charges. The precedent for such charges for discharges to sewers being received by the local authority to meet the cost of providing the treatment might well be followed by having these charges paid to the WA, which might use the funds received to provide public treatment of these effluents, or to treat the river, or to accept this pollution and use the funds so received to offset higher costs that this pollution would impose on users of the river who would be affected by the pollution.

The majority of the Commission, while supporting the principle that polluters should not have free use of the environment, were unwilling to subscribe to the initiation of effluent charges because they were not convinced that a system of charges would be as effective as consents and that the administration of such a system of charges would need an expertise which they did not believe existed.

The difference between the majority and minority was less a matter of substance than a matter of timing. While the Control of Pollution Act 1974 authorized the WAs to impose effluent charges, the government was explicit in postponing its implementation, quite probably because the WAs already had 'too much on their plates'.

That the imposition of effluent charges for the control of pollution is radical, at least in its implementation if not in its conception, is evident from the heroic but unsuccessful efforts made on its behalf by Resources for the Future, a non-profit Washington, D.C. corporation established in 1952 to advance the development, conservation and use of natural resources and the improvement of the quality of the environment through programs of research and education. Allen V. Kneese and Blair T. Bower, RFF economist and engineer respectively, have long been strong advocates of the use of economic incentives such as effluent charges for environmental quality control.[46] Not incidentally, they have also been articulate advocates of regional approaches to water quality management.

Up to now, effluent charges as a means for controlling water pollution have been given short shrift, except in The Netherlands and in the Ruhr area of Germany. The institutions created by the water reorganization make effluent charges far more feasible in England and Wales than in the United States, where philosophical acceptance may be greater. Some of the advantage of effluent charges are discussed below.

1. Effluent charges have the potential for minimizing the overall cost of pollution control at a given location on a stream by concentrating the reduction of pollution most heavily among those firms and activities whose costs of reduction are least.[47] Just as the regional ownership of the municipal wastewater treatment facilities in a river basin can minimize the investment in treatment to achieve any degree of water quality so, too, effluent charges applied to industries, not only in accordance with the cost of their treatment, but also in accordance with their location within the water basin, can minimize the costs of pollution abatement. Thus, an efficient approach will require that different industries reduce pollution by differing amounts depending upon the nature of the industry and the location of a particular plant.

2. The high price elasticity of water supply for industry is amplified when effluent charges are added to the charges for water supply. Not only can the effluent charges be reduced by the introduction of treatment costing less than the charges, but other approaches may be pursued, such as modification of production processes to require less water or to produce less waste, or by recycling water or by varying the nature of the raw materials or varieties of products with a view to limiting pollution. Examples are legion, but most illustrative may be the instance in Holland where effluent charges, gradually increasing with time on a fixed schedule, were introduced in 1970. The practice in a starch processing plant had been to wash down machinery and floors, using large quantities of water and adding substantial organic waste to the effluent. The initiation of effluent charges and the promise of a gradual increase in these charges were sufficient inducement to the industry to introduce the use of vacuum cleaners which, in addition to reducing water consumption and water pollution, returned previously wasted material to product.

3. With effluent charges, as contrasted with regulation by consent, regulatory agencies are not required to be as knowledgeable about industrial process or waste treatment. A system of effluent charges does

require monitoring, as does a system of consents. These can be routinely carried out by the industry, with only occasional checking by the regulatory agency in both instances.

4. Effluent charges encourage industry to re-examine its own operations on a continuing basis, and perhaps to make major changes at appropriate times when plant enlargements or process modifications are being undertaken for other reasons. An industry has no incentive to reduce pollution beyond what is required by their consent, and in fact would not be likely to do so, as it would incur costs that are not required. On the other hand, the potential for the reduction in effluent charges is a permanently dangling carrot that promises some financial return for every investment made in reducing pollution.

5. Economic research has tended to support the value of the effluent charge approach.[48] The effectiveness of effluent charges has been demonstrated by local authorities who have imposed such charges on dischargers into their sewerage systems, resulting in substantial reductions in discharges with little regulatory effort other than monitoring and the computation of costs. Effluent charges would mitigate one of the major problems afflicting regulatory procedures in the United States, namely, endless litigation over regulatory decisions, encouraged because delay in the courts offers a substantial saving to the industry by postponing capital investment. Effluent charges fairly arrived at would require little litigation.

6. The problem of setting limits for consents is always more intractable than establishing effluent charges. Pleas of economic stringency, political pressures, threats of unemployment if a factory is obliged to shut down because of the cost of meeting consent conditions, all have encouraged vacillation on the part of regulatory agencies. The political attractiveness of yielding has been quite apparent in recent developments in the United States, and some of this is already apparent in the United Kingdom. On the other hand, a system of effluent charges is not so likely to pose political problems for the regulatory agencies.

7. Effluent charges, particularly where water quality management is under the purview of regional WAs, can be an income-generating device. Consents do not generate funds, nor do the WAs have access to taxes or rates. Funds collected from effluent charges can be used for any one of a number of functions of the authorities: monitoring; the studies required to establish proper charging structures; and even the construction and operation of treatment facilities. Regional authorities in the Ruhr area of Germany have built and operated treatment facilities and charged the users for their services. In fact, the *Emschergenossenschaft* has constructed a facility to treat the entire Emscher River.

Charges for effluents discharged to sewerage systems
While effluent charges by local authorities for the use of sewers have been

common practice, these charges are often lower than industry's fair share of the total cost of providing the service, partly as a hidden subsidy for the industry, and partly because the industry may meet its share of the collection and treatment costs through property taxes. In response, the Congress incorporated in Public Law 92–500, the Water Pollution Control Act Amendments of 1972, a requirement that any local authority seeking construction grants from the federal government for water pollution control facilities must demonstrate that industry pays its fair share of the total treatment cost. The Environmental Protection Agency ruled that payment of property taxes would not meet this requirement and effluent charges were obliged to be instituted.

In the United Kingdom, the situation has not been much different. For example, the Severn Trent Water Authority announced in January 1975 that the cost of treating industrial effluents discharged to sewers within its area was £7·7 million per year, but the revenue actually collected on the basis of charging schemes established by its predecessors amounted to only £2·8 million per year. The STWA proposed to standardize effluent charges according to a formula which would include effluent volume and strength.

Such charging schemes might well offer a model for effluent charges to receiving waters because of their wide acceptance in almost all the industrialized countries of the world. In the United States, such formulae have varied widely among local authorities, often being calculated as a surcharge on the charge for flow alone, including such factors as suspended solids, to account for the cost of sludge disposal; BOD, to account for the costs of secondary biological treatment; and chlorine demand to account for the cost of chlorination where this is practiced. A similar approach, the so-called Mogden formula, is used in the United Kingdom.

A current example, which includes both the conditions and charges for discharge of industrial effluents into sewerage systems, is that adopted by the Anglian Water Authority. The controls are divided into two major categories: conditions and charging.

Conditions

Certain chemicals may be required to be totally excluded, but 'if *total* exclusion is not practical or needful it may be preferable to prescribe limits'. Among the chemicals so treated are cyanides, sulfides, organo-chlorine compounds, cadmium and mercury. In addition, limits are placed upon the concentrations of oil and grease, sulfates, and certain heavy metals, with the concentrations of these to be determined in each instance.

Other conditions for individual trade effluents could include maximum 24-hour discharges, peak hourly discharges, the requirements for pretreatment if necessary to eliminate certain forbidden materials, which in the case of the Anglian Water Authority are in all cases petroleum spirits and calcium carbide, and other substances that may be incorporated into individual consents. Furthermore, temperatures should not be higher than 45 °C, pH values not less than six nor greater than ten, and the discharge of condensation water is prohibited. The industry may be required to provide and maintain a special chamber for sample collecting and/or a continuous recorder, and the industry may be required to furnish the AWA records on the quantity and nature of its discharges.

Charging

For 1974–75, the charge was a minimum of £5 per annum or the following formula as a charge per 1000 liters of effluent discharged:

$$A + B + \frac{MC}{M_1} + \frac{SD}{S_1}$$

where A = The average cost to the AWA of receiving and conveying the industrial effluents to the AWA's treatment facilities, 1·63p/1000 liters.

B = The average cost to the AWA of primary treatment of 1000 liters of sewage, 0·85p/1000 liters.

C = The average cost to the AWA of biological treatment of 1000 liters of sewage, 1·17p/1000 liters.

D = The average cost to the AWA of treatment and disposal of sludge, 1·27p/1000 liters.

M = The strength of settled trade effluent; the sum of the chemical oxygen demand (COD) plus 4·5 times the total oxidizable nitrogen in mg/l.

M_1 = The mean strength of settled sewage at the AWA's treatment facilities, taken as 572 mg/l.

S = The suspended solids content of the trade effluent, in mg/l.

S_1 = The mean suspended solids content of the sewage at the AWA's treatment works, taken as 337 mg/l.

While the values in the formula were established authority-wide for the first year of operation, the AWA indicated that thereafter each division would establish its own values based upon its own costs.

The charging scheme is explicit in indicating how each of these terms is to be arrived at. For example, term A is 1/6 of the net revenue expenditure, including loan charging, for all sewerage and pumping stations other than those intended solely for surface water. Term B is the net revenue expenditure, including loan charges, on all pumping stations and force mains discharging directly to treatment facilities, all inlet works including screening, comminution and grit removal, all primary sedimentation units other than those for storm water treatment, all outfalls for effluents and all forms of tertiary treatment. Term C is the net revenue expenditure, including loan charges, on biological units, final sedimentation tanks, and returned sludge facilities.

EQUALIZATION AND SUBSIDIES

Apart from exchequer grants for specific purposes, the revenues of the WAs are to come from charges for services. Under the Act, the WAs may make different charges for the same service but, not later than 1 April 1981 charges should not '. . . show undue preference to, or discriminate unduly against, any class of persons'. The Jukes Committee tried to provide guidance to the WAs in promulgating charges. Two major problems arose almost immediately but were met in quite different ways: (1) subsidies; and (2) equalization. The principles enunciated by the government and incorporated in the Act explicitly prohibit subsidies and implicitly prohibit equalization, although some WAs have taken 'non-discrimination' to mean 'equalization'.

Subsidies

The debts inherited by the WAs were immediately incorporated into customer charges, with no assistance from the national exchequer, as the rate support grants were not available to the WAs. Calls for some type of subsidy arose throughout the country. Such subsidies were sought by the water industry in various forms, including assumption by the government of the inherited debts, a not unreasonable approach, as the government. when pressed, had assumed the debts of the nationalized steel, coal, and railway enterprises.

A write-off of the very large inherited debt would permit the WAs to reduce their charges almost immediately and would certainly make them look better in the eyes of the public they served, a very attractive proposition to the individual WAs and their chairmen. To a statement at the first National Water Conference that by '. . . writing [the inherited debt] off as far as the WAs are concerned and putting it on the national exchequer, we get a fairer distribution of repayment', Sir John Wills, chairman of the Wessex Water Authority responded that the NWC had considered the prospect of a write-off, but had declined to go that route because, in time, the inherited debt would be a small part of the total.[49] Because of the capital-intensive nature of the water industry, such a precedent would almost necessitate a fairly regular write-off in the future, and this was not a procedure that was felt to be appropriate to the image that the WAs wanted to establish among their customers.

Lord Nugent, chairman of NWC, in responding presumably for all WA chairmen, joined Sir John in stating: 'The whole history of the nationalized industries shows that if a national industry has to depend on government to shoulder its debt and write it off, this is never a once-for-all; it just goes on happening, because that industry then is subsequently prevented by successive governments of whatever complexion they are from charging the proper rate to pay its way. You gentlemen here who are managers of the new water industry must know what a desperate price that is to pay. Your independence really is gone. With the best will in the world the civil servants and ministers in the future, when they have accepted the burden of debt for an industry, forever remain interfering with the management of that industry. In so far as you value the independent management of your respective WAs and today I am delighted to say that your respective chairmen have vigorously held the line on this, they would sooner bear the burden of the debt and face the difficulty of passing on the debt services in higher charges rather than go cap in hand to government. This is a price they feel is worth paying in order to maintain the independent management of your respective authorities, and for my own part I would say long may that continue.' The United States is moving in the opposite direction, as is discussed in the next chapter.

Nevertheless, pressures for a subsidy for the water services will likely continue. For example, the Association of District Councils made a strong case for special relief to cushion domestic ratepayers from the effects of exceptional increases in water charges so that personal budgets are not disrupted.[50]

Nevertheless, in its two-year review of the water reorganization,[14] the government gave no hint of initiating national subsidies for the water industry, a move which would require parliamentary action and a significant change in philosophy from what was the basis for the water reorganization in the first place.

Equalization

From all early government statements, it must be concluded that equalization, the establishment of uniform charges throughout a WA area, let alone throughout England and Wales, could not have been contemplated. In their first report, the Jukes Committee stated:[5] 'Charging policies should ... be influenced not only by the need to cover revenue expenditure but also by the aim to make the consumers aware as far as possible of the real cost of services. ... It is desirable to provide water services only when their value to the user is greater than their cost to the community ... the value of services to the user is best indicated by the user's willingness to pay for them.'

Statements such as these certainly do not give any license or encouragement to equalization of charges. In fact, the Jukes Committee recommended that increases in expenditure in the first two years be recovered by applying a common percentage to the base charges of the prior authorities, a measure that exacerbated differences in areas where charges were at a high level prior to reorganization.

Gilliland pointed out that standardization of charging principles does not require standardization of charges.[27] However, whenever amalgamations have taken place in the past the differential charges that were initially inherited were gradually eroded until a standard unit charge applied throughout the new area of the undertaking. The reasons for this equalization were expediency and the view that all consumers should benefit equally from the improved administration and operation of the more efficient larger undertaking. Despite the principles expressed initially by government, Gilliland concluded that there was nothing in the consultation papers nor in the debates to suggest that equalization is *not* the intention of the Act.

An almost opposite interpretation is expounded by those who claim that standard unit charges are discriminatory as consumers in relatively high cost areas within a region would be subsidized by consumers in low cost areas. The theoretical justification of the latter interpretation is irrefutable in that consumers imposing greater costs on the system should be required to pay more. However, the practical implications of adopting any view other than equalization are formidable. The problems of having charges reflect the costs imposed by each use, whether a householder, agriculturalist or commercial/industrial undertaking, arise because of variations in:

1.   sources from which the water is abstracted,
2.   distances that water is transmitted before treatment,
3.   degrees of treatment needed,
4.   distances between consumer and treatment plant, and
5.   elevations of consumer's properties.

A charging structure taking into account such factors would be enormously costly to administer and this degree of sophistication is never seriously considered.

A compromise view would be based upon variations between different parts of a WA area, where greater costs in part of the area would reflect in the charges. Even this offered difficulties, such as defining the areas of differing costs, how many such areas to identify, and how to reconcile the historic and marginal costs for the areas. Public relations considerations also enter because, no matter how carefully the boundaries between areas are drawn, situations would arise where charges would differ between houses in close proximity. The public tends to accept this situation where authority boundaries exist but Gilliland wondered whether customers would accept these differences where adjacent services are provided by a single authority.

Gilliland concluded, with what was great perspicacity, that the implications of *not* moving toward an eventual equalization of charges were being given insufficient consideration by government. Moving from uniform increases based upon historic charges to any type of differential charging system within a region would likely cause great public dismay. The only rational approach may well be one that the public would accept, namely equalization within a region.

That the government got the message appears to be clearly evident in the Jukes Committee's third report, prepared after the impact of the first year's charges were fully appreciated.[6] Charging systems should serve to obtain the best balance between conflicting considerations. However, during the early years the WAs should avoid actions inhibiting the development of rational charging schemes that would be both fair and would achieve the best use of resources. Emphasis was placed on the crucial need to secure and sustain public acceptance of a WA's charging policies in that any system would have to appear to be equitable and reasonable.

The Jukes Committee faced great difficulty in defining 'equity'. Some believe that equity is achieved by relating charges to the costs imposed by the user, and that the business of the WAs is not to redistribute income by doing otherwise. Others argue that equity requires all to pay a similar charge for a similar service, irrespective of the cost of supply. They concluded: 'When, however, costs over an area are so similar or so interrelated that the costs imposed on the system by any consumer of a given amount of service are themselves similar, then that element in the charge to him reflecting those costs can and should be equalized'. Thus, the first genuflection towards 'equalization'.

Also incorporated in the Jukes Committee's third report was the need for 'simplicity, stability and predictability', with gradual changes in charging structures to avoid sharp increases to any one group of consumers, moving gradually toward equitable charging systems.

Equalization in the Southern Water Authority

The forces at work to promote equalization of charges were seen in the light of the experience of the Southern Water Authority, the first to move toward equalization. In October 1974, the SWA announced its charging policy: that charges should reflect the cost of providing the service and that each function should aim to recover its costs from its users; and equalization of charges should be adopted so that each consumer pays a fair and equitable charge.

Anticipating an outcry from communities with low historic water supply charges which would be forced to pay higher charges following equalization, and in accordance with the Jukes Committee's concern that changes should not be made 'with undue haste', a gradual equalization of charges was to be achieved through graduated charge increases that would eventually bring all communities' charges in line with the highest then extant. Three months later details for implementation were presented by staff to the authority, for equalization to be reached throughout the SWA area by 1 April 1981. However, the SWA opted for *immediate* equalization of water supply charges for both measured and unmeasured supplies, a move initiated by the ex-Mayor of Brighton, despite the fact that Brighton would face the greatest increase in charges.

Undeterred by anticipated protests from those local authorities, such as Brighton and Hove, which had previously enjoyed low charges, the pace of equalization of SWA quickened to the point where the target of the finance committee for complete equalization of charges for *all* services was moved forward to 1 April 1979.

The MP for Hove, Tim Sainsbury, initiated an adjournment debate in the House of Commons in protest against the higher charges for Hove resulting from equalization. Denis Howell responded for the government by affirming the recommendations of the Jukes Committee's third report that moves towards equalization be both gradual and limited in extent. 'It is not for me to defend the Southern Water Authority, because it is an autonomous body, a nationalized industry, set up by the Conservatives . . .'[51]

THE WELSH PROBLEM

Throughout the parliamentary debates on the Water Bill, repeated references were made to the special interests of Wales in the water reorganization. The Welsh problem is serious because Wales is amongst the most impoverished areas of the United Kingdom, with high rates of unemployment and little modern industry, quite similar to Appalachia in the United States. National policy is to encourage development in Wales. One Welsh resource is water, which has been used extensively for the benefit of people in England.

Because of their financial status, Welsh local authorities had been receiving high rate-support grants, with some subsidy going for water supply as well as for sewerage and sewage disposal. With the water reorganization requiring that charges meet all the costs, and with removal of all subsidies, the increase in charges fell most heavily on the Welsh. The bitter feelings engendered by the increased charges were exacerbated by the growth of Welsh nationalism and the election of Welsh Nationalists to parliament, whose influence far exceeds their numbers because of their strategic situation in alliance with Scottish Nationalists. All together, the nationalists constituted a balance of power as between the Labour and Conservative parties in 1974. Further complicating the issue was the promise of devolution, the establishment of separate governmental bodies for Wales and Scotland.

In March 1974, even before the reorganization was effected, questions were raised in parliament concerning the charges for water supply, sewerage and sewage disposal in Wales.[52] Questions were also raised as to why the

Welsh National Water Development Authority granted the Severn Trent Water Authority a 999-year lease at 5p per annum for the Elan Valley works in Wales. These works had been built by Birmingham. Ownership was transferred without cost to the WNWDA and the STWA will meet operation and maintenance costs of the facilities.

Nevertheless, as an MP from Wales stated: 'It is almost incredible that water should cost the residents of a town such as Rhayader, a small town in mid-Wales, five times what is charged to the residents of Birmingham. The residents of Rhayader live beneath the dam which supplies the water to Birmingham 80 miles away . . . Whatever kind of logic one may produce, it is not understood in the area, and in such a situation emotion tends to take over.'[53]

Industry raised a storm over ten-fold increases in its abstraction charges within the WNWDA area, which could negate the benefits of the government's regional policy for the development of Wales and which tended to make Wales less competitive as a location for new industry.[54] Examples of the increases in water charges included a paper mill in Cardiff whose charges were increased from £660 and £37, for abstraction and cooling water annually before the reorganization, to £67 000 and £38 000 respectively after. With increased water supply and sewerage and sewage disposal charges, the company faced a water bill of £140 000 during the first year. The abstraction charges for the Central Electricity Generating Board in South Wales rose from £843 to £174 074 and the National Coal Board's bill was raised from £1562 to £39 276. In response, the chairman of the WNWDA recommended a ceiling on charges in the first year of 50p per 1000 gallons.

An adjournment debate on the water charges in Wales took place in the House of Commons on 6 May 1974.[53] Cledwyn Hughes of Anglesey opened the debate by citing the increase in metered charges from 12·5p to 57p per 1000 gallons. He quoted from a lettter from an industry in Holyhead: 'A great deal of time, trouble, effort and money has gone into the establishment of an industry in Holyhead. We are substantial users of water and in the next year our water bill will rise by about £40 000, which this company cannot afford if it wishes to stay in business . . . there will be no alternative but to arrange the movement of this plant to a different area . . . All we are asking for is to be treated equally and justly instead of being penalized for being in a development area, which for some historical reason means we are now having to pay more for our supplies than our competitors . . . in the Midlands.'

The WNWDA became the least popular authority in Wales, despite the fact that it is Welsh. Salt is rubbed in the wounds when customers in Montgomeryshire, that part of Wales being served by the STWA, pay far less for water than their Welsh neighbors in the WNWDA area. The situation had become so incendiary that a proposal was made by the Plaid

Cymru, the Welsh nationalist political party, that a minimum of 10 pence per 1000 gallons be charged for water sent from Wales to England earning them the title of 'water sheiks'.[55]

Finally, the Secretary of State for Wales created a committee of inquiry, chaired by Sir Goronwy Daniel, with the following charge:

> 'To review the effects of the Water Act 1973 and other matters relevant to the increase in charges for water in the area of the Welsh National Water Development Authority; to consider all matters relevant to the future level of such charges; and to make recommendations.'

It was made clear by the Secretary of State in announcing the formation of the committee 'that the inquiry was not into the operations of the WNWDA, but into the effects of the Water Act 1973 and other relevant matters'.

Awaited with some trepidation, the report of the committee, made up of five Welshmen and one Englishman, was submitted to the Secretary of State for Wales in March 1975 but not released until August.[56]

The Daniel Committee report

The Daniel Committee report is of interest to all students of the water reorganization in that it constituted its first formal review and was a precursor to the government's own full-scale review.[14] In fact, with the publication of the Daniel Committee report, the government decided that the charging issue is of such complexity and importance to the water industry that it needed to be considered as a matter of priority and its review was moved forward.

The Daniel Committee pointed out that, prior to the reorganization, under both the Public Health Act 1936 and the Water Act 1945, water undertakers could not increase their charges above a stipulated maximum without first applying to the responsible ministers, and following with public local inquiries. Also, water supply undertakings were not required to meet all their revenue account expenditures through charges levied on consumers, and most such water supply authorities had powers to meet deficits by means of precepts or subventions on general rate funds.

However, under the Water Act 1973, there is no provision for consumers to appeal against the charges levied, and subsidies are prohibited. This change in accountability proved to be one of the major problems associated with the reorganization and was magnified in Wales.

In Wales, about half the local water undertakings had run their water supply operations at a loss, with the deficiencies being made up from the general rate funds, which were provided with a substantial subsidy for the water services from the rate support grant. The elimination of this source of support, in addition to a 50 percent increase in the cost of supply, combined to increase the price of water to the consumers in the WNWDA area an average of 121 percent after reorganization, as compared to an average increase of 40 percent in England. The water charges in many parts of Wales became far higher than in almost any locality in England, even though the WNWDA made an effort to cushion the full impact of the increase by limiting their maximum charges to 20p in the pound for unmetered supplies and 50p per 1000 gallons for metered supplies. The main issues are elaborated below.

Average increase in charges

The Daniel Committee concluded that the 121 percent increase in charges was inevitable but understandable as it represented a two-year price increase, as the counter-inflation policy of government had permitted no increases the previous year.

TABLE 9.10
Welsh National Water Development Authority—Unmeasured Water Supply Charges

Division	1973–74 Standard rate poundage p/£	1974–75 Standard rate poundage p/£	Poundage increase	Percentage increase
Anglesey	3·6	18·8	15·2	422
Cardiff	4·5	8·2	3·7	82
Cardiganshire	5·7	20·0	14·3	251
Carmarthenshire	5·0[a]	14·4	9·4	188
Central Flintshire	7·1	13·6	6·5	92
Conway Valley	4·3	6·8	2·5	58
Eryri	7·2	15·0	7·8	108
Gwent	5·6[b]	9·3[b]	3·7	66
Herefordshire	4·6	13·8	9·2	200
Merioneth	4·5	18·0	13·5	300
Mid Glamorgan	7·0[b]	12·6[b]	5·6	80
Pembrokeshire	6·0	9·6	3·6	60
Radnorshire and North Breconshire	5·6	20·0	14·4	257
South East Breconshire	4·0	15·9	11·9	298
Taf Fechan	6·3	16·8	10·5	167
West Denbighshire and West Flintshire	5·3	10·6	5·3	100
West Glamorgan	5·0	8·9	3·9	78

[a] A variety of rates applied and the one shown is that of the largest single undertaking—the Llanelli and District Water Board.
[b] Average rate poundages.

TABLE 9.11
Welsh National Water Development Authority—Comparison of Measured Water Supply Charges by Water Supply Division 1973–74 and 1974–75

Division	Standard 1973–74 charges p/1 000 gal	Standard 1974–75 charges p/1 000 gal	Increase in p/1 000 gal	Percentage increase
Anglesey	12·5	50·0	37·5	300
Cardiff	20·0	33·8	13·8	69
Cardiganshire	20·0	50·0	30·0	150
Carmarthenshire	15·0ᵃ	39·0	24·0	160
Central Flintshire	26·7	47·7	21·0	79
Conway Valley	15·0	23·8	8·8	59
Eryri	15·0	43·0	28·0	187
Gwent	22·0	34·3	12·3	56
Herefordshire	20·0	50·0	30·0	150
Merioneth	20·0	40·0	20·0	100
Mid Glamorgan	27·0	41·0	14·0	52
Pembrokeshire	17·5	29·2	11·7	67
Radnorshire and North Breconshire	20·0	50·0	30·0	150
South East Breconshire	15·0	50·0	35·0	233
Taf Fechan	12·5	49·5	37·0	296
West Denbighshire and West Flintshire	21·2	40·1	18·9	89
West Glamorgan	12·5	30·5	18·0	144

ᵃ A variety of charges applied and the one shown is that of the largest single undertaking—the Llanelli and District Water Board.

The differences in charges between water supply divisions

Tables 9.10 and 9.11 indicate the first year increases following upon the Jukes Committee recommendations, which enlarged differences in charges across Wales. Another factor amplified the distinctions amongst the WNWDA divisions: the larger, more financially secure areas, which had received no rate support assistance for water supply, such as Cardiff, required the smallest increases while those receiving considerable rate support, such as Anglesey, exhibited the highest percentage increases. The Daniel Committee was of the opinion that the WNWDA should not have followed the Jukes Committee recommendations, as they were not obliged to do so and the recommendations were certainly not appropriate to Wales.

The differences between classes of consumers

In order to offset the increased water charges, the Conservative government had proposed a scheme of differential rate relief which would

TABLE 9.12

Total Rate Burden in Selected Districts in the WNWDA Area

District	1973–74 Rate poundage					1974–75 Rate poundage						Difference between 1973–74 and 1974–75	
	Water rate	General rate[a]	Gross demand	Domestic element of rate support grant	Net demand	Water rate	General service charge	General rate	Gross demand	Domestic element of rate support grant	Net demand	Gross demand p/£	Net demand p/£
Isle of Anglesey	3·6	46·8	50·4	6	44·4	18·8	8·58	71·7	99·08	33·5	65·58	+48·68	+21·18
Cardiff	4·5	45·0	49·5	6	43·5	8·2	3·0	58·7	69·9	33·5	36·4	+20·4	−7·1
Ceredigion	5·7	33·2	38·9	6	32·9	20·0	12·5	56·77	89·27	33·5	55·77	+50·37	+22·87
Hereford City District	4·6	41·0	45·6	6	39·6	13·8	2·48	54·4	70·68	13·0	57·68	+25·08	+18·08
Leominster	4·29	32·1	36·39	6	30·39	12·16	8·6	52·79	73·55	13·0	60·55	+37·16	+30·16
Radnor	5·6	37·12	42·72	6	36·72	20·0	10·3	56·86	87·16	33·5	53·66	+44·44	+16·94
Rhuddlan	4·24	52·3	56·54	6	50·54	9·0	8·0	61·0	78·0	33·5	44·5	+21·46	−6·04
						(average)							
S. Herefordshire	4·6	33·38	37·98	6	31·98	13·8	8·6	51·93	74·33	13·0	61·33	+36·35	+29·35

[a] The rate shown is an average (weighted by population) of the various rates applying in the predecessor districts.

have amounted to varied support across the Welsh area ranging from 11p to the pound in Cardiff to 89·5p to the pound in Radnor. The Labour government considered that the differential system had serious defects and replaced it with a flat rate grant of 13p in the pound in England and 33·5p in the pound in Wales, a very helpful arrangement in Wales as is shown in Table 9.12. However, this rate relief helped public relations not at all, as the relief was offset against the general rates and the higher water rates were allowed to stand. The industrial, commercial, and agricultural consumers who were metered had to bear the full brunt of increases ranging from 52 to 300 percent. With selling prices under tight government control the higher charges for water could not readily be passed on. The government proposed to take account of the increased water charges during their next price review but, even if allowed, this would be a year late. While increased water charges encourage metered consumers to reduce water consumption, they are obligated to pay a minimum charge based upon the rateable value. With this minimum being sharply increased, often exceeding the metered charge, the incentive for water conservation is lost.

The difference in treatment of consumers within WNWDA and other WA areas

The seemingly different treatment accorded people in Wales as revealed in Table 9.13 and in Figs. 9.3 and 9.4 is the crux of the dispute. Part of the variation in charges for unmetered supplies can be attributed to generally lower rateable value in Wales, but charges for metered supplies reflect the

TABLE 9.13
Average Charges in Water Authority Areas in 1974–75

WA	Unmetered supplies p/£	Metered supplies p/1 000 gal
North West	5·3	26·0
Northumbrian	5·8	28·3
Severn Trent	5·1	25·7
Yorkshire	7·0	30·1
Anglian	5·8	31·1
Thames	3·1	29·2
Southern	5·0	30·8
Wessex	5·4	28·0
South West	7·4	34·1
WNWDA	11·5	37·5
Weighted average	4·9	29·0

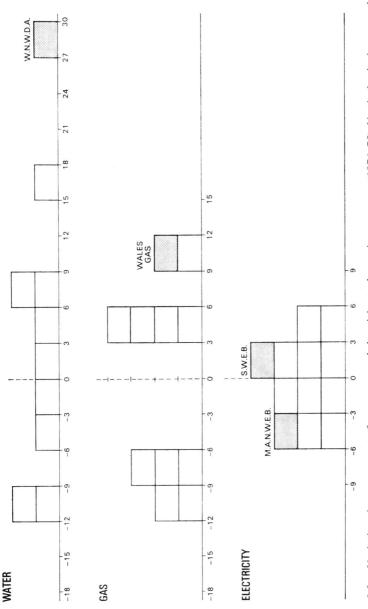

Fig. 9.3. Variations in average cost of water, gas and electricity to domestic consumers (1974–75). Vertical axis shows number of areas and the horizontal shows the percentage deviations from England and Wales average charges. Reproduced by permission of the Controller of Her Majesty's Stationery Office.

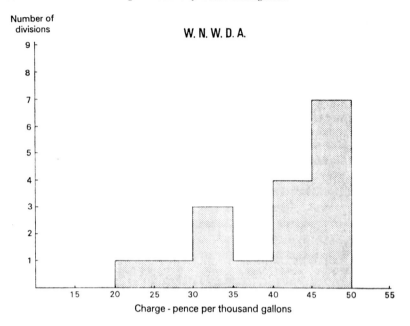

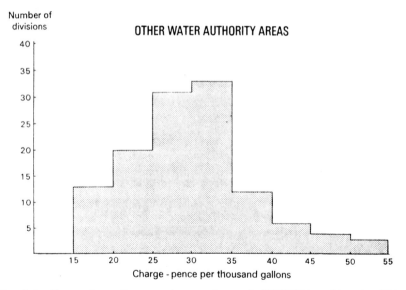

FIG. 9.4   Comparison of measured water charges in WNWDA and in other WA areas. Reproduced by permission of the Controller of Her Majesty's Stationery Office.

costs for providing the service. Within the WNWDA, the charge is almost 30 percent greater than the average for all of the WAs and about 45 percent greater than the average charges of the Severn Trent and North West Water Authorities, both of which take large quantities of water from Wales. The greater differences for Wales in the water industry than in either gas or electricity, as shown in Fig. 9.3, is difficult to explain in water-rich Wales. Only in two divisions of the WNWDA, in the Conway Valley, were charges less than the national mean of 29p per 1000 gallons, whereas in the Severn Trent and North West WAs, most divisions charge less than this mean.

As revenues equal expenditures, the conclusion must be drawn that the average charge in Wales is higher than in other WA areas because the average cost of supplying water is higher, despite the ample resources of water in Wales. However, the unit cost of water is more determined by the cost of distribution than the cost of resource development, and distribution costs tend to be lower in densely populated urban areas than in sparsely populated rural areas. Another determinant in cost is the time at which the investments were completed, inasmuch as the water industry is capital intensive. Therefore, the older the investment the lower the current cost of supporting that investment. For example, in 1973–74, the cost of supplying 1000 gallons of water in Birmingham was 14·01p, of which 34 percent represented debt charges. During the same period, the cost of supplying a similar quantity of water in Radnor in Wales was 104·46p, of which 60 percent was debt charges. The debt charge per 1000 gallons in Radnor was 13-fold greater than in Birmingham.

Equalization within the WNWDA

The Daniel Committee concluded that the system of charges used for the divisions of the WNWDA, based upon the Jukes Committee's first report,[5] could not be the basis of continued charging, particularly as the divisions are not financially responsible for meeting their costs. In Wales, the divisions with high charges are in low-density rural areas which have the sites and resources for providing additional water while the divisions which have a need for the supplies are in heavily populated areas where charges tend to be low. The latter group will need the good will of the former and equalization is one approach. Furthermore, because of the large population in the urban areas, the percentage increase in charges resulting from equalization is much less than the percentage reduction in high-cost areas. And equalization has merits of simplicity and acceptability to the public.

Accordingly, the Daniel Committee concluded that the WNWDA was correct in equalizing charges amongst their divisions, although they might have avoided some of the extreme changes brought on by equalization at 50p per 1000 gallons as shown in Table 9.14 by phasing the changes over a period of time instead of making them immediately.

TABLE 9.14

Effects of Equalizing Water Charges in WNWDA in 1975–76 on the Basis of a Standard Meter Charge of 50p/1000 gal

Supply division	Actual standard charges			Charges involved in levying a standard charge of 50p/1000 gal			
				Over 1973–74		Over 1974–75	
	1973–74 p/1000 gal	1974–75 p/1000 gal	Percentage change	Absolute p/1000 gal	%	Absolute p/1000 gal	%
Anglesey	12·5	50·0	+300	+37·5	+300	—	—
Cardiff	20·0	33·8	+69	+30·0	+150	+16·2	+48
Cardigan	20·0	50·0	+150	+30·0	+150	—	—
Carmarthen	15·0ᵃ	39·0	+160	+35·0	+233	+11·0	+28
Central Flints	26·7	47·7	+79	+23·3	+87	+2·3	+5
Conway Valley	15·0	23·8	+59	+35·0	+233	+26·2	+110
Eryri	15·0	43·0	+187	+35·0	+233	+7·0	+16
Gwent	22·0	34·3	+56	+28·0	+127	+15·7	+46
Hereford	20·0	50·0	+150	+30·0	+150	—	—
Merioneth	20·0	40·0	+100	+30·0	+150	+10·0	+25
Mid-Glamorgan	27·0	41·0	+52	+23·0	+85	+9·0	+22
Pembroke	17·5	29·2	+67	+32·5	+186	+20·8	+71
Radnor and							
N. Brecon	20·0	50·0	+150	+30·0	+150	—	—
S. E. Brecon	15·0	50·0	+233	+35·0	+233	—	—
Taf Fechan	12·5	49·5	+296	+37·5	+300	+0·5	+1
W. Denbigh and							
W. Flint	21·2	40·1	+89	+28·8	+136	+9·9	+25
W. Glamorgan	12·5	30·5	+144	+37·5	+300	+19·5	+64

ᵃ The charge for Llanelli & District Water Board.

Methods of charging

After considering a variety of charging systems, the Daniel Committee concluded that no immediate prospect of a better means of charging for domestic water supplies than the existing rateable value system is available. Some equity can be introduced by the WNWDA proposal of a fixed charge of £5 plus an equalized standard rate throughout the authority's area. Using rateable values leaves consumers with no incentive to economize on water use and, while universal metering may be impracticable, the Daniel Committee recommended that metering be extended to consumers whose bills are large enough to justify their installation.

Equalizing charges across the country

Many of the arguments for equalizing charges within WNWDA apply also to equalizing them amongst the WAs. The difficult terrain and low population density in Wales make for higher costs as contrasted with the easier terrain and higher densities in England, and the consequent higher charges are a disincentive to the government policy for industrial development in Wales.

The inhabitants of the rural headwater areas in Wales have become sensitive to the demands of the lowland populations in England for more land for reservoirs to serve them. Consequently, the English need to retain the good will of the Welsh if the water resources in Wales are to continue to be exploited for England. To ensure that water in Wales is no more costly than in England, the costs in Wales should be shared by England. The STWA already subsidizes their consumers in Montgomeryshire in Wales to the extent of 75 percent of their costs. Because Wales has a relatively small population, the increased burden on the English for subsidizing the Welsh would be small, as illustrated in Table 9.15, where three approaches to equalization are considered. A national average rate of 29p per 1000 gallons would reduce the charges in the WNWDA by 22·7 percent while raising the charges in the STWA by 12·8 percent.

Imposition of surcharges on water transferred from the WNWDA

Surcharges for water transferred from Wales have been proposed because the average WNWDA charges are over 40 percent higher than charges of the two authorities obtaining their water from Wales and because of the large amount of water used outside Wales as compared with that used within Wales. The principal arguments against applying surcharges for water going from Wales to England are that:

1.   much of the water in Wales flows naturally to England and could not easily be withheld,
2.   to achieve equalization, the surcharge might need to be so high that the receiving authorities would find it cheaper to use their own

TABLE 9.15

Effects of Equalizing Water Charges Between areas in 1974-75 on Various Assumptions

WA Authority	Actual average per 1000 gal charge in 1974-75	All authorities equalized to the national average of 29p/1000 gal — Percentage change compared with actual	*Effect on average charges if:* All equalized half way to 29p/1000 gal — Resulting average charge	Percentage change compared with actual	Average charge in WNWDA limited to 32p/1000 gal at the expense of the two lowest cost areas — Resulting charge	Percentage change compared with actual
North West	26·0	+11·5	27·5	+5·8	27·1	+4·2[a]
Northumbrian	28·3	+2·5	28·6	+1·1	28·3	—
Severn Trent	25·7	+12·8	27·3	+6·2	26·8	+4·3[a]
Yorkshire	30·1	−3·7	29·6	−1·7	30·1	—
Anglian	31·1	−6·8	30·1	−3·2	31·1	—
Thames	29·2	−0·7	29·1	−0·3	29·2	—
Southern	30·8	−5·8	29·9	−2·9	30·8	—
Wessex	28·0	+3·6	28·5	+1·8	28·0	—
South West	34·1	−15·0	31·5	−7·6	34·1	—
WNDWA	37·5	−22·7	33·2	−11·5	32·0	−14·7

[a] Assuming an allocation between these two authorities proportionate to their total consumption.

resources, in which case the Welsh resources would be left underused and would represent a loss to the entire economy and especially to Wales,

3. those who have already paid the full cost for the installations from which they get their supplies should not be required to pay a large additional price after their works have been taken away from them without compensation, and

4. surcharges would be expected to generate antagonisms that might lead to surcharges on goods and services moving in the other direction.

Increased charges for abstractions, which originally were trivial, need not discriminate between consumers inside and outside Wales. Also, the objections to a surcharge do not apply to establishing a commercial price for water supply, namely a price that is attractive to both the seller and the buyer, and would give the seller as well as the buyer a share of the benefits, and so could be said to accord with sound business practice on which the water industry is hopefully organized.

Recommendations of the Daniel Committee

The most significant recommendation of the Daniel Committee was that early action should be taken to reduce the difference in average water charges between the WNWDA and the other WAs by introducing legislation to give a Welsh Assembly executive responsibility for water supplies in and from Wales, with the pricing of transferred water from Wales being on a commercial basis or, if the Welsh Assembly is to have only advisory responsibility for water or if the present organization is to continue unchanged, then either commercial pricing should be extended to all water licensed to be exported from Wales or the Secretary of State should be given power to direct the WAs to operate a subsidy scheme adequate to reduce charges to WNWDA customers to a level not more than ten percent above the national average.

As a strictly interim measure, an exchequer subsidy sufficient to reduce charges to WNWDA customers to a level not more than ten percent above the national average should be given to the WNWDA.

The Daniel Committee report, and the call for relief for Wales, raised many questions that have implications for the water industry. Equalization within the area of any WA does not of itself challenge the principles upon which the Water Act was based. On the other hand, equalization amongst the WAs, which were created to obtain the benefits of local initiative and participation and responsiveness to local conditions would remove incentives for efficient use of resources within each WA.

The Welsh economic problem can be addressed without threatening the water industry structure through government policies that do not use water as a vehicle for subsidizing development. Assistance to Wales and its development should be explicit. In part, this is already provided by the higher rate support grants available in Wales as compared with England in recognition of the particularly severe impact of the reorganization of local government and the water services on Wales.

The Daniel Committee also addressed another aspect of the water reorganization, centralization of authority. With devolution and the imminent creation of a Welsh Assembly, a central water authority to include England and Wales would hardly be appropriate. A separate water authority for all of England would be even less appropriate as the problems between the Welsh and English would still exist. An English water authority *vis-à-vis* a Welsh water authority would certainly pose more political problems than exist at present.

The Welsh issue threatens the thrust of the reorganization. How the government deals with it and with the ancillary pressures for greater centralization of authority will presage the future of the water industry and the success of the regional water authorities for many years into the future. The government's proposals for addressing these and the other problems that have arisen in the first years of the reorganization are discussed in Chapter 11.

CHAPTER 10

The Relevance of the Reorganization for the United States

Why should the reorganization of water management and the creation of regional water authorities in England and Wales have significance for the United States? Advocates of regionalism are numerous and a wide variety of devices is available in the United States to encourage regional planning, yet the implementation of regional enterprise is moving haltingly at best. Such regional enterprises as do exist are warmly acclaimed, yet they are seldom emulated. The most admired regional effort in the United States is the Tennessee Valley Authority, Mecca for professionals from throughout the world. Yet in the 40 years since its creation, nothing like it has again appeared on the American scene, and a presidential aspirant threatens to turn it over to private enterprise.

This chapter is devoted to a brief assessment of American water management institutions, to ascertain whether the regional approach in England and Wales holds promise for the United States.

WATER MANAGEMENT IN THE UNITED STATES

The provision of water supply, sewerage and sewage treatment in the United States, as in Britain, began as a local government responsibility for the protection of health and welfare. As distinguished from Britain, where water supply and sewerage had always been separate functions, local government departments in the United States often have joint responsibilities for the provision of water supply and sewerage and sewage disposal.

The surveillance of local government operations in water supply, sewerage and sewage disposal originally was solely the responsibility of the states, with the state health department being the regulatory agency that prescribed the standards for design and operation of these facilities and monitored performance so as to protect the public health. At the federal level, the US Public Health Service, created in 1792 under the US Treasury for seeing to quarantine of disease from abroad, gradually increased its responsibilities by, *inter alia*, overseeing the quality of water used in interstate transportation. The Public Health Service also was the first federal agency to have any responsibility for water pollution control.

After many administrative reorganizations, the US Environmental Protection Agency, created in 1970, was given responsibility for the federal role in public water supply and water pollution control, as well as for air pollution control, solid waste disposal, noise and pesticides.

Water supply

Responsibility for providing water supply to households, commercial establishments, and industry is divided between the individual consumer, who often is required to provide for his own supply, and local government, whose responsibility for water supply often extends only to its political boundaries. Even within many political jurisdictions, individual consumers are left to fend for themselves, as in Suffolk County, described in the opening pages of this volume. The customary procedure for real estate developers in the post-war period in the United States was to provide each residence within a new development with its own well and septic tank so that the developers would have no responsibility for maintaining a public water supply or sewerage system after the residences were sold.

As difficulties were experienced, particularly from overflowing septic tanks and from wells that dried up, developers began to install their own small water supply systems and 'package' sewage treatment plants. The result has been a proliferation of small systems without any institutional base to assure sound design or operation. For example, in two of the most densely populated states in the United States, New Jersey and Rhode Island, half of the public water supply systems serve an average of fewer than 700 persons. The 1970 Public Health Service Community Water Supply Study indicated that the water provided by large numbers of small water supply systems did not meet the 1962 Public Health Service Drinking Water Standards, the greatest difficulty being associated with the small size of many of the systems.[1] While the federal standards did not apply to these supplies, most states had adopted these standards for their own communities. The large number of these small systems makes routine surveillance by the states virtually impossible, yet such small systems most need surveillance because they do not have the benefit of proper design and operation nor the resources to develop the best supplies.

The 1970 Community Water Supply Study resulted in the conception of a Safe Drinking Water Bill, but labor was not terminated until the end of 1974, when a television special, 'Drinking water may be dangerous to your health', attracted public attention. The television program was stimulated in good measure by the New Orleans drinking water situation. New Orleans draws its water from the Mississippi River at its 'mouth', where it drains 1.24 million square miles ($3 \cdot 2$ M km^2), some 40 percent of the area of the conterminous United States and is accordingly vulnerable to contamination by virtually every chemical used in the country. Many chemicals, some acknowledged to be carcinogenic, were identified in the supply. Epidemiological studies suggested a relationship between the consumption of Mississippi River water and cancer mortality, although the validity of this conclusion has been challenged.[2]

The publicity attendant to these revelations sparked Congress to the passage of the Safe Water Drinking Act of 1974 (Public Law 92–523) which extended to the federal government the responsibility for promulgating standards which would be applicable to all public drinking water supplies in the United States. The regulatory responsibility would be left with the states, if they so chose. However, the legislation did not address the major finding of the 1970 Survey, that smaller systems do not have the resources to provide adequate service. The problem was exacerbated by a new definition of public water supplies: all supplies serving 15 connections or 25 people, including water supplies for highway rest stops, camps, motels, and a wide assortment of other small supplies which will be difficult to locate, let alone regulate. In all, some 200 000 supplies, in addition to the 40 000 community systems, will now require surveillance. As contrasted with the approach taken in the Water Act 1945 in England and Wales, the Safe Drinking Water Act touches lightly on regrouping or regionalization. A glimmer of hope is discerned in the Environmental Protection Agency Strategy statement for implementation of the Act, which acknowledges that 'While regionalization may be a reasonable alternative only under certain limited conditions, it may prove to be a valuable alternative for some systems . . .'[3] Some initiatives have appeared at the state level. For example, North Carolina provides an incentive for the grouping of water supply and sewerage systems by providing funds for engineering planning of joint community efforts.

In the United States many major urban centers depend for water supply upon rivers that drain large areas and are subject to pollution from industry, agriculture and upstream urban development. In 1970, Philadelphia, Washington, Pittsburgh, St. Louis, Cincinnati and Kansas City, in addition to New Orleans, all drew their water supplies from major rivers which carry significant urban and industrial pollution. Cities that now draw from protected sources have been urged to extend their supplies by using polluted run-or-river sources. For example, New York City, which obtains its water supply from protected upland impoundments, is under pressure to draw upon the Hudson River which drains much of New York State. Just as no major strategy statement, such as that of the Water Resources Board urging a policy of developing resources from the downstream reaches of major rivers, has appeared in the United States, no equivalent group to the Steering Committee on Water Quality has recognized the problem and recommended action such as the seven days storage for raw waters drawn from polluted rivers for potable water supply.[4]

The health significance of using polluted waters for sources of water supply is being debated in the United States. The Science Advisory Board of the Environmental Protection Agency has concluded that the evidence to condemn polluted waters is not yet at hand. While the scientific issue as to the significance of the life-long ingestion of low levels of synthetic organic chemicals, many of which have been shown to be carcinogenic, mutagenic and teratogenic in experimental animals, is not likely to be settled for many years, the only approaches towards addressing the problem at present are through limited attempts to monitor for these chemicals and remove them from upstream discharges, and possibly to add activated carbon filtration to the water treatment process train. These approaches are not likely to effect any significant improvement in the near term, and with latency periods of the order of 20 years, by the time the hazard is revealed, if there is a hazard, it will be too late to protect a public already exposed.

With each separate local authority and developer responsible for water supply, no framework now exists for a national strategy that would address the problem of polluted sources. Each community is on its own, often being denied access to high quality sources that are geographically, economically, or politically out of its reach. A regional ownership model would facilitate the allocation of water resources according to their best use.

The alternative of preserving protected sources for potable purposes while using polluted sources for non-potable purposes is not yet receiving serious consideration. Some relief to demands on the limited resources of high quality waters is being offered in several places in the western part of the United States through the use of reclaimed wastewaters for industry and irrigation, replacing potable waters that had previously been used for these purposes. Colorado Springs, Colorado, provides about one-third of its treated wastewaters with additional treatment after which they are distributed through a separate distribution system to large industrial and commercial customers, such as power plants, golf courses, college campuses, and cemeteries. These customers had previously been using high quality potable waters and were pleased to be offered the alternative which was available at lower cost, while the city was thereby able to extend its upland water supply for drinking to a larger population.[5]

The financing of water supply systems in the United States has seldom been a problem, as local governments were almost always in a position to provide capital from revenue bonds which do not carry the restrictions associated with general obligation bonds. Many states prescribe limits above which local authorities cannot borrow against their property values, but such limits do not apply to revenue financing. Also, in order to move new housing schemes, developers are not hesitant to provide water supply systems as part of the utility package which generally includes streets, electricity, telephone and water, but often may not include sewerage. However, some states are beginning to require that the provision of sewerage and sewage treatment accompany the provision of water supply.

Subsidies for water supply have been restricted to rural communities through the Farmers' Home Administration, with such subsidies being in the form of grants, loans or a combination of these. However, no incentives are provided for water supply services for individual homes in rural areas or even in many densely populated areas. The only initiative for improving a water supply situation in such instances comes from the affected householders when they experience water service problems such as lack of water in drought periods, or poor quality when the aquifers from which they draw become polluted.

Water pollution control

As for water supply, the responsibility for sewerage and sewage treatment in the United States originally rested with local government. The impact of effluent discharges on receiving waters was a concern of the individual states. The only role for the federal government during the early decades of the 20th century, when water pollution became an issue of some concern, was in making studies of pollution of interstate waters such as the Ohio River. Responsibility in the federal establishment rested with the US Public Health Service where much of the scientific work in this field originated through the efforts of its commissioned corps of engineers and scientists.

When early concerns for stream pollution rested on health considerations, the Public Health Service was the appropriate agency to maintain this responsibility. However, with the explosion of the environmental movement in 1965, with its concern for the quality of the environment and the preservation of fish life and amenity, the responsibilities for pollution control were moved from the Public Health Service into a new Federal Water Pollution Control Administration within the Department of Health, Education and Welfare. One year later the agency was transferred to the Department of the Interior which emphasized a commitment to the environment as contrasted with a concern for the health implications of water pollution.

This shift from the PHS to HEW and from HEW to Interior reflected a charge that the physicians who dominated the PHS gave little attention to the water pollution control program which, after waterborne disease had been controlled, appeared to have little public health significance. The issues in water pollution control had become ones of water resource management.

With a brief hiatus as the Federal Water Quality Administration, the program was absorbed into the newly-created Environmental Protection Agency in 1970. During all of these changes, the cadre of professionals who had been with the PHS gradually left the program, either to remain as commissioned officers with the PHS in manning the few engineering responsibilities still retained by the agency, or to take early retirement and go into private practice. This emasculation of experienced staff took place with rapid growth of the program under new auspices. New personnel were being brought into EPA concluding with an explosion of growth resulting from passage of Public Law 92–500, the Water Pollution Control Act Amendments of 1972.

The continuous change in administrative focus within the federal government, accompanied by turmoil within the professional ranks manning the program, with pressure from the public for quick results, and the highly variable postures of the executive branch and Congress, resulted in an absence of continuity in the program and poor morale on the part of the large bureaucracy created to administer the program. The greatest uncertainty was on the part of those being 'managed', the regulatory personnel in the states, and those finally charged with making investments for the water pollution control, the officers of local governments and industries.

The crooks and turns of federal policy with regard to pollution control during the post-war period are too complex and confusing to be included here. The changing scene and the uncertainties may, however, be exemplified by illustrating one phase of the program, federal financing, with a brief exploration of the intricacies of PL 92–500.

The financing of water pollution control facilities

Initially, the construction of sewers was entirely a community responsibility, generally incorporated in other governmental public works functions such as street construction, with financing entirely through property taxes. When water pollution control became necessary, the costs of interceptors and the treatment plants were incorporated into the same financing structure with no special charges imposed on contributors to the sewerage system. However, as the pressure grew to build treatment facilities, particularly because of the consequences of pollution to others, the burdens began to be somewhat greater and were not so readily accepted.

With the hiatus in construction of public works during World War II, the needs in the post-war period were great, and new methods of financing were explored.

One answer was in extending the use of revenue bonds, which depend upon income from charging for the services to repay the loans. Revenue bond financing became exceedingly popular for the financing of such public facilities as turnpikes, bridges, and tunnels because this method of finance, particularly in an expanding economy, appeared to be painless. However, such revenue financing puts the burden for payment for these services on a limited population, those who actually use the facility, although some of the benefits accrue to non-users, such as those who own property in the vicinity of these facilities and who profit from their presence. When revenue financing began to be attractive for sewerage projects, the distortion in equity began to concern engineers and municipal officials.

At the annual meeting of the Section of Municipal Law of the American Bar Association in September 1947, the late Samuel A. Greeley, a distinguished American consulting engineer, presented a paper entitled 'Some fundamental considerations in revenue financing of water supply and sewage disposal projects with special reference to rate structures'. As a result, a joint committee of the American Society of Civil Engineers and the American Bar Association prepared a report which enunciated a fundamental financing principle:[6]

> 'The needed total annual revenue requirements of a water or sewage works shall be contributed by users and non-users (or by users and properties) for whose use, need, and benefit the facilities of the works are provided, approximately in proportion to the cost of providing the use and the benefits of the works.'

This principle would require that the extra size of water distribution mains to provide for fire-fighting would be paid for by non-users or properties, that is through general taxation, while that portion of the pipelines required for distribution of water for household, commercial, and industrial purposes would be charged to the users, and all the cost and maintenance of treatment facilities would be charged to users. Inasmuch as fire protection is a government service paid for from general taxation, this would require a transfer of funds from the fire department to the water department for the service. Similarly the major portion of the cost of a combined sewer is chargeable to the properties protected, while domestic sewers or that portion of a combined sewer that serves to carry household and industrial wastewaters would be paid for through service charges. Sewer service charges grew from being used for 20 percent of all municipalities in 1945 to 85 percent of all municipalities by 1969.

While often it was not feasible to prepare a financing package that would entirely satisfy the principles enunciated, an examination of the existing method of financing in a community would indicate what the next stage of financing might most properly be. For example, if all of the initial financing had been from general taxation, it would be appropriate for a subsequent stage in construction to be financed by revenue bonds paid for from service charges.

However, equitable methods of finance still did not assure that a local authority would be enthusiastic about funding sewage treatment facilities. To aggravate the situation, many local authorities made their sewerage systems available to industry at no cost, other than payment of property taxes, in order to attract these industries to provide employment and a larger tax base to provide funds for needed government services. (Local authority officials would never seem to learn that such additional income from the enlarged tax base seldom solved their problems, as the cost of providing services both to the industry itself and to the influx of population attracted by the industry, almost always exceeded the increase in tax receipts.)

The first significant federal endeavor in financing pollution control was the 1948 Water Pollution Control Act (PL 80-825), which provided loans for treatment plant construction but was heavily dependent upon states for pollution control regulation. Many states sought to be 'pollution havens', attracting industry with the promise of not having to invest in pollution control, while providing tax incentives and cheap non-union labor. Many large water-using, low-paying industries from the industrial northeast of the United States were thus induced to move to the south. With no pressure from industry to abate pollution, the state regulatory authorities had little leverage to impose pressure on their municipalities.

In an attempt to speed pollution control programs, the Congress enacted the Water Pollution Control Act Amendments of 1956 (PL 84-660), initiating appropriations for federal grants for the construction of municipal sewage treatment plants, with annual grants of $50 million. With the federal foot once in the door, these grants increased as shown in Table 10.1.

The law that authorized the last three-year $18 000 million construction grant support (PL 92–500) also required that where a grant was given, it was to amount to no more and no less than 75 percent of the total construction cost of the interceptors and treatment facilities. In addition, some states provided matching funds ranging from 10 to 15 percent, leaving the local authority to raise in its turn only 10 to 15 percent of the total construction cost. Needless to say, the true cost of wastewater treatment to the resident in a community is completely hidden and local decisions with regard to pollution control are dictated more by the availability of the federal funds than by any measure of true need. 'The rate of construction of publicly owned treatment works is determined principally by the level of Federal funding.'[7]

A massive bureaucracy was established for administering these construction grant funds. Complex regulations, stacked ten inches high, were prescribed for construction grant applications in an attempt to assure that the objectives of the program were being met. A typical application without the environmental impact statement or the plans and specifications, is 13 inches thick. Vigorous representations were made by municipal officials, state regulatory officials, consulting engineers, equipment manufacturers and construction contractors to the EPA because of their failure to implement the program and make the money that Congress had intended to be spent actually available. A glimpse of the nature of the problems at the federal level was a promise by the administrator of the EPA in mid-1975, three years after the Act was passed and the year when the last of the construction grant funds were to be committed, that the program would be 'got moving' by the immediate addition of 400 employees to the construction grants branch.

At hearings of the National Commission on Water Quality, which was mandated in PL 92–500 to review the Act, the Governor of North Carolina stated:[8]

'Since this law was enacted, the abatement of pollution in North Carolina waters has actually been severely hindered.

TABLE 10.1
US Federal Grants for Wastewater
Treatment Plant Construction

Years	Annual grant (*in $ million/year*)
1956–61	50
1962	80
1963	90
1964–66	100
1966–67	150
1968	450
1969	700
1970	1 000
1971	1 250
1973	5 000
1974	6 000
1975	7 000

'This has happened primarily because of the provisions in the Act which completely changed the philosophy of water pollution control from a program based on providing wastewater treatment as necessary to meet essential downstream uses to a program of providing treatment to meet effluent limitations.

'In addition, the entire process has been saddled with planning requirements that are next to impossible to meet and which are made worse by the bulk of unnecessary red tape. ...

'Finally, if something is not done soon to eliminate the confusion and break the bottleneck in the construction grant program, North Carolina will be hard-pressed to prevent the recurrence of serious water quality problems. It does little good for Congress to appropriate billions of dollars for this program if EPA, through its regulations and guidelines, is going to make it next to impossible for a project to be approved for funding.

'These comments have been pretty harshly directed toward EPA. But we also recognize that the agency has not been entirely at fault.

'The overly specific language of PL 92–500 has resulted in judicial opinions overruling EPA's attempts at more reasonable and more flexible administration. And the centralization of such far-reaching authority in this single-purpose environmental agency, so far removed from the practical effects of its decisions, has negated reasoned judgment on the social and economic impact of these decisions. ...'

Regardless of its administration, this method of financing is subject to serious criticism because it burdens taxpayers for expenditures that are not attributable to their own activities nor from which they are likely to be directly benefitted. More significantly, such financing hides from the people at the local level, who should be involved in making decisions about their own resources, the actual costs of the program. When PL 92–500 was enacted, little attempt was made to assess the benefits or costs, aside from the $18 000 million in construction grants. Estimates of such benefits are bound to be imprecise, but at least orders of magnitude might indicate what levels of expenditure society can justify. The first such attempt, made three years after the Act was passed, estimated that annual damages from water pollution in 1973 would range from $5500 million to $15 500 million with $11 500 million being the 'best' estimate. The major annual damages from water pollution which would be rectified by the program are to recreation, at $4000 million to $12 000 million, psychic costs at $1000 million to $2000 million and production losses of $100 million to $1400 million.[9]

The construction costs alone to alleviate these damages have been estimated to be on the order of $360 000 million in public investment alone. If the fixed charges from such construction were taken to be a conservative 12 percent, including both interest and amortization, annual capital charges of about $43 000 million would be required to eliminate annual damages of $11 500 million. In addition, substantial annual costs would be required for operation and maintenance of the public facilities, as well as for the construction and operation of industrial facilities. These expenditures are required fairly uniformly over the country while benefits are highly variable from place to place. The individual citizen, the city fathers, and the state officials often feel powerless to reduce their share of the costs under this Act, if they are to benefit from the construction grants program.

The shift to EPA, which is responsible for the control of air pollution, toxic materials including pesticides, solid wastes, and noise as well as water supply and water pollution control, has had the effect of diluting the impact of a single agency whose primary goal had been water pollution control. EPA exacerbated the situation by dispersing water pollution control activities throughout the agency. For example, the Office of Research and Development of EPA is responsible for R&D for all of the activities of EPA. The relationships with the states for water are fragmented among ten regional offices, each of which is responsible for all of the diverse activities of EPA. Thus, the chain of responsibility for a specific activity is obscure. Furthermore, personnel shift continuously between the categorical programs and functions of EPA in Washington and its far-flung research facilities and the regions.

Public Law 92–500, the Water Pollution Control Act Amendments of 1972

Labeled '... the most sweeping environmental measure ever considered by the Congress ...',[10] PL 92–500 was passed by the Senate by a vote of 86 to 0, by the House of Representatives by a vote of 380 to 14, vetoed by the President, and passed over his veto overwhelmingly in both houses.

This legislation, on which consideration was begun early in 1971 and which was passed late in 1972, just prior to the presidential election, is identified with Senator Edmund Muskie, then a leading aspirant for the Democratic party nomination for the presidency. The veto was prompted by the high cost of the legislation, $24 000 million, but the considerable public enthusiasm for environmental quality at that time made opposition on the part of members of the House of Representatives, all of whom were coming up for election, and in the Senate, one-third of whom were coming up for election, politically unwise. Little hint was given of the economic burdens that PL 92–500 would exact, not only by the appropriations required from the federal treasury, but for the funds required from local authorities and industries in meeting their share of the burden.

'The most complex and extensive environmental measure ever passed,'[11] PL 92–500 begins by declaring two goals:

'1. It is the national goal that the discharge of pollutants into the navigable waters be eliminated by 1985.

'2. It is the national goal that wherever attainable, an interim goal of water quality which provides for the protection and propagation of fish, shellfish, and wildlife and provides the recreation in and on the water be achieved by July 1, 1983.'

The law provided for the establishment of a National Commission on Water Quality to '... make a full and complete investigation and study of all the technological aspects of achieving, and all aspects of the total economic, social, and environmental effect of achieving or not achieving, the effluent limitations and goals set forth for 1983. ...' The Commission's report, in gestation during 1975, was published in 1976, after the authorized construction grants were to have been spent.[12]

PL 92–500 represents a significant change in the philosophy of pollution control in the United States, with the greatest impact being in the considerably expanded federal role in the program. In addition to substantially increased federal funding for the construction of publicly owned treatment facilities, a new regulatory mechanism is introduced requiring uniform technology nationwide based upon effluent limits together with a national permit system for all discharges. Another new element introduced into water pollution control programs, supported by federal funds, is regional planning.

Effluent limitations

Prior to PL 92–500, the approach to water pollution control taken by many states was through the classification of streams according to their best use, the establishment of stream standards to achieve the classifications, and a requirement that dischargers provide facilities so that the stream standards would not be contravened. Only a few states utilized effluent standards or limits, with most states maintaining considerable flexibility in permitting a wide range of treatment approaches so long as the stream standards were met. The uses were generally classified as follows:

Class A—Waters to be used for drinking,
Class B—Waters to be used for bathing,
Class C—Waters to be used for fishing,
Class D—Waters to be used for agricultural and industrial purposes,
Class E—Waters to be used for receiving wastewaters.

Each of these classifications would have its own set of stream standards appropriate to protecting that particular use. For example, Classes A and B would have coliform standards, but Classes C, D, and E would not. The dissolved oxygen requirements might be 5 mg/l for Classes A, B, and C, but 3 mg/l for Class D and 0 mg/l for Class E, with the provision, in the last instance, that septic conditions that would result in nuisance be prohibited. At the time these standards were promulgated, in the 1950s, even Class E represented a substantial improvement in stream quality in many places. With the thrust towards the achievement of environmental quality, many states eliminated Class E in the 1960s.

When the various reaches of the streams of a state were classified, the state regulatory agency would generally prescribe the treatment that was necessary to achieve the stream standards, but considerable flexibility on the part of the polluters was permitted, and effluent standards were not generally prescribed. For example, one useful approach appropriate to industrial discharges was the provision of large regulating basins for the effluent so that discharges to the receiving stream could be programmed to match the flow and condition of the stream.[13] The availability of dissolved oxygen monitoring instruments made such discharge regulation quite automatic, as a DO probe could be mounted at the critical point in the receiving stream, and the discharge of waste controlled to maintain a minimum DO.

Also, such stream classifications encouraged industry to locate on rivers where their impact would be minimal. Savings would accrue from locating on a large river where treatment and surveillance could be small as contrasted with another site where the maintenance of a high quality effluent for discharge to a small stream would require costly treatment and surveillance. Pollution control costs were often the deciding factor in the location of large water-using industries, such as pulp and paper mills.

Under PL 92–500, by 1977, all industrial facilities were to have the 'best practicable control technology' regardless of where located. By 1983, the 'best available technology', regardless of cost, is required of all industrial facilities, again regardless of where located.

All municipalities, by 1977, were required to have secondary (biological) treatment, although the precise definition of that degree of treatment had not yet been formulated, as a minimum, regardless of where the wastewaters are discharged, even if into the Mississippi River or into the ocean. For many discharges into large rivers or into the ocean it has been demonstrated that the improvement accomplished by secondary treatment over primary treatment would not be discernible either by any user of the water or by any routine analytical determinations. The removal of the biodegradable organic matter from a wastewater effluent, the only effect of secondary treatment, is not likely to be significant when that wastewater is diluted in a large turbid river.

The EPA defined secondary treatment to include chlorination, and accordingly many chlorination facilities were constructed at sewage treatment plants financed under the construction grants program. However, chlorination is now being re-evaluated because of a concern for the hazards from halogenated organics which have been found to be harmful to human and aquatic life. The fact that the chlorination of effluents might interfere with the stabilization of organic matter in the receiving waters has received little attention in the United States as contrasted with Britain, where chlorination of effluents is not practiced, even where effluents are discharged into waters to be used as sources of potable supplies.

The one relaxation of the uniform approach to effluents throughout the nation is in meeting the 1977 requirements of 'best practical control technology' for industry, where the economics of each individual situation is to be taken into consideration by the administrator of the EPA in setting individual requirements. With some 200 000 industrial facilities discharging wastewaters throughout the country, this regulatory approach promised to be, and has been, extremely burdensome, creating considerable uncertainty on the part of the industrialist as to how far in fact he will be obliged to go in each instance. This uncertainty has led to a slow-down in the provision of industrial treatment facilities that matched the slow rate of municipal construction occasioned by the dilatory implementation of the construction grants program. The conclusion of the staff of the National

Commission on Water Quality was that the 1977 goals will not be reached by industries or municipalities by 1977, although industry may do better achieving them 'perhaps by 1980'.

Planning of facilities for water pollution control

The planning provisions of PL 92–500 have received some modicum of approbation from the professionals in the field. For the purpose of encouraging and facilitating the development and implementation of areawide waste treatment management plans, the governor of each state is required to designate areas, and a single representative organization for each area, to formulate a management plan. These areas are based upon urban–industrial concentrations, but where such areas are not readily identifiable, the state is to be responsible for the management plan. However, despite the fact that responsibilities for drinking water and water pollution control both reside within the EPA, the planning for water supply seldom accompanies planning for pollution control. The regions established for areawide waste treatment management were not established on a hydrological basis nor with any thought to promoting efficient water supply development. River basin waste treatment plans are also required to be prepared, with these often including several of the planning areas.

In most instances, the representative agencies designated to prepare the plans have been 'Councils of Government'. Most states have established such COGs by dividing the state into regions for planning purposes, with each COG having representation from all of the municipalities and the counties within that region. The areas served by the COGs are almost always different from the areas for wastewater treatment management planning.

A more powerful planning device in PL 92–500 is in the construction grants program. In order for a municipality to receive a construction grant, a management plan must be approved which includes consideration of a wide range of options such as reclamation, land disposal, and treatment on an areawide basis. This last provision has been most productive in that it does encourage the several local authorities in an area and their engineers to work together with a promise of regrouping of facilities. Previously, local authority consulting engineers hesitated to encourage joint efforts because they faced the possible loss of clients.

Unfortunately, these several types of regional planning efforts are conducted by different agencies: the COGs conduct the regional areawide planning; the state regulatory agencies conduct the river basin planning; and the local authorities jointly conduct the treatment facilities joint planning. The planning efforts tend not to be well coordinated because of the diversity of agencies having responsibility and because of the timing. For example, in order to obtain construction grants, the local authorities feel obliged to press forward with their facilities planning before the areawide planning is completed. Nevertheless, this introduction of regional planning for water pollution control represents an important new initiative.

A CRITIQUE OF THE WATER POLLUTION CONTROL PROGRAM

A law passed so overwhelmingly would have been expected to have received great public and professional support. The profession did actually support PL 92–500 primarily because of the promise of massive construction grant funds which were felt to be important to local authorities, state agencies, consulting engineers, equipment manufacturers, contractors, and those who wanted to see water pollution abated. In straining for these grants, the concomitant vexations and burdensome regulations were not anticipated.

The administrators of EPA at the time PL 92–500 was being debated had asserted that it could not be implemented. It was widely appreciated that the goals, particularly for so-called 'zero discharge', were unattainable. Two philosophies for legislative action were at odds: (1) that goals should be set far beyond what can be attained to provide a steady spur to improvement and for attaining intermediate objectives: or (2) that laws that cannot be implemented and that have elements that are unreasonable encourage a disrespect for those parts of the law that may be sound, creating resistance to complying with any part of the law.

'Some see [PL 92–500] as the way to a cure for the nation's water pollution problems. Others call it an abomination, question whether it will ever be effective in its present form, and even call for its severe modification or outright repeal. ... All do agree that it is the subject of frequent, and often acerbic and emotional debates, especially with respect to industrial water cleanup guidelines and standards.'[14] Some of its complexity is revealed by the fact that three years after PL 92–500 was passed, 70 principal industrial categories had standards promulgated but these represent only the proverbial 'tip of the iceberg'. Standards are required for some 500 industrial sub-categories, with five sets of regulations necessary for each: for the best practicable control technology currently available, BPCTCA (1977); the best available technology economically available, BATEA (1983); pretreatment for existing sources which are to be discharged into sewerage systems; pretreatment for new sources to be discharged into sewerage systems, and new source performance standards. In all, more than 2500 sets of regulations need to be prepared.

Some measure of response is that, as of July 1975, industry had brought 243 suits against the EPA for those regulations it had established. These were based on the lack of reasonable rationale for the regulations, lack of opportunity for effective comment on proposed regulations, misuse of the 'exemplary' plant concept which is the basis for determining the best practicable technology, and the rigidity of single-numbered effluent limitations.

All together, industry has been extremely critical of PL 92–500 and the EPA's administration of it, principally on the basis of the economic impracticalities of many of the requirements and the over-regulatory attitude of the EPA which industry claims has considerably impeded progress toward pollution control.

Among the most articulate and well-informed critics of PL 92–500 has been the Water Pollution Control Federation, which had been a strong supporter of the legislation, particularly the construction grants phase of it, when it was being debated. The Federation, made up of 38 associations in the United States, plus many foreign associations, comprising more than 20 000 American members drawn from local authorities, state regulatory agencies, federal agencies, consulting engineering firms, educational institutions, equipment manufacturers, industries, contractors, and environmental organizations, has a considerable stake in water pollution control legislation and its administration. Their assessment resulting from lengthy deliberations, including sessions with congressmen, and state and EPA regulatory officials asserted that PL 92–500 and its implementation did not begin to approach public expectations for it. Certain common themes for improvement were repeatedly echoed:

1. the need to involve state and local officials more effectively,
2. the need to assess more realistically the efforts required against their effect on water quality, and
3. the need to reduce the burden of bureaucratic red tape.[15]

PL 92–500 and the EPA fail to consider local conditions, and state and local authorities assumed that elimination of local discretion was a sign of mistrust of local competence. Chlorination of effluents was cited as a classic example of these failings. The purpose of chlorination is the protection of public health, but chlorination appeared to be a goal in itself, required for effluents discharged even to dry stream beds. The requirement for a minimum of secondary (biological) treatment everywhere, including coastal areas, was cited as another example of wastefulness.

The permit system, tied to rigid effluent limits, was off to a shaky start, and once initial deadlines were missed, future deadlines were jeopardized. The Federation questioned the value of permits, particularly when they are hurriedly prepared without considering local conditions and without state review. Despite the admission by the EPA that the 1977 goal for universal secondary treatment is unattainable, the permits that are issued are obliged to prescribe effluent limits that satisfy the 1977 requirement. The Federation requested Congress to extend deadlines and to provide administrative relief for those who do not meet the deadlines as long as they demonstrate good faith efforts.

The most pervasive complaint was the frustration engendered by the staggering paperwork demands that accompanied implementation of the law. For example, Pennsylvania has found that office time spent by its technical and professional staff is increasing at six times the rate of its field work. Michigan, in a periodic computer audit of its activities, found that the administrative burden had caused a decrease from 73 to 58 percent in the number of industrial discharge stations visited. Total staff visits to the field dropped by two-thirds because of the requirements for paper work in the office.

The National Commission on Water Quality, charged in PL 92–500 with reviewing the law, recommended to Congress significant 'mid-course corrections' in March 1976, primarily with a view towards extending the several deadlines, providing flexibility and even waivers on a case-by-case basis, decentralizing regulatory and administrative functions, stabilizing the construction grants program at an annual $5000 million to $10 000 million level for five to ten years, and redefining the 'zero discharge' goal.[12] One member of the Commission, Senator Muskie, demurred from the recommendations and the EPA vigorously denounced the recommendations as a '... backward step ... unnecessary from a financial viewpoint, destructive from an environmental viewpoint, and in terms of the overall public interest just plain wrong.'[16] Whether Congress will revise the legislation significantly is uncertain as of this writing.

Created in 1968 to examine national water policies, the National Water Commission *inter alia* explored deficiencies in the construction grants program.[17] In its review of the 15-year history of the program, the Commission indicated that some cities had delayed construction while waiting for federal funds to become available or for grant percentages to increase. The Ohio River Valley Water Sanitation Commission (ORSANCO) was created in 1948 when only one percent of the wastewaters in the basin was being treated. By 1956, without federal grants, some 55 percent was being treated. Since then, progress has slowed as cities wait their turn for federal moneys. ORSANCO commissioners were particularly troubled because municipalities that had already instituted treatment would not be eligible for federal funds. 'Although federal aid as envisioned (in 1956) was designed specifically to help those communities which were in financial straits—the determination of which was left to the states in order that appropriate priority might be assigned—the fact is that after the law was enacted not many projects in the Ohio Valley moved forward until a grant was made available.'[18]

The Commission recognized that the public demand for cleansing of the nation's waters at an early date could only be met with federal construction assistance. Therefore, the Commission concluded that construction grants should be continued until the nation had eliminated its backlog of needed facilities and had fulfilled the current expectations of communities relying on federal funding. Thereafter, the grants program should be terminated and the responsibilities for construction, maintenance and operations, and repair and replacement should be borne by local government and paid for by user charges.

The National Water Commission has been the only official body in the United States to advocate termination of the grant program. Some engineers have been rash enough to suggest privately that construction grants be limited to that portion of a works which serves present populations, with local authorities funding all treatment requirements intended to meet future needs, the intention being to gradually shift away from construction grants as the needs of the present population are met. Such an approach would avoid the inequity that would result if the construction grant program were terminated before all of the present population had had an opportunity to get its 'fair' share from the federal treasury.

FEDERAL WATER RESOURCES AGENCIES

Several federal agencies have traditionally had major roles in water resources management, while others have been created to address certain problems. Illustrative of the widespread federal responsibility for water was the creation in 1965 of the Water Resources Council, now consisting of the Secretaries of Agriculture, Army, Commerce, Housing and Urban Development, Interior, and Transportation, all cabinet members; the Federal Power Commission; and the Administrator of the EPA; with participation by the Attorney General, the chairmen of the Council on Environmental Quality, the Tennessee Valley Authority, the River Basin Commissions and the Basin Inter Agency Committees, and the director of the Office of Management and Budget.

The Department of Agriculture, in addition to its primary concern for water for irrigation, is responsible for the Farmers' Home Administration, which makes loans and grants to rural communities for water supply and sewerage systems. The Corps of Engineers, under the Secretary of the Army in the Department of Defense, is both a civilian and a military construction agency with a major responsibility for providing facilities for flood protection and navigation, which also offer opportunities for multipurpose use, including water supply and recreation. In the 17 arid western states, the Bureau of Reclamation of the Department of the Interior is responsible for building reservoirs for irrigation which serve ancillary purposes such as water supply and power production. Also within the Department of the Interior is the US Geological Survey with responsibilities for mapping and hydrologic data collection. The USGS records the natural quality of the nation's waters, often engaging in special water quality studies. The water supply and water pollution control efforts of the federal government are in the EPA.

An initial objective of the Water Resource Council was the creation of federal–state river basin commissions for water resources planning. Also, the Council is required to establish procedures for federal participation in the preparation of comprehensive regional or river basin plans and projects. While the only federal agency with any responsibility for national water planning, the Council suffers from the fact that it is not in a position to move policies that would challenge the authority of any member agency. The director of the Water Resources Council is an employee of the chairman of the Council, traditionally the Secretary of the Interior, and neither the director nor the Council enjoys independent political status. With a limited budget and a professional staff of fewer than 20 persons, the Council has not been in a position to initiate the appraisal of programs and policies required of it.

Because of conflicts in future policies for water resources development in the United States that surfaced in the mid-1960s, the Bureau of the Budget, now the Office of Management and Budget, recommended creation of the National Water Commission: 'Only a national commission can effectively assess the many common aspects of water problems that we face, and only such a commission can outline the consistent courses of action which must be followed if this nation is to achieve the most efficient utilization of its precious water resources.' Accordingly, a National Water Commission, to have a life of five years, was established in the waning days of the Democratic administration in 1968. It was to review national water resource problems, economic and social consequences of water resources development, including their impact on regional economic growth and on esthetic values affecting the quality of life, and advise on such specific water resource matters as may be referred to it by the President and the Water Resources Council. The Commission was to be made up of citizens not associated with the federal government in any other capacity and having no commitment to any entrenched federal agency program.

Appointed in a Democratic administration and operating throughout its life in a Republican administration, the National Water Commission's report and recommendations embodied in a volume *Water Policies for the Future*,[17] was condemned to fall upon infertile soil. However, its dispassionate assessments of the water scene in the United States are likely to make the National Water Commission report a valuable guideline for future action within the government, when such actions can be taken in a more cordial climate.

The National Water Commission recognized that the Water Resources Council had become an important and useful body, but found that it was unable to review critically the policies and programs of the individual federal agencies, nor to confront policy questions and resolve them, particularly when they involved interagency conflicts. The Commission declared that the Council needs a policy-making component with an ability to enforce decisions when a consensus cannot be reached. It therefore recommended that the Water Resources Council have an independent full-time chairman on the White House staff and that the Council should be placed within the executive office of the President. Such placement would give the Council more 'clout' with the Office of Management and Budget and in promoting policies that may be repugnant to an individual agency. Failing the implementation of this recommendation, or another like it that would create a national water planning agency with executive power, and with the fragmentation of water resources programs and funds amongst many agencies, all of them strong and with separate but powerful constituencies, long-term plans or goals for water management are not likely to be enunciated or implemented.

The US Army Corps of Engineers

Three federal agencies are charged with designing and constructing water projects at the federal level: the Bureau of Reclamation in the Department of Interior, the Soil Conservation Service in the Department of Agriculture and the most powerful and ubiquitous water agency in the United States, the US Army Corps of Engineers. The Corps has divisions and district offices throughout the country and is charged with the planning, design, construction and operation of major and minor works having to do with flood protection, navigation, and harbors. The Corps has been responsible for building hundreds of major reservoirs throughout the country. In the process, the Corps has been thoroughly vilified by environmentalists who contend that the Corps' predilection for constructing reservoirs is changing the face of America for the worse. In order to justify many of its projects, the Corps has been obliged to incorporate facilities for one or more of the following in addition to flood control: power production, public water supply, irrigation, recreation, and low-flow augmentation for navigation. Credit for low-flow augmentation for pollution control was authorized after World War II and became an important element of major Corps projects. With the onset of the environmental movement and the resistance to the construction of reservoirs, particularly to replace adequate wastewater treatment, credit for benefits from low-flow augmentation for pollution control could not be included in Corps projects.

When the Corps assesses a project, often at the behest of a member of Congress representing the area involved, all of the benefits and costs are estimated, and if the benefit/cost ratio exceeds one, the project is sent forward to Congress for authorization. Financing is entirely from the federal government except that some recovery is expected from an electric or water utility for that part of a project used for hydroelectric power production or water supply. In projects that require cost-sharing on the part of the beneficiaries of a portion of a project, such as municipal and industrial water users, the cost-sharing is not required until the supply is used. Accordingly, because the costs of a reservoir with benefits for flood control and recreation, the two most important in the benefit/cost ratio, do not have to be met from local funds, Corps of Engineers projects are very attractive to Senators and Congressmen who often spearhead such projects, taking credit for them when they are constructed. Such 'pork barrel' projects bring resources and benefits to a region at no direct cost to that region. The benefits of Corps projects are almost never measured on the basis of the users willingness to pay. Many of these projects would never have been built if local funds, even in token amounts, would have been required for construction. They are attractive projects because the financial burden falls on the nation as a whole.

With such a powerful contribution potentially available from the Corps of Engineers, the Corps' success with Congress is easy to understand and its power has scarcely been diminished. With a reduction in the need for major flood control projects in the future, the Corps has shifted to an interest in regional plans for the land disposal of wastewaters, embracing somewhat grandiose schemes such as a project for the Chicago metropolitan area that would require 740 square miles of land in neighboring Indiana. Thus far, Corps pollution control projects in the civil sector have not been implemented.

Other federal water agencies

The Bureau of Reclamation has operated in the west much in the way the Corps of Engineers has operated in the east. The costs for irrigation are intended to be repaid, without interest, over a 50-year period. However, revenues from hydroelectric power from irrigation projects have been applied toward payment for construction. On many projects, irrigation water users actually repay only about 10 to 15 percent of the total allocated for irrigation construction costs, including interest. Thus, irrigation in the west is subsidized virtually to the extent that flood control is subsidized in the east.

Other substantial programs exist for the funding of local water projects. For example, the Department of Housing and Urban Development and the Farmers' Home Administration in the Department of Agriculture have provided up to 50 percent of construction costs for water supply and sewerage projects for local communities. The FHA is limited to rural communities under 10 000 people, but HUD can extend its grants up to 90 percent for communities below that size. In addition, in economically depressed areas, the Economic Development Administration can supplement other grants up to 80 percent, and up to 100 percent in lending for municipal water supply and sewerage. In all of these instances, the costs of operation are intended to be the responsibility of the local authority.

Other sources of funds have become available to municipalities for water supply and sewerage and sewage treatment under the guise of programs intended to accomplish other national goals. For example, federal assistance is available for facilities for new towns. Also, special funds for community development can be used for providing local sewerage. By far the largest and least identifiable source of funds is through so-called 'revenue sharing' whereby the federal government returns to local communities a certain share of revenue derived from federal taxation. Such funds can be expended for a wide range of local services, both for capital and for operation, including water supply and sewerage.

Federal intervention through a variety of devices for granting subsidies for meeting local government responsibilities has prevented the costs for the provision of water supply and sewerage and sewage treatment services, and particularly the latter, from being adequately identified so that choices can be made as to how financial resources are to be used. The EPA, in the administration of its construction grants program, insists on projects that are 'cost-effective', but only within the context of meeting specific effluent requirements and not with regard to competing social needs. If a community wants assistance from the federal government for categorical subsidies, it must comply with all of government's regulations or do without, even though its needs may be great. Communities expert in 'grantmanship' are able to accrue more such federal support than other communities whose needs may be much greater. Grantmanship aside, a community with 'muscle' derived from the political power of its local officials or through the power of its representatives in Congress is more likely to do well in the battle at the federal trough than are communities not so well favored.

The National Water Commission examined the matter of subsidies and called for a major reform of existing cost-sharing policies with the aim that:

policies should be consistent among alternative means for accomplishing the same purpose,

policies should be consistent among federal agencies for the same purpose,

policies need not require a uniform percentage of cost sharing for all water developments,

policies should require uniform terms for the repayment of non-federal cost shares,

policies should promote equity among project beneficiaries and tax payers, and

policies should not lead to the expansion of the federal role in water management.

While the Commission did not disapprove of subsidies, it believed that they are only justified if they serve some compelling social purpose and where conventional markets and pricing mechanisms cannot provide the benefits. The general rule the Commission proposed is that 'Direct beneficiaries of water projects who can be identified and reached should ordinarily be obliged to pay all project costs that are allocated to the services from which they benefit.'[19]

The increase in the federal role in subsidizing water-related projects is shown in Fig. 10.1, which does not include the impact of the substantial subsidies called for in PL 92–500.

One answer to the confusion and waste resulting from the plethora of federal agencies involved in essentially the same functions, often addressing the same constituents competitively, is the establishment of a single federal agency into which would be gathered all existing federal agencies responsible for design and construction of water projects. More persuasive arguments have been made for a new Department of Natural Resources which would incorporate all federal water-related activities.

REGIONALIZATION IN THE UNITED STATES

Local government in the United States is characterized by a diversity of government agencies varying in size from those serving hundreds to those serving millions of people, varying in area and in function over every spectrum of public service and combinations of these. With some 40 000 separate entities responsible for community public water supply, the total number of local government entities with responsibilities for planning, administration, and financing of public services approaches 100 000.

In the 56 Standard Metropolitan Statistical Areas that had 1960-populations of 500 000 or more, constituting a total population of 84 million, 11 254 local government units included 174 county governments, 2902 municipalities, 1470 township governments, and 3844 special districts. Among the latter were 2486 water-related special districts, of which 511 were for water supply alone, 395 for sewerage alone, and 117 for water supply and sewerage. Of the 2486 water-related special districts, 2351 were single purpose, including in addition to water supply and sewerage, flood control, drainage, irrigation, recreation, and fire protection.[20]

'The case of the New York metropolitan area, with its 1400 governments, is well known, but in none of the great metropolitan centers is there a metropolitan authority possessing power to plan the metropolis as a whole or to administer the services that require large-scale organization. The obstacles to reform are in part the indifference of state governments, in part the opposition of small suburban councils to being absorbed by or in any way subordinated to a metropolitan authority, and in part a belief that local government units must not be merged or otherwise tampered with unless a referendum has been held and a majority obtained in favor of the proposal.'[21]

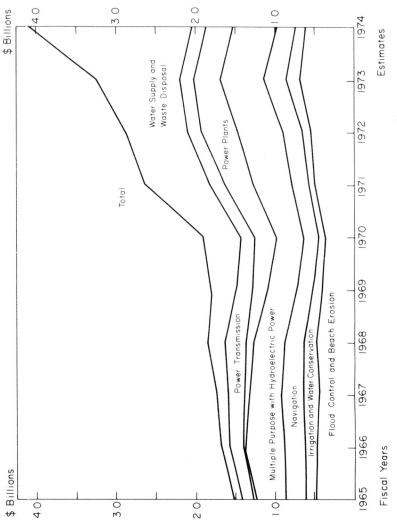

FIG. 10.1   Ten-year trend in federal water resources expenditures.

Nevertheless, many attempts have been made to overcome parochial interests. A most significant development, encouraging because it was fraught with emotion, was the consolidation of schools in the rural areas of the United States which led to large scale busing, not at all related to the promotion of racial integration. Rural one-room school houses denied children the full opportunity to exploit their capabilities, and their parents acceded to consolidated schools, despite the many hours of bus travel to schools in the 'big city', to obtain a better education for their children.

Although some critics have decried the large schools, particularly in the urban areas, no effort to return to the fragmented school system that had existed can be discerned. If so personal a service as education can be 'regrouped' or 'regionalized' in the United States, certainly water services can be. Consumers who receive adequate water services at a reasonable cost would have little interest in where the responsibility for these service falls, whether with local government or with some larger regional organization. Yet consolidation amongst water services in the United States has been notably slow, primarily because those responsible for the services have been reluctant to yield their powers and, up to now, state and federal leadership have generally been absent.

Some regional successes have been recorded. The Metropolitan Water District of Southern California, which is composed of 13 cities, 11 municipal water districts and the San Diego County Water Authority, serves a population of almost 10 million people over a distance of more than 150 miles (250 km), drawing its water from many sources, some of them quite distant. Sanitary districts are not uncommon, with the largest and oldest being the Metropolitan Sanitary District of Greater Chicago, which collects wastewaters from participating municipalities, including the City of Chicago, for treatment and disposal, with the sewerage systems being retained by the individual municipalities. Seldom do such large regional systems provide both water supply and sewage disposal services, and with separate ownership of the two services, seldom are the boundaries the same. About half of 63 water utilities from 28 states plus the District of Columbia, each serving populations in excess of 125 000, are billed for sewerage and sewage disposal services along with water supply service. Of 28 utilities serving over one million people, 20 were administered jointly.[22] The integration of water supply and sewerage services at the municipal level is far more advanced in the United States than it was in the United Kingdom prior to reorganization, but this was seldom accompanied by regionalization. The regional water supply system for Southern California is not related to the sewerage service and the regional sewage disposal system for Chicago is not associated with the water supply systems serving the area.

River basin planning

The major thrust for regional planning for water management was initiated as a result of interstate conflicts on the major rivers in the United States, almost all of which either form borders between the states or encompass, within their watersheds, all or parts of several states. The federal government took the initiative in establishing interstate agreements through its federal-interagency river basin committee. With the creation of the Water Resources Council and passage of the Water Resources Planning Act of 1965, river basin commissions were to be established throughout the United States. (The only areas excepted were those covered by the Tennessee Valley Authority and the Delaware River Basin Compact Commission.) Each such commission is to serve as the principal agency for the coordination of federal, state, interstate, local and private water development plans. These plans are to be submitted to the President and by him to Congress and the governors and legislatures of the participating states. An independent federal chairman and staff are provided for each of the commissions, the chairman being appointed by the President independent of any federal agency. Members of the commission are delegated from and salaried by other organizations. Each state and federal agency with a substantial interest in the river basin is entitled to a member. Thus, members of the commission represent diverse and often competitive interests and no mechanism exists whereby any one point of view can win the day. 'Bargaining takes place and an agreement is either worked out or the issue is deferred. River basin commissions are thus designed to achieve coordination without centralization of authority.'[23]

Financial control over the commissions resides with the member agencies, and many of these agencies often pursue their own objectives without reference to the river basin commissions. While the commissions may be more useful than *ad hoc* committees for planning, up to now they hardly seem to be viable regional authorities.

Interstate water compacts have provided more opportunities for the regional management of water related problems. Such compacts, in which the federal government is also represented, were first utilized in 1922 when the Colorado River Compact was first agreed upon to allocate water rights among the states in the Colorado river basin. In all, some 30 compacts have been promulgated, being particularly useful for pollution control. The earliest such compact, between New York, New Jersey and Connecticut, resulted in the Interstate Sanitation Commission to deal with water quality problems in New York harbor. This model was followed in 1948 by perhaps the most extensive pollution control agreement, that among eight states in the Ohio River basin, the Ohio River Valley Water Sanitation Commission. While these commissions do have enforcement authority, a serious limitation is that enforcement orders require concurrence by a majority of commissioners of the affected state.

The Delaware River basin compact represents a departure from the powers available to earlier agreements in that the Delaware River Basin

Commission may issue orders upon polluters to cease discharges which are in violation of its regulations. With licencing powers for discharges within its jurisdiction, the DRBC will approve any project which is consistent with its comprehensive plans for improving the waters of the basin. Also, the DRBC may construct, develop, operate and maintain facilities necessary to meet the obligations of the compact. The DRBC has the power to allocate the waters of the basin among the four signatory states, although unanimity amongst the Commissioners, the four governors, is required. The DRBC has broad financing authority but does not have the power to tax. DRBC approval of comprehensive plans for the basin places obligations on the state signatory parties to conform. With regulatory and allocation powers for both water supply and for water pollution control, DRBC has financed a demonstration project to prove the feasibility of regional wastewater management and its power to mandate such regional treatment could result in substantial reorganization in the Delaware River.

The Tennessee Valley Authority, established in 1933 as a public corporation to control floods, improve navigation, and produce electrical power in the Tennessee River basin, which covers parts of seven states, was at the time, and for that matter still is, the most innovative and successful water-related regional agency in the United States, and a model for the rest of the world if not for the rest of the United States. Its board of three directors is appointed by the President.

The TVA owns and operates all its water facilities including dams, navigation locks, power plants and related facilities within the basin. While it has been completely successful in that no major flood damage has occurred since the system of flood control dams was completed, and the area it serves with power can be seen to be economically well advanced as compared with surrounding areas, the TVA has come under attack because of its non-tax status and its competition with privately-owned utilities in the sale of electric power. Perhaps the reason that the TVA has not been emulated elsewhere in the United States, despite its success in meeting the objectives for which it was established, is 'the reluctance to enlist federal officials to shield activities from Congressional control and scrutiny by utilization of the corporate device.'[24] In any case, this approach is not likely to be adopted in the United States even though it would appear to represent the kind of regional management of water resources that would promise a high quality of water service.

Urban metros

The fragmentation of local government has posed serious problems in the provision of a wide range of local services. Regional government has long been recognized as a useful approach to achieving efficiencies and economies of scale, while ending conflicts among jurisdictions. Politically, regionalization has been difficult because it requires the yielding of local sovereignties. Many efforts at urban regionalization have failed because of resistance by inner city residents, generally Blacks, who are afraid of being electorally overwhelmed by white suburban populations and by the resistance of the suburbanites who fear that they will have to pick up the financial burdens of the inner cities.

'The idea of sharing public services has not had much appeal nationally. Few politicians seem willing to surrender the power, prestige, and patronage traditionally derived from running one's own departments.'[25]

Regionalization when it occurs is often unheralded, except by political observers and students of local government. Jacksonville, Florida, where disintegration of the central city was accompanied by a lack of common effort amongst the many small jurisdictions in the area, may be illustrative.[26]

'A decade ago Jacksonville was a dying community—its schools disaccredited, population shrinking, the business district in decay, the St. Johns River stinking with raw sewage, its air contaminated, and a lot of its public officials under indictment for petty corruption.

'Today the schools are in good shape, both air and water are being cleaned up fast, a hundred miles of crumbling sewer lines are being replaced, and new parks, swimming pools, health centers and mobile clinics are going up all over the place.

'Fire protection has improved so markedly that insurance rates have come down. More than 16 500 street lights have been installed and many of the streets in the poor—that is, the Black—sections of town have been repaved. New industries and jobs are flowing into the community, and office buildings ... are going up in the once dilapidated downtown district.

'At the same time, taxes have been reduced in five consecutive years, and if you compare the total tax burden—property, sales, income, and auto levies—in the 30 largest American cities, Jacksonville's are the lowest of all.' These changes were attributed to a new scheme of metropolitan government that replaced the weak, overlapping and confused patchwork of city, county, suburban and semi-independent agencies, accomplished under the leadership of private citizens rather than elected officials.

Other types of regionalization are also beginning to appear, even in rural areas, where the Rural Development District has appeared in Georgia, comprising groupings of counties that had been too small to provide effective government. The patterns of regionalization vary from place to place, but they have all served to simplify, strengthen, and amalgamate multitudes of local government units that were outmoded and impotent; they dealt only with regional problems, interfering as little as possible with local institutions; and they grew out of the initiative of private citizens who had never held nor expected to hold public office.

Nevertheless, resistance to regional government, even on a single-function basis, continues to be the hallmark of local government in the

United States. For example, New York City rejected out of hand a proposal by a New York State commission to take over the city's water supply and make it part of a regional water supply corporation.[27] New York City's environmental protection administrator asserted that, even with a provision that the city be given representation in the proposed water corporation, the program was still unacceptable. Following a series of hearings, the Temporary State Commission on the Water Supply Needs of Southeastern New York concluded that New York City could get along with less water and could save by such conservation measures as universal metering. On the other hand, New York City pointed out that its *per capita* consumption was less than that of Philadelphia, which has 100 percent metering. City officials fear that the Commission's plans would leave the city with inadequate water supply. Actually, New York City's water supply is drawn from a large region, calling upon a vast network of reservoirs in the upper Delaware River and in the Catskill mountains—all quite distant from the political jurisdiction of New York City. While New York City furnishes water to communities along the route of its aqueducts and in the vicinity of New York City, the Commission felt that there was not equality in treatment for all parts of the region because New York City was not considered responsive to upstate needs.

New York City draws its supply from protected sources and has not been required up to now to provide filtration. This high quality water is used for all purposes within the city, including purposes which could be satisfied with water of poorer quality. On the other hand, Philadelphia, the nation's fourth largest city, draws its water supply from the lower Delaware River which drains much of New Jersey, Pennsylvania, and part of New York. A regional organization for water management in this highly congested area might include the New York and Philadelphia metropolitan areas among others in the vicinity, permitting better use of the total water resource by directing the upland resources to uses requiring high quality, namely drinking water, throughout the area, including Philadelphia.

In examining recent experience in the United States and the United Kingdom in the management of environmental quality, Maynard Hufschmidt has concluded that: 'In the United States, practice in air and water quality management has lagged far behind the developed theory of regional management on an airshed or watershed basis. Although some attention is given to the regional management for achieving least-cost, or greatest net benefit solutions, United States policy has been moving toward adoption of uniform minimum national standards for both ambient air and water quality and for control of effluents, with inadequate regard for the cost-effectiveness of these approaches. ... One can summarize by noting that the United States is long on the theory of optimization and short on its practice; while the British, somewhat skeptical of optimization approaches that involve large investments of research and information, are more likely in the short run to develop a reasonable application of the theory, at least in the water resource field.'[28]

A COMPARATIVE ASSESSMENT OF WATER QUALITY MANAGEMENT IN THE UNITED STATES AND IN ENGLAND AND WALES

A useful framework for assessing the prospects for sound water quality management in the United States is to compare the situation in the United States with that in England and Wales with respect to each of the five principles enunciated in Chapter 1. If these principles have merit, the potential for following them should be a useful measure of the soundness of the programs. Although comparisons are inevitable, the intent is to indicate where changes in the American approach might be most appropriate.

1. The uniqueness of water projects

Each individual water project, if it is to serve society effectively and economically, is different from every other project. A factory for making paper, steel or shoes may be much the same wherever located but a water project must be fitted to the setting. Climate, precipitation, topography, density and distribution of population, industrial development, land use, recreational interests, and cultural pursuits vary from place to place throughout a nation, so that any efficient plan for water supply, water treatment, wastewater collection and disposal, or water recreation, needs to be considered uniquely.

When responsibility for water quality management in the United States rested upon the states, local and regional differences were considered in establishing requirements for water supply, for water pollution control and for meeting water-based recreational needs. With drinking water, for example, states in the southwest, where natural waters are characterized by high dissolved solids, tolerated levels in community water supplies much higher than is acceptable in the northeast, which is accustomed to having soft mountain water supplies. Even within a midwestern state, where most municipalities were required to provide secondary biological treatment for wastewaters because they discharged into small streams, those cities located on major rivers were only required to provide primary treatment, as the oxygen resources in the Mississippi and Missouri rivers are plentiful and not at all threatened by any amount of BOD. Wastewater treatment prior to discharge to such rivers was to prevent esthetic degradation of water quality by removal of floatable or settleable materials. Cities along the coasts were also under different strictures than inland cities because of the extensive water resources available for assimilation of wastewaters without impact on quality.

Some of the states, by intent or neglect, became pollution havens, encouraging industry to locate in their states on the promise that vigorous anti-pollution measures would not be instituted. With the environmental movement, and with a failure to alleviate water pollution in many different parts of the United States, the Congress responded with PL 92–500 which establishes virtually uniform requirements throughout the country, the only exception being where more treatment is demonstrated to be necessary.

All industries of the same type are required to provide the same treatment, wherever located. Guidelines for industries are developed based upon what certain exemplary industrial establishments have done. A mill located in a pollution-sensitive area might have installed extensive waste treatment facilities and modified its operations to minimize pollution because it had chosen that site to reap other advantages. However, this installation and others like it set the standard for all similar industries in the country wherever located, even if located where their effluents can cause no discernible harm. Such nationwide uniformity has been instituted in the name of equity and ease of administration. The equity is dubious because uniformity of pollution control, where all the other costs involved in industrial operations are not equitable, tends to distort sound investment planning. The ease of administration has turned out to be a chimera as each industry believes its situation to be unique and seeks legal redress against the administration of uniform requirements on the basis that the guidelines are not representative of their own establishment.

As Blair Bower has stated, levels of water quality to be achieved in any part of the country should bear some relationship to the present and anticipated uses of the water resource and to the related physical, economic, and esthetic benefits resulting from improved water quality.[29] With PL 92–500, pollution control requirements based upon protecting the best uses of streams have been abandoned to a goal that purports to make *every* stream fishable and swimable. The ambition of such a goal is far beyond the capacity of the nation to achieve and, inevitably if unofficially, priorities are now being established which in part depend upon the uses of the waters to be protected.

The National Commission on Water Quality '. . . was sensitive to the fact that this country has magnificently diverse conditions in climate . . . the environment . . . the economy . . . and society itself. We could in no way produce sufficient data to justify a standardized, rigid law based on averages.'[30] The Commission recognized the need for decentralization through authorizing the individual states to plan and implement its water pollution control program, with such decentralization inevitably recognizing regional differences. While the EPA is fighting these recommendations for abandonment of uniformity of approach in pollution abatement, it has made a valiant and largely successful effort to have the states take over responsibility for administering the 1974 Safe Drinking Water Act.

In England and Wales, the creation of ten water authorities, each responsible for establishing its own priorities, programs, and financing under only the most general guidance from the Department of the Environment, recognizes the different physiological, climatological, economic, and cultural differences across England and Wales. The varying approaches taken by the WAs provide a living laboratory for examining their relative effectiveness. Some WAs may give higher priority to providing improved water services while others may concentrate on improving the quality of their surface waters for recreational and amenity purposes.

A cogent example of the uniqueness of water projects is the case-by-case national approach followed in Britain for achieving water quality, a philosophy that was not a fruit of the reorganization, but certainly prospers under it. Baroness Birk stated the philosophy well in the House of Lords: 'It is an essential feature of the system we use for controlling polluting discharges that decisions about the precise levels of pollutants which may be allowed should be taken by WAs in the light of differing local circumstances. It makes a great deal of difference to the level of controls if the discharge is made into an inland river used for drinking supply, or into an estuary or the sea. This is not because we do not care about polluting the sea, but because the capacity of tidal waters with strong currents to absorb the pollutants without any harm is so much greater.... To ignore this fact, and to impose rigid, uniform standards on mills regardless of where they are situated is to risk wasting money treating effluent, sometimes to unnecessarily high standards. It also takes away the incentive for an industrialist to site factories where wastes can be most economically disposed of. ...'[31]

Similarly, in meeting specific water quality limits, a WA is in a position to determine how the desired level can best be attained. An optimal investment for the control of nitrates for downstream abstractions in the Thames will require different levels of nitrogen removal at different locations on the river, varying from no removal whatsoever at some points to high removals at others, the actual requirements being set to minimize the total investment in facilities in the basin. That the WA owns all the treatment facilities makes such an allocation not only theoretically possible but readily implementable.

While the United States is turning away from considerations of water use, as noted in Chapter 8, a National Water Council working party is proposing a new approach for establishing priorities in pollution abatement, preserving water for its highest uses and spending money only when a recognized benefit will result.[32]

2. The economics and efficiencies of scale

That the construction of engineering works, including water projects, exhibits significant economies of scale has always been recognized. In addition, economies of scale are achieved in the management and operation of water supply and pollution control undertakings. Even where physical water connections among many small works is not warranted because of distances between them, unified management is not only more economical but also more efficient in corralling professional talent for the enterprise.

In the United States, a majority of the approximately 75 000 separate water supply and sewerage and sewage disposal operations serve fewer than 1000 persons and cannot afford the quality of supervision that is necessary to assure effective planning, design, construction, management, and operation.

The 1974 Safe Drinking Water Act recognizes the need for proper surveillance but will be powerless to assure that it is provided to the smaller installations. In fact, the EPA's formula for grants to the states to assist in administering the Act assigns funds as a function of the number of separate systems in a state, thereby unintentionally rewarding fragmentation of water supplies.

However, the attitude towards water supply regionalization is changing. About two-thirds of the states have policies favoring regionalization, and some 75 percent of state engineers feel that regionalization will simplify state surveillance of small systems.[33] Nevertheless, small water supply systems are proliferating.

With regard to sewerage and wastewater treatment and disposal, PL 92–500 has specific provisions that offer priorities in funding for projects that serve more than one community, and joint community facilities planning is obligatory. The success of these initiatives is still uncertain, in part because of the general malaise of the construction grants program and the inverted time-table for pollution control and facilities planning. Moreover, funds for management and operation must come from the local community. Without a funding carrot, the incentive for regional management and operation has not been sufficient to overcome local sovereignty.

Furthermore, sewerage planning has become a surrogate for land-use planning in the United States, the latter being politically distasteful. Accordingly, local officials are hesitant to yield the one control they have for managing growth, the sewer and water lines, irrespective of whether they espouse 'pro-' or 'anti-growth' philosophies.

In England and Wales, decisions as to community growth rest on local authority decisions, and the WAs are obligated to meet sewerage needs of the local authorities. Pollution control and sewer location are not considered proper devices for controlling community growth.

The success of water supply regrouping as a result of the 1945 Water Act testifies to the advantages of regionalization of water supply services, which had brought a wholesome water supply to more than 99 percent of the total population of England and Wales. Sewerage and wastewater treatment and disposal, being local authority responsibilities, had been highly fragmented. A substantive accomplishment of the WAs after the reorganization was their taking inventory of their inheritance from predecessor authorities and immediately addressing the problems that appeared. Old and dilapidated works were abandoned and others were regrouped. 'Technically and scientifically the increase in scale of the new management units for sewage treatment and the concentration of existing resources of men and equipment have in general substantially raised the effectiveness of maintenance and process control where predecessor authorities were relatively small. The developing advantages of this change have been reflected not only in the possibilities of tuning up the performance of an authority's own treatment plants but also in an enhanced ability to deal objectively and helpfully with ... trade effluent.'[34]

That the regional organizations will promote the more efficient use of water resources, '... is already apparent [in] that the scope for integrating present supplies within the new areas will enable some schemes to be deferred.'[35] Some years will need to elapse before the WAs can expect to profit from the economies of scale of construction and from the more efficient allocation of resources within the larger geographical areas controlled by the WAs. *The Financial Times* (London) issued a special report on water, the feature article being devoted to the advantages of scale.[36] The reorganization was assessed in language generally foreign to financial publications: '... the restructuring ... is by far the most radical and, perhaps for that reason, may be more likely to endure' because the new WAs would be large enough to plan the future development of their water resources on an effective scale.

Institutional problems generally prevent optimal distribution of water resources when these resources are controlled by different authorities. Under the reorganization, optimal allocation of resources is relatively straightforward, with resulting major savings in capital construction. With the high place given the directorates of resource planning within the WA structures, examples of the optimal utilization of the water resources should develop.

In any large scale reorganization, with the creation of new administrative units, substantial increases in personnel would be expected. In fact, this has not been the case. In a special study of the pre- and post-reorganization manpower requirements, the Anglian Water Authority found that the total number of employees rose from 6888 to 6988, a 1·5 percent increase.[37] Against this exceedingly small increase, the AWA has achieved the following:

1. a greater capacity for in-house design work, effecting a saving in consulting fees,

2. the amalgamation of 21 water boards into 10 water divisions, realizing savings of £130 000 per annum in staffing costs, and

3. more efficient operational and maintenance standards and more effective and remunerative trade effluent control resulting from full-time staff available to even the smallest facilities.

For the water industry as a whole, 58 385 staff were employed after one year, about 60 percent of whom were manual workers. Prior to the reorganization, the estimates for the number employed had ranged to around 65 000. Although precise comparisons cannot be made, certainly no major increases in personnel were involved in the reorganization, while greater services are being offered, most particularly in improved operation of sewage treatment plant facilities and in the recreational and amenity uses of the nation's waters.

3. Integration of water supply and pollution control services

Historically, water quality, including particularly water supply and wastewater treatment, had been regulated in a single agency, the health department, in the United States. With the environmental movement, the regulatory emphasis on environmental pollution control resulted in the creation of new federal and state agencies leaving responsibility for water supply with the health agencies. The creation of the EPA brought these activities together once more at the federal level although they are still generally separate at the state level. However, even at the federal level, because of the separate legislation and their disparate histories, the administration of the programs is largely separate.

While many local authorities combine water supply and sewerage and wastewater disposal operations in single municipal departments, such regional metropolitan agencies that have been developed over the years are largely single function.

Integration of all water quality activities into single agencies, whether for ownership and operation or for surveillance, would seem today to be advantageous. Control of all elements of the hydrological cycle would permit more efficient management than would be possible if competing authorities owned and operated these elements. Wastewaters are becoming increasingly important as a 'new' resource, particularly for non-potable uses that were previously met with potable waters, and their utilization should be an integral part of overall water resource planning. Lastly, integration of these services will result in economies and efficiencies of scale, particularly in management and operation.

The creation of the new WAs, with integrated water management, was a major reformation in the British water industry, as water supply and water pollution control had been highly segregated responsibilities. Initially professionals viewed this change as merely cosmetic, expecting that within each WA the activities would be well separated with operating divisions responsible for each service. The reality was that even where single-purpose divisions were established with the first organization of the WAs, they very quickly became multifunctional so that now very few divisions remain single-purpose. The WA headquarters, with directorates of operations, resources planning, scientific services and finance, treat all water management as a unity. Even in the Anglian Water Authority, one of the few that maintains single-purpose divisions, the integration of the 'clean' and 'dirty' water services has permitted the postponement of expensive capital projects.

Of all the trauma associated with the reorganization, that of integrating the services was hardest on professionals in the industry. Yet of all the changes effected, integration now enjoys the greatest approbation.

In the United States, the common administration of all elements of environmental quality within the EPA should permit consideration of all environmental pollutants in an integrated fashion. The thrust of PL 92–500 and its administration is intended to consider the totality of pollutant potential from municipal, industrial, and agricultural operations. With both solid and liquid wastes being handled in the same federal agency, although generally in different agencies at local and state levels, the joint disposal of sewage treatment plant sludges with municipal refuse would seem to warrant a higher priority than it in fact has received. The creation of the WAs, with other pollution problems in other agencies, may make the integration of all pollution control activities more difficult than in the United States. An early failure of coordination between a local authority and a WA was the pollution of a water supply in the North West Water Authority by seepage from an illicit sanitary landfill which required temporary abandonment of the supply. However, the government has begun to address this problem.

4. Sound financial policies

A sound financing program should generate sufficient funds to cover the costs of the services, should promote the efficient utilization and allocation of the available resources, should not discriminate among classes of consumers, should reflect in its charges the costs incurred for providing the services, and should make subsidies for water services overt, if subsidies are needed. Subsidies for water should not be the vehicle for the amelioration of social inequities.

In the United States, the financing of public water supplies has generally met these criteria although in some instances the classic declining block rate of charges for water supply has been shown to benefit the large user, industry, at the expense of the residential customer. With the need for new water supply developments, always more costly than existing projects, interest has been expressed in designing charging schemes to meet marginal costs.

However, sound financing principles have been abandoned in meeting the costs for massive new initiatives in water pollution control. The federal construction grants program, exploding to commitments of some $6000 million annually, and often matched with state contributions, has violated every sound financial stricture. The heavy dependence on central government has resulted in a failure to generate sufficient funds to cover the local share, as local authorities will not move without assurance of a federal grant. With most of the capital costs, 75 percent from federal sources and 10 to 15 percent from many state treasuries, rather than from local funds, but with plans generated locally, little incentive exists for sound economic or natural resource planning, and the federal government has had to step in to try to assure, from a distance, that its funds are being spent wisely. Extensive federal regulatory requirements are accepted meekly, because otherwise the federal funds would not be forthcoming and because the federal agency imposing the requirements will meet most of the costs. Designs are promulgated that commit funds to higher capital costs and lower operating costs because only the latter must be met entirely from local funds. In a vain attempt to police those who use the federal funds: virtually every local authority, the states who supervise, and the consulting engineers, contractors, and equipment manufacturers who plan and build the facilities, the EPA has established a massive bureaucracy which, to those affected by it, seems only to have slowed the process and exacerbated the problem.

The grants program inevitably discriminates against one class of society—the middle class that provides most of the tax moneys that are used in the program. To the extent that the federal and state tax programs are inequitable, and that they are inequitable, cannot be gainsaid; to that extent the grants program discriminates among those who use and benefit from the facilities provided by the program. Furthermore, because the bulk of the wastewater treatment costs are met from general taxation and are not reflected in local charges, the true costs are hidden from the users and a wise selection from a variety of options for local expenditures becomes impossible.

While a financing policy for water should not address vast social issues by improving income distribution, it should not make income distribution more adverse. Though not intended, pollution control financing in the United States accounts for considerable adverse redistribution of income, without any discernible social purpose other than to accelerate the pace of pollution abatement. Those who use an environmental resource should pay for its use, i.e. polluters should pay and the prices of the final products and services should reflect the costs of protecting the environment from their production. In the United States, the approach of the government has been towards effluent limitations internalizing only those costs required to meet that limitation. No charge is made for the use of the water resource, either by its abstraction or by its pollution, even where standards are met. Only if the goal of PL 92–500, to cease discharging pollutants, is met would this characteristic of a sound policy be satisfied. However, achievement of the goal of eliminating pollution by 1985, or by any forseeable date, is widely accepted as not being possible. In England and Wales, inasmuch as the polluted water is the property of the WA, and all of the polluters within the authority are required to pay for all of their water services, a system of charges which would require that the polluter pay is feasible.

Perhaps the most daring aspect of the reorganization in England and Wales is in the provisions for financing the WAs. Up to the time of reorganization, sewerage and sewage disposal, which represent more than half the total costs of the water services, were local authority responsibilities benefitting from subsidies from the national exchequer in the form of rate support grants. Overnight, these subsidies were removed, and each consumer was obliged to meet directly the full costs of all of the water services. This difficult step was undertaken because it was an essential part of a sound financing program which was intended to generate sufficient funds to cover the costs of the services and to have the charges reflect the true costs incurred. Such financial assistance as the government feels obliged to provide for its citizens is provided through mechanisms other than the water services.

Unfortunately, the difficult economic situation in which the country found itself, the high rate of inflation, the backlog of needs, and the removal of national subsidies, all resulted in a substantial increase in water charges. In response, some WAs began to consider equalization of charges throughout their areas, which cannot be considered a sound policy for inducing the most efficient use of resources. If the charges are to be the same to a consumer wherever he is located, industries have no incentive to choose a site where water services would be least costly. However, the need to demonstrate equity amongst customers in a given administrative area is pervasive. Because equalization amongst the WAs would rob them of their autonomy, the question is still at issue, but is not likely to be adopted in the long term.

The Water Act 1973 enables metering residential customers while the Control of Pollution Act 1974 enables effluent charges for discharging into surface waters. Metering and effluent charges promise, if adopted, to offer a rational approach to the financing of the water services. Serious consideration will be given to those measures, as WA structure and financing are suited to them, although the Labour government is not in favor of utilizing these tools at this time.

Metering of residential customers is common in the United States even in the smallest of communities. However, effluent charges are not used in the United States other than for discharges into sewerage systems, and present administrative arrangements make the introduction of effluent charges for discharges directly to surface waters quite difficult. The allegation that an effluent charge is payment for a license to pollute may be appropriate in the American setting, but need not at all be so interpreted when collected by a WA, as the income from the effluent charge can be used directly for the benefit of those affected.

It is in sound financing that the prospects in the United States for improvement are most dim. The substantial subsidies for sewage treatment plant construction have distorted the water pollution control program to the point that it bears almost no relationship to the benefits to be achieved, to the priorities amongst competing needs for pollution control, nor to the priorities of other competing social needs. Unless the construction grant program can be phased out, and this is quite difficult because some communities would have received substantial support while after a phaseout others would not, little hope for a rational program exists. The recommendations of the National Water Commission offer the best guidelines for the phasing out of construction grants, but until this is seriously considered, the prospects for change in financing are small.

5. The preference for pure rather than polluted sources for potable water

So long as each local authority is obliged to seek its own least-cost solution, conflicts inevitably arise between the upstream discharger and the downstream abstractor. When the only concern with water quality was to prevent water-borne infectious disease, upstream pollution was manageable through conventional treatment, including chlorination. However, when the problem became that of the increasing concentration and diversity of synthetic organic chemicals, which are not removed in treatment or in passage downstream, the use of polluted sources assumes another dimension.

In the United States, considerable attention is being given to the threat of water quality from synthetic organic chemicals. One approach to this problem is to remove these contaminants at their source, a formidable task which is not at all feasible in large river basins. A second approach is their monitoring and removal by treatment, not at present technically feasible, and not likely to be so in the reasonable future. A third approach, dual water supplies, dismissed in the past as being too costly, is receiving fresh attention. The high costs and the uncertainties involved with using polluted sources, together with the limited resources of high quality water available, have made the consideration of dual supply systems less forbidding. The new respectability of this approach is revealed by the mounting of a full-day seminar on dual systems held at the American Water Works Association 1976 Conference.[38]

A fuller appreciation of the consequences of using polluted sources may well become the stimulus for integration and regionalization of water supply and wastewater disposal in the United States, to the end that communities, because of unfortunate location, need not be condemned to using second-class water for drinking.

In England and Wales, the new WAs provide an institutional arrangement which permits dealing with the problem of chemical pollutants effectively in that decisions can be made for the river basin as a whole as to the most efficient places to discharges effluents and to abstract water supplies.

The Water Resources Board, before its demise, had recommended a strategy that incorporated upstream reservoirs for the regulation of rivers with the intention that public water supplies be drawn from the downstream reaches of these rivers, with little attention being given to the quality implications of this strategy. However, the National Water Council indicated that the water industries' '. . . more scientific preoccupation, [is] the assurance of the quality of public water supplies for drinking purposes'.[39] The considerable attention given to this issue at the first National Water Conference in March 1975 is also testimony to this concern.

The dual supply studied under the Trent Research Programme, which considered using the Trent River as a source of industrial rather than potable water supply, is an interesting model. Such a hierarchy of water quality is not nearly as feasible in a fragmented water industry as it is where regional water authorities have control over entire river basins, and where second class waters of dubious quality can be used for industrial purposes to replace, and therefore extend, the usefulness of protected sources that can then serve larger residential populations with potable water.

This issue will be the subject for debate on both sides of the Atlantic in the years ahead, but the institutional arrangements in England and Wales promise easier implementation should this approach be found to have merit.

If these principles are accepted as desiderata in a water quality management program, then England and Wales would score about 80 percent as contrasted with about 20 percent for the United States. More significant, though, are the directions. In the United States, the massive federal subsidies, with the accompanying bureaucratic structures that derive from their administration, combined with a uniform national approach, serve to hamper the creation of a sound national strategy for managing water quality.

Added to these problems is the fragmentation of authority amongst many tiers of government and overlapping geographical jurisdictions, with most authorities being far too small to implement sound policies and programs. Efforts on the national scene in the United States seem to be devoted to patching up the existing system with frequent reorganizations within the EPA and highly variable and selective enforcement of laws and regulations. Pressures for 'mid-course' corrections are being exerted by environmentalists on the one hand who would like stiffer, more punitive measures of control, as contrasted with municipal and industrial officials who would like relief from rigid regulations and greater local autonomy. Above all, what seems most to be missing on the American scene is confidence and trust between officials of the federal establishment and those of local governments and industry, with the state regulatory agencies caught in between. The most rational set of recommendations for the future, those of the National Water Commission, are largely unheralded and ignored, but are sufficiently sound that in time the United States may turn to some of them in an effort to create institutions and policies upon which to build a sound program of water management.

CHAPTER 11

The Future—Problems and Prospects

The reorganization has provided England and Wales with institutions that have strong potential for building on the five principles of water management outlined in Chapter 1: the uniqueness of water projects; their economies and efficiencies of scale; the integration of water supply and water pollution control services; sound financing; and the preservation of the purest waters for potable purposes. At the very least, the water industry in England and Wales is pointed in the right direction, giving promise that these principles will be adopted if not sooner then later, and if not totally, then mostly.

Such massive restructuring was bound to create problems, some anticipated and others unexpected. Uncommonly serious economic perturbations buffeted Britain during initial implementation of the reorganization. Nature also conspired against the new WAs in their third summer with the worst drought in recorded history. Many contended that only the reorganization enabled England and Wales to ride out these difficulties by permitting a more efficient use of both financial and water resources than would have been possible under the old fragmented system of control. Some local water supply projects could be put off because exploitation of resources on a regional basis made them redundant. Limited financial resources and the absence of outside subsidy forced the WAs to explore ways of establishing priorities so as to derive the greatest benefit from each investment of scarce funds.

These problems, how they are being addressed, and what the future portends are the subject of this chapter, concluding with consideration of the government's own review of the reorganized water industry.[1]

THE PROBLEMS OF THE REORGANIZATION

'A radical transformation of perhaps the most vital public service of all has taken place quickly and efficiently without any faltering in the standard of that service.'[2] So stated Lord Nugent in the first annual report of the National Water Council. That so massive a reorganization, affecting the lives of some 65 000 water services staff serving 50 million people, involving changed positions and uprooting of homes, new organizations and new lines of authority, new methods of finance, and totally new pioneering organizational structures, could take place so smoothly can be attributed to the history of developmental change in the water industry in England and Wales combined with the thorough discussion of the issues prior to the reorganization, and an adequate, if hurried, nine-month period between passage of the Water Act 1973 and its implementation. Most of those who were opposed to the reorganization have now joined to make the new system work.

Nevertheless, many problems have surfaced. Some are attributable to the nature of the reorganization itself, such as accountability to the public and the relationships between the water authorities and the local authorities whose residents they serve. Other problems can be traced to external forces such as the deterioration of the national economy and the growth in Welsh nationalism.

Relationships with the local authorities

The sharp increases in water charges, regardless of their justification, created strong resentment because of the seeming immunity of the WAs to complaints from local authorities and the public. The constitution of the WAs, with a majority of local authority members, was intended to demonstrate accountability. Resting somewhat between the local authority, with all elected members, and a nationalized industry, with all appointed members, the WAs were in an ambivalent position in responding to charges of indifference to their customers. Faced with the responsibility for continuing existing water services, the local authority members of the WAs found themselves assuming positions little different from those of the appointed members. Not being able to examine critically the real issues behind the increased charges, local authority officials, local newspapers, and citizens' groups tended to focus their complaints of excessive spending on peripheral issues.

Typical were the comments of Maureen Colquhoun, a Labour MP, who reported widespread resentment amongst local authority councillors at the way in which WAs were spending money without being accountable to any electors.[3] She indicated considerable support for a motion in the House of Commons that the WAs should be brought under the control of local councils as a matter of urgency which arises from 'their attitudes to spending money, not like water, but like champagne and the fact that they are neither publicly elected nor accountable to anyone'.

Brian Thorpe, chief executive of the Southern Water Authority, suggested *ad hoc* advisory committees or other forms of consultation with local authorities and their representatives:[4] 'These are the very early days of a new type of organization and there will be those who will press upon us the need to move nearer to local government and there will be others who will seek to press us more firmly towards the nationalized industries. We are neither a local authority nor an area board of a nationalized industry. In answer to the question *"Quo Vadis?"* perhaps the answer ought to be a gathering of confidence in ourselves, producing a willingness to press for a brave venture as contained in the Water Act 1973 to be given a fair chance to succeed.'

The anomalous position of the WAs, with only limited responsibility to the DoE, led finally to parliament asserting that the affairs of the WAs should come under the scrutiny of the Select Committee on Nationalised Industries. 'The committee affords an opportunity to members to study the affairs of industries whose affairs are otherwise outside the day-to-day control of Ministers and parliament. The select committee seeks to understand the general principles on which an industry conducts its affairs, with special reference to any instruction or guidance that it may have to any particular problems with which the industry finds itself confronted.'[5] The DoE pointed out that hearings before the select committee would give the water industry a chance to answer criticisms leveled against it. The significance of this move was not lost on the local authorities who feared a further diminution in their impact on the operations of the WAs.

Regardless of accountability, the relations with the local authorities will pose continuing problems. The WAs have a dual interest in local authority planning: firstly, they are responsible for providing the water services to meet the development requirements of local authorities; secondly, they need to exercise a degree of control over developments that might increase pollution risks. The particular difficulty of the WA lies in the fact that '. . . it could appear invidious if a housing development were delayed because of the inadequacy of sewage works in preventing a deterioration in river quality, when the WA is responsible for both. Indeed, the resolution of such conflicts was one of the objectives of reorganization'.[6]

The need for machinery for collaboration and consultation appeared to have been clear from the start, particularly in the integration of WA programs with local authority planning, which would involve both county and district councils and necessitate close collaboration at all stages of the planning process. 'It is perhaps a matter of regret that the WAs are not required, like the new area health authorities, to establish joint consultative committees with local authorities.'[7]

One year after reorganization, all three local authority associations indicated their dissatisfaction with the recommendations of the NWC on relations between the local authorities and the water industry, by pointing out that the NWC did not even mention the establishment of local joint advisory committees originally recommended by the DoE. The NWC proposed to advise that WAs fix at least one meeting a year between the chairman and chief executive of the WA and each local authority in the area, in time to coincide with the publication of the WA's annual report, such meetings to be supported by more informal day-to-day contacts. The situation varies from place to place, as the Greater Manchester Association of Metropolitan Authorities had already reached agreement with the North West Water Authority for three meetings a year, the first such including subjects such as charges, planning, liaison, recreation, pollution control and sewerage.

One illustration of the problem was the considerable publicity given the Severn Trent Water Authority announcement that it may oppose important housing and industrial development within its area because it cannot find the funds for key sewerage schemes.[8] While housing was exempted from a major cutback on public spending in the government budget, the WAs were not exempted. Later, the STWA announced that it would be able to finance services for high priority housing developments, but would cut back on the provision of first-time sewerage in rural areas.[9]

In an attempt to provide guidance in connection with the government's high priority for housing, the late Anthony Crosland, then Secretary of State for the Environment, asserted in response to questions in parliament about the lack of supporting services for new housing developments, that the government 'have made it clear to the WAs that their first priority must be developments to help new housing. The second priority must be industrial development. A continued improvement in the quality of our rivers must come as a third priority . . .'.[10] Whether the WAs will accept this degree of direction from government is uncertain.

The agency agreements for the district councils to manage sewerage on behalf of the WAs created problems. One of the reasons for making this commitment, largely objected to at the time by officials of the water industry, was to permit the district councils to maintain a nucleus of engineering personnel. Sir John Wills, chairman of the Wessex Water Authority, spoke for many chairmen when he indicated that the data the WAs were getting from the district councils were just not adequate to provide the guidelines necessary for their planning.[11] WA officers generally do not give the agency concept more than about five years, except in the few instances where large authorities are able to maintain strong professional engineering staff for the purpose. While this appears to be a self-fulfilling prophesy, it is no doubt a reasonable prognosis.

The impact of solid waste disposal on water quality and the failure up to now of joint planning for handling these often conflicting responsibilities has constituted a problem. A hopeful sign of improved relations was the advocacy by Peter Black, chairman of the Thames Water Authority, for the sharing of treatment and disposal facilities available for the treatment and sea disposal of industrial effluents.[12] The government took cognizance of the issue with the publication of a circular, *The Balancing of Interests Between Water Protection and (Solid) Waste Disposal*, offering guidance to both local and water authorities.[13]

The emotional context in which the relationships between the district councils and the WAs exist was revealed in the annual conference of the District Councils Technical Association, where it was averred that 'both sides might get on just as well, and possibly understand each other better, if they passed their messages in bottles thrown into the nearest clean or dirty waterway'.[14] The lack of grass roots accountability and meaningful local authority member participation on the WAs were decried.

All in all, the relationships between the WAs and the local authorities will require constant nurturing, particularly on the part of the WAs, if grave resentments are not to develop on the part of local authority personnel and the citizenry who identify more with their local authority than with their water authority.

Land-use planning

In England and Wales, land-use controls enjoy a considerable reputation, being the envy of professional planners from industrialized countries throughout the world. The 'green belts' have helped protect the integrity of rural areas from the spillover from urban centers and altogether the amenity values of the countryside are cherished. However, the location of new towns has been criticized because of unconcern for their impact on water resources. In 1962, the location of the new town of Milton Keynes on the upper reaches of the Great Ouse was challenged because of the detrimental effect of industrial development in the new town on downstream abstractions from the river. The decision to accept this environmental risk was attributed to political considerations. In an attempt at mitigation of the problem, a board of scientific advisors was appointed by the government to review the siting of all new industry in Milton Keynes and its operations as they might affect water quality. However, the impact of urbanization itself on water quality was ignored. The WAs can now expect to play a significant role in land-use planning as they have leverage unavailable to any authority in the past.

Financing and the economic situation

The financing of the water services and the increased charges constituted grave challenges to the success of the reorganization. The shock of the changeover, from a partially subsidized service to full payment for the services rendered, and the considerable inherited debt, may be ameliorated in time as, except for investments required to replace aging facilities, future increases in charges will reflect primarily inflation and the level of new services provided.

To abate some of the most severe outcries, several WAs have already instituted equalization for part or all of their water service charges, and others may be expected to follow suit. As costs rise, charging on the basis of property value may appear less equitable than when charges are low, and pressures for metering will undoubtedly increase. Also, to provide some leverage for controlling industrial effluent discharges, particularly in the face of a slowdown in providing additional publicly-owned facilities, greater impetus may be given to a consideration of effluent charges to industry for discharges into public waters.

Given the difficult financial condition of the nation, the government placed severe limitations on capital investments. In light of this, the NWC and the WAs have asked that the government not implement, for a period of three years, the provisions of the Control of Pollution Act 1974, which would make WAs liable to prosecution with respect to discharges from their facilities which infringe consent conditions originally imposed by the predecessor river authorities. Whether this delay will have an effect on the rate at which industrial polluters are brought to account remains to be seen.

The precarious economic situation presents the WAs with an opportunity to demonstrate the economic efficiency of the new organizational structure by utilizing existing resources, facilities and personnel in an optimal manner. Except where acute polllution problems exist, the limitation on construction of new facilities may well be advantageous to the WAs in giving them an opportunity to digest their inheritance and plan soundly for the capital investments that they will be making in the future.

The Welsh problem

The severe financial strains of the water reorganization in Wales actually threatened the reorganization. The increases in charges after reorganization were far greater in economically depressed Wales than in England. Also, charges for water services are higher in Wales, where water is plentiful, than in England where water is imported from Wales. The seriousness of the Welsh problem was not lost on government, which created the Daniel Committee to study the problem (Chapter 9), and after its report was released advanced its own review of the water reorganization.

The main recommendation of the Daniel Committee called for reducing differences in average water charges between the WNWDA and the other WAs, a move which would inevitably threaten the integrity of the WAs.

Another recommendation of the Daniel Committee was tied to the creation of a Welsh Assembly as part of the government program of devolution of government in Scotland and Wales.[15] The Daniel Committee would have a Welsh Assembly take responsibility for water supplies in and from Wales. If that part of the STWA now in Wales were transferred to the Welsh Assembly, the definition of the WA areas would be on political rather than hydrologic boundary lines. The chief executive of the WNWDA, Dr H. H. Crann, stated that 'bitter experience in the past has demonstrated that effective river management, the cornerstone of efficient water services, can only be accomplished with undivided catchment areas'. Altering the WNWDA boundaries would 'set the clock back by half a century'.[16]

The other Daniel Committee option, pricing transferred water on a commercial basis, would be a departure from sound pricing policy, but would not, of itself, lead to uneconomical utilization of resources. Should the commercial price be high, the pressure for transfers from Wales to England would be seriously reduced and greater efforts would be made by the WAs in England to satisfy their needs from within English borders. This would optimize resources development within England, but would leave Wales with a resource used to a fraction of its capacity, and water not used in Wales runs off to England and the sea and is lost. So optimization would be on a smaller canvas.

Centralization versus independent water authorities

The Welsh problem helped focus on another problem—whether the independent WAs could negotiate with one another on resources issues that extended beyond their boundaries. In its initial proposals in December 1971, the government had stated that it was '. . . [not] necessary to interpose a national body between Ministers and the small number of strong regional WAs they propose. . . . Where water does need to be moved from one region to another the regional authorities involved should have no difficulty in settling matters between themselves'.[17]

It is ironic that the author of that statement when in the DoE, J. E. Beddoe, as chief executive of the STWA, was party to the 'wrangle' between the STWA and the WNWDA over the Craig Goch water project in Wales, an enlargement of an existing reservoir which had been conceived by the Water Resources Board as a means for meeting increased water demands in the midlands, in Wales and even possibly in the Thames region. The demand by the WNWDA for heavy surcharges against the STWA for water already being transferred threatened the Craig Goch scheme and led to serious examination of the need for a centralized authority.

Labor

For employees of local government to unionize and, if unionized, actually strike, had been at one time unconscionable. Unionization of public employees is now common, both in Britain and in the United States. Strikes of sewage treatment employees in Britain and strikes of police and firemen in the United States have already had significant public impact.

So long as the water industry was fragmented, labor actions were not likely to be nearly so effective as they now can be. Laborers serving small local authority sewage treatment facilities are relatively powerless to initiate a labor action. However, when they are united in large agencies which include water supply, their power becomes exceedingly great.

The WAs have attempted to create a setting that would minimize the threat of labor actions. For example, the STWA authorized trade union branch officers to be relieved of their duties until reorganization was completed in order that they might be available to assist their members during the reorganization. Every attempt was made to give assurance that the reorganization would be conducted in such a way as to open opportunities for STWA people to the maximum extent possible.

Whether an enlightened approach to labor relations will reduce the potential for labor actions remains to be seen. With little control over inflation, and with government control over wages, the WAs are vulnerable. The secretary of the Joint National Council for Water Services Senior Staffs asserted that a national strike of water industry workers was, if not exactly imminent, then not very far away.[18] Reorganization has concentrated management, providing easier targets for the unions. Such a strike would likely be politically motivated and sound personnel management policies might have little to do with resolving the issues.

Poacher–gamekeeper issue

The conflict of interest of the WAs in being both polluter and regulator created remarkably little controversy within the industry. The Royal Commission on Environmental Pollution did propose the establishment of a new central regulatory agency, Her Majesty's Pollution Inspectorate, to take over responsibilities for air pollution control, now divided between local authorities and the DoE Alkali Inspectorate, and all pollution arising from industrial processes. HMPI would collaborate with the WAs in seeking to reduce the discharge of effluents but would not trespass on the WA responsibilities for establishing consent conditions.[19]

While the Royal Commission proposals do not address the poacher–gamekeeper conflict directly, the issue did arise in the House of Lords debate on the government's review of the water industry, decrying the absence of consideration of the issue in that document.[20]

The European Economic Community

The posture in Britain for policing effluent discharges that has been characterized by adapting consent conditions to the local situation will no doubt be affected by Britain's participation in the European Economic Community, the common market. The EEC is pushing for uniform standards and regulations for wastewater discharges, being particularly anxious to have these written into national legislation so as to avoid apparent inequities in the responsibilities that industries in the common market countries are obligated to assume.

The type of regulation being sought by the EEC is exemplified by the rigorous microbiological, physical, and chemical standards being envisaged by the EEC for discharges into natural bathing waters. Although the WAs have an obligation for protection of coastal bathing waters, the control of discharges into the sea would not normally be accorded a high priority. The actual health risk from bathing in British coastal waters, which would not meet EEC directives, is considered to be slight,[21] but meeting the standards prescribed is estimated to cost on the order of £100 million.[22] The ironic part of this situation is that the pollution of the more extensively used coastal waters of France and Italy is much more severe than anywhere in the United Kingdom. Moreover, Italy might well adopt the regulations requested by the EEC, but, based upon performance to date, they are not likely to invest very much in meeting the standards prescribed. On the other hand, if regulations are adopted into national law, the British would be more inclined to respect the standards.

The British delegation to the EEC refused to give its approval to a draft decision on toxic chemical discharges. The EEC document *Dangerous Substances in the Aquatic Environment* proposed a blacklist of toxic, persistent and bio-accumulable chemicals which should on no account be discharged into seas, lakes, or rivers; and a grey list of less dangerous substances for which there should be fixed emission limits.[23] The original approach of the EEC had been to work towards water quality objectives rather than fixed effluent standards, with each member country left free to decide its own limits. The approach finally adopted by the EEC appears to resemble the standard setting approach taken by the EPA in the United States. Effluent standards are comprehensive and rigorous but little attention has been given to the likelihood that these standards can or will in fact be attained. Apparently, it will be sufficient for the EEC to have them written into national legislation.

Were the EEC approach to be adopted, some of the advantages of regionalization would be lost, as optimal solutions for attaining water quality would no longer be permissible.

The differences in philosophy between the EEC and the United Kingdom came to a head in Brussels at the Council of Environmental Ministers meeting on 8 December 1975.[24] Denis Howell, Minister of State in the DoE, leading the UK delegation, declared that the United Kingdom was not able to accept an approach for uniform effluent emission standards. United Kingdom practice, which fixes local emission standards to water quality objectives, was claimed to better protect the environment and make more efficient use of resources, Britain, the only advocate for this approach won an important compromise, highly lauded at home, whereby member states will be able to choose between the two approaches.

RESPONSE TO CRISIS

The sixteen months from May 1975 thru August 1976 were the driest in England and Wales since meteorological data collection was initiated in 1727, with estimates indicating the drought, in some areas, to have been the most severe in a millenium. *We Didn't Wait for the Rain* . . .[25] attests to the effectiveness of the new arrangement for water management in meeting the challenge of the drought and the water shortages that inevitably resulted.†
The WAs were able to develop all the available resources in their areas without regard to local political boundaries and to reallocate and redistribute these resources for their fullest use.
The responses to the water shortages can be placed in two broad classifications:[26] (1) water resource management; and (2) water use reduction. Almost all the WAs adopted one or more measures in each classification, often simultaneously, although the details of implementation varied.

Water resource management

The WAs had embarked upon capital programs of building both raw and finished water interconnections between previously separate undertakings soon after the water reorganization was implemented. The onset of the drought provided impetus to the program. Many smaller systems, that before reorganization had suffered from frequent water shortages because of inadequate storage, were able to draw on other systems that were better supplied with storage capacity. These transfers were easily accomplished because, as Severn Trent Water Authority officials put it, 'All the cash was now in one pocket'.
By the summer of 1976, all the 54 reservoirs in the Southwest Division of the Yorkshire Water Authority were interlinked. While some interconnections were of an emergency nature, most will remain to be used as part of a regional water network reducing the impact of future droughts. The safe yield of water for a major urban complex was increased without an investment in additional resources development. Without this 'switchability' many pockets within the YWA would have been dry by midsummer.
A second major initiative was the development of new bore-holes or wells. Groundwaters had been a neglected resource because the yields of individual wells are uncertain and not large as compared with developed surface sources. Yet, in times of shortage, water from underground can be developed incrementally at lower marginal cost and in less time than new surface sources. The construction of surface storage reservoirs is slow and

---

† Had there not been shortages in 1976, the authorities could fairly have been charged with over-investing in capital facilities, facilities whose full capacities would be called upon less than once per century.

costly and not at all suited to small increments in supply. Furthermore, the streams they are intended to impound would be low during a drought, so that impoundments are only appropriately built before the onset of a drought.

Water use reduction

The first reaction to drought in almost all instances is a push for reduction in water use, beginning with a ban on lawn watering. In Britain, where the pattern of rainfall makes lawn watering less essential than in the United States, and few homes have fixed lawn sprinkling systems, such a ban did not effect a significant reduction in water use.

Intensive publicity campaigns were adopted by all the WAs to urge conservation upon residential, commercial and industrial users, but the most effective measure to reduce water use was the reduction in system pressure. A 50 percent reduction in pressure reduces the discharge through fixtures and leaks by almost 30 percent. Certain users, such as hospitals, were protected by complex valving from these reduced pressures.

The last ditch measure, before cut-offs in service would have been required, was the installation of standpipes from which users would be forced to carry water to their homes. Hospitals, industries, essential commercial establishments and fire fighting were excluded. The first standpipes were to go into areas with the biggest 'pay-off', densely populated modern housing estates, with large numbers of water-using devices, where large numbers of people would have easy access to standpipes In mid-September, 1976, 20 000 households in North Devon were cut off from piped supplies and obliged to use standpipes while the other WAs had standpipes ready but the drought ended before they were needed.

Intermittent interruptions in service to conserve water were widely considered. The Welsh National Water Development Authority instituted cut-offs in part of its area for 13 hours daily, from 7 p.m. to 8 a.m. The North West Water Authority viewed overnight cut-offs as ineffective and uneconomical, and had they needed to go this far, domestic supplies would have been cut off for 36 out of every 48 hours, beginning at 8 p.m. on one day and ending at 8 a.m. on the second day following.

Because of the absence of residential metering, the institution of targets or economic incentives for residential users was not possible. During water shortages in the United States, customers are often mailed their use figures for the same month during the previous normal year and urged to achieve a specified reduction. This was done with industrial and commercial users in England and Wales, the only users that are metered.

The impact of the drought on the quality and amenity values of the surface waters, on the economy, and on health and welfare has not yet been studied systematically. How frequently should shortages be allowed to occur? If they are readily dealt with and cause no severe problems, perhaps the capital investments that are required to limit the shortages to one year in 100 can be reduced so as to tolerate shortages one year in 50, or 20, or 10, with significant capital savings.

All in all, the drought did call attention of the populace to the water reorganization and the role of the new water authorities at a time when they needed public understanding.

THE FUTURE

'The industry is in good heart and resolved to take full advantage of its opportunities to provide economic and reliable services.'[2] These words of the chairman of the National Water Council represent fairly the spirit that pervades the WAs and the water industry generally. 'The rightness of the basic concept of the hydrological cycle for the structuring of authorities and their activities must be regarded as substantially endorsed even on such short experience ... [and is] producing that fresh, powerful, and unfettered approach to the problems of pollution and to the cost-effective remedies which Parliament undoubtedly had in mind ... the assembling in single authorities of relevant skills at the highest levels is starting to show signs of great advantage. For, while some advances will depend on capital investment, others will yield and are yielding to good management seized with opportunities that opened out before it.'

This promising future was clouded by the government's decision to initiate review of the reorganization after less than 18 months of operation, which undoubtedly created strain and uncertainties amongst personnel in the water industry, as the potential for further reorganization cannot be far from the minds of those most involved.

THE GREEN-EDGED WHITE PAPER—THE GOVERNMENT'S REVIEW[1]

Being enacted by a Conservative government, the Water Act 1973 was inevitably to come under critical review when the Labour government assumed power. One question was whether further major reorganization or only minor course corrections would be proposed. Another was whether the review would appear as a 'white paper', expressing the government's intentions, or as a 'green paper', open for discussion. While published in a green cover, with a request for comments on the proposal to be submitted to the DoE by the end of July 1976, the document was viewed as a 'green-edged white paper' with the government's intentions being clearly elaborated.[27]

In the words of Denis Howell, Minister of State, the document '... deliberately avoided the suggestions—and there are plenty of them—that we should tear things up by the roots and start again. What we have attempted to do, and I believe it will win general acceptance, is to build on what is good for the existing structure and avoid disruption for the staff of the WAs who have worked so hard to get the new structure going . . .'.[28] Most of the major proposals had been widely forecast and some were, in fact, broadly welcomed.[29] The main thrust was for creation of a stronger agency at the center, a National Water Authority, as had been fervently called for by the Labour opposition during the parliamentary debates, and for some measure of equalization as a response to the Daniel Committee recommendations. Other proposals concerned the private water companies and the British Waterways Board which had been excluded from the reorganization.

The National Water Authority

The NWA would replace the National Water Council, the Central Water Planning Unit, and the Water Research Centre and would have merged with it the British Waterways Board. The new powers and duties of the NWA would be:

1. to prepare a 20-year national strategy for water services for submission to the Ministers,
2. to review the plans of the individual WAs, although the WAs would have direct access to the Ministers in the event of differences with the NWA,
3. to advise the Ministers on WA plans and programs,
4. to prepare annual capital investment programs,
5. to recommend to the Ministers plans for allocating water resources among regions,
6. to develop charging and financial policies for the industry, and
7. to promote and report on the efficient operation of the WAs.

Thus the NWA would fill a lacuna in providing a mechanism for dealing with water planning that required the participation of two or more WAs. Such powers might have avoided the 'wrangle' between the WNWDA and the STWA over the Craig Goch project.

This proposal did arouse some concern for the continued independence of the WAs, given expression by Lord Nugent, chairman of the NWC: 'The proposal to bring directly under the NWA the planning and research capacity of the industry is likely to be generally acceptable, but the other new powers for the NWA will have to be closely examined to ensure that they do not significantly impede the necessary freedom of local decision and action of WAs.'[30] This view was affirmed by the NWC in its review of the government document.[31]

Some observers read into the government's review a desire to reopen the water management strategy of downstream abstractions proposed by the Water Resources Board. Banks believes and hopes that major strategic schemes will lean heavily towards the concept of upland water flowing unpolluted to the demand areas.[32]

The takeover of the Water Research Centre would pose problems in that the WRC is a membership organization, offering direct services to agencies other than the WAs and outside England and Wales. Despite vigorous defense of the WRC in the House of Lords, strong opposition to this proposal is not likely to develop.[33]

Charging and finance

The government emphasized that the water industry as a whole should continue to be financially self-sufficient and should operate without subsidy. The government also decided that for one WA to put a surcharge on water transferred to another WA '. . . would be bound to prejudice any national strategy for the rational and economic use of water resources; it would lead to efforts for self-sufficiency at regional level uneconomic in financial, resource and environmental terms'. Transfers should continue to be made on a no profit/no loss basis.

After examining these and other equalization schemes, the government proposed to reduce the wide variations in average bills paid in the WAs by an interim device of pooling the historic (up to 31 March 1976) financing costs attributable to the provision of unmeasured (primarily residential) supplies. This would have the effect of reducing the range in charges from the existing 44 percent above average in the WNWDA and 17 percent below in the TWA to 16 percent above and 14 percent below respectively.

Restricting equalization to historic costs alone has the important virtue of preserving for each WA the financial incentives for the management of its current capital expenditure and operating and maintenance programs. Further, the portion of total costs to be pooled will steadily diminish with time.

The NWC responded that equalization which obligated WAs to costs outside their control would erode their autonomy. Hence, the proposed equalization of historic costs should be clearly stated to be 'once and for all and final'.

The water companies

The Labour Party had consistently maintained that retaining the privately-owned water companies (that serve about 22 percent of the population) was wrong in principle and anomalous in practice. Accordingly the government decided to integrate the companies into the WAs, with fair compensation (estimated at about £300 million), as soon as practicable. Despite protestations of the companies that they are viable and efficient, they are not likely to long survive unless the money for their purchase does not become available.

Service to unconnected properties

The House of Lords' judgement that the Water Act entitles WAs to charge persons only for services performed, facilities provided, or rights made available, meant that properties not directly connected to sewers were not liable for charges for sewerage and sewage disposal. However, sewerage and disposal services confer a substantial benefit in terms of public health and an improved environment which is enjoyed by all members of the community whether or not connected to the sewers, and therefore the government holds that all properties should make some contribution to the costs of these services and proposed amending the Water Act to authorize such charges.

In addition to inviting comments on these proposals, the government solicited views on other issues, including the following:

1. *Membership of the proposed NWA.* The membership, to be appointed by the Ministers, would include a full-time chairman, some full-time members (the NWC has no full-time members), some part-time members, and some or all chairmen of the WAs. The NWC was insistent in the not unreasonable stand that if conflicts between the projected NWA and the WAs were to be avoided, then all the chairmen of the WAs must be members of the NWA.

2. *Membership of the WAs.* This has been a contentious issue from the beginning, ending with a compromise by the Conservative government providing a majority (often of one) of elected local authority officials. Strong feelings of insufficient accountability continued to be expressed, especially as some district councils and major cities are not represented on the WAs. Meanwhile, the Labour government stated, as it did not when it was in opposition, that appointed members are important to the WAs. Full local authority representation plus members appointed because of their qualifications would make the WAs unmanageably large and no change is likely to be offered.

3. *The need for statutory advisory committees.* Such committees were considered during preparation of the Water Bill and then dropped when local authority members assumed majorities on the WAs. With local authorities vitally concerned with the priorities accorded services for local development, particularly housing, advisory committees might well serve a useful liaison function. The government proposed to institutionalize some type of consultation machinery, and sought advice on form and membership of appropriate bodies. The NWC agreed that liaison is necessary but indicated that almost all the WAs had created some type of arrangement, and it was not necessary for the government to prescribe a specific form.

4. *Arrangements for agency agreements between district councils and WAs for sewerage.* As these arrangements were not all working well,

information leading to possible modification in the agreement was sought by government. The NWC recommended that agency agreements be selective at the discretion of the WAs, and not compulsory.

5. *Arrangements for requisitioning sewers.* The Water Act, in requiring the WAs to provide sewers to householders, developers and local authorities by requisition, so long as certain conditions are met, including repayment of costs over a period of up to 12 years, has created some financial problems for the WAs and this needed to be reviewed.

6. *Contributions from developers for flood plain protection.* WAs are often called upon to protect from flood those properties which were developed against their advice. While the WAs do not now have the power to call for a financial contribution for flood protection from the land developer, it might be considered fair for such a contribution to be made.

Whatever the responses to the government's consultative review, little fundamental change in the philosophical thrust of the reorganization is expected. The large, decentralized, hydrologically-based, independently-financed, water authorities will continue to provide the institutional basis for water management in England and Wales. Only so much central cohesion is likely to be built into the system as is necessary to avoid creating strong political pressures on the Ministers for national uniformity. The Labour government had an opportunity to 'back-track' on the principles that were the basis for the reorganization promulgated by their Conservative predecessors. In proposing only minor adjustments, the government demonstrated its support for the new organization of water management, which is thus likely to be that followed for some time to come, sufficient time certainly to offer a fair measure of opportunity for its evaluation.†

CONCLUSION

The regionalization of water management in England and Wales, in providing a rational structure for water management generally and for water quality management particularly, cannot help but be a model for other countries throughout the world. Few countries, including the United States, will be in a position to adopt the entire package. But even those just

† As this volume was going to press, the government issued its White Paper *The Water Industry in England and Wales: The Next Steps.*[34] In general, the proposals in the government's 1976 *Review* were affirmed, with the exception that take-over of the private water companies by the WAs was to be deferred because such a proposal would not gain sufficient parliamentary support. When, or even whether, the other proposals in the White Paper would be placed before parliament was uncertain.

initiating water management schemes in the developing countries of Asia, Africa, and Latin America will be in a position to profit from this experience.

For the industrialized countries, lessons may be learned from the process of reorganization as much as from the new structures. For the developing countries, the advantages of regional rather than the highly centralized organizations and the issues of self-financing and integration of services to economize on resources of funds and personnel will be of value. Hardly anyone involved in any phase of the water industry anywhere in the world will fail to be interested in some aspect of this revolution in water management and its outcome.

This volume represents an attempt to examine the process of regionalization as well as the new institutional arrangements, because the process of change may be as important as the change itself and far more difficult than managing the change after it occurs. Also, the trials of the process will tend to be lost in time while the new structure will be refined and its full value will only be discerned some years from now, when other students of water management will be in a better position to evaluate its success.

A Summary of the Precursors to the Water Reorganization in England and Wales

1935–36 *Parliamentary Joint Committee on Water Resources and Supplies*
Minister of Health appointed the Central Advisory Water Committee with Field Marshall Lord Milnes as chairman.

1943 *Milne Committee Report*
Recommended establishment of river authorities to integrate water pollution control, water conservation and rivers control.

1944 *Government White Paper*, 'A National Water Policy'
Accepted the essence of the Milne Committee Report in recommending the creation of river boards to include responsibility for water pollution control, land drainage and control of fisheries while recommending that the Minister of Health be responsible for central planning and water conservation.

1945 *Water Act*
Gave to the Minister of Health (later the Minister of Housing and Local Government and still later the Secretary of State for the Department of the Environment) the responsibility for water conservation and provision of water supply in England and Wales, and particularly to promote water supply regrouping or regionalization.

1948 *River Boards Act*
Created 32 river boards in England and Wales to take responsibility for pollution control in rivers, land drainage (flood control), navigation and fisheries.

1951 *Rivers (Prevention of Pollution) Act*
Made new provisions for maintaining and restoring the wholesomeness of non-tidal rivers by authorizing establishment of a system of 'consents' for discharges, applicable only to new or altered discharges.

1960   *Clean Rivers* (*Estuaries and Tidal Waters*) *Act*
Established control over new or altered discharges into tidal rivers and estuaries.

1961   *Rivers* (*Prevention of Pollution*) *Act*
Extended the 1951 Act, and included pre-1951 discharges.

1962   *Central Advisory Water Committee, Proudman Committee Report,* 'The Growing Demand for Water'
Drew attention to the growing demand for water and the need for a national policy and an administrative structure to see to it. Also recommended the establishment of river authorities which would license and charge for water abstractions from rivers.

1962   *Government White Paper,* 'Water Conservation in England and Wales'
Accepted Proudman Committee recommendations except that an advisory central body was recommended, rather than an executive body.

1963   *Water Resources Act*
Established Water Resources Board and 29 river authorities. The WRB was to have planning and advisory responsibilities, while the river authorities were to license and charge for abstractions, plan, construct, and operate wastewater works, and take over pollution control responsibilities, among others, of the river boards.

1964   *Creation of Water Resources Board*

1965   *Creation of River Authorities*

The Timetable for the Reorganization—Signal Events

February 1969	Government established the Working Party on Sewage Disposal (the Jeger Committee).
March 1969	Joint Symposium 'Future Organization of River, Sewage and Water Authorities' conducted by The Institution of Water Engineers, the Institution of Public Health Engineers and the Institute of Water Pollution Control—London. *Proceedings* were published in 1969.
September 1969	Government reactivated the Central Advisory Water Committee, authorized in the Water Act 1945.
March 1970	Report of the Working Party on Sewage Disposal, *Taken for Granted*.
April 1971	Report of the Central Advisory Water Committee, *The Future Management of Water in England and Wales*.
2 December 1971	Department of the Environment Circular 92/71, *Reorganization of Water and Sewage Services: Government Proposals and Arrangements for Consultation*.
January to September 1972	Government issued a series of seventeen consultation papers.
June 1972	The Secretary of State for the Environment appointed a management structure committee (Ogden Committee) to give guidance to the proposed water authorities.
23 January 1973	Government introduced Water Bill in the House of Commons, accompanied by publication of *A Background to Water Reorganization in England and Wales* by the Department of the Environment and the Welsh Office.
5 February 1973	Second reading of the Water Bill in the House of Commons.

20 February to 12 April 1973	Nineteen sittings of Standing Committee D of the House of Commons on the Water Bill.
20 March 1973	Government created a Steering Group on Water Authority Economic and Financial Objectives (to be known as the Jukes Committee) to advise on the economic and financial policies that should be adopted by the regional water authorities.
1 and 2 May 1973	Report Stage and Third Reading of Water Bill in the House of Commons.
21 May 1973	Second Reading of the Water Bill in the House of Lords.
June 1973	Report of Ogden Committee: *The New Water Industry Management and Structure.*
11, 14 and 19 June 1973	Debate on the Water Bill in the House of Lords, sitting in Committee.
2 July 1973	Report Stage on Water Bill in the House of Lords.
9 July 1973	Third Reading of the Water Bill in the House of Lords.
10 July 1973	The Secretary of State for the Environment announced the names of the persons he intended to appoint as chairmen of the National Water Council and the water authorities in the event the Water Bill became law.
17 July 1973	The House of Commons considered amendments to the Water Bill adopted by the House of Lords and approved the Bill.
18 July 1973	The Water Bill received Royal Assent.
26 July to 14 August 1973	The new water authorities brought into formal existence by Constitution orders, with the members already appointed.
3 August 1973	The National Water Council brought into formal existence.
16 August 1973	Government issued Department of the Environment Circular 100/73: *Water Authorities and Local Authorities* which dealt with transfer of property and staff, sewerage, environmental health, land drainage, cooperation between water authorities and local authorities, financing of water services, etc.
August 1973	All the water authorities held their initial meetings.
12 September 1973	First report issued by the Steering Group on Economic and Financial Objectives: *The Water Services: Economic and Financial Policies.*

September 1973	Interviews and appointment of water authority and National Water Council chief executives.
December 1973	Publication by the Water Resources Board of its final statement on water strategy: *Water Resources in England and Wales.*
1 April 1974	The water authorities took over ownership and operation of all water facilities and services in England and Wales, except British Waterways Board canals and statutory water companies.

APPENDIX 3

Water Services—Administration

This 'Data Sheet' appeared as a supplement to *Municipal Engineering*, 11 March 1977, and is reproduced by kind permission of the Editors.

This data sheet is the first of a second series replacing 7.01 (29 September 1967), 7.02 (13 October 1967), 7.03 (27 October 1967) and 7.04 (10 November 1967). These second series sheets deal with statute law concerning the reorganized water services related to: the system of administration (statutory bodies); natural flow (drainage); water resources and supply; sewerage; sewage treatment and pollution control; river management and the use of water for recreation and amenity.

This sheet deals with the system of administration; a chart indicates the general hierarchy in the chain of control established by the Water Act 1973. The Act was primarily an administrative measure and the system set up was elaborated in a series of subsequent reports (Ogden, Jukes and Woodham—see bibliography). The Water Act 1973 did not attempt to consolidate existing law contained in : Public Health Acts 1936 and in 1961 (sewerage and sewage disposal); Water Acts 1945 and 1948 (water supply); Water Resources Act 1963 (resource development and conservation); Rivers (Prevention of Pollution) Acts 1951 and 1961, Public Health (Drainage of Trade Premises) Act 1937 and Clean Rivers (Estuaries and Tidal Waters) Act 1960 (pollution control). The law on land drainage has since been consolidated in the Land Drainage Act 1976, which came into force on 17 January 1977. The Control of Pollution Act 1974, Part II, amended and consolidated most of the law related to water pollution control, but only a few minor provisions have been implemented.

ADMINISTRATIVE SYSTEM—BASIS

Functions

The Water Act 1973 radically restructured the water services in England and Wales by creating 10 autonomous multipurpose water authorities (nine regional authorities in England and the Welsh National Development Authority) and transferring to them the functions previously exercised by

1393 sewerage and sewage disposal authorities, 157 water undertakings and 29 river authorities concerning: water resources, water supply, sewerage, sewage disposal, water pollution prevention, land drainage, flood protection, fisheries, and water recreation and amenity.

River basin and water cycle concepts

The nine English water authorities are: North West, Northumbrian, Yorkshire, Severn Trent, Anglian, Thames, Southern, Wessex and South West. The boundaries of the water authorities were based on generally accepted self-sufficient hydrometric areas comprising groups of river basins within which the authorities are responsible for all aspects of the water cycle.

Ministerial responsibilities

The overall responsibility for water authorities is shared between the Secretary of State for the Environment (SofS) and the Minister for Agriculture, Fisheries and Food (Minister); the latter is responsible for land drainage, flood protection and fisheries, and the SofS for the other functions. Both are jointly charged to promote a national policy for water in England and Wales.

STATUTORY CORPORATE BODIES

The Water Act 1973 set up and defined two central advisory bodies: The National Water Council (NWC) and the Water Space Amenity Commission (WSAC).

1. National Water Council

Constitution

The NWC consists of a chairman appointed by the SofS, 10 other members with special relevant knowledge of whom not more than eight are appointed by the SofS and not more than two by the Minister, and the chairmen of the water authorities. Appointed members may not hold office for more than five years at a time.

Duties

The NWC is required to:

consider and advise any minister on anything related to the national water policy;

consider and advise any minister and the water authorities on matters of common interest to WAs;

promote and assist WAs' performance, especially as to research and the preparation of s24 reviews, plans and programmes;

undertake training and education for the water services in England, Wales, Scotland and Northern Ireland;

consider whether to establish a UK scheme for the testing and approval of water fittings; Water Act 1973 s4(5).

Powers

If authorized by two or more WAs, the NWC may act for WAs and provide similar services to statutory water bodies and companies in Scotland, Northern Ireland, Channel Islands and Isle of Man; Water Act 1973 s4(12).

The NWC has power to do anything, including spending, borrowing or lending money, which is calculated to facilitate the discharge of its functions; Water Act 1973 Sch 3 s23.

As self-governing bodies, water authorities are constrained only by either directions of a general character given by the SofS or the Minister related to the execution of the national water policy or to matters of national interest, or by a decision under a statutory instrument related to the stopping or restriction of any activity; Water Act 1973 s4(10).

2. Water Space Amenity Commission

Constitution

The WSAC consists of the chairmen of the water authorities and not more than 10 other members, including one from the Countryside Commission, the English Tourist Board, the Sports Council, and others representing bodies of persons with special interests in water-based recreation and amenity. The whole is under a chairman appointed by the SofS from the members of the NWC.

Duties

The WSAC is required to:

advise the SofS on recreational and amenity aspects of the national water policy;

advise the NWC and WAs;

submit proposals for the consideration of the WAs;

assist the WAs in the preparation of s24 plans and programmes; Water Act 1973 s23(3).

The WSAC is funded by the NWC to the approval of the SofS, who also determines the staff complement and scale of accommodation.

3. Water Authorities

Constitution

Each water authority consists of a chairman appointed by the SofS, a majority of members appointed by local authorities (related to the number of metropolitan and non-metropolitan counties within the WA's area), not less than two or more than four appointed by the Minister and others appointed by the SofS.

Duties

Water Authorities are required to:

exercise the functions of their predecessor river authorities, e.g. pollution prevention in inland, estuarine and tidal waters, trade effluents, abstractions; Water Act 1973 s9;

conserve, redistribute or augment water resources; secure their proper use; transfer as necessary or expedient resources to another water authority; Water Act 1973 s10;

supply water in their area; Water Act 1973 s11;

provide the necessary public sewers for effectually draining their area and sewage disposal works or other means for effectually dealing with the contents of the sewers; Water Act 1973 s14;

provide public sewers, subject to conditions, for the drainage of domestic premises when required by the owners or occupiers or developers; Water Act 1973 s16;

maintain, improve and develop salmon and freshwater fisheries; Salmon and Freshwater Fisheries Act 1975 s28;

exercise general supervision over all matters related to land drainage; Land Drainage Act 1976 s1;

secure the use of water and land associated with water for the purposes of recreation and in that regard put their own rights to the best use for those purposes; Water Act 1973 s20;

have regard to the desirability of preserving natural beauty and conserving flora, fauna, and geological and physiographical features of special interest, and buildings of architectural, archaeological or historic interest, in relation to proposals for any of their functions; Water Act 1973 s22;

survey the water in their area, its management, its use and quality in relation to existing and future use; prepare estimates of demand for 20 years ahead and action plans for that period; prepare programmes for the discharge of their function over a period of not more than seven years; and regularly review their plans and programmes; Water Act 1973 s24;

make arrangements for carrying out research related to their functions and they may give financial support to relevant research organizations; Water Act 1973 s24(11);

undertake the training and education of their employees so as to advance their skill; Water Act 1973 s26;

assist county and district councils in the event of emergencies and disasters; Water Act 1973 s28;

taking one year with another, break even on their revenue account; Water Act 1973 s29.

Additional special duties

1. *Water supply*
The Water Act 1973 left statutory water companies undisturbed (there are 28 public supply companies serving a fifth of the population and three companies mainly concerned with industrial supplies) and placed a duty on water authorities to discharge their water supply functions within company areas through the appropriate water company; Water Act 1973 s12.

2. *Sewerage*
Water authorities and district councils are required to endeavour to make arrangements for the district council to discharge the sewerage function on behalf of the water authority; Water Act 1973 s15.

3. *Land drainage*
Water authorities must arrange for their land drainage functions, except for drainage charges, precepts and borrowing, to be discharged by a regional land drainage committee; Land drainage Act 1976 s1.

4. *Fisheries*
Water authorities must establish regional fisheries advisory committees and such necessary local advisory committees and consult them on the discharge of the authority's fishery functions; Salmon and Freshwater Fisheries Act 1975 s28.

Powers
A water authority has power to do anything, including spending, borrowing or lending money, which it calculates will facilitate the discharge of its functions; Water Act 1973 Sch 3 para 2.

1. *Borrowing*
Unlike local authorities, water authorities are restricted to three sources for long-term borrowing for capital projects:

  from the National Loans Fund in sterling;
  from the European Investment Bank in foreign currencies;
  from other foreign sources subject to Treasury and Bank of England
    approval; Water Act 1973 Sch 3 paras 3 and 4.

2. *Charges*
Water authorities may fix different charges for the same services provided, but, not later than 1 April 1981, their charges must not show undue preference to or discriminate against any class of persons; Water Act 1973 s30.

3. *Goods and services*

Water authorities are *public bodies* within the meaning of the *Local Authorities (Goods and Services) Act* 1970 and consequently WAs and local authorities may provide goods and services to each other. Similarly, WAs and water companies may enter into agreement to provide goods and services; Water Act 1973 s7.

4. *Water supply*

Water authorities may supply, by agreement, water outside their limits of supply; Water Act 1973 s13.

BIBLIOGRAPHY

Ogden report. *Staffing and management in water authorities*, HMSO.
Jukes reports 1, 2 and 3. *Financial objectives of water authorities*, HMSO.
Woodham report. *Water authority accounts*, HMSO.
Background to water reorganization, HMSO.

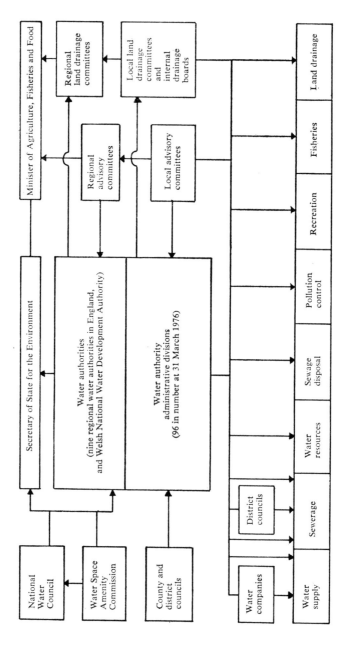

The administration of the water services—chain of control.

APPENDIX 4

Abbreviations

ABS	alkyl benzene sulfonate	EEC	European Economic Community
ARA	Association of River Authorities	EPA	Environmental Protection Agency
AWA	Anglian Water Authority	FHA	Farmers' Home Administration
BOD	biochemical oxygen demand	GLC	Greater London Council
BWA	British Waterworks Association	GP	General Practitioner (doctor)
BWB	British Waterways Board	gpd	gallons per day
		HEW	Health, Education and Welfare
CAWC	Central Advisory Water Committee	HMPI	Her Majesty's Pollution Inspectorate
CBI	Confederation of British Industry		
COD	chemical oxygen demand	HMSO	Her Majesty's Stationery Office
CoG	Council of Governments	HUD	Department of Housing and Urban Development
CWPU	Central Water Planning Unit		
DHSS	Department of Health and Social Security	IMTA	Institute of Municipal Treasurers and Accountants
DICTA	District Councils' Technical Association	IPHE	Institute of Public Health Practitioners
DO	dissolved oxygen		
DoE	Department of the Environment	IRA	Irish Republican Army
DRBC	Delaware River Basin Commission	JWP	joint working party
		LAS	linear alkyl sulfonates
DWF	dry weather flow		

MAFF	Ministry of Agriculture Fisheries and Food	RANN	Research Applied to National Needs
MANWEB	Merseyside and North Wales Electricity Board	RCC	Regional Consultative Council
mgd	million gallons per day	RFF	Resources for the Future
MP	Member of Parliament (UK)	SS	suspended solids
MWB	Metropolitan Water Board	STWA	Severn Trent Water Authority
NALGO	National Association of Local Government Officers	SWA	Southern Water Authority
		SWEB	South West Electricity Board
		TVA	Tennessee Valley Authority
NHS	National Health Service	TWA	Thames Water Authority
NTA	nitrilo-tri-acetate	USGPO	US Government Printing Office
NWA	Northumbrian Water Authority	USGS	United States Geological Survey
NWC	National Water Council	WA	Water Authority
NWWA	North West Water Authority	WNWDA	Welsh National Water Development Authority
ORSANCO	Ohio River Valley Water Sanitation Commission	WRA	Water Research Association
PAH	polynuclear aromatic hydrocarbon	WRB	Water Resources Board
		WRC	Water Research Centre
PCB	polychlorinated biphenyl	WSAC	Water Space Amenity Commission
PG	Planning Group		
PHS	Public Health Service	WWA	Wessex Water Authority
PL	Public Law	YWA	Yorkshire Water Authority
PMU	Provisional Management Unit		

Glossary

British	*American*
agency agreement	an agreement for one agency to provide services on behalf of another
Alkali Inspectorate	agency for industrial air pollution control
billion (10^{12})	million million (10^{12})
thousand million (10^9)	billion (10^9)
clerk	manager or administrator, generally the top staff position in a local authority
consents	permits
drain	house or building wastewater connection
Green Paper	government proposals open for discussion
land drainage	flood protection
leading article (in newspaper)	editorial
local authorities: district, borough and county councils	towns, cities and counties
main	water distribution pipe
main drainage	sewerage
precepts	charges against authorities for services
rates	property taxes
public health engineering	engineering for sewerage and water pollution control
sewage	wastewater
statutory water company	investor-owned water supply company
tied housing	housing for staff belonging to authority
tip	refuse dump or sanitary landfill
trade effluent	industrial wastes

British	*American*
undertaking	system
waste	refuse
water conservation	water resources development
water rate	water charges based on property values
water waste	leakage
White Paper	government position paper

References

Chapter 1
1. *Time*, 4 January 1971, pp. 21–2.
2. *New York Times*, 18 January 1972, p. 12.
3. Daniel A. Okun, 'Water Management in England. A Regional Model', *Environmental Science and Technology*, Vol. 9, October 1975, pp. 918–23.
4. Sir Eric Ashby, 'Prospect for Pollution', *Journal of the Royal Society*, June 1973, pp. 443–54.
5. Daniel A. Okun, 'Phosphates in Detergents—Bane or Boon?', *Environmental Affairs*, Boston College Environmental Law Center, Vol. 2, No. 1, 1972, pp. 64–74.
6. K. F. Roberts, discussion presented to the Institution of Water Engineers, 14 May 1975.
7. 'Pollution Control: RWAs Under Transatlantic Fire', *Municipal Engineering*, 4 October 1974, p. 1867.
8. National Water Commission, Water Policies for the Future, USGPO, 1973, p. 459.
9. Frank J. Trelease, *Federal–State Relations in Water Law*, prepared for the National Water Commission, National Technical Information Service, Springfield, Va, PB 203/600, 1971, p. 11.
10. *Democracy and Devolution: Proposals for Scotland and Wales* (Cmnd 5732), HMSO, September 1974; *Our Changing Democracy: Devolution to Scotland and Wales* (Cmnd 6348), HMSO, November 1975.
11. Dick Francis, *Enquiry*, Harper & Row Publishers, 1969.
12. 'No Surprise: Politics in Civil Service', *New York Times*, 10 August 1975, p. E3.
13. *New York Times*, 7 September 1975, p. 36.
14. Frederick Toplis, 'National Water Supply. Suggestions for Dividing England and Wales into Watershed Districts', *Journal Society of Arts*, 4 July 1879, pp. 696–709.
15. Department of the Environment, Welsh Office, Ministry of Agriculture, Fisheries and Food, *Review of the Water Industry in England and Wales*, a Consultative Document, 1976.

Chapter 2
1. Central Advisory Water Committee (Milne Committee). *Third (Final) Report*, HMSO, August 1943.
2. Ministry of Health and Ministry of Agriculture and Fisheries, *A National Water Policy*, HMSO, April 1944.

3. Daniel A. Okun, 'Regrouping of Water Supplies in the United Kingdom', *Public Works*, Vol. 198, No. 6, June 1967, pp. 153–4.
4. Department of the Environment, *Taken for Granted*, Report of the Working Party on Sewage Disposal (Jeger Committee), HMSO, 1970.
5. Central Advisory Water Committee, Subcommittee on the Growing Demand for Water, *Final Report*, HMSO, 1962.
6. Ministry of Housing and Local Government, *Water Conservation. England and Wales*, HMSO, 1962.
7. Lorna Rose Barr, 'Area Reorganisation of Water Management in England and Wales', M.A. Thesis, University of Victoria, June 1973, p. 46.
8. *Ibid.*, p. 53.
9. Water Resources Board, *Annual Reports*, HMSO, 1964–1974.
10. Water Resources Board, *Water Supplies in Southeast England*, HMSO, 1966.
11. Water Resources Board, *Water Resources in England & Wales*, HMSO, 1973.
12. Water Resources Board, *Seventh Annual Report*, HMSO, 1971, p. 47.
13. Water Resources Board, *Ninth Annual Report*, HMSO, 1972, pp. 72–9.
14. Water Resources Board, *Tenth Annual Report*, HMSO, 1974, pp. 47–55, 66–9.
15. Judith Rees, 'Industrial Abstraction and the 1963 Charging Schemes', *Report to the Water Resources Board*, 1974.
16. Lyle E. Craine, *Water Management Innovations in England*, Resources for the Future, Johns Hopkins Press, 1969.
17. *Local Government in Britain*, Central Office of Information, Reference Pamphlet 1, HMSO, London, 1975.
18. Derek Senior, 'Whose Water Cycle?', *Built Environment*, November 1974, pp. 557–9.
19. Department of the Environment, Water Act 1973: Water Authorities and Local Authorities, Circular No. 100/73, 16 August 1973.
20. Christopher Worman, 'Beginning of the End for Local Government?', *The Times* London, 1 April 1974.
21. Tony Eddison, 'Has Reorganization Eased the Burden? Present Tense—Future Indefinite?', *The Surveyor*, 4 April 1975, pp. 11–13.
22. Bob Wallis, 'Inside Views on Gains in the First Year', *The Surveyor*, 4 April 1975, pp. 14–16.
23. 'The Nation's Health', *The Times* London, pp. I–VIII, 25 April 1974.
24. 'A Guide to the NHS', *New Society*, London, 1974.

Chapter 3

1. J. E. Beddoe, personal interview, 18 December 1943.
2. The Institution of Public Health Engineers, the Institution of Water Engineers, the Institute of Water Pollution Control, *Future Organization of River, Sewerage and Water Authorities*, March 1969.
3. Department of the Environment, *Taken for Granted*, Report of the Working Party on Sewage Disposal (Jeger Committee), HMSO, 1970.
4. Central Advisory Water Committee, *The Future Management of Water in England and Wales*, HMSO, 1971.
5. Department of the Environment, 'Reorganization of Water and Sewage Services: Government Proposals and Arrangements for Consultation', Circular 92/71, 2 December 1971.

6. A. V. Kneese and R. J. Frankel, 'Economics of Water Reclamation', *Institute of Water Pollution Control Symposium on Water Conservation and Reclamation*, 1967.
7. Peter Banks, 'Efficient Organization is not Sole Criterion', *Municipal Engineering*, 12 January 1968, p. 39.
8. Peter Banks, 'Costs Must not be Overlooked in Debate on Reorganization', *Municipal Engineering*, 20 September 1968, p. 1837.
9. Royal Commission on Local Government in England 1966–1969, (Cmnd 4039), HMSO, 1969.
10. Peter Banks, 'CAWC Report', *Municipal Engineering*, 13 September 1973, p. 1613.
11. Lord Nugent, Ernest Balsom Lecture, Institution of Public Health Engineers, 23 April 1971.
12. Peter Banks, 'Danger to Essential Progress While New Bodies are Set Up', *Municipal Engineering*, 10 December 1971, p. 2361.
13. Royal Commission on Environmental Pollution, Second Report, (Cmnd 4894), HMSO, 1972.
14. Peter Banks, 'Revolutionary Changes but No Great Debate', *Municipal Engineering*, 22 September 1972, p. 1929.
15. 'Local Government Promised "Substantial Role" in New Authorities', *Public Service & Local Government Appointments* (London), 22 August 1972, p. 7.

Chapter 4

1. Frank Roberts, 'Water Bill Proposes to Set up Ten Regional Authorities with Clear Local Majorities', *The Times* (London), 23 January 1973.
2. Department of the Environment, *A Background to Water Reorganization in England and Wales*, HMSO, 1973, p. 8.
3. Hansard, House of Commons, Parliamentary Debates, 2–8 February 1973, col. 48.
4. *Ibid.*, col. 130.
5. *Ibid.*, col. 145.
6. *Ibid.*, cols. 151–2.
7. House of Commons Parliamentary Debates, Standing Committee D, Water Bill, 1973, col. 60.
8. *Ibid.*, col. 61.
9. *Ibid.*, col. 63.
10. *Ibid.*, col. 80.
11. *Ibid.*, col. 81.
12. *Ibid.*, col. 83.
13. *Ibid.*, col. 83.
14. *Ibid.*, col. 84.
15. *Ibid.*, col. 82.
16. *Ibid.*, col. 128.
17. *Ibid.*, cols. 138–44.
18. *Ibid.*, col. 186.
19. *Ibid.*, cols. 187–91.
20. *Ibid.*, cols. 217–21.
21. *Ibid.*, col. 298.

22. *Ibid.*, col. 299.
23. *Ibid.*, col. 556.
24. *Ibid.*, cols. 564–7.
25. *Ibid.*, cols. 576–8.
26. *Ibid.*, cols. 612–4.
27. *Ibid.*, cols. 615–7.
28. *Ibid.*, col. 667.
29. *Ibid.*, col. 677.
30. *Ibid.*, cols. 678–9.
31. *Ibid.*, col. 768.
32. *Ibid.*, cols. 858–60.
33. *Ibid.*, col. 963.
34. *Ibid.*, col. 972.
35. *Ibid.*, col. 973.
36. *Ibid.*, cols. 979–80.
37. *Ibid.*, cols. 980–1.
38. *Ibid.*, cols. 981–2.
39. House of Commons, Parliamentary Debates, Hansard, HMSO, 1–2 May 1973.
40. *Ibid.*, cols. 1008–2.
41. *Ibid.*, cols. 1041–9.
42. *Ibid.*, cols. 1049–54.
43. *Ibid.*, cols. 1025–42.
44. *Ibid.*, cols. 1055–9.
45. *Ibid.*, cols. 1100–2.
46. *Ibid.*, col. 1138.
47. *Ibid.*, cols. 1277–81.
48. House of Lords, Parliamentary Debates, Hansard, HMSO, 21 May 1973.
49. *Ibid.*, col. 982.
50. *Ibid.*, cols. 983–4.
51. House of Lords, Parliamentary Debates, Hansard, HMSO, 9 July 1973, col. 535.
52. *Ibid.*, col. 537.

Chapter 5

1. Leonard W. F. Millis, Presidential Address to the British Waterworks Association, 19 June 1973, *British Water Supply*, July 1973, pp. 3–5.
2. Institute of Water Pollution Control, Annual Conference Torquay, 11 September 1973.
3. Department of the Environment, 'Administrative Brief for Water Authorities', Water Authority Circular No. 1/73, 31 August 1973.
4. 'Everest Has Been Climbed!', *Municipal Engineering*, 13 July 1973, p. 1537.
5. Department of the Environment, 'Reorganization of the Directorate of Water and the Directorate-General of Water Engineering', Water Authority Circular No. 3/73, 5 November 1973.
6. Department of the Environment, *Water Act* 1973: *Water Authorities and Local Authorities*, Circular 100/73, 16 August 1973.
7. Department of the Environment, *The New Water Industry Management and Structure*, HMSO, 1973.

8. Douglas H. Banks, personal interview, 4 June 1974.
9. Informal conversations with British consulting engineers.
10. 'Jack Beddoe: Always Happy to Go Back to Water', *Municipal Engineering*, 27 July 1973, pp. 1643–4.
11. 'Ogden—Reflected Bains with Strong Highlights', *Municipal Engineering*, 27 July 1973, p. 1640.
12. John Finch, 'Presidential Address', *Water Pollution Control*, Vol. 73, No. 1, 1974, pp. 5–13.
13. 'Discussion: The Water Act 1973', a panel at the Annual Conference of The Institute of Water Pollution Control, *Water Pollution Control*, Vol. 73, No. 3, 1974, pp. 256–61.
14. Notes taken by the author while attending the opening and closing plenary sessions of the Water Industry General Management Program, October 1973.
15. 'IWPC Conference Gives Reorganization a Cool Reception', *Surveyor*, 27 September 1974, pp. 11–15.
16. Department of the Environment, *The Water Services: Economic and Financial Policies*, HMSO, 1973.
17. Department of the Environment, *The Water Services: Estimates and Accounts*, HMSO, 1974.
18. D. R. Newbury, 'Water Authorities Budgets', *Public Finance and Accountancy*, Vol. 1, No. 12, October 1974, pp. 330–3.
19. J. E. Beddoe, Water Supply Industry Training Board, Presentation at Tadley Court, 4 February 1974.
20. National Water Council, *Bulletin*, No. 1, 19 April 1974.
21. National Water Council, *Bulletin*, No. 4, 10 May 1974, par. 217.
22. National Water Council, *Bulletin*, No. 2, 26 April 1974, par. 118.
23. National Water Council, *Bulletin*, No. 2, 26 April 1974, par. 135.
24. *Surveyor*, 29 March 1974.
25. Lord Nugent, from remarks made to officers of Thames Water Authority, Tadley Court, 25 January 1974.

Chapter 6

1. 'How the RWAs Line Up', *Surveyor*, 1 March 1974, pp. 37–48, 50–5.
2. Department of Environment, *The New Water Industry Management and Structure*, HMSO, 1973.
3. 'RWAs Go Their Different Ways', *New Civil Engineer*, 22 November 1973.
4. Department of the Environment, Directorate General of Water Engineering, 'Southern Water Authority Technical Brief', April 1973.
5. *Mid-Sussex Times*, 21 February 1974.
6. Thames Water Authority, *Annual Report and Accounts* 1974–75, p. 7.
7. *Sunday Times* (London), 11 August 1974.
8. Anglian Water Authority, *Annual Report and Accounts* 1974–75, p. 14.
9. Les Freeman, 'Northumbrian: Creating an Image', *Water*, October 1974, pp. 29–31.
10. Peter Liddel, 'The New Water Industry: At the Sign of the Tickled Trout', *Municipal and Public Service Journal*, 8 March 1974, pp. 249–55.

11. J. G. Lloyd, 'Preliminary Consideration of the Field of Action and the Staff Structure of the Directorate', North West Water Authority, 30 November 1973.
12. 'Water Reorganization Round-Up', *Surveyor*, 22 November 1974, p. 42.
13. Welsh National Water Development Authority, *First Annual Report* for the Period Ending 31 March 1975, October 1975, par. 4.3.2.4.
14. 'Into 1976 With the Regional Water Authorities', *Water Services*, January 1976, pp. 30–6.
15. K. F. Roberts, 'Wessex: Variations on a Theme', *Water*, No. 1, October 1974, pp. 24–5.
16. A. B. Baldwin, 'Yorkshire: Building Upwards', *Water*, No. 1, October 1974, pp. 26–8.

Chapter 7

1. D. E. Weald, 'Towards a National Communications Network', *Water*, No. 2, January 1975, pp. 6–9.
2. G. T. King, 'People Matter in the Water Industry', *Water*, No. 1, October 1974, pp. 19–21,
3. M. Greenfield, 'National Water Council—Watchdog or Lapdog', *Municipal Journal and Municipal Engineering Supplement*, 4 April 1975, pp. 21–2.
4. John Ardill, 'Watchdog for Water', *Water*, No. 1, October 1974, pp. 8–10.
5. Peter Scott, personal interview, 6 March 1974.
6. 'Executive Body Needed for Water Resource Planning', *Municipal Engineering*, 26 September 1975, p. 1832.
7. National Water Council, *National Water Conference Proceedings Report*, Bournemouth, 1975.
8. Michael Hanson, 'Water for Recreation', *Municipal Journal and Municipal Engineering Supplement*, 4 April 1975, pp. 15–18.
9. 'Water Authorities' Research Needs', *Water*, No. 5, October 1975, pp. 16–26.

Chapter 8

1. Royal Commission on Health of Towns, *First Report*, 1844.
2. Keith Smith, *Water in Britain*, Macmillan (London), 1972, pp. 140–7.
3. Daniel A. Okun, 'Health Aspects of Water Management', *Public Works and Society*, Proceedings of the 1972 Joint Conference of the American Society of Civil Engineers and the Institution of Civil Engineering (UK), 1974, pp. 133–66.
4. Metropolitan Water Board, *London's Water Supply*, 1903–1953, London, 1953.
5. Metropolitan Water Board, *Forty-Fifth Report on the Results of the Bacteriological, Chemical and Biological Examination of the London Waters for the Years 1971–1973*, 1974, p. 67.
6. Department of the Environment, *Second Report of the Steering Committee on Water Quality*, HMSO, February 1973.
7. World Health Organization, International Agency for Research on Cancer, Vol. 3, 1973.
8. W. M. Lewis, 'Polynuclear Aromatic Hydrocarbons in Water', *Water Treatment and Examination* (Britain), Vol. 24, 1975, pp. 243–77.

9. N. A. F. Rowntree, 'River Control and the Development of Surface Water Resources in England and Wales', *Conservation of Water Resources*, Institution of Civil Engineers, 1963, pp. 155–9.

10. K. Smith, 'The Availability of Water on Teeside', *Journal of the British Waterworks Association*, Vol. 49, 1967, pp. 481–9.

11. Water Resources Board, *Water Resources in England and Wales*, 2 volumes, HMSO, 1973.

12. Department of the Environment, Dee Estuary Scheme Phase IIa, Supplementary Report, 1974.

13. U. T. Burston, and T. J. Coats, 'Water Resources in Northumbria with Particular Reference to the Kielder Water Scheme', Institution of Water Engineers, 14 May 1975.

14. National Water Council, *Water Resources in England and Wales—Views of the National Water Council on the Report of the Water Resources Board*, 1975.

15. Water Resources Board, *Water Strategy for the Future*, March, 1974.

16. Daniel A. Okun, 'The Promise of Water Reorganisation', *Water*, National Water Council, No. 1, October, 1974, pp. 3–7.

17. US Environmental Protection Agency, *Organic Chemical Pollution of Freshwater*, Water Quality Criteria Data Book Vol. 1, Arthur D. Little, USGPO, 1970.

18. National Institutes of Health, 'Chemical Mutagens as a Possible Health Hazard', Genetic Study Section, Bethesda, Maryland, undated.

19. W. C. Hueper, 'Cancer Hazards from Natural and Artificial Water Pollutants', *Proceedings, Conference on Physiological Aspects of Water Quality*, US Public Health Service, Washington, DC, 1960.

20. P. Stocks, *Regional and Local Differences in Cancer Death Rates*, No. 1, London General Register Office, 1947.

21. J. S. Diehl and S. W. Tromp, *First Report on Geographical and Geological Distribution of Carcinogens in the Netherlands*, Leiden Foundation for the Study of Psychophysics, 1953; S. W. Tromp, 'Possible Effects of Geophysical and Geochemical Factors on the Development and Geographic Distribution of Cancer', *Schweiz A. Path*, Vol. 18, 1955, pp. 929–39.

22. H. F. Dorn and S. J. Cutler, *Morbidity from Cancer in the United States*, US Public Health Service Monograph No. 56, 1959.

23. P. Talbot and R. H. Harris, 'The Implications of Cancer-Causing Substances in Mississippi River Water', A report by the Environmental Defense Fund, Washington, DC, November 1974.

24. Metropolitan Water Board, discussion in 3 above, p. 162.

25. Department of the Environment, *First Annual Report of the Steering Committee on Water Quality*, HMSO, 1971.

26. Hugh Fish, 'A New Look at Pollution Prevention on Lowland Rivers', *Water*, National Water Commission, No. 3, April 1975, pp. 2–4.

27. J. C. Brown, 'Pollution—Problems, Priorities, Methods, and Money', *National Water Conference Proceedings Report*, Bournemouth, 1975, pp. 4–7.

28. F. L. Shaw, 'Pollution—Problems, Practices, Methods and Money', *National Water Conference Proceedings Report*, Bournemouth, 1975, pp. 9–11.

29. 'Rethinking the Philosophy of our Water Quality', *Surveyor*, 19 September 1975, p. 9.

30. 'Cutting the Pollution According to the River', *Surveyor*, 7 May 1976, p. 25.
31. Trevor Hughes, 'Issues that the Water Authorities Must Face', *Water*, National Water Council, No. 2, January 1975, pp. 3–5.
32. David Walker, 'Water Pollution Control—the Priorities', *Water*, National Water Council, No. 8, May 1976, pp. 8–12.
33. Department of the Environment, *The Monitoring of the Environment in the United Kingdom*, Central Unit on Environmental Pollution, HMSO, 1974.
34. 'Instruments, People, or Fish—Which are the Best Pollution Indicators?', *Surveyor*, 4 October 1974, pp. 7–8.
35. United Nations Economic and Social Council, *Water for Industrial Use*, Report No. E/3058, FT/ECA/50, 1958.
36. J. W. Seddon, 'Presidential Address', *Journal of the Institution of Water Engineers*, Vol. 27, 1973, pp. 237–42.
37. A. K. Deb and K. J. Ives, 'Dual Water Supply Systems', Report submitted to the Science Research Council, 1974.
38. Water Resources Board, *Dual Water Supply Systems*, The Trent Research Programme, Vol. 9, 1972.
39. M. Lindley, S. J. Boyer and H. S. Hawkins, 'The Design and Promotion of a Scheme Using Mixed Water from the Rivers Ancholme, Witham and Trent for Industrial Supply to Humberside', *Journal of the Institution of Water Engineers*, Vol. 28, 1974, pp. 272–98.
40. J. K. Jackson, 'Dual Water Supply in the Trent River Basin', *Journal of the Institution of Water Engineers*, 1970, pp. 133–50.
41. J. G. Lloyd, 'Making the Most of our Inheritance', *National Water Council Conference Proceedings Report*, Bournemouth, 1975, pp. 56–9.
42. Brian Appleton, 'Water—Recycling Concept Comes Under Fire', *New Civil Engineer*, 10 April 1975.
43. Daniel A. Okun, 'A Potential for Water Reuse—Dual Supplies', *Proceedings American Water Works Association Seminar on Reuse*, 8 June 1975, pp. 1–21; 'Planned Reuse of Polluted Waters and Wastewaters', *Effluent and Water Treatment Journal* (Britain), July 1974, pp. 373–6; 'Planning for Water Reuse', *Journal American Water Works Association*, Vol. 65, 1973, pp. 617–22; 'The Hierarchy of Water Quality', *Environmental Science and Technology*, Vol. 2, 1968, pp. 672–5.
44. American Water Works Association, *Proceedings Seminar on Dual Distribution Systems*, 20 June 1976.
45. Water Resources Board, *The Trent Research Programme*, Vol. 1, HMSO, 1973, p. 25.
46. Ministry of Housing and Local Government, *Pollution of the Tidal Thames*, HMSO, 1961.
47. Ministry of Housing and Local Government, 'Technical Problems of River Authorities and Sewage Disposal Authorities in Laying Down and Complying with Limits of Quality for Effluents, More Restrictive than those of Royal Commission', Circular No. 37/66, 1966.
48. Department of the Environment, *Report of a River Pollution Survey of England and Wales 1970*, HMSO, Vol. 1, 1972; Vol. 2, 1972; Vol. 3, 1974; updated 1973, 1975.

49. C. Lumb, 'Control of River Pollution: Administrative Measures', *Proceedings of Symposium on Conservation and Reclamation of Water*, Institute of Water Pollution Control, November 1967, pp. 84–94.

50. G. Ainsworth, 'Control of River Pollution: Practical Measures', *Proceedings of Symposium on Conservation and Reclamation of Water*, Institute of Water Pollution Control, November 1967, pp. 95–105.

51. Institute of Water Pollution Control, 'Memorandum of Evidence to the Royal Commission on Local Government in England', *Water Pollution Control*, Vol. 66, No. 2, 1967, p. 131.

52. National Water Council, *Bulletin*, No. 28, 18 July 1975, par. 4902.

53. Welsh Office, Report of the Working Party on Possible Pollution in Swansea Bay, 1974.

54. Medical Research Council, *Sewage Contamination of Bathing Beaches in England and Wales*, HMSO, 1959.

55. Royal Commission on Environmental Pollution, *Third Report Pollution in Some British Estuaries and Coastal Waters*, HMSO, September 1972.

56. Elizabeth Porter, *Pollution in Four Industrialized Estuaries*, Royal Commission on Environmental Pollution, HMSO, 1973.

57. Department of the Environment, *Taken for Granted*, Report of the Working Party on Sewage Disposal, HMSO, 1970.

58. Institute of Municipal Treasurers and Accountants, *Sewage Purification and Disposal Statistics 1964–65*, London, 1966.

59. Chartered Institute of Public Finance and Accountancy, *Water Statistics*, 1972–73; *Sewage Purification Disposal Statistics*, 1972–73.

60. Robin Wiseman, 'Sewage Works: A Legacy of Neglect', *New Civil Engineer*, 22 August 1974, pp. 28–31.

61. Severn Trent Water Authority, *Water Quality* 1973, 1974.

62. Yorkshire Water Authority, *Water Quality Inheritance*—1 *April* 1974, 1974.

63. J. E. Beddoe, personal interview, 18 December 1973.

64. Richard Lillicrap, in 'Risk of Outbreak of Waterborne Disease has Increased', *Municipal Engineering*, 29 November 1974, pp. 2352–3.

65. Severn Trent Water Authority, *Guide to Water Quality* 1973, 1974.

66. *Sewage Disposal, Municipal Engineering Supplement*, 18 October 1974.

67. Norman J. Nicolson and Leslie B. Wood, 'The Impartial Assessment of Performance of the Sewage Treatment Works of a Regional Water Authority', *Sewage Disposal, Municipal Engineering Supplement*, 18 October 1974, pp. S2003–S3006.

68. 'Nitrate in Lee Proved Reorganization's Value', *Municipal Engineering*, 20 September 1974, p. 1747.

69. 'No Outside Watchdog for Thames WA's Pollution Control', *Municipal Engineering*, p. 1366, 18 July 1975.

70. Royal Commission on Environmental Pollution, *Fourth Report, Pollution Control: Progress and Problems*, December 1974.

71. Lord Ashby, personal interview, 11 October 1973.

72. Gerald Wall, 'Control of Pollution Act—A Model for Lawmakers', *Municipal Engineering*, 9 August 1974, p. 1564.

72. J. McLoughlin, 'The Control of Pollution Act 1974', *Journal of Planning and Environmental Law*, February 1975, pp. 77–85.

74. J. F. Garner, *Control of Pollution Act* 1974, Butterworths, 1975, p. 55.
75. Confederation of British Industry, *Control of Pollution Act* 1974—*A Synopsis of its Requirements*, 7 March 1975.
76. Jon Tinker, 'River Pollution: The Midlands Dirty Dozen', *New Scientist*, 6 March 1975, pp. 551–4.
77. H. C. Butcher, Senior Technical Adviser of the Confederation of British Industry Company Affairs Directorate, personal interview, 13 March 1975.
78. Severn Trent Water Authority, *Water Quality* 1974/75, 1976.
79. *New Scientist*, leader, 11 March 1976.
80. Department of the Environment, Press Notice T4175, 3 February 1975.
81. 'WAs Hope Pollution Act Will Stay on the Shelf', *Municipal Engineering*, Vol. 152, 11 July 1975, p. 1315.
82. *Surveyor*, 13 December 1974, p. 3.
83. *Ibid*, p. 33.
84. Department of the Environment, Central Unit on Environmental Pollution, *Controlling Pollution*, Pollution Paper No. 4, HMSO, 1975, p. iii.
85. National Water Council, *Bulletin*, No. 32, 15 August 1975, par. 5222.

Chapter 9

1. G. B. Shaw, Preface to *The Irrational Knot*, 1905.
2. H. Fish, 'Pollution Control Financing in the United Kingdom and Europe', *Journal Water Pollution Control Federation*, Vol. 45, April 1973, pp. 734–41.
3. Department of the Environment, *The Water Services: Estimates and Accounts*, HMSO, 1974.
4. E. J. Gilliland, 'New Directions for Public Accountancy', *Municipal and Public Services Journal*, 26 April 1974, pp. 503–4.
5. Department of the Environment, *The Water Services: Economic and Financial Policies*, First Report to the Secretary of State for the Environment, HMSO, 1973.
6. Department of the Environment, *The Water Services: Economic and Financial Policies*, Third Report to the Secretary of State for the Environment, HMSO, 1974.
7. National Water Council *Bulletin*, No. 13, 4 April 1975, par. 3454.
8. *Municipal Engineering*, Vol. 152, 21 February 1975, p. 346.
9. *The Times* (London), 28 June 1974.
10. K. F. Roberts, 'Reorganisation—Reflections After a Year of Change', Institution of Water Engineers, Summer General Meeting, 14 May 1975, pp. 16–33.
11. 'Sewerage Charge Cuts Announced by Howell', *Municipal Engineering*, 6 December 1974, p. 2395.
12. 'High Court Judge Waives £18 Million Sewer Charges in Test Case', *Surveyor*, 9 May 1975, p. 4.
13. '£60 m Must be refunded by WAs Following Daymond Appeal Rejection', *Surveyor*, 5 December 1975, p. 3.
14. Department of the Environment, Welsh Office, Ministry of Agriculture, Fisheries and Food, *Reviews of the Water Industry in England and Wales—A Consultative Document*, 1976.

15. National Water Council *Bulletin*, No. 10, 12 March, par. 8372.
16. E. J. Gilliland, 'The New Water Industry—Economics and Finances', *Municipal and Public Services Journal*, 8 March 1974, pp. 256–63.
17. National Water Council *Bulletin*, No. 6, 14 February 1975, par. 2840.
18. E. J. Gilliland, 'Financing the New Water Authorities', *Water Services*, February 1975, pp. 46–9, 54.
19. National Water Council, *Paying for Water*, April 1976.
20. 'Dallas Rate Survey', *Journal American Water Works Association*, Vol. 67, May 1975, pp. 232–8.
21. John J. Boland, 'Toward More Rational Water Rates', *Proceedings North Carolina Conference on Water Conservation*, University of North Carolina Water Resources Research Institute, September 1975, pp. 19–31.
22. American Water Works Association, *Journal*, Vol. 69. February 1977 issue is devoted to 'Meters and Metering'.
23. J. J. Warford, 'Water Supply', Chapter 6 in *Public Enterprise*, ed. by R. Turvey, Penguin Modern Economics, 1968, pp. 212–36.
24. A. V. Kneese and Charles L. Schultze, *Pollution, Prices and Public Policy*, Brookings Institution, 1975, pp. 19–22.
25. G. M. Fair, J. C. Geyer and D. A. Okun, *Elements of Water Supply and Wastewater Disposal*, 2nd ed., John Wiley and Sons, 1971, pp. 33–40.
26. S. H. Hanke, 'Water Rates: An Assessment of Current Issues', *Journal American Water Works Association*, Vol. 67, May 1975, pp. 215–19; Fred P. Griffith, Jr, 'An Innovative Approach to Rate Making', *Journal American Water Works Association*, Vol. 69, February 1977, pp. 89–91.
27. E. J. Gilliland, 'Principles of Charging for Water Services', Report to the Policy and Resources Commission, Thames Water Authority, 13 September 1974.
28. J. A. Rees, '*A Review of Evidence of the Effect of Prices on the Demand for Water Services*', Directorate General of Economics and Resources, Department of the Environment, June 1973.
29. B. R. Herrington, 'The Costs of Domestic Metering', *Water Services*, September 1974, pp. 306–10.
30. R. J. Smith, 'Some Comments on Domestic Metering', *Journal of the Institution of Water Engineers*, Vol. 28, 1974, pp. 47–53.
31. R. C. Jenking, *Fylde Metering*, Fylde Water Board, Blackpool, 1973.
32. John Lingard, 'The Case for Universal Metering', vs. Sir Wm. Dugdale, 'The Case Against Universal Metering', *Water*, No. 4, July 1975, pp. 6–10.
33. Sir John Wills, 'Management in the Water Industry', *National Water Council Conference Proceedings Report*, Bournemouth, 1975, p. 32.
34. Daniel A. Okun, 'Tomorrow's Methods to Provide Tomorrow's Service', *Journal of the American Water Works Association*, Vol. 58, 1966, pp. 938–52.
35. Peter F. Stott, *National Water Council Conference Proceedings*, Bournemouth, 1975, p. 32.
36. G. M. Fair, J. C. Geyer and D. A. Okun, *Water and Wastewater Engineering*, Vol. 1, John Wiley & Sons, *Water and Wastewater Supply Removal*, 1966, pp. 5–15.
37. J. A. Rees, *A Review of Evidence on the Effect of Prices on the Demand for Water Services*, Directorate General of Economics and Resources, Department of the Environment, June 1973, p. 5.

38. S. H. Hanke, 'Demand for Water Under Dynamic Conditions', *Water Resources Research*, Vol. 6, October 1970, pp. 1253–61.
39. National Water Commission, *Water Policies for the Future*, Water Information Center, Inc, 1973, p. 252.
40. C. W. Howe and F. P. Linaweaver, Jr, 'The Impact of Price on Residential Water Demand and its Relation to System Design and Price Structure', *Water Resources Research*, Vol. 3, 1967, pp. 13–22.
41. F. P. Linaweaver, J. C. Geyer and J. P. Wolff, *A Study of Residential Water Use*, Report prepared for the Federal Housing Administration, Department of Housing and Urban Development, Washington, DC, 1966.
42. R. Porges, 'Factors Influencing Per Capita Consumption', *Water and Sewage Works*, Vol. 104, May 1957, pp. 199–204.
43. J. A. Rees, *Factors Affecting Metered Water Consumption; a Study of Malvern U.D.C*', Final Report to the Social Science Research Council, August 1971.
44. P. R. Herrington, *Water Demand Study Final Report* for the Water Resources Board, University of Leicester, July 1973, p. 59.
45. Royal Commission on Environmental Pollution, *Third Report, Pollution in Some British Estuaries and Coastal Waters*, HMSO, September 1972.
46. Allen V. Kneese and Blair T. Bower, *Managing Water Quality: Economics, Technology, Institutions*, Johns Hopkins Press for Resources for the Future, 1968.
47. Allen V. Kneese and Charles L. Schultze, *Pollution. Prices and Policy*, The Brookings Institution, Washington, DC, 1975, pp. 87–8.
48. *Ibid.*, p. 90.
49. *National Water Council Conference, Proceedings Report*, Bournemouth, March 1975, p. 27.
50. National Water Council *Bulletin*, No. 21, 30 May 1975, par. 4285.
51. National Water Council *Bulletin*, No. 9, 7 March 1975, par. 3071.
52. National Water Council *Bulletin*, No. 1, 19 April 1974, pars. 3943 and 3952.
53. National Water Council *Bulletin*, No. 5, 17 May 1974, par. 265.
54. 'Industry Storm Over WNWDA'S Tenfold Price Increases', 11 July 1975, p. 4.
55. 'Welsh Water Sheiks', *Municipal Engineering*, 10 January 1975, p. 56.
56. Welsh Office, *Committee of Inquiry Into Water Charges in the Area of the Welsh National Water Development Authority* (Daniel Committee Report), HMSO, 1975.

Chapter 10

1. Environmental Protection Agency, *Public Health Service Community Water Supply Study*, 1976.
2. P. Talbot and R. H. Harris, 'The Implication of Cancer-Causing Substances in Mississippi River Water', a report by the Environmental Defense Fund, Washington, DC, November 1974.
3. Environmental Protection Agency, *National Safe Drinking Water Strategy, One Step at a Time*, May 1975.
4. Department of the Environment, *First Annual Report of the Steering Committee on Water Quality*, HMSO, 1971.

5. Daniel A. Okun, 'Planning for Water Reuse', *Journal of the American Water Works Association*, Vol. 65, 1973, pp. 617–22; 'Planned Reuse of Polluted Waters and Wastewaters', *Effluent and Water Treatment Journal* (Great Britain), July 1974, pp. 373–6.

6. 'Fundamental Considerations in Rates and Rate Structures for Water and Sewage Works, *Ohio State Law Journal*, Vol. 12, Spring 1951, p. 151; also published as Bulletin No. 2 of the American Society of Civil Engineers, 1951.

7. National Commission on Water Quality, Staff Draft Report, November 1975, p. I-16.

8. James E. Holshouser, Jr, testimony to the National Commission on Water Quality, Atlanta, Georgia, 9 July 1975.

9. F. H. Abel, D. P. Tihansky, and R. G. Walsh, *National Benefits of Water Pollution Control*, Washington Environmental Research Center, Office of Research and Development, Environmental Protection Agency, Undated, but released in 1975.

10. J. C. Davies III and B. S. Davies, *The Politics of Pollution*, Bobbs-Merrill, Indianapolis, 2nd ed, 1975, p. 44.

11. *Ibid.*, p. 193.

12. National Commission on Water Quality, Report to the Congress, USGPO, 18 March 1976.

13. Daniel A. Okun, James C. Lamb III, and C. C. Wells, Jr, 'A Waste Control Program for a River with Highly Variable Flow', *Journal Water Pollution Control Federation*, Vol. 35, August 1963, pp. 1025–43.

14. 'The Effluent Guidelines Scorecard', *Environmental Science and Technology*, Vol. 9, October 1975, pp. 908–9.

15. *PL 92-500: Certain Recommendations of the Water Pollution Control Federation for Improving the Law and its Administration*, Water Pollution Control Federation, Washington, DC, 10 October 1974.

16. John R. Quarles, Jr, 'Mid-Course Correction–Minor Adjustment or Major Retreat?', in *Public Law 92-500–Mid-Course Correction*, Water Pollution Control Federation, 1976 Government Affairs Seminar, 6 April 1976.

17. National Water Commission, *Water Policies for the Future*, USGPO, 1973.

18. Edward J. Cleary, *The ORSANCO Story*, Johns Hopkins Press, 1967, p. 112.

19. *Water Policies for the Future*, p. 495.

20. M. L. Albertson, L. S. Tucker, and D. C. Taylor, eds, *Treatise on Urban Water Systems*, Colorado State University, July 1971, Chapter 11a, 'An Introduction to Urban Water Management', M. B. McPherson, p. 116.

21. 'City Government', *Encyclopedia Britannica*, Vol. 4, 1974, p. 646.

22. 'Dallas Rate Survey', *Journal American Water Works Association*, Vol. 67, May 1975, pp. 232–8.

23. *Water Policies for the Future*, p. 417.

24. *Ibid.*, p. 430.

25. B. D. Ayres, Jr, 'Atlanta Tries Not to Catch a Bad Case of Urbanitis', *New York Times*, 24 August 1975, p. E5.

26. John Fischer, 'In Some Areas, Today's Temperature is 98·6°', *New York Times*, 1 August 1976, p. 27.

27. David Byrd, 'City Spurns the Regional Takeover of Water Supply', *New York Times*, 13 December 1974.

28. M. M. Hufschmidt, 'Management of Environmental Quality: Observations on Recent Experience in the United States and the United Kingdom', in *Economic Analysis of Environmental Problems*, National Bureau of Economic Research, 1975.
29. Blair Bower, notes from a lecture at the University of North Carolina on 6 November 1972.
30. Raymond Kudukis, *Keynote Address*, Water Pollution Control Federation, 1976, Government Affairs Seminar, Washington, DC, 6 April 1976.
31. National Water Council *Bulletin*, No. 42, 24 October 1975, par. 5054.
32. 'Fish Swims Against Department of the Environment River Current', *New Civil Engineer*, 6 May 1976, pp. 7–8.
33. Frank A. Bell, Jr, Clifford W. Randall, and Frank Homerosky, Jr, 'Survey of State Programs and Attitudes on Regionalization for Public Water Systems', American Society of Civil Engineers Conference, Seattle, Washington, July 1976.
34. National Water Council, *First Annual Report and Accounts*, 1974/75, 1975, p. 15.
35. *Ibid.*, p. 23.
36. 'Water Supplies', *Financial Times* (London), 28 January 1974, pp. 32–3.
37. Anglian Water Authority, 'Manpower Statistics', Report No. 8.2/75, 5 February 1975.
38. American Water Works Association, *Proceedings Seminar on Dual Distribution Systems*, 20 June 1976.
39. National Water Council, *First Annual Report and Accounts*, 1974/75, p. 25.

Chapter 11

1. Department of the Environment, Welsh Office, Ministry of Agriculture, Fisheries, and Food, *Review of the Water Industry in England—A Consultative Document*, 1976.
2. National Water Council, *First Annual Report and Accounts*, 1974/75, Chairman's Foreword, 1975.
3. John Anderson, 'Water Authorities Spending Money Like Champagne', *Public Service and Local Government Appointments*, 10 December 1974, p. 2.
4. Brian Thorpe, 'Management in the Water Industry', *National Water Council Conference Proceedings*, Bournemouth, 1975, pp. 22–4.
5. 'RWAs Move Further Along Road to Full Nationalization', *Municipal Engineering*, p. 1273, 4 July 1975.
6. K. F. Roberts, 'Reorganization—Reflections After a Year of Change', *Institution of Water Engineers*, 14 May 1975.
7. A. Simpkins, 'The New Water Industry—Links With Local Government', Municipal and Public Services Journal, 8 March 1974, pp. 266–73.
8. 'No Cash for Drainage. Threat to Midlands Housing Program', *Public Service and Local Government Appointments*, 7 May 1974, p. 1.
9. 'Shortage of Cash Will Curtail STWA Sewers', *Surveyor*, 5 September 1975, p. 5.
10. National Water Council *Bulletin*, No. 27, 11 July 1975, par. 4755.
11. Sir John Wills, 'Management in the Water Industry', *National Water Council Conference Proceedings*, Bournemouth, 1975, pp. 20–1.

12. 'Call for Greater Cooperation on Sharing Waste Facilities', *Surveyor*, 11 July 1975, p. 5.

13. Department of the Environment, *The Balancing of Interests Between Water Protection and Water Disposal*, Circular 39/76, 13 April 1976.

14. Bill Randall, 'Water Authorities Get a Roasting at Dicta Conference', *Municipal Engineering*, 2 May 1975, p. 853.

15. *Our Changing Democracy, Devolution to Scotland and Wales* (Cmnd 6348), HMSO, November 1975.

16. 'Welsh Assembly Will be Responsible for Water', *Surveyor*, 15 August 1975, p. 3.

17. Department of the Environment, *Reorganization of Water and Sewage Services: Government Proposals and Arrangements for Consultation*, Circular 92/71, 2 December 1971.

18. John Naughton, 'National Water Strike is not Far Away–Slater', *Surveyor*, 9 May 1975, p. 12.

19. Royal Commission on Environmental Pollution, *Fifth Report, Air Pollution Control: An Integrated Approach*, HMSO, January 1976.

20. House of Lords Parliamentary Debates, Hansard, 26 May 1976, cols. 275–6.

21. Medical Research Council, *Sewage Contamination of Bathing Beaches in England and Wales*, HMSO, 1959.

22. '£100 Million for Water Fit for Bathing', *Municipal Engineering*, 11 July 1975, p. 19.

23. 'Department of the Environment Fights Battle of the Standards', *Municipal Engineering*, 10 October 1975, p. 1919.

24. Department of the Environment Press Notice, 'EEC Agreement on Pollution Proposals', 9 December 1975.

25. C. D. Andrews, *We Didn't Wait for the Rain...*, National Water Council, December 1976, 49 pp.

26. Daniel A. Okun, 'Management of Water Under Crisis Conditions', *Water*, No. 12, January 1977, pp. 2–5.

27. House of Lords, Parliamentary Debates, Hansard, 26 May 1976, col. 341.

28. Denis Howell, 'Review of the Review', *Water*, No. 8, May 1976, pp. 2–3.

29. *Surveyor*, 26 March 1976, pp. 1 and 3.

30. National Water Council *Bulletin*, No. 12, 26 March 1976, par. 8608.

31. National Water Council, 'Review of the Water Industry in England and Wales, A Consultative Document—Response to the Government', July 1976.

32. Peter Banks, 'Water Review Opens up Debate on Quality', *Municipal Engineering*, 14 May 1976, p. 749.

33. House of Lords Parliamentary Debates, Hansard, 26 May 1976.

34. Secretary of State for the Environment, Secretary of State for Wales and Minister of Agriculture, Fisheries and Food, *The Water Industry in England and Wales: The Next Steps*, HMSO, July 1977.

Index

9. P/ST.

12

339-370 (P/ST)